Marketing

Marketing
a complete guide

Malcolm McDonald
& Martin Christopher

with **Margrit Bass**
and contributions from
Susan Baker & Simon Knox

First published 2003 by
PALGRAVE MACMILLAN
Houndmills, Basingstoke, Hampshire RG21 6XS and
175 Fifth Avenue, New York, N.Y. 10010
Companies and representatives throughout the world

PALGRAVE MACMILLAN is the global academic imprint of the Palgrave Macmillan division of St. Martin's Press, LLC and of Palgrave Macmillan Ltd. Macmillan® is a registered trademark in the United States, United Kingdom and other countries. Palgrave is a registered trademark in the European Union and other countries.

ISBN 0–333–99436–1 hardback
ISBN 0–333–99437–X paperback

This book is printed on paper suitable for recycling and made from fully managed and sustained forest sources.

A catalogue record for this book is available from the British Library.

A catalog record for this book is available from the Library of Congress

10   9   8   7   6   5   4   3   2   1
12 11 10 09 08 07 06 05 04 03

Printed and bound in Great Britain by
Creative Print & Design (Wales), Ebbw Vale

Contents

List of figures

List of tables

List of case studies

Preface and acknowledgements

Our purpose in developing *Marketing: A Complete Guide* was to provide a practical textbook on marketing which will be of primary interest and value to those managers who have little formal training in the topic but who:

- ▶ are impacted by marketing in their own jobs;
- ▶ are undertaking a marketing role for the first time;
- ▶ are taking on greater marketing responsibility; or
- ▶ have an interest in marketing

Such managers have neither the time nor the inclination to decipher jargon-ridden specialist volumes where theory seems to have drowned out the often mundane practice of marketing.

Equally, students on a formal course will find this book useful because we have deliberately taken a comprehensive view of marketing within the context of business and society. There is just enough theory to underpin the topics in each of the five modules, although we have quite consciously not included many academic references which, in our view, tend to break up the flow of logic in many texts.

That is not to say, however, that we have not given credit to the original work of others. Indeed, this unusual work is the result of a lengthy and rigorous process of developing teaching materials for marketing modules on the core MBA programme at Cranfield School of Management over a period of thirty years. Hence, it is a distillation of the work of generations of scholars, particularly those with whom we have worked at both the Bradford and Cranfield Schools of Management.

The overhead slides and tutors' guides which were developed alongside earlier versions of this text enabled the contents to be tried and tested on many of the world's blue chip companies and the current text is the result of many years of research, teaching and consultancy – that is, the implementation of our concepts in the world of practice.

Earlier versions of this text were the result of collaboration with Gordon Wills, David Walters, Sherril Kennedy, David Corkindale and our current, much-respected colleagues at Cranfield: Adrian Payne; Simon Knox; Helen Peck; Moira Clark; Susan Baker; Roger Palmer; and Lynette Ryals. In particular, we are grateful to Professor Simon Knox and Dr Susan Baker for allowing us to use some of their work in our latest text.

Above all, however, we are grateful to Margrit Bass, of Native Arrows (Hopi Lodge, Bow Brickhill, Bucks), who took on the prodigious task of editing our work and of rewriting substantial parts of it in order to give it a thoroughly up-to-date look and feel. Her professionalism and high standards are reflected in the current text, which we hope you will enjoy and find useful in your busy lives.

MARTIN CHRISTOPHER
MALCOLM McDONALD

Overview

Before considering in more detail the purpose that marketing serves in the organization and how this role is fulfilled, let us remind ourselves of the definition of marketing. Marketing is essentially a matching process between the needs and expectations of customers, and the organization's ability and capacity to satisfy them. For this matching process to take place successfully, the organization must understand *who* is the customer and *what* value is required, and *how* best to deliver this value on a sustainable basis in line with the organization's overall corporate objectives. Marketing is thus a process for:

▶ Defining markets, and more specifically, target markets/segments.
▶ Identifying the value customers require by quantifying the needs of these customer groups, or market segments.
▶ Creating value propositions to meet these needs, involving the setting of marketing objectives and strategies.
▶ Communicating these value propositions to all those people in the organization responsible for delivering them, and securing their buy-in (commitment and co-operation).
▶ Delivering these value propositions through products/services, supported by appropriate customer communications and customer service.
▶ Monitoring the value actually delivered against that required, utilizing information, knowledge and performance measurement.
▶ Enhancing value through adjustments to organizational structure and culture, and corporate ethos and ethics, as a result of experiential learning and marketing research.

A map of this marketing process is shown overleaf.

From the marketing map, it will be clear that the marketing process is cyclical in that monitoring the value delivered will update the organization's understanding of the value that is required by its customers, while enhancing value through continual capacity-building will

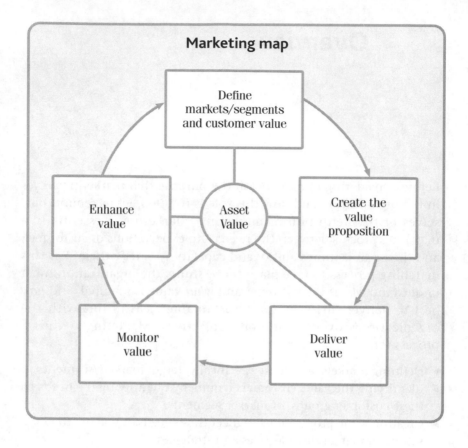

Marketing map

enable the organization to develop its potential to sustain the delivery of that requisite value. The cycle may be predominantly an annual one, with a marketing plan documenting the output from the 'define markets/segments and customer value' and 'create the value proposition' processes, but equally, changes throughout the year may involve fast iterations around the cycle to respond to particular opportunities or problems. At the same time, the five individual subprocesses (define/create/deliver/monitor/enhance) contained within the overall marketing process will inform and support each other.

We have used the term 'create the value proposition' rather than 'create value' to make plain that we are referring here to the decision-making process of deciding what the offering to the customer is to be – what value the customer will receive, and what value (typically the purchase price) the organization will receive in return. The process of delivering this value, such as by making and delivering a physical product or by delivering a service, is covered by 'deliver value'.

Thus it can be seen that the first two subprocesses ('define markets/ segments and customer value' and 'create the value proposition') are concerned with strategic marketing planning; that is, developing marketing strategies. The next two subprocesses ('deliver value', and 'monitor value') relate to the actual delivery in the market place of what was planned and then measuring the effect. A fifth subprocess, here described as 'enhance value', refers to the recognition of learning derived from experience, and the assimilation of this learning into the organization's make-up and operations to improve its marketing performance – and, by implication, its asset value.

It is well known that not all of these marketing activities will be under the control of the marketing department, whose role varies considerably between organizations. The marketing department is likely to be in charge of the first two subprocesses, 'define markets/segments and customer value' and 'create the value proposition', although even these need to involve numerous functions, albeit co-ordinated by specialist marketing personnel. However, responsibility for delivering value is the shared domain of the whole company, requiring cross-functional expertise and collaboration. It will include, for example, product development, manufacturing, purchasing, sales promotion, distribution, sales and customer service. Similarly, the subprocesses of monitoring and enhancing value will occur throughout the organization and involve every individual, function and unit.

The various choices made during this marketing process are constrained and informed not just by events and trends in the outside world, but also by the nature and strength of the organization's own asset value. By 'asset value' we mean both the organization's *tangible* assets, such as plant equipment, stock and financial holdings; and its *intangible* assets, such as the skills and ingenuity of its people, the strength and width of its brand(s), and the power and performance of its information management and operational systems. In other words, an organization's asset value extends beyond its mere balance sheet value to encompass all those qualities and abilities to which we attribute value. We see asset value in action, for example, during corporate acquisitions, when companies are valued at figures (and bought for sums) that far exceed their 'actual' worth. Because asset value lies at the core of the marketing process, understanding what it is and what it means is essential to charting the organization's development.

The five arrows connecting the subprocesses comprise the input/ output of each subprocess. For example, the output of 'defining markets/segments and customer value' is the target of prospective customers the organization wishes to reach, and the associated value expectation. This then becomes the input to the next subprocess, shaping and driving the creation of the value proposition. In turn, the output of that subprocess is the marketing plans, which become the input to 'deliver value', and so on. The dual role played by these connectors highlights the seamless integration of the subprocesses that comprise the marketing process.

Let us consider briefly what each of these subprocesses in the marketing process entails and how they all work together to create and deliver customer value – and consequently, to grow the organization's asset value.

Define markets/segments and customer value

This subprocess is suggested as the staring point for organizations, be they developing or reviewing their marketing process. It involves defining the markets the organization is in, or wishes to be in, and how these markets divide into segments of customers with similar needs. The choice of markets will be influenced by the organization's corporate objectives as well as its asset value. To identify markets and segments, the organization will collect information about market characteristics, such as the market's size and growth, current profitability, and estimated future potential.

Once each market or segment has been defined, it is necessary to understand what value the customers within the segment want or need; that is, the benefits sought through product ownership. This involves identifying customers' current requirements and making predictions about their future needs. Knowledge about customers' purchase history, lifestyle and life stage can be helpful in developing patterns of likely buyer behaviour, which can then be used to pursue proactive as well reactive marketing strategies. It may emerge that subsets of the customers within a market have very different requirements, in which case the market may need to be segmented further.

The organization must also establish how well it and its competitors currently deliver the value the customers seek in order to understand competitor value positioning. From these market and competitive analyses the relative attractiveness of the different markets or segments can be evaluated.

Create the value proposition

This subprocess is about selecting and prioritizing the range of markets and market segments in which the organization is to operate, and accordingly creating appropriate value propositions. These decisions will take into account both market/segment attractiveness and the organization's actual and potential ability to meet the needs of customers within those market/segments. They will also be shaped by the overriding corporate objectives. The setting of marketing objectives and strategies, and the production of marketing plans to articulate them, therefore dominate this subprocess.

Organizations normally start by defining the value they hope to receive from the market or segment, in terms of, for example, market share, market volume, market value or profit contribution by segment. They must also define the value to be delivered to the customer in return, or the product/service benefits the customer cares about. These price/value propositions must then be set in a realistic context; that is, they must be accompanied by a definition of how the customer value is to be delivered and communicated.

Once these issues have been resolved, an estimate of the expected results of the marketing strategies can be made in terms of the costs to the organization and the impact of the price/value proposition on sales. This final step closes the loop from the earlier step of setting marketing objectives, as it may be that iteration is required if the strategies that have been defined are now considered insufficient to meet the financial objectives.

The output from the 'create the value proposition' subprocess is typically a strategic marketing plan, or plans, covering a period of at least three years. In some cases, specific plans are produced for each of the four 'P's, such as a pricing plan, a distribution plan, a customer service plan or a promotions plan. However, even when no marketing plans are produced, the organization is taking decisions implicity about what constitutes the offer to the customer and how this offer is to be communicated and delivered. The content of the marketing plans has to be communicated to, and agreed with, all departments or functions responsible for delivering the customer value articulated in the plans.

Deliver value

This subprocess puts the plans into action. It focuses on the tactical, value-delivering activities of inbound logistics, operations, outbound logistics and service. Encapsulating these activities is the overall discipline of relationship management. The need to manage customer relationships effectively is driven by the fact that it is customers, not products, that generate profits, and there is direct link between customer retention and profitability.

Value delivery thus concerns how the offer is communicated to the customer, and how a two-way dialogue is facilitated with the customer. Inherent within this are a number of decisions, including which media and channels to use, and whether or not (and how) they should be integrated; what levels of service should be provided, given the need for individualization as well as cost-effectiveness; what is the requisite size and nature of the sales force; and how can custom be developed through customer retention programmes.

Monitor value

The delivery of value through the implementation of the marketing plans results in performance, which then needs to be monitored closely for quality gaps and improvement opportunities. This subprocess therefore seeks to establish whether the value identified as *required* by customers was indeed *delivered* to customers, and whether the company *received* the return on investment it had expected. The value delivered can be monitored against the value proposition which was defined during the subprocess 'create the value proposition'. As all aspects of value should be measured in terms of the customer's perspective, this subprocess will involve obtaining customer feedback in order to understand the value *perceived* by customers. In addition, the overall effectiveness of the marketing strategies by which the value was delivered may be evaluated.

By monitoring performance against internal indicators and industry standards, the organization will be able to ascertain the scope and level of its professionalism. To be 'future robust' in an increasingly challenging marketing environment requires substantial competence, skills, courage and conviction. Ensuring that such qualities and aptitudes exist in an organization is crucial for maintaining commercial viability as well as growing asset value.

Enhance value

This subprocess builds on current levels of professionalism in order to enhance value and thus raise the organization's market potential. It brings the marketing process full circle. While most organizations profess to learn from experience, surprisingly few demonstrate serious commitment to examining their performance and processes, and taking the action required to redress weaknesses and reinforce strengths. Furthermore, the source of learning need not be confined to the organization itself. Other organizations in similar or disparate industries can also provide valuable lessons and guidance.

The key areas open to improvement include the structure and culture of the organization, and the ethos and ethics by which it operates. The way in which departments and functions are constructed, and the extent to which they collaborate and integrate, can have a marked impact on the organization's ability to enhance value. For example, the sharing of information, ideas and expertise across functions and processes is what enables augmented value to be realized. Careful management is needed to maximize the use of limited resources in achieving customer-based objectives. Strong leadership is required to overcome natural resistance to change, and the barriers presented by outdated attitudes and practices. The maxim 'average products deserve average success' might also be applied to organizations.

Summary

In an effort to assist organizations to gain a fuller understanding of the meaning of marketing and a firmer hold on the 'mechanics' of marketing, we have developed a map of the marketing process. This map is intended to simplify some of the complexities of marketing and to provide a 'point of entry' on what can often seem a 'spinning carousel'. It is not meant to diminish the significance or scale of the many activities, principles and beliefs that constitute marketing.

Some relevant features of the map are worth highlighting:

The map is inherently cross-functional 'Deliver value', for example, involves every aspect of the organization, from new product development through inbound logistics and production to outbound logistics and customer service. Hence IT support for marketing involves more cross-functional commitment than many other application areas, with important implications for how to organize projects.

The map represents best practice, not common practice Well-embedded processes in even the most sophisticated companies do not address explicitly many aspects of the map. Hence IT projects need to tackle the difficult issues about how to discover best practice, and how to adapt it to the needs of the organization – issues far outside the expertise of the average computer analyst, who is used to analysing an existing process and providing IT support for it.

The map is evolving One-to-one communications and principles of relationship marketing demand a radically different sales process from that traditionally practised. Hence, exploiting new media such as the Internet requires a substantial shift in thinking, not just changes to IT systems and processes. This reality is illustrated by the following example.

Marketing managers at one company related to us their early experience of operating a website, designed to enable them to reach new customers considerably more cost-effectively than through the traditional use of their sales force. When it was first launched, prospective customers would visit the website, make their purchase decisions based on the information provided there, and place their orders online. So far, so good. But, stuck in a traditional model of the sales process, the company would allocate the 'lead' to a salesperson, who would telephone the prospective customer using the contact details given online and make an appointment to see them in three weeks' time. Those prospects who did not move on to another online supplier were subjected to a sales pitch that was totally unnecessary, as the customer had already decided to buy. Those that were still not put off were registered as online customers. By this time, however, the company had lost the opportunity to improve its margins by using the sales force more judiciously. In time, the company realized its mistake: unlike those prospects which the company identified and contacted, which might indeed need 'selling' to, many new e-customers were initiating the dialogue themselves, and simply required the company to respond speedily and appropriately. Leaving online sales to online processes allowed the sales force free to concentrate on building relationships with major clients.

The following chapters set out how this marketing map works. Each of the five subprocesses (define/create/deliver/monitor/enhance) makes a specific contribution to the marketing process, and this is explained clearly by breaking the subprocess down into manageable parts. The subprocesses also interact and interrelate, giving the marketing map a dynamic, iterative dimension. Attention must therefore be paid to *all* the subprocesses, for their ultimate value emanates from their coalescence.

Responsibility for how this map is used, and the benefit to be derived from using it, does, of course, rest with the user. We hope your marketing journey is a rewarding one and wish you every success!

Further reading

Baker, M. (1999) Marketing – philosophy or function? in M. Baker (ed.) *IEBM Encyclopaedia of Marketing*, International Thomson Press; London.

McDonald, M. and Wilson, H. (2002) *The New Marketing: Transforming the Corporate Future*, Butterworth-Heinemann; Oxford.

Defining markets/ segments and customer value

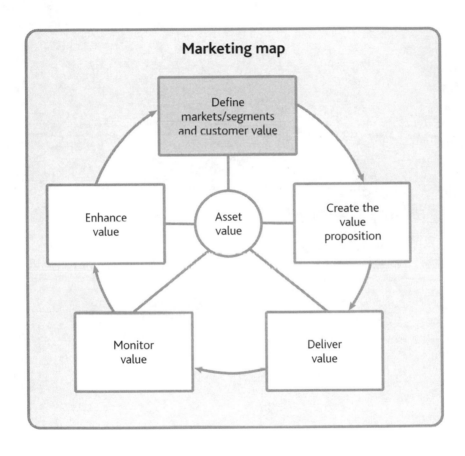

Marketing map

Define markets/segments and customer value

Asset value

Create the value proposition

Enhance value

Deliver value

Monitor value

1 Consumer buyer behaviour

In this chapter we study the:

- ▶ complexity of consumer buyer behaviour
- ▶ factors influencing consumer buyer behaviour
- ▶ types of consumer buyer behaviour
- ▶ role of consumer 'involvement' and consumer perception
- ▶ consumer purchase decision-making process
- ▶ cognitivist and behaviourist viewpoints
- ▶ underlying requirement for consumer research

Understanding consumer buyer behaviour

Understanding consumer buyer behaviour is intrinsic to the successful management of the marketing mix and the building of long-term, profitable customer relationships. It is, after all, consumers who make up markets. In order to offer the right consumers the right products at the right time, providers of products and services need to understand their preferences, prejudices, motivations and buying habits. They need to appreciate that every purchase decision is a *choice* decision and that it encompasses a wide variety of factors. As human beings, we make our choice using a combination of rational judgements, based on facts and previous experience, and subjective feelings that determine our likes and dislikes. As discussed later, in Chapter 3, consumers are not always the buyers and this chapter adopts the definition of consumers as being the end users of the product or service.

In trying to comprehend why people buy what they buy, marketers have to make judgements about the importance they ascribe to consumers' expressed beliefs about certain products and services. All over the world, people form attachments to different products and services, and research suggests that they do not purchase strictly on the basis of performance alone. In the purchase of a washing machine, for example, the decision to buy may depend on how well the appliance cleans clothes, its ease of use, or its reliability. Alternatively, the buyer may be persuaded by the machine's appearance, the sound of the door as it shuts, the excellent after-sales service, or the brand name.

It is an accepted fact that consumers buy certain brands for valid non-functional reasons which have to do with emotional values, or associated services and benefits (best described as the 'augmented brand'; see Chapter 9). It is the job of the marketer to assess which of the product's/service's attributes weigh most heavily in the purchase decision and to exploit this knowledge.

Katherine Hamnett, a well-known clothes designer, has expressed the opinion that designer logos 'can make people think that success can be theirs through acquisition, they believe that Nike can change their world, that Tommy Hilfiger can bring them wealth'. She supports the notion that an intangible value is ascribed to products by consumers, describing how clothes might make people feel rich or look rich.

These observations raise questions about the impact of brands on consumers. While the power of the brand is explored in greater detail in Chapter 9, it is necessary at this juncture to raise the following questions: if consumers believe that one brand delivers more benefit than another, then is it only logical that they are prepared to pay more for it? Can consumers be described as 'irrational' when attributes unrelated to performance predominate in the purchase decision-making process? Consumer buyer behaviour may well be shaped more by perception than reality – as Hamnett highlights – and it is imperative that marketers take this truth on board.

A model of consumer buyer behaviour

Buyer behaviour within markets has to be understood before marketing strategies can be developed. However, constructing a standard model of consumer buyer behaviour can be somewhat problematic. While the inputs and the outputs of decision-making can readily be identified and, to a certain extent, measured, the intangible element which concerns buyer characteristics and choice determinants is often more elusive. At best, it can be described as a 'black box' (Kotler *et al.*, 1996). Predicting consumer buyer behaviour may be an imprecise science, but some simple models have been created to assist marketers

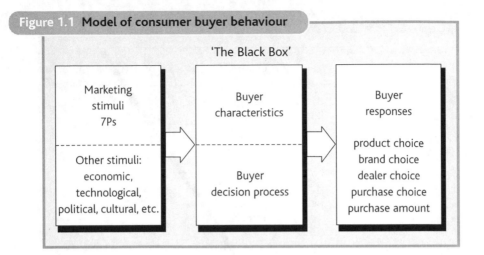

Figure 1.1 **Model of consumer buyer behaviour**

'The Black Box'

| Marketing stimuli 7Ps | Buyer characteristics | Buyer responses |

Other stimuli: economic, technological, political, cultural, etc.

Buyer decision process

product choice
brand choice
dealer choice
purchase choice
purchase amount

in gaining a deeper understanding of consumers in order to acquire and retain their custom.

The inputs in Figure 1.1 can be distinguished between internal stimuli over which the marketer has control – the components of the expanded marketing mix: product, price, place, promotion, people, process and physical evidence (also known as the 7Ps) and customer service – and external stimuli. These latter influences tend to be of a political, economic, social or technical nature. In making a purchase decision, consumers respond to the stimuli deployed by the selling company. The greater the company's knowledge is about the reactions these stimuli elicit, the greater the competitive advantage for that company.

Outputs refer to buyer responses. Outputs can be identified and assessed in terms of the purchase decision, such as the choice of brand, the place of purchase, the quantity purchased, and the terms and conditions of purchase.

A comparison of inputs and outputs raises questions about who buys and how they buy. These issues have led researchers to examine closely buyer characteristics in order to identify the critical drivers in the purchase decision-making process.

Influencing Factors

Part of the process of understanding consumer buyer behaviour involves appreciating the context in which consumers make their purchase decisions. Pervasive social influences can be viewed on two levels: the macro

Figure 1.2 Social influences on consumer buyer behaviour

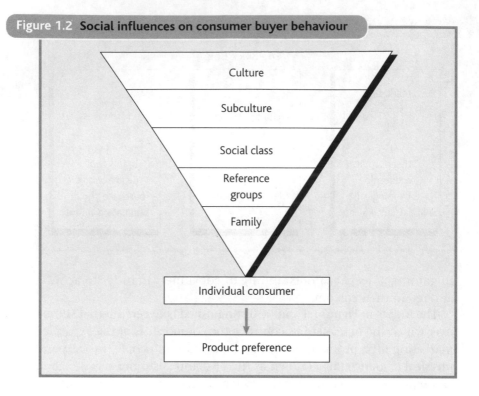

level and the micro level. Macro influences embrace culture, subculture and social class, while micro influences comprise the consumer's more immediate social environment of reference groups and the family. Let us consider each level in turn, as portrayed in Figure 1.2.

Macro social influences

Macro social factors play a role in shaping the values, beliefs, attitudes and behaviours of individual consumers, and provide useful bases upon which to segment markets. They have direct implications for designing effective relationship marketing strategies, especially where management of the marketing mix spans national boundaries. The annals of international marketing contain numerous examples of companies, many of them respected brand owners, who have failed to manage their product/service portfolios successfully because their marketing efforts have neglected to take into account the respective cultures concerned. For example, General Motors' marketing of the Nova car in Spain was destined to bring disappointment, for 'nova' literally means, 'won't go' in Spanish. Simon Anholt, founder of World Writers, said at a Marketing Society event in October 1997:

> Culture is the things that people think, it is the things they believe in, it is the things that motivate them, it is the things that make them what they are. Language is just the way they say it, and if you get the culture right, then the language is sure to follow.

Culture

Culture can be defined broadly as 'a complex of learned meanings, values and behavioural patterns' (Peter and Olson, 1987) that are shared by a society. The relationship between the consumer and the product, often described as the 'product/self relationship', is culturally specific and thus of great interest to marketers seeking to identify the factors that influence purchasing and consumption. As the saying goes, the devil is in the detail.

Consider the Christmas holiday. It appears on the calendars of many countries, yet differences occur in the minutiae of each celebration. For example, the manufacturer of a major chocolate brand made serious mistakes in the first year of trying to manage a pan-European Christmas marketing campaign because it failed to appreciate that Christmas is celebrated differently across the Continent. In the Netherlands, Sinterklaas visits on 6 December, while in the UK, Father Christmas arrives on 24/25 December. Christmas and Epiphany are celebrated later in Greece and Russia.

Euro Disney also experienced a number of teething problems when it first opened on the out skirts of Paris in 1992. Research revealed, among other things, that while Americans prefer 'grazing' (or snacking) all day as they tour the theme park, Europeans want a full meal between 12 noon and 2 pm. Not recognizing this difference in eating patterns, park caterers were faced with big, unexpected queues for food in the early afternoon. To redress this situation, the company had to create more suitable eating opportunities for visitors. In addition, the two main daily parades of Disney characters had to be rescheduled for 11.30 am and 4 pm to avoid a clash with the lunch period.

Cultural influences play as important a role in domestic markets as they do in international ones. However, because marketers operating within their home countries tend to be very familiar with the prevailing culture, they may find it harder to recognize the significant cultural factors that influence domestic buyer behaviour.

Subculture

A subculture is a cultural group within a larger culture that has beliefs or interests that are at variance with those of the larger culture. Many types of distinction are used to classify subcultures, including ethnicity, religious or political affiliation, age and so on.

Taking age as an example, marketers often distinguish categories of consumers in terms of their age group. People within certain age ranges frequently behave similarly, but in ways which set them apart from other consumers. The youth market, for example, is described in terms of life stage characteristics. Young people are noted for their willingness to experiment with new identities. They exhibit a tendency to seek peer approval constantly, to be preoccupied with sex, and to find conflict with their parents. In terms of lifestyle, today's teenagers are the first computer-literate generation. They are well-travelled, possess unprecedented assertiveness, and are concerned with world issues and global perspectives. Young people currently have the highest earning power ever recorded for their age group, and outward manifestations of their subculture, such as accessories of music and apparel, are exceedingly important to them. These easily-identified and insatiable consumers represent every marketer's dream!

Interestingly, youth subculture is not restricted to any particular nationality, and is found in countries across the world. Teenagers comprise the most global market of all. Their tastes, language and attitudes are converging and, as consumers, they purchase a common portfolio of products. The teenager's bedroom is often 'a universal shrine' to pet products and icons, most of which are American in origin. With numbers of consumers in this market segment totalling 57 million in Mexico, Brazil and Argentina; 42 million in Japan, Korea, Singapore and Vietnam; 28 million in the USA; and 50 million in Europe, the opportunities for marketers with the right products and the right approaches to marketing them are immense.

Social class

The concept of social class is drawn from sociology, where a social group is organized according to a recognized hierarchy based on the individual's status within the group. While the impact that social class has on consumer behaviour is a topic of considerable debate, marketers favour social class as a form of shorthand to describe their typical consumers. In the UK, for example, consumers are classified into six social classes, mainly determined by the occupation of the

Table 1.1 UK socio-economic classification scheme

Class name	Social status	Occupation of head of household
A	Upper Middle	Higher managerial, administrative, professional
B	Middle	Intermediate managerial, administrative or professional
C1	Lower Middle	Supervisors or clerical, junior managerial, administrative or professional
C2	Skilled Working	Skilled manual workers
D	Working	Semi-skilled and unskilled manual workers
E	Subsistence level	Pensioners or widows, casual or lower-grade workers

head of the household, as given in Table 1.1. This method of classification has remained in use for a number of years, despite unease at its decreasing relevance to current society.

These systems of consumer classification tend to be culturally bound, having been developed on a parochial basis. They do not lend themselves to international comparison. Within Europe, there have been attempts to use a harmonized set of demographics, which focus on the terminal education age of the main income earner in the household, their professional status, and the average net monthly level of household income. However, collecting this kind of data from across European markets can prove problematic in countries such as the UK, where it is common practice for survey respondents to think in terms of their gross annual salary, rather than the net monthly income of their household. These issues surrounding the difficulties of marketing research are discussed further in Chapter 4.

The need to find a more appropriate method of defining social class is the driving force behind the recent unveiling of a revised classification by the UK government. This is described in Case study 1.1.

Case study 1.1 **Climbing the social classes**

Since before the First World War, UK government statisticians have ranked people in terms of their employment: professional; managerial and technical; skilled non-manual; skilled manual; partly skilled; and unskilled. Some 87 years after their introduction, these six social classes were redefined in 1998 by the Office for National Statistics, during a three-year project sponsored jointly with the Economic and Social Research Council. The project report highlighted the fact that changes in the nature and structure of both industry and occupations had rendered the distinction of social class based on skills outmoded and misleading. The new social classifications reflect more accurately current employment conditions, such as reduced job security and greater career uncertainty.

The revised eight major social classes are:

1 Higher managerial and professional occupations
    1.1 employers and managers in larger organizations
    1.2 Higher professionals
2 Lower managerial and professional occupations
3 Intermediate occupations
4 Small employers and own-account workers
5 Lower supervisory, craft and related occupations
6 Semi-routine occupations
7 Routine occupations
8 People who wish to work but who never have.

Updating the social classification system has had the effect of elevating the rank of working women and public-sector employees. Teachers and police officers also have been regraded; teachers now belong to Class 1, while police officers, who were previously on a par with skilled workers, are now classed as 'associate professionals'.

Micro social influences

Purchasing decisions are also influenced at the micro level by the people closest to the consumer, namely family, friends, relatives and peers. These people feature significantly in the consumer's immediate social environment and can be grouped into two types of influencer: reference groups, and family. Their effect on consumers' attitudes and purchasing behaviour can be considerable.

Reference groups

Reference groups are made up of people who share the consumer's social circumstances and who are personally relevant to the consumer; they influence the way that the consumer thinks, feels and behaves in respect to choosing between different products and services. Classic examples of reference groups are school or college friends and peers. The tendency for young people to own certain brands of footwear, for example, is highly likely to be driven by the desire to conform to the norm for their peer group.

Some companies use reference groups explicitly in their marketing activities. For example, companies such as Tupperware that use in-home selling techniques actively encourage reference groups to exercise their power in the purchasing decision. It is also common practice for health and fitness clubs to build their client registers through special promotions where current members are encouraged to recommend or recruit new members. In this case, reference group endorsement is used to market the club's facilities.

Family

Market research traditionally uses the individual consumer as the unit of analysis, but there are types of purchasing decision where the family becomes the decision-making unit. Studies of this phenomenon attempt to describe the various roles played by family members and the complexity of interactions that take place in reaching a collective decision. For example, the choice of restaurant for a family's meal out may well be influenced by the children within the family, whose motivation may stem from the appeal of a promotional offer. McDonald's, for example, is one of the largest toy retailers in the world, tying in promotional give-aways with the release of blockbuster Disney movies.

In fact, it is estimated that, in the USA, children prompt purchases amounting to a staggering US$260 billion per annum. This power exerted by children in the market place, directly through the purchases made by immediate family members and indirectly through gifts received from wider family and friends, is known as 'pester power'.

In seeking to understand the dynamics of the family decision-making unit, two issues are key: demographic changes in 'the family'; and the family life-cycle. Family statistics are altering in response to changes in the composition of the household and the nature of child rearing, increased female employment, and lower birth rates. This has necessitated a move away from the traditional picture of the family unit, that of two married parents where the mother is at home bringing up the children and the father is out at work. These demographic trends have profound implications for marketers, who are faced increasingly with the challenge of identifying and satisfying families' needs without having any firm idea of what the 'family' is.

Present trends indicate that families will continue to be smaller, more affluent, and more geographically mobile. At the time of writing, children enjoy the highest ever level of material goods, and this is set to continue, presenting tremendous scope for youth-orientated brands. Additionally, opportunities are opening up as people become increasingly willing to pay for services that maximize their use of time: for example, the home delivery of groceries, after-school clubs for children, and so on.

A popular tool for analysing family purchasing behaviour is the family life-cycle, which describes the typical changes that take place in families over a period of time. Traditionally, the family life-cycle has concentrated on life-stage events such as marriage and the arrival of children, and schooling and the departure of children (often referred to as the 'full nest' and 'empty nest' life stages). However, given the evident changes in demographics, the family life-cycle is no longer a straightforward linear model, but something resembling a complex network of life patterns that may be connected by (out), non-traditional or repeated life stages. The traditional family life cycle is:

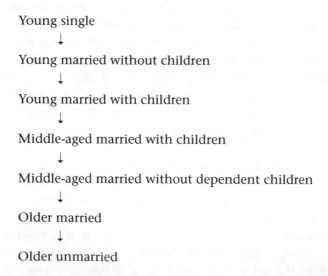

Young single
↓
Young married without children
↓
Young married with children
↓
Middle-aged married with children
↓
Middle-aged married without dependent children
↓
Older married
↓
Older unmarried

It is crucial that marketers are able to recognize changes at each of these life stages so that they can re-evaluate the positioning of existing products and services, and identify opportunities for new products and services. For example, the marketing of 'white goods' is generally targeted at young couples, who are likely to require domestic appliances when setting up a home together.

Consumers

Influencing factors that have a more direct impact on consumer behaviour are those concerned with the individuals themselves. They include personal attributes, such as age, stage of life, occupation, economic circumstance, lifestyle, personality type, and psychological forces with respect to beliefs, attitudes and motivations. For example, the same individual may display distinctly different buyer behaviour when purchasing a bottle of wine for home consumption than when buying a gift for a dinner party. Equally, consumers may display a completely different set of purchase motivations and preferences when faced with a so-called 'distress purchase', such as buying petrol when the petrol gauge in the car hits zero, compared to simply topping up a half-full tank.

Market research data on consumer buyer characteristics can be presented to marketers in the form of a typology of buyers for a particular set of products or services. These consumer profiles, with their memorable labels such as 'sporting thirties' and 'young survivors', can be assimilated quickly into marketing strategies. They offer an abbreviated method of expressing a complex set of consumer characteristics and typical buying behaviours.

Case study 1.2, of a typology of British shoppers, shows how the personal attributes of consumers can be summarized in a way that is meaningful to marketers.

Case study 1.2 A typology of British shoppers

Bluewater is Europe's largest and newest shopping complex. Opened in Kent, to the east of London, in 1999, at a cost of £350 million, the centre incorporates more than 320 shops, in addition to restaurants, cafés, a crèche, a 12-screen cinema, a boating lake, picnic area, mountain bike trails and numerous cash points. Approximately 80 000 customers are expected to visit the complex each day and, with an estimated average spend of £25, it is anticipated that Bluewater will become a valuable business for its Australian owners, Lend Lease.

No aspect of the Bluewater project has been left to chance. For five years, researchers investigated consumer buyer behaviour using a variety of methods in order to create psychographic profiles of anticipated shoppers for the shopping centre planners. The research was directed by a pyschotherapist with a background in marketing, and has resulted in the identification of seven definitive types of British shopper. These are:

County classics	House-proud; shop at John Lewis and Jaeger; interested in success, concerned about what others think of them and cynical about fashion; numerically the largest cluster
Club executives	BMWs and Boss suits are part of their iconography; career orientated; expect service to be efficient
Sporting thirties	Interested in sports; with a disruptive tendency, really don't want to shop – prefer the bar instead
Home comfortable	Elderly customers with traditional tastes; like to be served by people their own age
Young fashionables	In search of an identity; interested in cosmetics, personal grooming and outward appearance
Young survivors	Want low-cost amusement; may use shopping to boost their self-esteem
Budget optimists	Don't need to have their egos massaged; looking for a sense of trust in their transactions.

Bluewater's research into consumer behaviour was designed to ensure that the shopping centre's offerings would be aligned to shoppers' needs. Attention has been devoted to making every aspect of the shopping experience customer-friendly and customer-focused. Shoppers enter the complex through hotel-style 'welcome' halls, where they are advised by concierges, who will do everything from escorting them to a particular shop to carrying their bags and reminding them where they left their car in the 13 000-space car park.

Bluewater's investigations also identified gender issues common to certain groups of shoppers. These traits have been addressed through special measures such as ensuring that certain stores (for example, Marks & Spencer, which the shopping psychologists reported 'is where men tend to get bored and want to go home'), are placed conveniently next to gadget shops such as Dixons or the bar of a TGI Friday. (This section was sourced from articles appearing in the UK press during March 1999.)

Types of consumer purchase decision

Understanding the purchase decision-making process as a fundamental part of creating a relationship with consumers requires an examination of the role and interaction of two important dimensions: the concept of involvement and the degree of difference that consumers perceive to exist between competing brands. These are important elements in both the acquisition and retention of consumers.

'Involvement' is a term used to describe how personally meaningful the purchase is to the consumer. It implies that the act of purchasing will be a conscious activity and that an element of effort will have been invested in making the final choice. The role of consumer 'involvement' refers to the factors listed in Figure 1.3.

Figure 1.3 The role of consumer involvement

- high degree of risk (performance, cost, psychology)

- high degree of brand differentiation

- hedonism and pursuit of pleasure

- lifestyle products

- special interest products (hobbies and leisure pursuits)

Purchases with high involvement are made by consumers who perceive there to be a high degree of risk. Risk may be judged on the basis of performance (will it work?), cost (is the price too high?) or psychology (is it right for me?). Generally, a high involvement situation is where the purchase is linked strongly to the pursuit of pleasure, as with a hobby or lifestyle product, or an infrequent purchase, such as a bed. Conversely, purchases with low involvement involve little risk and tend to be habitual, practical purchases of consumables, such as bread or laundry detergent.

Types of consumer buyer behaviour

When the degree of consumer involvement is combined with knowledge of whether consumers perceive many or few differences between brands, it becomes possible to identify four distinctive types of buying behaviour. These are depicted in Figure 1.4 and may be summarized as:

► complex buyer behaviour;
► dissonance-reducing buyer behaviour;
► variety-seeking buyer behaviour; and
► habitual buyer behaviour.

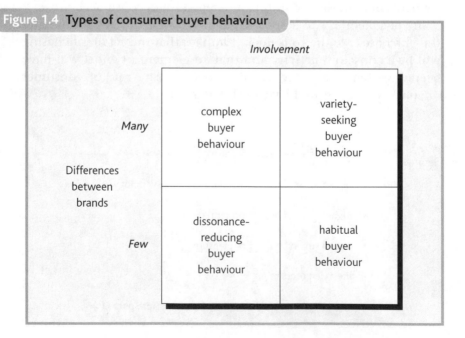

Figure 1.4 Types of consumer buyer behaviour

Complex buyer behaviour Often marked by consumer confusion, this behaviour is demonstrated when consumers are highly involved in a purchase and perceive significant differences among brands. For many people, the purchase of a personal computer (PC) falls into this category. The rapid pace of technology is reflected in an overwhelming variety of features and applications, and to make an informed choice about which PC is best requires a personal investment of time and energy. Marketers are presented with an opportunity to influence the purchase decision at the stage where consumers seek information about a product's attributes and differential value. Well-trained sales staff can also influence the purchase decision proactively by providing consumers with guidance and advice. If the purchase is managed well by the selling organization, the chances are that the consumer will return to them for future purchases, thus increasing the customer's lifetime value to the organization. The purchase decision-making process can therefore be seen to pass through the stages of 'awareness', 'trial' and 'repeat buying'.

Dissonance-reducing buyer behaviour 'Dissonance' describes the after-sales feelings of the consumer who believes that there has been some sort of shortfall between the purchase expectation and the purchase delivery. This post-purchase disappointment is often related to the product's actual performance. Dissonance-reducing behaviour is demonstrated where consumers are highly involved with the purchase, perhaps because it is something expensive which they would seldom buy, and where they perceive there to be few differences between brands. Bed purchases are one good example. In order to address this type of behaviour, marketers need to concentrate their efforts on before- and after-sales communications to ensure that consumers feel confident about their choice of brand. This is essential to 'win over' consumers and move them up the ladder of loyalty (see Chapter 14). Dissonance-reducing behaviour must be managed at all costs, to prevent consumers from generating negative publicity by word of mouth.

Variety-seeking buyer behaviour This is characterized by low consumer involvement and the perception of significant brand differences. This type of consumer will switch brands regularly within the same product category. Such behaviour is not driven by dissatisfaction with the brand, but rather by a desire to sample other brands. In order to be successful in such markets, marketers need to encourage habitual buying by ensuring that target brands or products dominate the shelf space, that distribution strategies minimize stockouts, and that communications and promotional activities constantly provide reminders and reinforcements. Once again, brand visibility and availability provide the key levers in building a relationship with variety seekers.

Habitual buyer behaviour This behaviour occurs where there is low consumer involvement and few perceived differences between brands. This behaviour tends to be associated with low-cost, frequently purchased products, such as flour. Consumers simply make their choice by reaching out for the same product time and again, and more out of habit than loyalty. Opportunities for relationship building may be perceived to be small, but the shrewd marketer will focus on promotions which serve to build a sense of brand familiarity and which stimulate trial usage of the product. In these circumstances, it is important that the brand is always displayed prominently on the shop shelf, and that out-of-stock situations are avoided. Visibility and availability are the vital elements in managing habitual buyers.

The consumer purchase decision-making process

While different types of buyer behaviour can be shown to exist, it is quite another matter to be unequivocal about why people buy what they buy. Decision-making is generally regarded as a linear process, starting with the recognition of a need. In the purchase decision-making process, as outlined in Figure 1.5, the first step is where buyers acknowledge that they have a need, or a problem that requires a solution. This realization can be triggered through internal stimuli, such as hunger pangs, or external stimuli, such as recalling a favourable review of a restaurant or noticing aromas emanating from a restaurant

Figure 1.5 Model of consumer purchase decision-making process

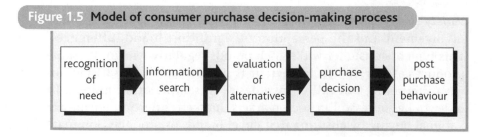

recognition of need → information search → evaluation of alternatives → purchase decision → post purchase behaviour

kitchen. This initial acknowledgement is usually followed by an information search: the consumer reads the menu displayed outside the restaurant and evaluates the offerings. The consumer will then reach a conclusion and either enter the restaurant and order a meal, or move on down the road to a different dining establishment. After eating the meal, the consumer will demonstrate some form of post-purchase behaviour by making an assessment of his or her level of satisfaction with respect to expectation, perhaps leaving a tip that reflects the outcome of that assessment.

Of course, most consumers pass through the decision-making process without giving it much thought. In instances where consumers are making a repeat purchase, they would enter the purchase decision-making process at one of the later stages.

Approaches to consumer buyer behaviour

A substantial amount of research has been conducted to try to explain consumer buyer behaviour. How a marketer should interpret and use the vast amount of consumer data available depends on whether they believe it is more beneficial to direct marketing activities according to consumer psychology or according to consumer behaviour. This dilemma is related to perceptions of how consumers learn about products and services. The differences here are that a cognitivist approach focuses on what consumers think and feel, while a behaviourist approach is concerned with understanding overt consumer behaviour, or what consumers actually do.

These two approaches hold different implications for designing consumer research studies and subsequent marketing strategies. The focus of research and promotional activity will depend on whether the marketer adopts a cognitivist or a behaviourist view of consumer buyer behaviour.

At a simplistic level, marketers of a cognitivist persuasion tend to favour image-based advertising and promotions, which appeal to consumers' values. They will offer brand benefits in ways that play on consumers' thoughts, feelings, attitudes and beliefs. Behaviourists, on the other hand, tend to use conditioning behaviour, where the marketing message is reinforced through skilful advertising. For example, the association between the Marlboro man and the Marlboro cigarette is now so strong that in some cases the company no longer includes the brand name in its advertisements. This is because the brand has succeeded in transferring the meaning of an unconditioned stimulus to a conditioned stimulus.

So, which marketing approach is right? Historically, advertisers have adopted the behaviourist philosophy. However, they are now shifting the emphasis towards creating a mood and eliciting an emotion, while still recognizing the importance of the association of products with symbols, colours and images. The debate is ongoing.

Summary

An understanding of the buyer behaviour of individual consumers is necessary in order to make sense of markets, and essential in planning a marketing strategy. This requires that marketers work with the consumers' perception of reality.

Models of consumer buyer behaviour can, at best, help to promote this understanding, and demonstrate how consumers may be persuaded to buy one product rather than another. The development of models involves 'de-layering' the social influences that have an impact on culture, subculture and social class. Forces which have a more immediate effect on consumer behaviour are close associates, namely reference groups and family. Of paramount importance to the purchase decision is the make-up of the consumers themselves, encompassing their age, occupation, lifestyle, personality type and psychological motivation.

The interaction of two key dimensions – consumer 'involvement' and consumer perception of differences between brands – produces four distinct types of buyer behaviour: complex, dissonance-reducing, variety-seeking, and habitual. Understanding how best to manage buyers of these persuasions enables marketers to develop long-term, profitable relationships with consumers.

Typical stages in the consumer purchase decision-making process can be identified, although these will not always represent conscious actions in the minds of consumers. It is the task of marketing research (see Chapter 4) to make these steps explicit in order that they may be better addressed and exploited.

Marketers must decide whether they favour a cognitivist or a behaviourist approach to understanding consumer buyer behaviour if they are to give clear direction to marketing activities which support consumer relationships, such as market research, market segmentation, branding and marketing communications.

Further reading

Ajzen, I. and Fishbein, M. (1980) *Understanding Attitudes and Predicting Social Behaviour*, Englewood Cliffs, NJ: Prentice-Hall.

Lambkin, M., Foxall, G., Heilbrunn, B. and van Raajj, F. (eds) (1998) *European Perspectives on Consumer Behaviour*, London: Prentice-Hall (a definitive collection of European-authored research on consumer behaviour).

References

Kotler, P., Armstrong, G., Saunders, J. and Wong, V. (1996) *Principles of Marketing*, Englewood Cliffs, NJ: Prentice-Hall.

Peter, J. and Olson, J. (1987) *Consumer Behavior and Marketing Strategy*, Homewood, Illinois: Irwin (2nd edn 1990).

2 Organizational buyer behaviour

Consumer versus industrial purchase decisions

Earlier we referred to the purchase decision-making process as having three stages; awareness, trial, and repeat buying. It is perhaps more accurate to describe this process as being typical of most consumer purchases. For industrial purchases, the buying process can be more complex and involve more stages, as Table 2.1 shows.

The need for the purchase invariably starts from within the buyer's organization as some kind of problem or need. The remaining 'buy stages' gradually unfold, sometimes over a period of weeks or even months. This process is clearly very different from walking into a shop and saying, 'I'll have one of those, please', paying, and walking out.

What makes the industrial purchase decision more complex is the fact that there is rarely just one person involved. Because of the technological, production, financial, safety and quality ramifications of buying a new piece of plant or machinery, for example, a number of people have to be satisfied that the correct buying decision is being made.

Table 2.1 Industrial buying process

Stage	Description of industrial buyer's actions
1	Recognizes needs or problems; works out general solution
2	Works out the characteristics and quantity of what is needed
3	Prepares detailed specification
4	Searches for and locates potential suppliers
5	Analyses and evaluates tenders, proposals, plans, etc.
6	Selects 'best' supplier
7	Places trial order
8	Evaluates trial order
9	Negotiates main contract subject to trial results
10	Monitors deliveries, quality, etc.

Change drivers in the business environment

A company involved in freight forwarding recently benchmarked how its customers perceived the added value it contributed towards their business development. The evaluation revealed that some of its main customers, including global companies such as Compaq and Intel, are in the process of developing efficient end-to-end supply chains, from component supply to end-customer delivery. Consequently, these customers will be seeking to work with suppliers who offer logistics capabilities across a wide range of products and services to serve them on a global basis. The company's research also confirmed suspicions that this fundamental shift in customer expectations and purchasing requirements was leading to a large-scale rationalization in the number of logistics companies their customers used. The world-wide logistics director of a US computer company said, 'Six years ago, we had 35 significant logistics suppliers (including freight forwarders); we are now reducing this to about five. International product flow should be within the capability of anyone; information flow and a willingness to provide customized services is where competitive advantage can be achieved.'

Table 2.2 Supplier rationalization across companies

Company	Number of suppliers		% change
	Current	Previous	
Xerox	500	5 000	90
Motorola	3 000	10 000	70
General Motors	5 500	10 000	45
Ford	1 000	1 800	44
Texas Instruments	14 000	22 000	36

Source: *Wall Street Journal*, issues in 1999.

Faced with increasing customer demands, the challenge to suppliers now is to develop their businesses globally and to work closely with leading customers so as to align their logistics offer with customer requirements. Customers in other markets are pursuing similar purchasing strategies among their own suppliers. Table 2.2 shows the extent of supplier rationalization in a range of global companies and markets.

The globalization of businesses is only one of many drivers that are changing the environment in which companies make purchasing decisions. Our research at Cranfield shows that there are four other major forces that suppliers must take into consideration when dealing in business-to-business markets: customer expertise, sophistication and power; lack of market growth; process thinking; and time-based competition.

Customer expertise, sophistication and power As we have seen from the previous logistics example, customers are becoming more and more demanding in their expectations of quality, reliability and compatibility. The growing desire for customization stems partly from a better knowledge base, facilitated by developments in communications and IT, and partly from the concentration of buying into fewer hands.

Lack of market growth In many mature markets, such as North America and Europe, market saturation has been reached. This state is characterized by over-capacity, increased competition and eroding margins. Under these conditions, customers are calling for greater operational efficiencies and 'value for money' from a smaller portfolio of preferred suppliers.

Process thinking A direct outgrowth of the technology explosion in information handling and electronic data interchange (EDI) has been the switch from a single-product approach to a systems orientation. The shift from marketing ready-made, tangible products to marketing by reputation, based on manufacturing capabilities and service delivery against exact client specifications, has fundamental implications for how companies organize to meet their customers' purchasing requirements.

Time-based competition Time horizons continue to become more compressed while the pace of change accelerates. The development of business systems, such as flexible manufacturing and just-in-time (JIT) deliveries, has encouraged companies to compete in terms of the speed with which they can deliver products and services to the market place.

In this rapidly changing climate of business-to-business marketing, how should companies go about managing customer relationships more effectively?

At a recent conference on relationship marketing held at Cranfield, Richard Hodapp, at that time of Managing Process Inc., reminded the audience of the need for business marketers to engage more fully in the customers' purchase decision-making processes as well as to provide customers with better products and services. While management endeavours to increase product and service content to inspire market share gains, this strategy is likely to produce only incremental gains, as it relies solely on technologies, product development procedures and marketing know-how. In Figure 2.1, this is referred to as 'product development strategy'.

However, enhanced knowledge of, and involvement with, customer purchasing processes (designated 'customer relationship strategy' in Figure 2.1) can lead to more significant market share gains. Comprehending *what* the scope of purchasing decision-making is and *where* the customer is at in the decision-making process can be hugely instrumental in influencing the purchase outcome. What is more, close relationships with customers leading to a detailed knowledge of their operations, are invisible to competitors but they can promote significantly product and service developments that fit more closely with customers' emerging requirements.

Meeting customer needs through a greater understanding of their requirements is similar to the approach consumer marketers use when they develop their products for the supermarket shelves. Without an appreciation of consumers' changing attitudes, buying behaviours and

Figure 2.1 Product content versus involvement in the customer purchasing process

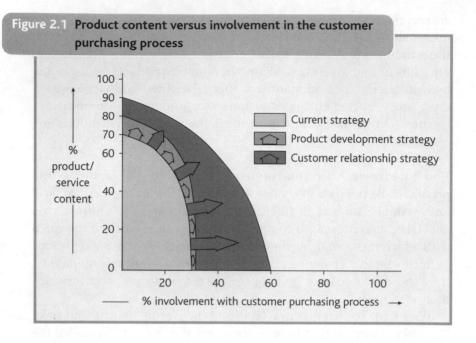

brand loyalty (see Chapter 9), the launch of a consumer product is likely to be unsuccessful. However, while the general approach to fulfilling customer needs may be similar, *how* the business purchase gets made and *who* influences the decision is fundamentally different from consumer marketing. A comparison of business-to-business and consumer marketing, as shown in Table 2.3, serves to illustrate this point.

Let us now take a closer look at four key aspects of organizational buyer behaviour: the decision-making unit (DMU); the decision-making process (DMP); behavioural segmentation of customers; and managing buyer–supplier relationships.

The decision-making unit (DMU)

The size and composition of the DMU, being the management team involved in the purchasing process, varies according to the size of the company (as shown in Table 2.4) and the strategic nature of the purchasing decision.

In certain situations involving the first-time purchase of large-scale capital goods and services, as many as forty people from across the company may become involved at different stages of the

Table 2.3 A comparison of business-to-business and consumer marketing

	Business products	Consumer products
Customer base	Few, with concentrated buying power	Numerous, widely dispersed and limited buying power
Buying behaviours (Decision-making unit)	Group decisions Many buying influences	Individual and family involvement
(Decision-making process)	Many purchasing procedures	Impulse, planned or experiential
Buyer/supplier relationships	Very close relationships over time Pre-sale consultancy and problem-solving After-sales services/support	Short duration with very little close contact
Product	Technical complexity Standard or customized Detailed specifications	Standard
Price	High unit price Negotiating/bidding Standard items from list	Low unit price from list
Promotion	Emphasis on personal selling	Mainly mass advertising and promotion
Distribution/logistics	Mainly direct for make-to-order customized items Standard items often available from stock through distributors	Stock items through a network of wholesalers and retail distributors

Table 2.4 The DMU by company size

Number of employees	Number of DMU members	Average number of contacts made by suppliers' salespeople during purchase
0–200	3.40	1.72
201–400	4.85	1.75
401–1000	5.81	1.90
1000+	6.50	1.85

decision-making process. The structure of the DMU can also be examined in terms of the different functions that are represented. These *roles* can be placed broadly into seven categories: policy-makers; purchasers; users; technologists; influences; gatekeepers; and deciders.

Policy makers Those individuals within the company who have the authority and responsibility for agreeing certain general policies that directly affect purchasing behaviour. The central purchasing of strategic items across a number of business units, such as media buying in Unilever, is one example of a company policy. The outsourcing of IT is often directed by similar policy decisions.

Purchasers The actual buyers who are formally authorized to order products or services from suppliers. The purchaser's role can range from filling in purchase requisition forms to being the purchasing team leader responsible for making the final recommendation to senior management or the main board. Any assessment of the importance of the purchasing agent must consider the organization's attitude towards the purchase function, together with the level of risk associated with the purchase.

Users The people who ultimately use the product or service. It is likely that they will be concerned primarily with product performance and ease of use. If installation or application is technically demanding for the customer, then the provision of post-sales consultancy and support will become crucial, to the point of overriding commercial considerations such as price and delivery times.

Technologists The engineers or specialists, such as actuaries, and those with specialist knowledge who appraise the technical aspects of competitive offers and advise on key performance indicators (KPIs). It is the KPIs which enable the DMU to differentiate and judge suppliers against the company's own specifications – standards which the technologist is likely to have defined.

Influencers The people who influence the DMP, either directly or indirectly, by providing information and criteria for the evaluation of alternative buying actions. Influencers can work inside the company or act as external advisers. For example, companies will quite often employ a systems integrator as a consultant in a major IT purchase to guide the DMU from the earliest stages of the purchasing process. Sometimes the DMU may visit a company that has made a similar purchase to discuss their experiences of using the product and the supplier against KPIs.

Gatekeepers People who control the flow of information to others within the company and the DMU. For example, buyers may have the authority to prevent salespeople from seeing users and deciders. Other gatekeepers include technical personnel and even personal secretaries.

Deciders Those with the authority to approve purchases. The decider is likely to be a senior manager where a complex purchase or company policy is involved. Otherwise, in more routine purchases, the buyer is usually the decider.

From a supplier's perspective, the make-up of the DMU is critical. The company's marketing efforts will reflect the individual priorities and interests of the constituent members as well as the overall group dynamics. In other words, in meeting the collective concerns of the DMU, trade-offs will be made during the purchasing process that will alter the perceptions of what are the key technical, problem-solving and relational benefits required from suppliers.

This need to deliver against key benefits is illustrated by an example, shown in Table 2.5, of the marketing of oil lubricants to a cement company. Even though the purchase is relatively straightforward, the DMU consists of six people, who display six distinct roles.

Table 2.5 Marketing oil lubricants to a cement company

DMU role	DMU job title	Benefits sought
Specifier/user	Engineer	No technical problems
User/influencer	Storeman	JIT deliveries, palleted barrels
Decider	Buyer	Lowest price
Gatekeeper	Finance Manager	System uses a purchase order number and pays according to usage
Influencer	Cement Sales Manager	Quid pro quo for new cement business
Gatekeeper	General Manager	An innovative supplier that contributes to a lean supply chain

Organizational and product influences on the DMU

Various organizational 'demographics', such as a firm's size, purchasing policy or use of electronic data processing (EDP) and communications such as the intra- and extra-net, can change the composition of the DMU and *how* and *what* it buys.

Historically, much of the purchasing in companies consisting of many different business units has been carried out at the business unit level. Recently, however, some large companies have tried to centralize purchasing in order to obtain more purchasing clout as well as substantial savings. Case study 2.1, featuring PepsiCo, provides an example of this move towards central purchasing.

Case study 2.1 A move towards central purchasing

PepsiCo aims to save US $100 million a year out of a total cost of US $2 billion by combining the buying power of its separate businesses.

Paul Steele, European vice-president of sales and marketing, said; 'When we went through the list it was surprising. For example, Pizza Hut buys an enormous quantity of cardboard for the pizza boxes. Pepsi-Cola buys cardboard for soft drink trays. We're looking at whether we can leverage the scale.'

They will now try the same with buying flour, salt, spices and cooking oil across their restaurant businesses, which historically have developed separately. Now that they have the scale, central purchasing across preferred suppliers becomes a very exciting proposition.

Source: adapted from Diane Summers, *Financial Times*, 29 September 1994.

Product factors that influence buyers' decisions include frequency of purchase, the strategic nature of the product or service being considered, and loyalty to suppliers. Generally, there are three types of buying situations that have an impact on the way that the DMU is organized and how products and suppliers are selected: Straight rebuy; modified re-buy; and new-task purchase.

Straight re-buy The buyer reorders without requesting any product or service modifications. The buyer simply chooses a supplier from an approved list based on past buying satisfaction. Because it is a routine reordering situation, the supplier may propose an automatic reordering system both to save purchasing time and to reduce the risk of losing profitable, regular purchases.

Modified re-buy Although the company has prior experience of the product, the particular purchase situation demands some degree of customization, such as changes in the product specification, price, terms or supplier. Approved suppliers, including those currently under contract to the customer, may use the purchasing opportunity to make a better offer to the customer in order to win new business (see Case study 2.2).

New-task purchase A company buying a product or service for the first time may have no experience of supplier capabilities or performance evaluation. Consequently, the greater the cost or risk, the larger the DMU and its informational requirements. The new-task situation represents the marketer's greatest opportunity and challenge: the aim is to reach as many key buying influencers as possible, and to provide help and information.

Case study 2.2 A modified re-buy in systems cleaning

In the late 1990s, the Canadian company, DiverseyLever, had a leading market share in the provision of systems-cleaning services for plants of multinational food companies around the world. Many of its customers used different suppliers on a country-by-country or plant-by-plant basis as well as within each plant. Some of the plants required up to fourteen different cleaning procedures to clean a range of areas, from surfaces of temperature-controlled, high-speed filling lines to washrooms and canteens.

In a strategic review of their key customers' needs, DiverseyLever's marketing and sales management recognized the opportunity to develop a unified cleaning programme. Using the slogan 'one plant, one solution', and working with a leading customer who could also see the benefits of simplifying their cleaning procedures for health and safety purposes, DiverseyLever developed a specialist business unit which combined *elements* (products, services and equipment)

Case study 2.2 *continued*

and *systems* (applications) with *expertise* (multi-skilled cleaning teams) to deliver a customized cleaning *programme* for the customer's entire plant. As knowledge was accrued and trials were extended to other plants, the customer decided to outsource the cleaning of its entire North American business to DiverseyLever.

In time, as the appropriate key account management structure develops, DiverseyLever hopes to provide a service to the customer on a country-by-country basis. In the meantime, other multinationals are inviting DiverseyLever to provide them with customized systems cleaning services, and demand will no doubt grow as health and safety legislation around the world becomes more complex.

The decision-making process (DMP)

Buyers who face a new-task buying situation are likely to adopt a formal decision-making process (DMP), which may involve up to eight separate stages. Purchases that are modified or straight re-buys may skip some of these stages. Referring to Table 2.6, let us now look at the DMP for the typical new-task purchase.

Although the DMP is shown to be a linear sequence of progressive stages, in practice the stages are rarely neatly sequential or discrete. Sometimes the stages may occur out of sequence or simultaneously, or not at all if it is a fairly straightforward re-buy. None the less, the DMP does provide a helpful guide to the distinguishing features of each of the typical buying stages.

Clearly, there is a relationship between the composition of the DMU and the DMP. Generally, as the *risk* associated with the organizational purchase *increases*:

▶ The DMU becomes more complex, with participants having more authority.
▶ DMP members will have greater levels of experience and heightened motivations.
▶ Suppliers with strong reputations and proven product solutions will be favoured.
▶ Information searches and sources, particularly personal and non-commercial communications, will be used increasingly to guide and support decisions.

Table 2.6 The eight stages of the DMP

Buying Stage	Characteristics
1 Problem recognition ↓	► Changing business needs ► Supplier review ► Current product/service dissatisfactions
2 General need ↓	► Innovation ► Cost savings ► Improved performance
3 Specification ↓	► Buyer/supplier dialogue ► 'Qualifying' criteria ► 'Differentiating' criteria
4 Supplier search ↓	► Risk profile of purchase ► Information gathering ► Consideration set
5 Proposals submission ↓	► Qualification of suppliers ► Choice set ► Proposal solicitation
6 Supplier selection ↓	► Proposals reviewed ► Buyer/supplier negotiations ► Selection and ratification
7 Order specification ↓	► Blanket contract/order ► Order fulfilment procedures ► Relationship development
8 Performance review	► Benchmark supplier performance ► Evaluation performance ► Endorse, modify or discontinue

► DMU role stress and conflict will increase, with bargaining negotiations taking place among members.
► Buyer–supplier relationships and communication networks become critical to fostering an atmosphere of co-operation and reducing perceived risk

As business marketers become more involved with organizational buying procedures and customer practices in general, market segmentation can be improved, enabling the marketing mix to be tailored more specifically to the needs of distinctive customer groups. This requirement for customization is a characteristic of competitive, mature markets. The product life cycle, or PLC (see Chapter 7), contends that prices drop with customer familiarity and an unwillingness to pay for consultation services from suppliers. In addition, heightened competition results in the availability of equivalent products at similar or lower prices. Steadily, as the market becomes more of a commodity, customer differentiation is needed to target offers more effectively. In highly competitive markets, segmentation based on buyer behaviour characteristics can be used to help strengthen buyer-supplier relationships and reach the right levels of customization. Although we shall be dealing with market segmentation in more detail in the next chapter, it is appropriate here to explore an organizational buyer behaviour approach.

Segmenting business customers in mature markets

Given this market dynamic, customers in mature markets may be aligned along the two dimensions of price and cost-to-serve according to their purchasing characteristics (see Figure 2.2). Customers who demand a low price can be offered a 'no frills' product with minimal service. Customers who value a customized offer will pay a higher price for tailor-made adaptations to products and services. Price differentials founded on product quality differences alone tend to be small because competitors are able to offer more or less equivalent products.

In keeping with this rationale, suppliers operating in mature markets may expect their customers' buyer behaviours to follow the path of the *value line* in Figure 2.2. Zone C of this line represents the unbundled offer or core product, while zone B denotes a

Figure 2.2 Buyer behaviour matrix

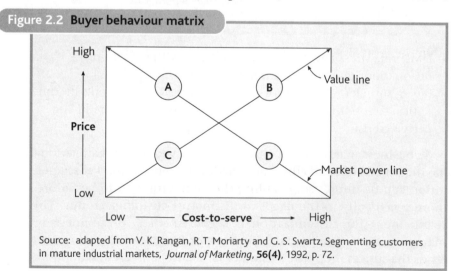

Source: adapted from V. K. Rangan, R. T. Moriarty and G. S. Swartz, Segmenting customers in mature industrial markets, *Journal of Marketing*, **56(4)**, 1992, p. 72.

customized offer based on a range of value-added services. In both cases, the value-for-money of the offer is equitable to the buyer and the seller.

From the buyer's perspective, an alternative strategy exists which is linked to the *market power line* in Figure 2.2. Customers see only the price dimension of the matrix, because they are price-driven and do not know or consider the supplier's cost-to-serve. Customers are likely to shop around for the best price, given that products themselves are largely undifferentiated, and to offer the bait of guaranteed purchase volume and large order sizes in order to drive prices down even further. Scrutinizing customers such as these choose to operate in zones D or C, depending on their knowledge of competitive offerings and their own market power.

In terms of supplier performance, operating in zone A implies that the supplier retains market power. This may be because of their having a truly superior product offering which competitors are unable to match for reasons of technological excellence or patent protection. In such circumstances, the supplier is able to support a high price. Remember, customers in zones A and B seek value through the superiority of the products or services that the supplier provides.

All locations *above the value line* indicate that the supplier meets the value requirements of the customer segments it serves and generates superior profits. In the areas *below the value line*, customer segments will be less profitable for the supplier, and possibly loss-making.

The buyer behaviour matrix serves to illustrate the possibilities of unearthing profitable customer segments using diagnostics closely associated with their patterns of buyer behaviour. Equally, as unprofitable customer segments are exposed, marketing and sales management will need to develop their marketing strategies, mindful of the costs of serving such price-conscious customers. Marketing planning may well involve the rationalization of customers who display blatant switching behaviours and who regard supplier relationships as purely transactional.

With increased turbulence in the market place, it is clear that firms are generally moving away from transaction-orientated marketing strategies and towards relationship-orientated marketing as a means of enhancing commercial performance and customer value. At Cranfield, we believe that the next source of competitive advantage will stem from the types of relationship that firms develop with their suppliers.

Relationship marketing and organizational buyer behaviour

Earlier in the chapter we noted the trend towards 'lean' supply, in which companies have reduced their supplier base significantly (see Table 2.2). With a smaller number of suppliers to manage, it becomes possible for buyers and suppliers to develop closer, longer-term relationships to increase competitiveness. There are three underlying reasons why stronger customer relationships can help to build competitive advantage:

1 *Systems cost reduction* – closer relationships achieved through multiple linkages between a preferred supplier and the customer enable better work practices, such as JIT deliveries, and reduced inventories and order cycle times. As trust increases and sales volatility decreases, cost savings resulting from improved work practices can be shared by both parties.
2 *Increased effectiveness through innovation* – as supplier relationships solidify, the customer may ask key suppliers to invest in technology that will allow the supplier to provide a quality platform, offer direct deliveries and engage in information exchange. Suppliers are naturally more willing to innovate by investing in such assets and services when they enjoy a strong relationship with the customer.
3 *Enabling technologies* – electronic linkages, ranging from automatic reordering and invoicing to the use of the Internet for immediate inter-company communications, enable suppliers to become closer and more responsive to their major customers. IT also allows the cost of transactions to be tracked. Consequently, suppliers are better able to determine which customers are cost-effective to serve (see Figure 2.2).

It is sometimes useful to picture supplier relationships as a continuum, with four levels of engagement defined according to the contribution the relationship makes to the buyer's competitiveness (see Figure 2.3). At each relationship level, the supplier provides products and services as well as capabilities, such as R&D, risk management and training. However, as the relationship develops and there is increased interdependency, the offering becomes more weighted towards the supplier's capabilities. Let us consider each relationship level in turn.

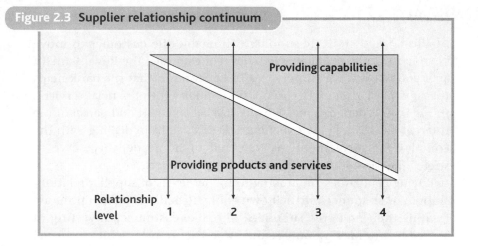

Figure 2.3 Supplier relationship continuum

Level 1

This basic level describes a traditional supplier who has a trans-actional relationship with the customer. The supplier sells specified products to the customer on the basis of price, service and quality. In most instances, the supplier adds limited value to the cus-tomer's overall competitiveness. This is a traditional buyer–seller relationship.

Level 2

Here, the supplier works co-operatively with the customer to reduce total costs and to increase the customer's competitiveness. Procter and Gamble's work with US food retailers on achieving everyday low price (EDLP) across its product portfolio is an example of this level of engagement.

Level 3

Working in partnership with the customer, the supplier takes responsi-bility for a significant component of the customer's value-adding capabilities. The customer will also be dependent on the supplier for innovation. Strategic sub-assembly deals in the automotive industry characterize this level of supplier relationship.

Level 4

At this level, a strategic supplier can enable the customer to move beyond its traditional competencies. For example, the Royal Bank of Scotland is a strategic supplier to Tesco Stores in that the bank helps the supermarket chain to extend its credibility into financial services. In the USA, Federal Express delivery has become part and parcel of the Internet-based shopping experience. FedEx's skills in dealing with the complex logistical problems involved in home delivery serve to stretch the capabilities of home-shopping providers.

Buying companies are moving to higher levels of supplier relationships in order to increase their own ability to add value. Such firms are treating their preferred suppliers more like customers, investing in shared technology, resources and expertise so as to achieve mutual benefit. In short, buyer–supplier relationships with common business interests require shared relationship marketing and planning skills. The growing trend towards long-term business relationships both indicates and influences changes in organizational buyer behaviour. The tendency towards long-term partnerships represents one of a number of current trends in organizational buyer behaviour.

Other key trends in organizational buyer behaviour

Customers want what customers want

Increasing levels of customization mean more co-operation and co-engineering, with the transfer of people and know-how across both sides of the buyer–supplier relationship. The commitment, 'Our people are your people', becomes part of the supplier's offer.

Qualifiers and differentiators

The product- and service-related aspects of the supplier's offer have become hygiene factors, as they no longer serve to differentiate. Differentiation now flows from the problem-solving and relational capabilities suppliers are able to demonstrate over a period of time.

Customer value, not risk reduction

As customers have grown more sophisticated in their purchasing processes, they have become less averse to risk. Unfettered by the need

Figure 2.4 The buyer's changing role

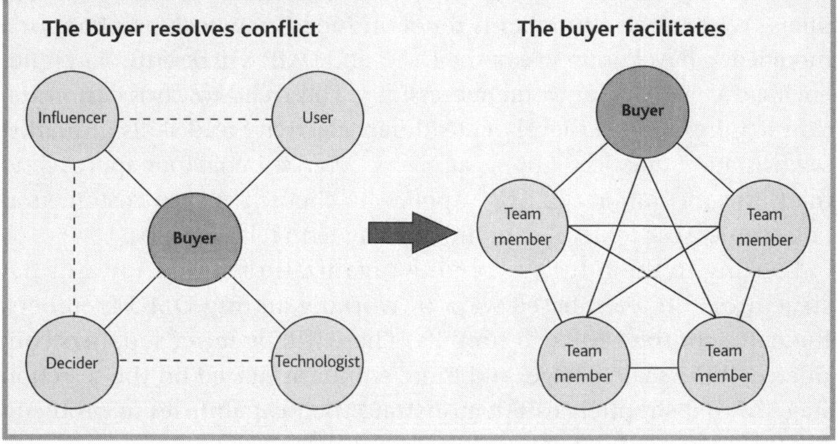

The buyer resolves conflict

The buyer facilitates

to manage downside risk, suppliers have come to be seen as a resource to enhance the end-customer's perceptions of value. In some markets, such as laptop computers and PCs, this has led to the co-branding of products and related services.

Conflict, what conflict?

The shift to flat structures and team-based working in organizations is altering perceptions of the buyer's role and how the DMU functions in a purchasing decision. Conflict, role stress and trade-offs among DMU members become less evident as co-operative solutions replace traditional divides. The buyer's role is changing from one of managing conflict to one of facilitating a cross-functional team (see Figure 2.4).

Summary

With the onslaught of ever more rapid and radical changes to the business environment, it has become imperative that business marketers understand their customers' needs fully. Knowing how people buy makes it easier to sell to them, and possibly to anticipate future market demands. In mature markets, characterized by increasing levels of commoditization, customers are looking for positive added value from their suppliers in order to be able to discriminate between alternative products and services.

The move towards lean supply and relationship marketing is heralding an era of customization and open co-operation between buyers and suppliers. Whether the supplier is tendering for a new-task purchase or a modified re-buy, knowledge of the DMU and DMP will be critical in influencing the purchase outcome successfully. This trend towards customization requires a higher level of customer selectivity and skills in market segmentation practices among suppliers. A buyer behaviour approach to market segmentation can help suppliers to choose between customers as both parties seek to develop profitable long-term relationships.

Looking to the future, as buying organizations move towards flat structures and team-based ways of working among DMU members, the nature of the DMP will simplify. There will be fewer suppliers considered at the search stage, and more emphasis placed on the selection stage so that suppliers can demonstrate their capabilities in problem-solving and building relationships with the DMU.

For an in-depth discussion of managing key supplier–buyer relationships, see Chapter 12.

Further reading

Bunn, M. (1993) Taxonomy of buying decision approaches. *Journal of Marketing*, **57** (January), pp. 38–46.

Hill, R. and Hillier, F. (1977) *Organisational Buyer Behaviour*, Macmillan, London.

Robinson, P., Faris, C. and Wind, Y. (1967) *Industrial Buying and Creative Marketing*, Allyn & Bacon, Boston.

References

Denison, T. and McDonald, M. (1995) The role of marketing past, present and future. *Journal of Marketing Practice: Applied Marketing Science*, **1(1)**, pp. 54–76.

Knox, S. and Maklan, S. (1998) *Competing on Value: Bridging the Gap between Brand and Customer Value*, Financial Times Pitman, London. [http://www.competingonvalue.com]

Kotler, P., Armstrong, G., Saunders, J. and Wong, V. (1999) *Principles of Marketing*, 2nd European edn, Prentice Hall, London.

Thompson, K., Mitchell, H. and Knox, S. (1998) Organizational Buying Behaviour in Changing Times. *European Management Journal*, **16(6)**, pp. 698–705.

3 Market segmentation

The importance of market segmentation

We have seen so far that marketing is an attitude of mind concerning customer satisfaction rather than a set of techniques simply to 'sell' products or services. No matter how good the product or service on offer, if there are not enough customers to buy it, there is no business.

Equally, when an organization starts giving customers the consideration they deserve and finds out more about them and their needs, it often discovers that they do not possess the resources or skills to take advantage of *all* market opportunities. In other words, a particular organization may not be as competitive as others when it comes to some *particular types* of customer, whereas it might be very competitive when it comes to others.

As few companies can be 'all things to all people', it is necessary to define in precise and actionable terms just who are the organization's customers, both now and in the future. Knowing where sales and profits are coming from is key to understanding current market positions and assessing potential market directions. In consumer and industrial markets, it is increasingly imperative to create and present a different offer to each group of customers, or, in the language of marketing, market segments. By sorting customers into economically manageable and 'prioritisable' segments, market segmentation enables an organization to target its limited resources on the most promising opportunities.

Most companies experience a phenomenon called the Pareto effect, or the 80/20 rule, where some 20 per cent of customers account for 80 per cent of business. However, this does not mean that the best potential customers reside in the top fifth of the market, and care must be taken to identify and address each market segment appropriately in the context of the market as a whole.

The difference between customers and consumers

Market segmentation is one of the key determinants of successful marketing, and is fundamental to the matching process between customers' wants and needs and the supplying organization's ability to satisfy them. In order to understand market segmentation, it is necessary to be clear about the difference between customers and consumers; the meaning of 'market' and market share; and the sequential relationship between the various steps of the market segmentation process and its ultimate contribution to securing competitive advantage.

Let us start with the difference between customers and consumers. The term 'consumer' is generally interpreted to mean the final consumer, who is not necessarily the customer. For example, parents who buy breakfast cereals are probably the intermediate customers, acting as agents on behalf of the eventual consumers (their families). In order to market cereals effectively, it is imperative that the marketer understands what the final consumers want, as well as what the parents want.

Given that we can appreciate the distinction between customers and consumers, and the need to be alert to any changes in the consumption patterns and requirements of final consumers, the next question becomes: 'Who are our customers?'

Direct customers are those individuals or organizations that buy direct from us, such as distributors, wholesalers, retailers and so on. However, as intimated in the previous paragraph, there is a tendency for organizations to confine their interests, and hence their marketing, to those who actually place the orders. Adopting a 'tunnel vision' approach to marketing can be a major mistake, as can be seen from Case study 3.1.

Case study 3.1 **The decline of a fertilizer company**

A fertilizer company that had grown and prospered during the 1970s and 1980s because of the superior nature of its products reached its farmer consumers via merchants (wholesalers). However, as other companies copied its leading technology, the merchants began to stock competitive products and were able to drive prices and margins down. Had the fertilizer company paid more attention to the needs of its different farmer groups and developed products especially for them based on farmer segmentation, it would have continued to create demand pull through differentiation. As it was, the fertilizer company's products became commodities and market power shifted almost entirely to the merchants. The company is no longer in business.

There are countless other examples of companies that have ceased trading because they did not pay sufficient attention to the needs of customers further down the supply chain and thus failed to provide any real value to their direct customers. An example of good practice is given in Case study 3.2.

Case study 3.2 **Procter & Gamble implement good practice**

Procter & Gamble (P&G) in the USA, which supplies the giant food retailer, Wal-Mart, exemplifies good practice. As can be seen from the simple diagram below, P&G creates demand pull (hence high turnover and high margins) by focusing its operations on serving the needs of consumers. The company is also very attentive to the needs of its direct customer, Wal-Mart. Wal-Mart is able to operate on very low margins because, as the bar code is swiped across the till, P&G produces an invoice, manufactures a replacement product and activates the distribution chain, all by means of integrated IT processes. This simultaneous and instantaneous system has reduced Wal-Mart's costs by hundreds of millions of dollars.

P&G $\Rightarrow$ CUSTOMERS $\Rightarrow$ CONSUMERS

Closely related to the question of what the difference is between customers and consumers is the question: 'What is our market share?'

Market definition and market share

Most business people understand that there is a direct relationship between having a relatively high market share and receiving a high return on investment (ROI). (Buzzell *et al.* 1995) This relationship is shown in Figure 3.1.

Before attempting to evaluate market share, it is very important to define the term 'market': for example, BMW is not in the same market as Ford, although both companies manufacture automobiles. Correct market definition is crucial for the purposes of measuring market share and market growth, specifying target customers, recognizing relevant competitors, and formulating marketing objectives and strategies.

The general rule for defining 'market' is that it should be described in terms of a customer need and in a way that covers the aggregation of all the alternative products or services that customers regard as being capable of satisfying that same need. For example, we would regard the company canteen as only one source providing a meal

Figure 3.1 **The relationship between market share and return on investment (ROI)**

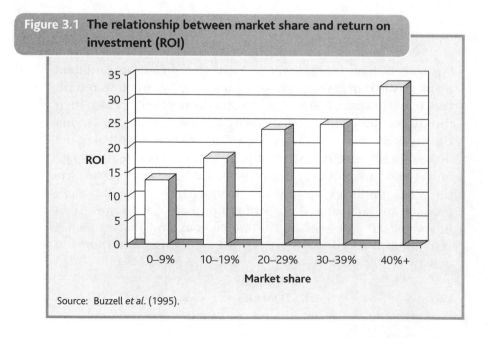

Source: Buzzell *et al.* (1995).

at lunchtime; the alternatives include external restaurants, public houses, fast food outlets and sandwich bars. The market definition emphasis, therefore, is clearly on the word 'need'.

Aggregating currently available products/services, however, is simply an aid to arriving at the definition, one that will probably require revision as new products are developed that better satisfy users' needs. For example, the button manufacturer who believed its market to be the 'button market' was no doubt disappointed at the arrival of zips and Velcro! A needs-based definition would have enabled the company's management to recognize the fickleness of current products, to accept that one of their principal tasks was to seek out better ways of satisfying their market's need for fastenings, and to evolve their product offer accordingly. IBM would have saved itself a lot of trouble if it had realized earlier that mainframes were products, not markets.

As well as highlighting the importance of getting the market definition right, these examples illustrate the necessity of arriving at a meaningful balance between a broad market definition and a manageable market definition. Too narrow a definition can restrict the range of new opportunities that could be exploited through segmentation, while too broad a definition could make marketing planning meaningless. For example, the television broadcasting companies are in the 'entertainment' market, which also consists of theatres, cinemas and theme parks. Because 'entertainment' is a fairly broad definition, television broadcasters may find it more manageable, when looking at segmenting their market, to define their market as 'home entertainment'. This definition could then be further refined into the pre-school, child, teenager, adult or family home entertainment markets.

Having established what we mean by 'market', we can then proceed to measure, manage and maximize it. To calculate market share, the following three criteria may be used:

Product class – cigarettes; computers; fertilizers; carpets;
Product subclass – filter; personal computers; nitrogen; carpet tiles; and
Product brand – Silk Cut; IBM; Intel; Heuga.

Silk Cut as a brand, for the purpose of measuring market share, is only concerned with the aggregate of all other brands that satisfy the same group of customer wants. Nevertheless, the manufacturer of Silk Cut also needs to be aware of the sales trends of filter cigarettes and the cigarette market in total.

One of the most frequent mistakes made by people who do not understand what market share really means is to assume that their company has only a small share of some market, whereas, if the company is commercially successful, it probably has a much larger share of a smaller market.

We must never lose sight of the purpose of market segmentation, which is to enable us to create competitive advantage for ourselves by creating greater value for our customers. For example, a London orchestra that defines its market as the aggregation of all London classical orchestras, rather than as all entertainment, has a relevant and realistic market definition that potentially will enable it to out-perform its competitors and grow profitably. The company in Case study 3.3 obviously did not understand the significance of market segmentation.

Case study 3.3 A European airline fails to focus

The chairman of a European airline, alas now bankrupt, once told his assembled general managers that his ambition was for his airline to be the best in the world and to provide customer service to the point of obsession. The problem was that his airline did not compete in many markets, and an unfocused customer obsession policy led to a provision of service the company could not afford. High-flown and ungrounded statements such as this chairman's can do more harm than good!

Market segmentation process

Market segmentation is the means by which a company seeks to gain a differential advantage over its competitors. A methodology is required to achieve market segmentation.

Markets usually fall into natural groups or segments, which include customers who exhibit broadly similar needs. These segments form separate markets in themselves and can often be of considerable size. Taken to its extreme, each individual consumer is a unique market segment, as all people differ in their requirements. However, it is clearly uneconomical to make unique products to meet the needs of individuals, except in the most exceptional of circumstances. Consequently, products are made to appeal to groups of customers who share approximately the same needs.

The universally accepted criteria of what constitutes a viable market segment are as follows:

▶ Segments should be of an adequate size to provide the company with the desired ROI;
▶ The members of each segment should share a high degree of similarity in their requirements, yet be distinct from the rest of the market;
▶ The criteria for describing segments must be relevant to the purchase situation; and
▶ Segments must be reachable by means of communication channels, distribution channels, or both.

While these criteria may seem obvious, market segmentation is one of the most difficult marketing concepts to put into practice. Yet, without effective segmentation, the company is susceptible to the 'me too' condition, where it offers the potential customer much the same product as any other company, which is likely to be the lowest-priced article. This can be ruinous to profits, unless the company happens to have lower costs, and hence higher margins, than its competitors.

There are basically three stages to market segmentation, all of which have to be completed if any progress is to be made. In the first stage, the company takes a detailed look at the way its market operates, and identifies how customer decisions are made about competing products or services. Successful segmentation is based on a detailed understanding of decision-makers and their requirements (see Chapter 2). The second stage is essentially a manifestation of the way customers actually behave in the market place and consists of answering the question, 'Who is buying what?' The third stage seeks to resolve the issue of 'Why do they buy what they buy?', and then to search for market segments based on this analysis of identified needs.

Market mapping

A useful way of tackling the complex issue of market segmentation is to start by drawing a 'market map' as a precursor to a more detailed examination of 'who buys what'. An example of a very basic market

Figure 3.2 A simple market map

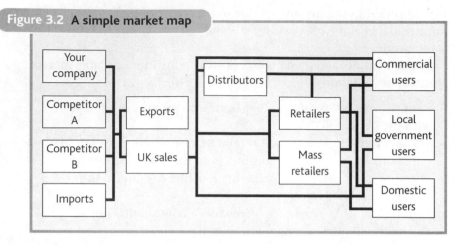

map is given in Figure 3.2. Note that this market map combines domestic and business-to-business end users, as some of the distribution channels are common to both of them.

A market map portrays the distribution, or supply and value chains that link the supplier and the ultimate consumer, or end user. It takes into account the various buying mechanisms found in the market, including the part played by 'influencers' (see pp. 28–9, 52).

In general, if an organization's products or services go through the same channels to similar end users, then one composite market map can be drawn. If, however, some products or services go through totally different channels and/or to totally different markets, then more than one market map must be produced.

It is probably sensible to treat different business units individually, as their respective business value or volume justifies a specific focus. For example, a farming co-operative that supplies seeds and fertilizer as well as crop protection, insurance and banking services will require a separate market map for each of these product groups, even though they all appear to go through similar channels to the same end users. In other words, it is advisable to start the mapping process (and subsequent segmentation process) at the lowest level of disaggregation within the organization's structure.

It is very important that the market map tracks the organization's products/services, along with those of its competitors, all the way down the supply chain to the end user, even though the organization may not in fact sell to the end user directly. A simple example of this is an insurance company that does not sell to the consumer directly. Another example is a radiator company that does not sell directly to builders.

In most markets, the direct customer/purchaser will not be the end user. For example, the doctor we visit when seeking treatment is, in many respects, a contractor when it comes to prescribing medicine. The doctor is the designated bridge between the pill maker and the pill taker. The distinction is important because, to win the commission, in this case, the patients' custom, the doctor will have needed to understand the patients' requirements and, in treating them, would have addressed those requirements on the patients' behalf. To omit the final users (the patients) from the market map would, therefore, have ignored an array of needs which the supplier (the pharmaceutical company) must be aware of (and must include in its offer) to ensure that its name appears on the contractor's (doctor's) list of preferred suppliers. The inclusion of a contractor on a market map is illustrated in Figure 3.3. In this particular market map the introduction of contractors has now reduced the similarity between the domestic and business-to-business end users. Mass retailers continue to be shared with a proportion of the commercial users, but this new contractor stage only operates in the business-to-business field.

Making certain that the market map follows through to the end user is also important in situations where products/services are purchased for end users by their company's purchasing department. In such instances, the market map should track the products/services beyond Purchasing to the departments where the end users are found, listing each end user department separately, as they have either utilized

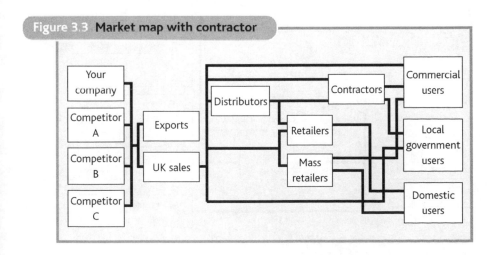

Figure 3.3 Market map with contractor

the product/service differently, or utilized it to achieve a different objective. (Where a single end user department, or individual, uses the products/services in multiple applications, that user should appear only once on the market map.) The market map should include, where appropriate, the inherent purchasing procedures, such as committees, authorizations, sealed bids and so on, as shown in Figure 3.4. In this market map, the physical delivery of the product to the final user (car retailer to car user) is insufficient in representing the sales routes and purchasing procedures encountered. The market map also assumes that all the final users who appear beyond 'Purchase Procedure 1' are subject to the same purchasing route. If this is not the case, ensure that your market map reflects the reality. For example, all the departments in a company may use mail, but the advertising department may 'purchase' its mail through their direct mail agency and therefore bypass the normal purchase procedures. The market map in Figure 3.4 also illustrates a particular purchase procedure that involves a purchase committee as well as the financial director and they have therefore been combined into one box. As these diagrams demonstrate, most market maps will have at least two principal components:

▶ The channel; and
▶ Consumers (final or end users).

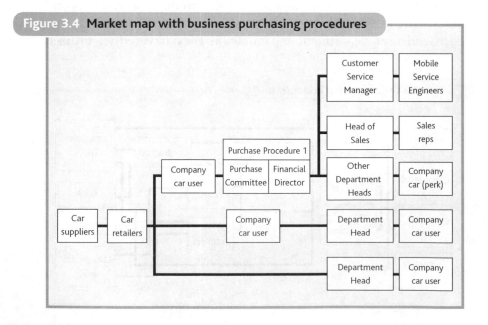

Figure 3.4 Market map with business purchasing procedures

Be sure to draw a total market map, rather than just the part you deal with currently, to gain a comprehensive understanding of the market's dynamics. For example, beware of writing in only the word 'Distributor' if there are, in fact, different kinds of distributors that behave in different ways and that supply different customers. This point is explained further under the subsequent heading 'Leverage Points'.

With quantification playing an important role later on in the process, it is useful to mark along each 'route' the volumes and/or values (vol/val) that pass along that route (guesstimate if necessary). Also, note your market share, if known, as illustrated in Figure 3.5. This market map combines domestic and business-to-business end users, as some of the distribution channels are common to both of them.

The market map should incorporate all the transaction stages or 'junctions' en route that support the flow of products between suppliers and end users. These stages will therefore include points at which a transaction takes place and/or where influence or advice is given or where decisions occur. (The latter two may not constitute a transaction.)

Figure 3.5 Market map with volumes and/or values on each route

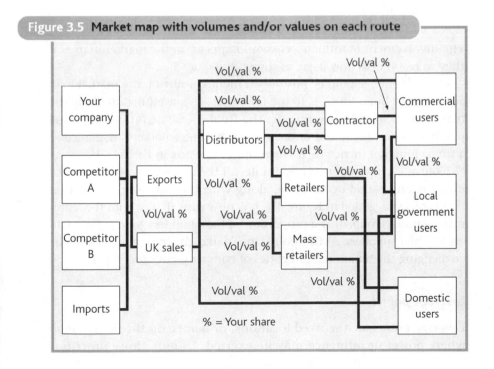

Figure 3.6 Market map with influencers

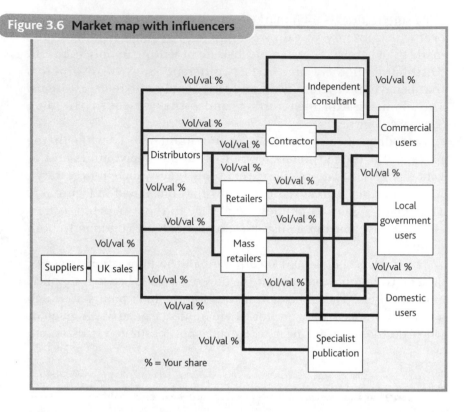

The involvement of influencers should appear on the market map as if they were a transaction stage, as shown in Figure 3.6.

Each junction should be positioned hierarchically on the market map according to how close it is to the final user. The last junction along the market map would, therefore, be the final user. The junctions in the purchase procedure found in business-to-business markets are graded as a single junction (hence their enclosure in one box in Figure 3.4).

Note at each junction, if applicable, all the different types of companies/customers that occur there, along with the number of them that there are, as suggested in Figure 3.7. It is now clear that, within the 'commercial users' group, only a proportion of local builders go to mass retailers for their suppliers. At this point, the market mapping routine may be challenging the traditional categories of company/customer types.

Leverage points

Leverage points are the fixed locations, or points, on the market map where power or influence may be exerted. To note those junctions

Figure 3.7 Market map with different company/customer types, their volumes and/or values, number of each type, and your market share

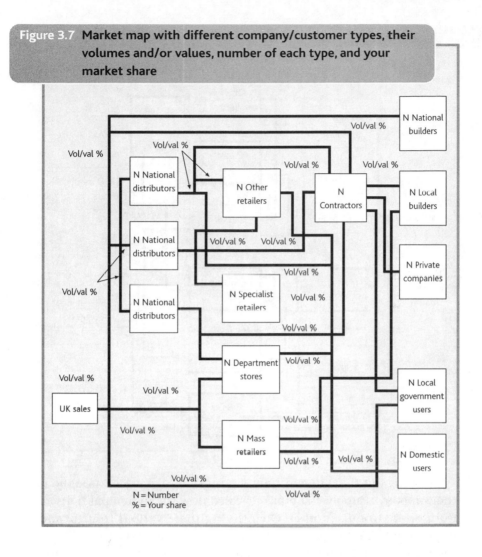

where decisions are made about which of the competing products/services should be purchased, highlight them with a thick bold outline, as shown in Figure 3.8. Also, attach to each company/ customer type the appropriate number of business units/individual purchasers it incorporates. In those instances where one company/ customer type has been split into two boxes in order to distinguish between a leverage point and a non-leverage point (for example CB1 and CB2) guesstimate the volume/value passing through each.

Figure 3.8 Leverage points at two junctions on a market map

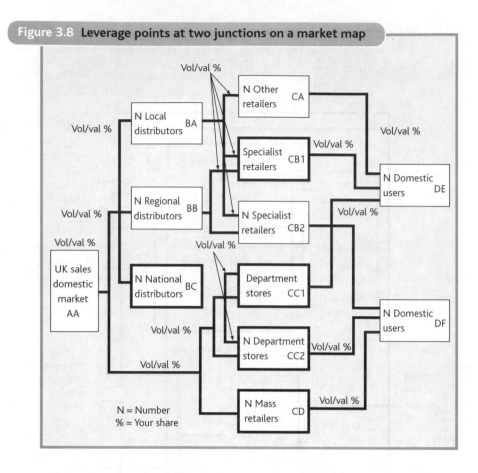

Mapping out the different transactions that take place throughout the company's supply chain has revealed how the individual transactions relate to one another. Quantifying these various 'routes' and determining the company's share along them has served to identify the most important supply routes and the progressive changes in the company's market position.

By pinpointing where in the supply chain decisions are taken which consider the products/services of competing suppliers, we can establish at which stages, or junctions, customers are expressing preferences, and thus where segmentation could occur. For most companies, it is recommended that segmentation should first be implemented at the junction furthest away from the supplier/manufacturer where decisions are made. Most importantly, however, marketing mapping provides a clearer understanding of the structure of the market and how it works.

Who buys and what they buy

Who buys

A useful method for dealing with this step in the market segmentation process is to refer to the market map and, at each point where leverage is exhibited, attempt to describe the characteristics of the customers who belong to that point. The analysis may consist of a single characteristic or a combination of features, depending on the market concerned.

Such customer analyses aim to identify the shared attributes within customer groups, which can then be used to guide the development of effective communication strategies. No matter how clever we may be in isolating segments, unless we can find some common ground upon which to base our promotional activities and methods of information exchange, our marketing efforts will be to no avail.

The use of demographic descriptors can be helpful in identifying commonalities. For consumer markets, these include age, sex, education, stage in the family life-cycle, and socio-economic group (A, B, C1, C2, D, E). As an example, a full list of the UK socio-economic groups is provided in Table 3.1. This repeats Table 1.1 on page 9, with the percentage of adults in the population added.

Table 3.1 is based on the British census and, while this example is peculiar to the UK, similar socio-economic groupings and percentages

Table 3.1 Socio-economic groups

Class name	Social status	Occupation of head of household	Percentage of adults
A	Upper Middle	Higher managerial Administrative Professional	3
B	Middle	Middle managerial Administrative Professional	10
C1	Lower Middle	Supervisory Clerical Junior managerial Administrative Professional	23

Table 3.1 *continued*

Class name	Social status	Occupation of head of household	Percentage of adults
C2	Skilled Working	Skilled manual workers	33
D	Working	Semi and unskilled manual workers	22
E	Subsistence level	Pensioners Widows Casual Lowest paid workers	9

exist for most advanced economies. This method describes people by their social status as represented by their occupations. Not surprisingly, A, B and C categories, which include most of the professions and senior managers, are light television viewers; consequently, if these categories are your target market, it does not make much sense to advertise your product or service on television. However, they can be reached effectively by means of certain newspapers and magazines, where they comprise the principal readership. Thus the correlation between these socio-economic groupings and readership and viewing patterns can be useful in helping manufactures to communicate cost-effectively and conveniently with their target market by means of advertising.

It is obvious that, at different stages in life, we have different needs, and these distinctions provide another useful means of describing our market. Banks and insurance companies have been particularly adept at developing products for specific age groups. In this respect, because socio-economic groups are becoming less relevant as predictors of behaviour (for example, all classes now play golf and travel abroad), there is an emerging concept of 'contexts', including 'wellness', 'awareness', 'Euroness', 'traditionalism', 'expectism' and 'home-centredness', each one being related to a life stage such as 'single', 'nester', 'developer' and 'elder'. Thus, Laura Ashley would clearly suit the 'traditionalism' context, while Body Shop would probably appeal to the 'wellness' context.

ACORN (A Classification of Regional Neighbourhood) groups, which classifies all households according to fifty-four different neighbourhood types based on census data, is particularly useful to the retailing business because, when employed in conjunction with market research, it can be used to predict consumption patterns accurately in specific geographical locations.

SIC (Standard Industrial Classification) categories, defined by number of employees, turnover and production processes, can be useful demographic descriptors for industrial markets.

What they buy

In respect of what is bought, the value of the market map should now become apparent. Market mapping is about representing, diagrammatically, the actual structure of markets in terms of volume, value, the physical characteristics of products, the place of purchase, the frequency of purchase, the price paid, and so on. Outlining the market's construction serves to indicate whether any groups of products (or outlets, or price categories and so on) are growing, static or declining; in other words, where there may be opportunities or obstacles.

Case study 3.4 represents market segmentation at its most elementary level, yet it is surprising how many companies run apparently sophisticated budgeting systems based on little more than crude extrapolations of past sales trends, and which only hint at marketing strategies. Such unclear and inflexible systems usually cause serious commercial problems when market structures change, as in the case of the carpet company, which changed direction too late and went bankrupt. The same fate befell a shoe manufacturer who continued doggedly to manufacture similar products, in similar materials, for similar kinds of outlets, irrespective of the rapid changes that were taking place in the footwear market.

Case study 3.4 A carpet company 'wakes up' to segmentation

A carpet company, whose sales were declining, discovered through analysis that although the overall market was buoyant and rising, the particular outlets to which it had sold traditionally were accounting for a declining proportion of total market sales. Furthermore, demand for high-priced products was falling, as was demand for the particular fibre types manufactured by the company. All this added up to a decline in sales and profitability, and prompted the company to refocus its marketing efforts towards some of the growth sectors of the market.

Having determined the market's make-up, the next task is to list all relevant competitive products/services, whether or not you manufacture them. It is important to unbundle all the components of each purchase to ensure that the list of 'what is bought' is comprehensive. The listing of purchases particular to a market should consider the following product/service features:

▶ Applications;
▶ Physical characteristics;
▶ Where they are bought;
▶ How they are bought; and
▶ When they are bought.

Consider the following examples:

Lawnmowers	Hover, cylinder, rotary, petrol driven, manual, electrically driven, 12-inch cut, 16-inch cut, any mower with a branded engine, extended warranty, with after-sales service, and so on.
Paints	Emulsion, gloss, non-drip coat, 5-litre cans, 2-litre cans, environmentally friendly, bulk, and so on.
Petrol stations	Self-service, forecourt service, with loyalty programme, and so on.

As part of this step of listing 'what they buy', and without attempting to link it with the earlier step of listing 'who buys', list all the channels through which the listed range of products/services are bought.

The list of supply channels (where bought) might include: direct/mail order, distributor, department store, national chain, regional chain, local independent retailer, tied retailer, supermarket, wholesaler, mass distributor, specialist supplier, street stall, via a buying group, through a buying club, door-to-door, local/high-street/out-of-town shop, and so on.

It is also necessary to draw up a list of the different frequencies of purchase (when bought) which might include: daily, weekly, monthly, seasonally, every two years, at 50 000 miles, occasionally, as needed, only in emergencies, degrees of urgency, infrequency, rarely, special events, only during sales, and so on.

Then draw up a separate list covering the different methods of purchase (how bought) and, if applicable, the different purchasing organizations and procedures observed in the market:

Methods of purchase – credit card, charge card, cash, direct debit, standing order, credit terms, Switch, outright purchase, lease-hire, lease-purchase, negotiated price, sealed bid and so on.
Purchasing organization – centralized or decentralized; structure and distribution of power in the decision-making unit (DMU), which could apply equally to a household or to a business. For example, the decision to purchase is made at one level, the choice of suitable suppliers is made at a second, technical level, the negotiation of price is left to the purchasing department, and the final decision is taken by senior management.

The next step in the market segmentation process is to build a representative model of the market by recording all the unique combinations of 'what is bought' and to identify for each of these 'micro-segments' the different customer characteristics associated with them, or 'who' buys. This step often produces a large number of micro-segments, each of which should have a volume or value figure attached. These micro-segments can be reduced in number by distinguishing important from unimportant features, and then removing the latter. A full explanation of this procedure can be found in Chapters 4 and 5 of McDonald and Dunbar (1998).[1] Some preliminary screening at this stage is vital in order to reduce this long list of micro-segments to manageable proportions.

Why they buy

The third stage of analysing customer behaviour is to gain an understanding of why customers behave the way they do in order that we can better sell to them.

Benefit analysis

The most useful and practical way of explaining customer behaviour has been found to be that of *benefit analysis*, or the identification of the benefits customers seek in buying a product/service. For example, customer choice may be based on utility (product), economy (price), convenience and availability (place), emotion (promotion), or a combination (trade-off) of all these. For how else can the success of firms such as Rolls-Royce, Harrods and many others be explained? Understanding the benefits sought by different groups of customers helps us to organize our marketing mix in the way most likely to appeal to our target market.

Differential benefits

While it is important for an organization to go through this process of benefit analysis, it is vital that, in doing so, *differential benefits* are identified. Differential benefits are those benefits that are not provided by competitors and that offer the greatest prospect of a competitive edge over them. If a company cannot identify any differential benefits, then either it is offering a product/service that is identical to the offerings of competitors (which is unlikely), or it has not done the benefit analysis thoroughly enough. Differential benefits hold the key to success – which will only follow where the differential benefits are in fact desired by target customers.

Having identified the relevant benefits, it is now appropriate to take each significant micro-segment selected in the second stage (who buys and what they buy) and to list 'why' they buy. In other words, what benefits is each customer group seeking by buying what they buy?

Cluster analysis

Our market segmentation is now almost complete. The final step in the third stage ('why they buy') is the culmination of all previous steps in the segmentation process: to look for clusters of segments that share the same, or similar, needs and to apply to them the organization's minimum volume/value criteria in order to determine their viability.[2]

While this concluding step can be difficult and time-consuming, any care lavished on this part of the market segmentation process will pay handsome dividends at later stages of the marketing planning process (see Chapter 6). Following is a useful summary of the issues surrounding market segmentation:

What is bought	Physical characteristics
	Applications
	Where bought
	When bought
	How bought
Who buys	Demographics
	Socio-economics
	Brand loyalty
	Heavy/light users
	Personality, traits, lifestyles

Why   Benefits
                                       Attitudes
                                       Perceptions
                                       Preferences

Segmentation case studies

Case studies 3.5 and 3.6 are provided to illustrate how superior profitability can result from successful market segmentation.

Case study 3.5   A national off-licence chain reconsiders its portfolio

In the early 1990s, a national off-licence chain with retail units in major shopping centres and local shopping parades was experiencing a decline in both customer numbers and average spend. The original formula for success of design, product range and merchandising, copied meticulously in each outlet, no longer appeared to be working. The chain had become a classic example of a business attempting to be all things to all people, but managing to satisfy very few of them. Rather than waiting and hoping for the best, the company embarked on a project designed to provide a deeper understanding of both its actual and potential customer base.

In the first stage of this study, one of the more sophisticated geodemographic packages (CCN's MOSAIC) was employed to profile the residential regions within each shop's catchment area. Not unexpectedly, many geodemographic differences were found to exist, and the business quickly accepted that the same retail formula was unlikely to appeal to all the various target markets represented.

Instead of looking at each shop separately, the company subjected the catchment area profiles for each shop to a clustering procedure in order to group similar catchment areas together. The cluster analysis produced twenty-one different catchment area groupings, each of which was then profiled in terms of its potential to buy different off-licence products using purchasing data from national surveys. (The company's own in-house retailing data would, of course, only reflect the purchasing patterns of its existing customers, or, at worst, a proportion of their requirements if the data was limited to the company's current product range.)

However, stocking the requisite range of products in the relevant geographical locations would not necessarily serve to attract the respective target markets. The company was already associated with one type of offer, which, in addition to including a particular range of drinks, also included the basic design of the shops and overall merchandising.

The project, therefore, moved into a second phase, in which the target customers' attitudes and motivations to drinking were explored, and relative values were attached to their choice determinants. This was achieved through an independently commissioned piece of market research and resulted in the market being categorized into a number of psychographic groups. The categories included 'happy and impulsive' shoppers, 'anxious and muddled' shoppers, 'reluctant but organized' shoppers, and 'disorganized, extravagant shoppers'.

Linking the findings on customers' attitudes and motivations to the demographic data enabled the original twenty-one clusters to be refined into a few distinct segments, each of which required a different offer.

The company then had to decide between two alternative strategies:

(a) To focus on one segment using one brand and to relocate its retail outlets accordingly through a closure and opening programme; or
(b) To develop a manageable portfolio of retailing brands, leaving the shops relatively intact, and re-brand, re-fit and re-stock as necessary.

The company decided to pursue the second strategy.

Realizing that geodemographic profiles can alter over time, and that customer needs and attitudes can also change, the company now monitors its market carefully and is prepared to modify its brand portfolio accordingly. For the time being, the company's five retail brands suit the five identified target market segments satisfactorily, and sit comfortably together in the same shopping centre.

Based on John Thornton, Market Planning Manager Threshers, Market Segmentation from Bottoms up (*Research Plus*, December 1993).

Case study 3.6 A brewer discovers its market segment is its market niche

A privately owned brewery in the UK was enjoying exceptional profitability in its industrial sector. In terms of output, it was by no means the largest brewery in the UK, and in terms of geographic cover, it only operated within a particular metropolitan area.

At one of the regular meetings of the Board, it was agreed that the company clearly had developed a very successful range of beers and it was time to expand into new geographic areas.

The expansion programme met with aggressive opposition from other brewers, however, particularly the very large brewers. This came as no great surprise to the Board, who, before embarking on expansion, had built up a large 'war chest' of mainly past profits in order to finance the plan.

As with all good marketing-focused organizations, the progress of the marketing plan was monitored regularly against pre-set targets by a specially appointed task force headed by the company's CEO. In addition, the Sales and Marketing Director, who was a key member of the task force, held regular meetings with his own senior staff to ensure the continuous evaluation of the sales and marketing strategies being pursued.

The marketing plan under-performed severely and was eventually abandoned.

In the post-mortem that followed, the brewery discovered the reason behind its traditional success and why that success could not be extended to other areas of the UK. To its loyal customers, the beers' 'local' flavour was a prime attraction. Historically, the brewer's market had been the metropolitan area in which it operated, where competitors comprised local brewers in other areas, or owners of established local breweries.

Without the brewery realizing it, the UK beer-drinking market had already segmented itself. The brewer's segment was known as the 'regional chauvinist'. Thus the company was able to secure considerable market share, and hence its long-held profitability. Had the company appreciated earlier the significance of this segmentation structure, it would have spent its 'war chest' more effectively and achieved its growth objectives.

These two case studies illustrate the importance of intelligent segmentation in guiding companies towards successful marketing strategies. However, without the benefit of hindsight, the problem for most of us is how to arrive at a definition of 'market segmentation' that will enable us to create differential advantage. This has been the purpose of this chapter.

Summary

In today's highly competitive world, few companies can afford to compete only on price, for a product has not yet been sold that someone, somewhere, cannot sell more cheaply – and in any case, in many markets, it is rarely the cheapest product that succeeds. What this means is that we have to find some way of differentiating ourselves from the competition, and the answer lies in market segmentation.

The truth is that very few companies can afford to be 'all things to all people'. The main aim of market segmentation as part of the marketing process is to enable a firm to focus its marketing efforts on the most promising opportunities. But what may be an opportunity for Company A is not necessarily an opportunity for Company B. Thus the firm needs to develop a typology of the customer or segment it prefers, based on a myriad of criteria, including:

► Size of the firm;
► Its consumption level;
► Nature of its products/production/processes;
► Motivations of the decision-makers (for example, desire to deal with big firms); and
► Geographical location.

The purpose of segmentation is to enable a company to:

► Define its markets broadly enough to ensure that its costs for key activities are competitive; or
► Define its markets in such a way that it can develop specialized skills in serving them to overcome a relative cost disadvantage.

Both strategies must relate to a firm's distinctive competence and to those of its competitors.

Correct market definition is crucial for:

► Share measurement;
► Growth measurement;
► The specification of target customers;
► The recognition of relevant competitors; and
► The formulation of marketing objectives and strategies.

The objectives of market segmentation are:

► To help identify appropriate marketing strategies through the analysis of market trends and buyer behaviour;
► To help determine relevant and realistic marketing and sales objectives; and
► To help improve marketing decision-making by enabling managers to fully consider future options.

Notes

1. A PC-based package called *Market Segment Master*, the registered trademark for this process, has been developed to support the segmentation process summarized in this chapter. For further details, please contact Professor Malcolm McDonald at Cranfield University School of Management, Cranfield, Bedford MK43 OAL, UK (fax: (0) 1234 752691), (email: *m.mcdonald@cranfield.ac.uk*); or Ian Dunbar at the Market Segmentation Company, Chandos House, 26 North Street, Brighton BN1 1EB, UK (fax: (0) 1273 737981), [http://www.marketsegmentation.co.uk].
2. This section is based on John Thornton, Marketing Planning Manager, Threshers, 'Market Segmentation from Bottoms Up', *Research Plus*, December 1993.

Further reading

Evans, M. (1999) Market segmentation, in M. Baker (ed.), *The Marketing Book*, Butterworth Heinemann, Oxford. (a more up-to-date review of market segmentation).

Jenkins, M. and McDonald, M. (1977) Market segmentation: organisational archetypes and research agendas. *European Journal of Marketing*, **31**(1).

Tynan, C. and Drayton, J. (1987) Market segmentation. *Journal of Marketing Management*, **2**(3) pp. 303–35. (a review of market segmentation, including a comprehensive list of references).

References

Buzzell, R., Gale, B. and Sultan, R. (1995) Market share – a key to profitability. *Harvard Business Review*, **53** (January/February), pp. 97–106.

McDonald, M. and Dunbar, I. (1998) *Market Segmentation: How To Do It – How To Profit From It*, 2nd edn, Macmillan, London.

4 Marketing research

What is marketing research?

Marketing research and market segmentation are key elements in understanding markets. Marketing research is the process that links the marketer to the market by providing information and insights to aid marketing decision-making. Marketing research both drives the market segmentation process and is influenced by it. While most managers never have to carry out market survey work themselves, they do need to know how the marketing research process functions in order to exploit its value fully.

In particular, marketers adopting a multiple markets approach (see Chapter 13) will wish to understand how the research process can assist in building long-term and profitable relationships in principal markets. The output of the marketing research process should be twofold: first, an analysis that identifies key customer groups; and second, an understanding of what constitutes customer value among each of these groups, and how that value can be created, delivered and leveraged in a way that is perceived to be superior to competitive offerings. It is especially important that appropriate research methods are used in order that the data generated is relevant to the strategic decisions that are to be made.

So, what is marketing research? It is the systematic gathering, recording and analysis of data related to the marketing of goods and services. It is used to identify marketing opportunities and obstacles, to generate marketing actions, and to monitor marketing performance. As such, marketing research is crucial to understanding the processes of relationship marketing and customer relationship management. Marketing research is concerned with the whole marketing process. Market research is research about markets. In this chapter we shall refer to it as 'marketing research'.

Marketing research, however, should not be viewed as simply an input into better decision-making. When used correctly, it can become a significant marketing asset, conferring competitive advantage. Many companies have demonstrated an awareness of the value of marketing research by extending the remit of their market research teams to cover marketing information systems or even knowledge management.

Before turning to the types of marketing research available, let us place marketing research more firmly in the marketing context.

The marketing environment

We have defined marketing as the concept and process of matching the abilities of the supplying company with the needs of the customer so that both parties get what they want. The limitations that militate against this matching process working well are likely to be weaknesses within the company and external factors, which can be seen as threats. However, on the positive side, companies also possess strengths, and the business environment is rarely completely hostile. As one commercial opportunity dies, another will appear. The successful company plays on its strengths, which it tries to build on, and works to reduce its weaknesses. At the same time, it identifies and concentrates on the available opportunities, while consciously negotiating a way through the threats.

There are likely to be several important factors that can affect the extent to which it is possible for an organization to balance its resources and efforts with customer needs. The milieu in which the organization is operating is referred to as the *marketing environment* and consists of the following components:

- Customers;
- Competitors;
- Social and cultural trends;
- Political, fiscal, economic and legal policies;
- Technology; and
- Institutional patterns.

The two most obvious components of the marketing environment – customers and competitors – are examined in much more depth elsewhere in this book. The ability to know who our actual and potential customers are, and to understand in what ways different groups of customers have different needs is obviously central to any organization's success. Equally, since what competitors do will always affect a business, it is necessary to find ways of monitoring their activities and of building that information into decision-making.

This special consideration of customers and competitors, however, is not to imply that the other components listed are not important. Indeed, it is the purpose of this chapter to examine their impact on the organization, and then to look at ways of monitoring them, starting with social and cultural trends.

Social and cultural trends

Different countries – and, in domestic markets, different regions – have different preference patterns that spring from culture and tradition. For example, preference shown by customers for one product over another may be based purely on cultural traditions or trends. Consider for a moment European breakfast habits. The Dutch prefer cheese, the British like toast and the Danes enjoy crispbread. If there are problems when marketing domestically, the problems are that much greater when it comes to differentiating between cultures. Intuitive skills in domestic markets can make a great contribution to marketing programmes, but behaviour according to the same cultural criteria in foreign markets can lead to the most elementary and expensive marketing mistakes. Take Wal-Mart's entry into the German market as an example. Applying the same 'rules' as for the USA (for example, 'Greeters', the 'Ten Foot Rule', 'Packers' and the like) was totally alien to the German shoppers' culture. Not only did Wal-Mart lose hundreds of millions of dollars over a four-year period, but they were voted consistently bottom in supermarket popularity ratings by German consumers. By 2001, Wal-Mart had begun to adapt its policies to the local culture.

Material culture
This is often responsive to increased national wealth and its consequent rewards, as well as the current state of discretionary income and its impact on purchasing inclinations and abilities. Language is another aspect of culture that requires the most careful attention, in the choice, for example, of brand names and in the communication of ideas. Different cultures respond differently to the acquisition of conspicuous wealth, towards changes in lifestyles and towards taking social risks.

Education
This determines whether or not written communication is possible. High levels of illiteracy make instructions on packaging pointless; training programmes for distributors and agents must take careful cognisance of the problems that result. The conduct of marketing research will also pose its own problems, which can be severely restricting because such a high premium must, of necessity, be placed on objectively collated data in the face of an uncertain cultural situation.

Religion
Like language, religion is a readily identifiable aspect of cultural differences that we find both within and across national boundaries. Its taboos and predilections must be ascertained, and their impact on economic behaviour studied with care. For example, anything to do with liquor in some Muslim countries must be handled with great sensitivity. Attitudes and values, most especially towards marketing, advertising and sales, will need to be ascertained and understood.

Business practices
These vary between cultures and nations, as do acceptable modes of dress. For example, the conventions for making business appointments in South America and the Middle East not only vary, but are alien to most European business people. Punctuality, or at least respect for this convention, is interpreted differently across national boundaries. While a safari suit and long socks might be acceptable business dress for men in many hot climates, exposed knees and lower arms would be considered a mark of disrespect by many native businessmen of the Gulf states. Contract negotiation, itself an art, must be adapted accordingly. What may be common negotiating practice 'at home' might be wholly unacceptable to business people in the country in which one is trying to develop a commercial presence.

Social organization

This can be seen most clearly at work in the family or in the company's purchasing department. Certain cultures respect age and status, while others have developed a meritocratic stance. Some have a greater respect for womenfolk than others. Some operate through a greatly extended concept of family, whereas in other cultures the family has almost broken down as an effective social institution, even for bringing up children.

Ultimately, successful intercultural marketing activity is built upon an understanding of how culture interacts with the four 'P's, discussed in pp. 134–5 and elsewhere in this book.

Political, fiscal, economic and legal policies

The political, fiscal, economic and legal policies of the governments of the countries in which we sell our goods also determine what we can do. For example, inflation reduces the discretionary spending power of consumers, and this can result in market decline. Legislation concerning such things as labelling, packaging, advertising and environmentalism all affect the way in which businesses are run and all these things have to be taken into account when we make our plans.

One of the most obvious and visible examples of government policies has been the impact in certain countries of heavy taxation on tobacco, and the banning of cigarette advertising. This has forced tobacco companies to seek less hostile markets in other pats of the world, but most have also diversified into other products and services in order to continue their historical growth in turnover and profits. Also, publicity about, and in many cases legislation against, unhealthy ingredients in food has caused significant changes in purchasing behaviour. In the USA and the UK, for example, per capita consumption of chicken now exceeds that of beef. This is a prime example of an industry not being sufficiently aware of changing environmental trends and allowing a competitive industry to overtake them.

Turning for a moment specifically to the internal environment, *tariffs* are taxes on imports levied in order to earn revenue and protect home industries. They affect the price of imported goods, making them less competitive than locally produced goods. Companies affected by tariffs often react by using marginal cost-pricing policies, by modifying the product, by repositioning the product in a high-priced market segment or by CKD shipping (completely knocked down) for local assembly, thus attracting a lower rate of duty.

Quotas are direct barriers to imports. They are much more serious because the firm has less flexibility in responding to them. Apart from attempting to obtain a fair share of quotas, virtually the only response is to set up local production if the market size warrants it.

Exchange control This means that foreign exchange is in short supply and the government is rationing it. If a company is manufacturing in a country with exchange controls, it has to make sure it is able to obtain exchange for imported supplies of raw materials or component parts; or else develop local supplies irrespective of possible higher costs and indifferent quality. Also, such a country is unlikely to give high priority to profit remittance, while currency fluctuations can either wipe out a company's profit or create a windfall virtually overnight.

Non-tariff barriers In the form of customs documentation, marks of origin, product formulation, packaging and labelling laws, these can similarly have a dramatic effect on a company's freedom over the management of its marketing effort.

Political instability, boycotts, customs, unions and other environmental factors can also have a drastic effect on a company's marketing policy. For example, one German company selling consumer products in Latin America lost most of its market share when the tariff was raised from 20 per cent to 50 per cent. The options discussed by the local management at an emergency meeting were to continue paying the high duty and change the product positioning to a high price segment; to import the primary ingredients and assemble locally; to ask for a lower price from the home factory; or to give up the market completely. Eventually, the company realized that it had to take a longer-term view that took account of the potential in the total Latin American Free Trade Area (LAFTA), and that this should have been done at the market entry stage rather than after a heavy investment had been made in only one market. Eventually the company set up manufacturing facilities in one of the LAFTA countries, and South America is now a profitable market for the company. But, above all, the company learned the hard way that it just did not enjoy the same degree of control over its international marketing as it did over its home market.

Technology

Technology is changing constantly. We can no longer assume that the current range of products will continue to be demanded by our customers. For example, the introduction of non-drip paint had a profound effect on what had traditionally been a stable market. People discovered that they could use paint without causing a mess, and eventually the product was demanded in new kinds of outlets such as supermarkets. Those paint manufacturers who continued to make only their traditional kind of paint and to distribute it through traditional outlets went into decline very quickly.

In the 1970s, companies such as Gestetner were badly affected by the encroachment into their traditional areas of business by more effective small photocopying machines, and the printing industry has been revolutionized by the development of desktop publishing. The advent of the computer, of course, has revolutionized just about every facet of business life, and no organization can afford to be technologically ignorant or complacent. The merging of telecommunications and computer technology has caused a fundamental reappraisal of a variety of industries, with new ones springing up to replace those that do not keep pace with the speed of technological change.

Information technology (IT), in particular, has enabled suppliers to offer 'faster, better, cheaper' solutions to customers' problems, while at the same time allowing customers to transact and interact with suppliers on a more informed and empowered basis. The result has been the generation of closer, long-term business relationships that deliver mutual value. For example, the impact of IT on management information and communications systems has given rise to integrated ordering processes in the business-to-business arena, and customised bank statements and self-service banking in the business-to-customer sector.

Institutional patterns

Institutional patterns are another aspect of the marketing environment that contemporary marketers have inherited from previous years of trading activity. Since we have been talking about food and technology, this point can be illustrated by two well-known examples.

Until the late 1960s, the major pattern of food distribution throughout Europe was for relatively small grocers or multiple stores to operate through highly local retail outlets. The advent of mass car ownership transformed this pattern in two decades to one of large-scale supermarkets in almost every developed country. In so doing, several other traditional retail institutions have been undermined – the pharmacist, the butcher, the greengrocer, the fishmonger, the dairy, the hardware merchant, and even the baker.

But even at the time of writing, changes are taking place. Super markets that present themselves only as discount retailers are losing out to those who are making more specialized offers to a more discerning public. The result is that in the UK, for example, Boots, St Michael and Tesco have become brand names in their own right, while a whole new generation of specialist retailers is beginning to emerge.

The Giro method of banking, invented in Austria and widely practised throughout Europe for half a century, only reached the UK in the 1960s. It is only now that the Giro system is beginning to make any real impact on the pattern of banking behaviour among the two-thirds of the population who made no use at all of the clearing banks at the time of Giro's introduction, and to whom the convenience of banking services had hitherto effectively not been available.

The essential point is that the environment in which human kind operate is not controlled by humans. It is dynamic, and hence must be monitored constantly. Let us turn briefly to the methods that are available to us to help monitor the environment.

Monitoring the marketing environment

The element of risk

A prime management concern in marketing is the *conversion of uncertainty into risk*. Uncertainty implies an inability to state the likelihood of any possible outcome occurring. By implication, all outcomes must be treated as being equally likely. Under *uncertainty* the manager must consider, say, the chance of failure in a new product launch to equal the chance of success. *Risk*, on the other hand, suggests that the likelihood of outcomes might be assessed more precisely. The marketing manager might feel that a particular new service launch has only 5 per cent chance of failure. Our ability to make successful decisions is enhanced if we are operating under conditions of known risk rather than uncertainty. If this conversion of uncertainty into risk is the prime marketing management task, the second is surely the reduction, or at least the minimization, of that risk.

To achieve either of these goals, the manager requires information. Good information is a facilitator of successful marketing action. Seen in this way, marketing management becomes essentially an information-processing activity. Marketing research is therefore concerned with much more than simply telling us something about the market place. Rather, it is a systematic and objective search for, and an analysis of, information relevant to the identification and solution of marketing problems. Marketing research both depends upon and ensures that a two-way information flow exists between the customer and the organization.

Types of marketing research

Marketing research can be *ad hoc* or ongoing. *Ad hoc* marketing research refers to situations where the identification of a research problem leads to a specific information requirement. So, when a French manufacturer of proprietary pharmaceuticals found that sales of its long-established cough remedy were failing, it decided to conduct a study of consumer attitudes and beliefs about cough remedies, and used the information gained to relaunch the brand.

Ongoing marketing research, as the name implies, provides more of a monitoring function, resulting in a flow of information about the market place and the company's performance in it. The Confederation of British Industry (CBI) maintains a regular monitor, based on surveys, of business confidence and investment intentions in the UK, for example.

There are many forms of marketing research to consider, which break down into four basic types:

▶ Internal – analysis of sales records, advertising levels, price versus volume and so on.
▶ External – use of sources outside the organization to complement internal research
▶ Reactive – responses to questionnaires, structured interviews and so on.
▶ Non-reactive – interpretation of observed phenomena, for example, filming customers in a store, listening to customer panels and so on.

As there are pros and cons for each type, a mix can be useful. For example, sales records can provide valuable insights, but are not good predictors of future performance as they are restricted to historic performance. Telephone interviews are quick and relatively inexpensive,

Figure 4.1 A framework for marketing research

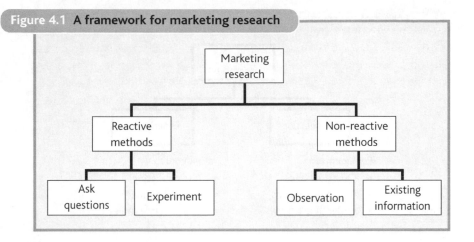

but limited in the amount of technical information that can be obtained. Figure 4.1 provides a summary and useful framework for discussing the types of marketing research activity that are encountered most frequently.

Internal marketing research This is based on an analysis of company data gained from information such as sales trends, changes in the elements of marketing – price, for example – and advertising levels. Advances in database management (see Chapter 19) have greatly enhanced the speed and accuracy with which complex data analyses can be produced, enabling marketers to develop strategies that are more timely and customer-specific.

External marketing research This is conducted within the market and the wider competitive environment in which the company operates. Compared to internal marketing research, it generally accounts for the majority of total market research expenditure. External information gathering should always be seen as a complement to internal information and not as an alternative.

Reactive marketing research As the term implies, this is information about the market place and the customers who inhabit it. It can involve the asking of questions, such as in a survey or during an interview, or it can involve experiments. Figure 4.2 summarizes the main forms of reactive marketing research.

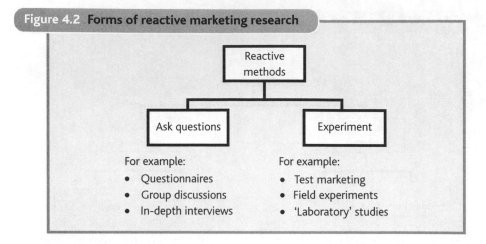

Figure 4.2 Forms of reactive marketing research

Reactive methods

Ask questions

For example:
- Questionnaires
- Group discussions
- In-depth interviews

Experiment

For example:
- Test marketing
- Field experiments
- 'Laboratory' studies

Questionnaires Questionnaires are the favoured means of data gathering. They are a flexible instrument and can be administered by an interviewer or by the interviewees themselves. As we know only too well from the experience of being stopped in the street, approached via the fax or telephone, faced with postal surveys or confronted with questionnaires when visiting websites/using the Internet, this process can take place in various situations. However, before embarking on this method of marketing research, it is useful to be aware of the pitfalls that can result from the use of a questionnaire that has not been pre-planned and checked carefully.

Loaded questions can have a distorting effect, as can ambiguous phrases. Even the order of the questions may upset the final result. The errors in the final population estimates from a questionnaire administered to a sample are called *bias* or *systematic error* of the estimates. In other words, the true characteristics of the population – for example, relative preferences between several types of industrial compressor – may be different from the estimate produced by the sample survey. This bias may result from the way in which the sample was chosen, or from the means by which the survey data were collected.

Such pitfalls can be reduced by designing the questionnaire carefully and then *pilot testing* it. In other words, give the survey a trial run on a subgroup of the intended sample to isolate any problems, ambiguities or omissions that may arise in responses.

Group discussions Group discussions may be a more appropriate way to gather market information, as they attempt to draw insights for marketing action from smaller-scale, more detailed studies. Such studies are intended to provide qualitative cues, rather than quantitative conclusions.

In such circumstances a group discussion is a loosely structured format where the leader – often a trained psychologist – attempts to draw from the group their feelings about the subject under discussion. The group is chosen to be representative of the population in which the researcher is interested, although, naturally, any conclusions emerging from the discussions can only form the basis of qualitative generalizations about that population. Such interviews need not be conducted in groups. They can be equally effective in pairs or alone with the interviewer.

Single interviews Single interviews are an alternative way of deriving information. Sometimes they are extended or in-depth interviews, and have the advantage that both the interviewer and interviewee can explore certain lines of discussion more rigorously if this is perceived to be of mutual benefit, whereas a group discussion must always maintain a degree of structure if it is to be meaningful. Such a form of single indepth interview will be used more often when information regarding specialized markets is required in industrial marketing research.

Experiments Experiments are another type of reactive marketing research. Earlier in this book we assessed the benefits of test-marketing new products. Marketing experiments can also help us to gain a better understanding of how marketing processes work.

For example, a manufacturer of confectionery wanted to know if the effect on sales of a 'money-off' offer was greater than spending a similar sum on in-store merchandizing improvements. The information needed to answer the question could only be obtained from the experiment, whereby a number of stores were selected in different areas of the country and used as the testing ground for these alternative promotional approaches. The stores chosen for the experiment were as near alike as possible in terms of turnover on the brand in question and served similar types of customers.

One-third of the stores ran the 'money-off' promotion, one-third used the improved in-store merchandizing, and the remaining third carried on selling the product without any changes. After a period of two months, the manufacturer felt able to draw conclusions about the relative effectiveness of the two promotional methods by comparing store results with those stores where no changes were made.

Market experimentation need not necessarily involve the setting up of large-scale experimental designs such as the one just discussed.

Sometimes, laboratory-type situations can be used to test marketing stimuli. Often, advertisements will be pre-tested in such laboratory conditions. Samples of the target audience for an advertisement will be exposed to the advertisement and their reactions to the sample sought. Eye cameras, polygraphs and tachistoscopes are just some of the devices that have been used successfully to record physical reactions to marketing stimuli.

While the theory of experimentation in the marketing context is sound enough, there are a number of drawbacks to its operation in practice. It is very often difficult to set up experimental situations that are microcosms of the total market. There is always the problem of controlling all the variables in the experiment – such as, for example, the actions of competitors – and, of course, the cost of setting up and maintaining market experiments can be prohibitive.

Non-reactive marketing research These methods are based on interpretation of *observed phenomena* or extant data. By definition, they do not rely upon data derived directly from respondents. Figure 4.3 summarizes the main forms of non-reactive marketing research.

Desk research Desk research should, in fact, be the starting point of any marketing research programme. Desk research involves the use of existing information to determine the extent of prior knowledge about the subject being studied. There is often a wealth of material to be obtained from published and unpublished sources, which can reduce the need to 'reinvent the wheel'. Official statistics, such as those published by governments, the OECD, the European Union

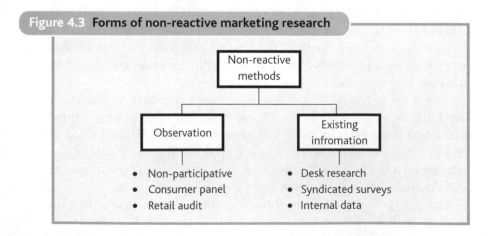

Figure 4.3 Forms of non-reactive marketing research

(EU) and the UN, can provide detailed data on markets and patterns within those markets. Other sources, such as newspapers, technical journals, trade association publications and published market studies, will provide a 'fill-in' to any later fieldwork that might be needed. Internal data derived from sales figures and sales reports can also be a guide to the direction that later studies might need to take.

Observation Observation can be a very effective marketing research technique. How people behave in the real world and how they react to stimuli can often be discovered best of all through watching and interpreting their reactions. Some observational methods, such as a camera in a supermarket, do not involve the direct participation of the researcher, and this can be a limiting factor. Often, the areas of activity in which we are most interested may only occur infrequently and the observation must be sustained over a period in order to capture a single activity.

Participant observation 'Participant' observation, a phrase borrowed from anthropology, involves the observer attempting to become a part of the activity that is under observation. This form of marketing research is very limited in its scope, although one British research organization, Mass Observation, did some early pioneering work in this area in a number of studies, a famous example being a major study of consumer behaviour in public houses.

Retail audit Retail audit is used widely as a secondary source of observation data. This has been developed and perfected as a technique over a period of time and, properly controlled, it can be a very accurate source of marketing information on brand shares, market size, distribution coverage and sales trends.

The audits conducted by A. C. Nielsen Ltd are perhaps the most widely known, and work on a simple basis. Within a particular product field, a representative sample of stockists is chosen and their co-operation obtained. The investigator visits the stockists at regular intervals and notes two things: the current levels of stock of the product group being audited; and the invoices or delivery notes for any goods in that group delivered since the previous visit. With the information on stock levels obtained on the *last* visit, it is a simple matter to determine the sales of each item being audited during the period between visits – that is, opening stock plus deliveries between visits less closing stock equals sales during that period.

The consumer panel The consumer panel is another similar source of data. This is a sample group of consumers in a particular product field who record in a diary their purchases and consumption over a period of time. This technique has been used in industrial as well as consumer markets, and can provide continuous data on patterns of usage as well as other data such as media habits.

Primary and secondary research

It is also important to understand the difference between *primary* and *secondary* research. Collecting information directly from individual respondents is known as primary research. Primary research may be: qualitative, answering the question 'Why do customers buy what they buy?'; quantitative, investigating 'Who, what, where and how many?'; or quali-quant – a combination of both.

In contrast, secondary, or desk, research involves scanning available information sources to see what has already been published. Because secondary data is often out of date, insufficiently detailed or not analysed from a perspective relevant to the research concerned, it should never be used in isolation.

Integrating marketing research with marketing action

How should managers approach this issue? In the first place it is necessary to view marketing information as a resource. This means that we must be concerned with the problems of producing, storing, distributing and constantly updating it. Marketing information has a limited shelf life – it is perishable. Like other resources, information has a value in use. The less the manager knows about a marketing problem, and the greater the risk attached to a wrong decision, the more valuable the information becomes.

This latter point is an important consideration in assessing marketing research budgets. It implies the need for a cost–benefit appraisal of all sources of marketing information. There is no point in investing more in such information than the return on it would justify. Naturally, it is easier to determine the costs than the benefits. The managerial benefits of marketing research are difficult to pin down. They can be expressed in terms of additional sales or profits that might be achieved through the avoidance of marketing failures which could otherwise result if there is a lack of information. As Case study 4.1 demonstrates, a cost–benefit approach can be a valuable means of quantifying the value of marketing research in a managerial context.

Case study 4.1 A cost–benefit appraisal of using marketing research

One company involved in the development of an industrial application of heat exchangers in West Germany believed that there was a 20 per cent chance that the product might not succeed, leaving them with a development and marketing bill of DM 2 million. From this they inferred that the maximum *loss expectation* was DM 400 000 (that is, 20 per cent of DM 2 000 000), and that it was worth paying up to this sum to acquire information that would help them avoid such a loss. Such a cost–benefit calculation implies that the information they could acquire would in itself be totally reliable. Because such *perfect information* is rare, and in this case could not be obtained, they budgeted a smaller sum for marketing research, which effectively discounted the probable inaccuracy of the information.

The use of marketing research by European companies has grown considerably since the late 1980s. Its use is not confined to manufacturers selling into consumer markets; some of the most interesting work to have been conducted in recent years has been on behalf of industrial marketing organizations, service companies such as banks, and social organizations such as voluntary and government agencies.

With this growth of marketing research has come an increasing sophistication in the use of the techniques available to the researcher, now a professional whose advice is looked for increasingly in marketing decision-making. Similarly, the growth of companies that provide specialist marketing research services has multiplied, so it is now a major industry in its own right. This means that managers have the facility available to them to monitor the effectiveness of their marketing performance and to gain a better feel for what opportunities exist in the market place (see Chapters 19 and 20.)

Finally, let us have a brief look at the difficulties of marketing research in the international context.

International marketing intelligence

International marketing intelligence is simply the systematic gathering, recording and analysis of data about problems relating to the marketing of goods and services internationally. It is concerned with the following:

► Where to go;
► How to enter;
► How to market (the 4 'P's); and
► Traditional marketing research questions within each market.

International marketing intelligence involves marketing research covering additional factors not usually present in domestic marketing; and the study of many foreign markets individually.

This form of marketing research is often referred to as *comparative analysis*. It is a way of organizing information on international markets, and involves comparing and grouping countries in ways useful to decision-making, thus maximizing the use of a company's international experience. For example, grouping countries according to their geographic proximity, which some companies do for the purpose of marketing control, can be a mistake if the countries are not homogenous in characteristics important to the company's marketing. Grouping countries according to their stage of economic development, for example, can be a useful way of filling data gaps, as the missing values can be assumed to be similar to those available in the small group. Also, the expense of researching in many small markets can often be avoided by carrying out research in a sample of countries and extrapolating the results to other countries in the same group. The following example encapsulates the benefit of comparative analysis.

A large electronics company carried out a comparative analysis of its markets world-wide by first identifying the characteristics that were important to its international marketing decisions, then grouping different countries according to their similarity in these dimensions. It found three distinct groupings and began to develop marketing strategies for these, rather than develop separate marketing strategies for each individual country, as the company had previously. The result was reflected in great savings for the company and an improvement in the company's control.

There are a number of problems in international market research not normally present in domestic research. These centre around cultural problems and economic problems. In some parts of the world, only oral communication is possible, with several languages being spoken. Quite apart from these considerations, it is often almost impossible to interview women. For example, in most Islamic countries, women are not allowed to talk to men without their husbands being present. Mail and telephone surveys are impossible in some countries, either because they are illegal, or because they are impractical. This leaves virtually only personal interviews, often difficult because of geographic and cultural problems.

Published data is less available and often unreliable, because different base years and different definitions are often used. Add to this the cost of researching foreign markets, and it will be seen at once that international market research is not just a simple extension of domestic techniques, although it must be said that as far as questionnaire design and sample sizes are concerned, exactly the same rules apply.

Preparing the marketing research brief

Do we need a research brief?

Regardless of who carries out the work, it is important that a clear brief should be produced against which the subsequent work will be undertaken and judged. The research brief – which should be produced in both written and verbal form – is a key document and the starting point. In its preparation, the following two questions are important:

▶ What do we want to know? and
▶ What will we do with the information when we get it?

In this way, clearly defined objectives will be set and adhered to.

What should it contain?

First, the commissioning company should think very carefully about what and how much it wishes to disclose in the brief. Ideally, the brief should be open, precise and factual – but there may be particular points that are best omitted; for example, the precise budget.

A good briefing document, preferably accompanied by product/ service literature, may cover between one and five pages. Its elaboration/discussion at a briefing meeting should clarify points, confirm contents and remove any written ambiguities. At the end of the meeting, if a quotation is to be submitted, the consultant/agency should both see and show a firm commitment to the project.

A good research brief should contain the following:

▶ Background information on the market, the company, its products/services, market standing and so on.
▶ Research objectives – perhaps both primary and secondary. In this section it may be useful to define precise question areas to be covered by the research.
▶ Desired time scale: overall project completion date, together with any interim report times or key decision dates (for example, product development stages or interfaces with other departments).
▶ Report format/presentation requirements (if desired): this is a good opportunity, if the commissioning company wishes, to indicate preferences.
▶ Company liaison/contact; information to be made available in support of the research.
▶ Market-place confidentiality or openness required from the research.

It is not suggested that the briefing document be seen as a 'straightjacket', but rather as a series of well-thought-out guidelines. As such, the expertise of the agency/consultancy should be sought in the briefing meeting, both with regard to the information and requirements of the brief, as well as in discussion of the best methods of achieving the brief's objectives.

What else might we do?

While it is not suggested that the brief should define exactly some areas – for example, research methodology or precise budget allocation – although it could be helpful if some verbal discussion on these points were to take place during the briefing meeting. Given the expected expertise of the agency/consultancy, it is a very fair approach to provide a comprehensive briefing and ask for a written proposal offering the best solutions, including recommended methodologies, expected time frames and cost involved.

While guidelines as to the probable research budget are very helpful, indications of precise budget allocations frequently tend to be met by proposal documents/terms of reference just under or exactly equal to the figures given!

Some commissioning organizations set a proposal deadline or tender submission date. At the briefing stage, it may be best to indicate the competitive quoting levels involved, without necessarily defining or naming these precisely.

This stage should be seen as a further opportunity to confirm importance and commitment. Remember, the client retains the prerogative to reject all proposals, or require modifications to them. Normally, the costs involved in the briefing meeting and preparation of the research proposal are seen by the consultants/agencies as part of their prospecting/business development costs and involve no client charges (whether the proposal is accepted or not), unless specifically previously agreed.

Preparing the research proposal

What is the research proposal?

Basically, the research proposal – a written document and personal presentation – is a best response to the marketing research brief. As such, it represents an ability to communicate, and this should be a selection factor – remember that the organization subsequently commissioned to carry out the research is providing an indication or preview of its listening, communication and presentation skills. This assessment opportunity for the client should not be overlooked!

The research proposal should provide a specification of what the research organization will do, how it will carry out the work and what it will cost. It is important that it conveys its understanding of what is expected, and its competence to provide the work most efficiently. This understanding and competence should be in both written and verbal forms if presented personally.

What should it contain?

A good research proposal should include:

▶ *Background information*: to convey a clear understanding of the project and the issues involved.
▶ *Objectives*: these should be clearly listed and defined very precisely against the needs of the problem.

▶ *Work programme and methodology*: these should cover how the objectives will be achieved and the way the work programme will be completed; they should detail sample size, research stages and questionnaire methods.

▶ *Fees/payment terms and time scales*: these should be clearly stated and broken down to show expenses and the work schedule.

▶ *Company details and research personnel involved*: to include research company competence and brief biographies of personnel, plus, if relevant, any business terms.

▶ *Summary of research project benefits* and the agency's confidence in its competence to 'deliver' what is required.

How should the sponsoring organization respond?

Acceptance of the proposal should be in writing. It should authorize the work and confirm the points of agreement and costs involved. This should provide a binding agreement as to what is to be done and at what cost – thus, it is hoped, eliminating any subsequent disagreement between the two parties.

Summary

From this brief summary of research methods and techniques in marketing it can be seen that the scope of marketing research can be considerable. Yet, at the same time, we must recognize that even the most carefully designed and conducted studies can at best only provide *imperfect information* of market phenomena. However, that being said, marketing research remains the link between the identification of market opportunities and successful exploitation of them by organizations, whatever their specialism or function. It is the principal means of monitoring the environment in which the matching process takes place.

The gathering of data is only the first step in marketing research. Data must be given direction before it can become relevant information, and information is only relevant if the company has some purpose in mind, and some marketing problem to solve. Information allied to purpose becomes *intelligence*: information that is consumable and usable by management in converting uncertainty into measurable risk. Conversion of uncertainty into risk, and the minimization of risk, is perhaps marketing management's most important task – and marketing research is vital in this process.

Whatever research method(s) is/are adopted, the research should be carried out with accuracy, thoroughness and professionalism. High research standards will ensure that the findings are valuable and usable. It is important to remember that the aim of marketing research is to help direct business strategy, which seeks to build and improve relationships with customers by leveraging product and service quality to have maximum impact on consumer satisfaction levels. Case study 4.2 demonstrates the crucial role that research plays in developing business strategy.

Case study 4.2 Abbey National: the role of research in developing strategy

Abbey National developed a research brief to investigate consumer perceptions of key brands in the financial and retail market. The investigation was aimed specifically at finding out what differentiation existed, and what consumers were looking for in brands so that Abbey National could design new advertising and in-branch merchandising material successfully. The company worked with an advertising agency as well as with separate qualitative and quantitative agencies on the £200 000 research project. Over 200 product and service initiatives were evaluated, and twenty were tested quantitatively. The study identified those initiatives that customers most favoured: staff do not take their lunch hour at the same time as customers take theirs; the reduction of queues through the introduction of 200 express service assistants; fair banking; flexible mortgages; and the consistent use of plain English in all communications.

The project served to detect the most popular and promising of Abbey National's brands, some of which were then further developed and promoted in a television campaign using the strapline 'Because life's complicated enough'. Abbey National's advert sought to demonstrate the company's desire to make things easier for its customers and thus to differentiate its offerings from those of competitors. As a result of the study, an ongoing programme was put in place to monitor Abbey National's perceived image and advertising success so that further customer-focused initiatives could be developed.

Source: *Research*, February 1998.

Further reading

Aaker, D. A. and Day, G. S. (1990) *Marketing Research*, 4th edn, New York, John Wiley.

Baker, M. (1991) *Research for Marketing*, Macmillan, London.

West, C. (1999) Marketing research in M. Baker (ed.), *The IEBM Encyclopaedia of Marketing*, International Thomson Press: London (an excellent summary of marketing research).

5 Competitive analysis

Determining competitive strategy

Success in the market place is dependent not only upon identifying and responding to customer needs, but also upon a company's ability to ensure that its response is judged by customers to be superior to that of its competitors. In other words, the development of marketing strategies must be based upon both customer satisfaction and competitive differentiation.

Just as we can remember the key components of the marketing mix by the shorthand of the 'four P's', so too can we focus on the basic elements of competitive strategy by reference to the three 'C's. The three 'C's in question are the Customer, the Competition and the Company. Figure 5.1 illustrates the triangular relationship that exists between the three 'C's.

Competitive strategy can therefore be seen as a search for differential advantage as perceived by customers. The key here is *perception*, since the ultimate test question is: how does the customer evaluate our offer compared with competitive offers? This basic principle is the foundation for market *positioning*. A key component of the strategic process in marketing is the identification of an appropriate competitive 'position' in the market

Figure 5.1 Marketing and the three 'C's

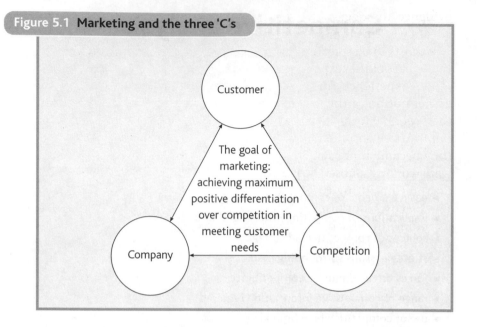

place. In essence, the position of a brand or offer is simply the customer's perception of the similarity or dissimilarity of a company's brand in relation to competitive offerings. As such it will be influenced by the particular marketing mix of product features, promotional appeals, price levels and place (distribution) factors that the company selects.

How do companies achieve this competitive advantage? Many commentators and academics have investigated this fundamental question and their findings tend to point in the same direction. Put very simply, successful companies have a cost advantage or a 'value' advantage – or a combination of the two. The cost advantage means that the company can produce and distribute its products at a lower cost than the competition; while the value advantage means that the company's offer is perceived as providing differentiated benefits to customers – the product has greater 'added values'. Let us examine briefly these two fundamental sources of competitive advantage.

Cost advantage

In many industries there will typically be one competitor who will be the low-cost producer, and, more often than not, that competitor will have the greatest sales volume in the sector. There is substantial evidence to suggest that 'big is beautiful' when it comes to cost advantage. This is partly because of economies of scale, which enable fixed costs to be spread over a greater output, but more particularly to the impact of the 'experience curve'.

The experience curve is a phenomenon that has its roots in the earlier notion of the 'learning curve'. Researchers discovered during the Second World War that it was possible to identify and predict improvements in the rate of output or cost effectiveness, of workers as they became more skilled in the processes and tasks on which they were working. Subsequent work by Bruce Henderson, founder of The Boston Consulting Group, extended this concept by demonstrating that *all* costs, not just production costs, would decline at a given rate as volume increased. In fact, to be precise, the relationship that the experience curve describes is between *real* unit costs and *cumulative* volume. Further, it is generally recognized that this cost decline applies only to 'value added' – that is, costs other than bought-in supplies. The experience curve in its general form is shown in Figure 5.2.

There are many implications of this relationship for the development of marketing strategy, not least in the determination of pricing strategy. However, its importance in this current discussion is in the fact that, if one company's relative market share is greater than that of its competitors then, other things being equal, it should be further down the experience curve. In other words, it will have a cost advantage. Such a cost advantage can either be used to lower prices, thus putting pressure on competitors, or to earn higher margins at the same price as competitors.

Figure 5.2 The experience curve

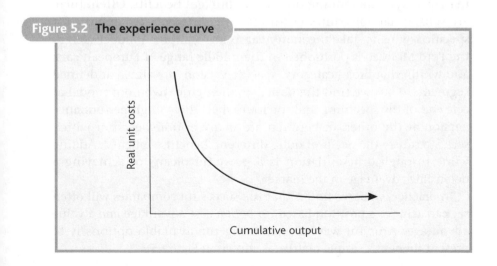

Later in this book, it will be suggested that it will generally be preferable to use such a cost advantage to reinvest in the product rather than to use it to initiate price wars, and thus run the risk of reducing the product to the status of a 'commodity'.

Value advantage

We have already observed that 'customers don't buy products, they buy benefits'. Put another way, the product is purchased not for itself but for the promise of what it will 'deliver'. These benefits may be intangible; that is, they relate not to specific product features but rather to such things as *image* or *reputation*. Alternatively, the delivered offering may be seen to out-perform its rivals in some functional aspect.

Unless the product or service we offer can be distinguished in some way from its competitors, there is a strong likelihood that the market place will view it as a 'commodity', and so the sale will tend to go to the cheapest supplier. Thus, the importance of seeking to attach additional values to our offering to mark it out from the competition becomes more apparent.

What are the means by which such value differentiation may be gained? Essentially, the development of strategy based on additional values will normally require a more segmented approach to the market. As discussed in Chapter 3, when a company scrutinizes markets closely, it frequently finds that there are distinct 'value segments'. In other words, different groups of customers within the total market attach different importance to different benefits. Often, there are substantial opportunities for creating differentiated appeals for specific segments. Take the motor car as an example. A model such as the Ford Mondeo is positioned in the middle range of European cars; and within that broad category, specific versions are aimed at defined segments. Thus we find the basic, small-engine, two-door model at one end of the spectrum, and the four-wheel-drive, high-performance version at the other. In between are many options, each of which seeks to satisfy the needs of quite different 'benefit segments'. Adding value through differentiation is a powerful means of achieving a defensible advantage in the market.

In practice, what we find is that the successful companies will often seek to achieve a position based on *both* a cost advantage *and* a value advantage. A useful way of examining the available options is to present them as a simple matrix, as shown in Figure 5.3.

Figure 5.3 **The sources of competitive advantage**

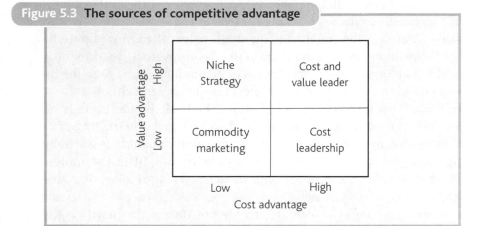

Let us consider the options in turn. For companies who find themselves in the bottom left-hand quadrant of our matrix, the world is an uncomfortable place. These products are indistinguishable from their competitors' offerings and they have no cost advantage. These are typical 'commodity' market situations and the only ultimate strategy is to move to the right of the matrix (that is, to cost leadership) or upwards into a 'niche'. Often, the cost leadership route is simply not available. This will be the case particularly in a mature market where substantial market share gains are difficult to achieve. New technology may sometimes provide a window of opportunity for cost reduction, but in such situations it is often the case that the same new technology is available to competitors.

Cost leadership, if it is to form the basis of a viable long-term marketing strategy, should essentially be gained early in the market life-cycle. This is why market share is considered to be so important in many industries. The 'experience curve' concept, described briefly above, demonstrates the value of early market share gains – the higher the share relative to competitors, the lower the costs should be. This cost advantage can be used strategically to assume a position of price leader and, if appropriate, to make it impossible for higher-cost competitors to survive. Alternatively, price may be maintained, enabling above-average profit to be earned, which is potentially available to develop further the position of the product in the market.

The other way out of the 'commodity' quadrant of the matrix in Figure 5.3 is to seek a 'niche', or segment, where it is possible to meet the needs of customers through offering additional values. Sometimes, it may not be through tangible product features that this 'value added' is generated, but through service. For example, a steel stockholder who finds himself in the commodity quadrant may seek to move up to the niche quadrant by offering daily deliveries from stock, by providing additional 'finishing' services for his basic products, or by focusing on the provision of a range of special steel for specific segments.

What does not seem to be an established rule is that there is no middle ground between cost leadership and niche marketing. The relationship between size, differentiation and profitability is generally agreed to be as depicted in Figure 5.4. Being caught in the middle (that is, neither a cost leader nor a niche-based provider of added values) is generally bad news.

Finally, perhaps the most defensible position in the matrix is the top right-hand corner. Companies occupying that position have products that are distinctive in the values they offer as well as being cost competitive. Arguably, many Japanese products, particularly in consumer markets, have achieved this position. Clearly, it is a position of some strength, occupying 'high ground' that is extremely difficult for competitors to attack.

Market share strategies

In discussing the advantages and disadvantages of pursuing niches or volume, it is important that the issues surrounding 'market share' are fully understood. That there is a strong relationship between market share and return on investment has been confirmed by the analysis of data from thousands of companies

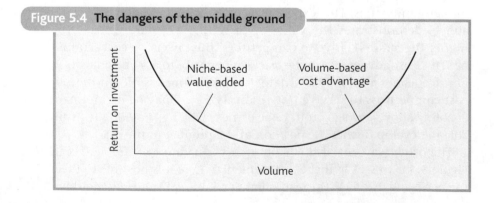

Figure 5.4 **The dangers of the middle ground**

participating in the PIMS study (Profit Impact of Marketing Strategy). This study, in searching for explanations of variations in profitability between firms, identified a strong correlation between market share and ROI.

However, a warning should be sounded. It may well be that profitable companies have high-market-shares, but it does not follow that all high-market-share companies will be profitable. Quite simply, this is because market share can be 'bought'. It can be bought through price reductions, increased marketing effort and product development. All this can be good practice unless it is at the expense of long-term profit. Some companies have failed to recognize that investing in market share is really only viable early in a product/market life-cycle. Similarly, other companies have been caught out when the product /market life-cycle turns out to be much shorter than had been anticipated. In summary, market share strategies are long-term, and in volatile markets such strategies must be pursued with care.

A further issue surrounds the question, 'Share of *which* market?' In other words, of what is market share a measure? The answer is that it all depends on how we define the total market. A holiday tour operator specializing in the organization of cultural tours of sites of antiquity, accompanied by a professor of archaeology, is not operating in the same market as a tour operator offering ten days in Majorca for £200, yet they both offer holidays.

The definition problem is helped if we use the concept of the 'served' market. The served market is best described in terms of the specific needs that we seek to meet rather than some generic product category. Some have called market share in this context 'share of mind', meaning that when potential customers are contemplating a purchase to meet a specific need, they limit their choice to offerings they consider competitive. The marketing challenge may thus be seen as one of how to increase 'share of mind' among specific target groups.

Competitive drivers

As markets mature, as growth rates stabilize, or markets enter recession, the only way to grow a business faster than the growth of the market is at the expense of the competition. This implies a need to understand in the greatest possible detail the competitive context and the characteristics of specific competitors. Here the work of Michael Porter, a Harvard

Business School professor, is particularly valuable in providing a framework for the systematic exploration of the competitive context. Figure 5.5 summarizes the main forces driving industry competition.

Figure 5.5 Forces driving industry competition

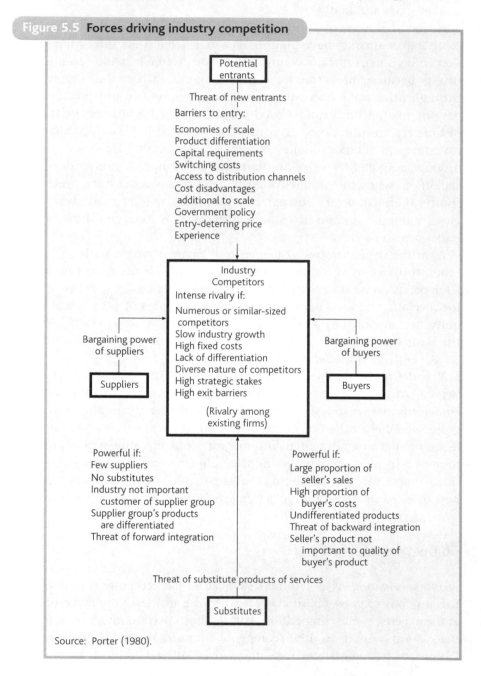

Source: Porter (1980).

These key determinants of competitive position are as follows:

Market competition

Obviously, the more numerous or equally balanced the competitors, the more intense will be the rivalry within the market. If this is combined with a slow industry growth rate, and if fixed costs relative to variable costs are high, then the prognosis is for a high level of aggressive competition, probably accompanied by severe price-cutting. A further influencing factor will be the extent to which the competing products on offer are seen as substitutes by the market place, with few switching penalties for buyers.

Of key importance will be the relative cost structures of the major players in the market; these will be determined not just by market share, but also by capacity utilization and production technology.

In certain circumstances, the fall of a giant in the industry, such as Enron, will cause reverberations across a number of associated companies and industries. Similarly, the so-called dot.com revolution of the 1990s shook many competitors out of their complacency and forced many of them into a 'root and branch' reappraisal of their products and services.

Threat of new entrants

In analysing markets, one of the factors to be appraised is the existence, or absence, of 'barriers to entry'. In other words, how easy is it for new entrants to enter the market? Typically, barriers might be provided by economies of scale, so that, without a minimum market share, unit costs will be uncompetitive. Similarly, heavy start-up costs – whether through the need for capital investment or high levels of marketing expenditure – can provide a barrier. Government regulation, as, for example, in the telecommunications industry, might also prove an effective barrier.

Conversely, markets may be easy for new competitors to enter where product differentiation is low, or where technology changes can overcome cost barriers. In the latter case, a good example would be the way in which new technology had made it possible for new daily papers to be launched in an industry that previously had high entry barriers. Industry convergence also opens up markets to new entrants, as in the case of Tesco's expansion from food retail into non-traditional services such as personal finance and fashionwear/clothing.

Substitute products

One factor that can alter the strategic balance in a market place considerably is the development of products that meet underlying customer needs more cost-effectively than do existing products. The development of synthetic fibres had a major impact on the demand for natural fibres, for example. Similarly, the advent of home video recording through video cameras has virtually eliminated the demand for home movie products.

Bargaining power of buyers

The competitive climate of a market will clearly be influenced by the extent to which customers wield power through purchasing strength. Thus a market that is dominated by a limited number of buyers, or where a buyer takes a larger proportion of the seller's output, will substantially limit the seller's opportunities for individual action or development. The UK grocery market illustrates the situation well, with a handful of major retail chains being able to exert considerable influence over manufacturing suppliers' marketing policies, and thus their profitability. Another source of competitive threat from buyers will exist when opportunities arise for backward integration up the value chain by buyers.

There is also the profound impact of unforeseen events on behaviour in the market place, such as the downturn in air travel following the terrorist attacks of September 2001, and the consequent demise of some leading major carriers and the rise of smaller, budget airlines.

Bargaining power of suppliers

Many of the potential threats that exist from buyers can also come from the suppliers to an industry. If the supply of critical materials is controlled by a few suppliers, or if an individual company's purchases from a supplier constitute only a small part of that company's output, then freedom of manoeuvre may be limited. Again, if opportunities exist for forward integration by suppliers, this constitutes a further source of potential competitive pressure.

Competitive information

Competitive analysis at this level requires access to a wide range of information, necessitating a continued monitoring of all sources of data. The range of competitive intelligence that should be gathered is listed below. Some of the issues listed appear to be obvious, and yet it is surprising how often we lack accurate information about them. Ideally, a 'data bank' on the competitive environment should be established; use should be made of annual reports, annual statutory returns, Dun & Bradstreet reports (or their equivalent), trade press and financial reports, and publications from trade associations, as well as company catalogues and advertisements, to discover:

- Who are the competition … and Where are they?
- Who else might become a competitor?
- Their shares of market segments and trends.
- Their product line, performance, quality, service.
- Their management, its skill, philosophies.
- Size and development of their sales force and how they organize the sales effort.
- Their promotion strategy.
- Their pricing policy, terms, discounts.
- Their distribution and service strategies.
- Their technological capability.
- Their financial strength.
- Their objectives.

Information can often be gathered from customers and suppliers about competitors' actions or intentions. If personnel are recruited from competitors, they should be debriefed as far as professional ethics allow. In fact, it is often surprising to see just how much openly available competitive intelligence can be gathered by making use of publicly-available databases.

Table 5.1 gives some indication of the sources of competitor information, most of which is readily accessible. What organizations typically lack is an effective *marketing intelligence system* that collects, interprets and disseminates this information on a regular and systematic basis. This is not so in the case of the Japanese External Trade Organization (JETRO), a subsidiary of the Ministry of International Trade and Industry (MITI), which has eighty offices around the world, all of which gather competitive and relevant information for transmission back to Japan. The larger Japanese companies also operate world-wide monitoring systems, which, quite legally, screen and index all material, patents, licences and academic journals in their fields of interest.

To be a viable basis for marketing strategy, competitive analysis must be organized and managed as an ongoing activity – not just an

Table 5.1 Sources of competitor information

	Public	Trade/Professionals	Government	Investors
What competitors say about themselves	▲ Advertising ▲ Promotional materials ▲ Press releases ▲ Speeches ▲ Books ▲ Articles ▲ Websites ▲ Personnel changes ▲ Recruitment advertisements	▲ Manuals ▲ Technical papers ▲ Licences ▲ Patents ▲ Courses ▲ Seminars	▲ Company House reports ▲ Lawsuits ▲ Office of Fair Trading and Monopolies Commission	▲ Annual meetings ▲ Annual reports ▲ Prospectuses ▲ Stock/bond issues ▲ Speeches to security analysts
What others say about them	▲ Books ▲ Articles ▲ Websites ▲ Case studies ▲ Consultants ▲ Newspaper reports ▲ Environmental groups ▲ Unions ▲ Ex-employees	▲ Suppliers/vendors ▲ Trade press ▲ Industry studies ▲ Customers ▲ Subcontractors	▲ Lawsuits ▲ Government ministries ▲ National plans	▲ Security analysis ▲ Reports ▲ Industry studies ▲ Credit reports

ad hoc response to a particular circumstance. The important topics of conducting a *marketing audit* and having a *marketing information system* are addressed in Chapter 19.

Competitive benchmarking

The ultimate test of the efficiency of any marketing strategy has to be sales – not just measured against volume targets, but rather in terms of profit. Those companies who strive for market share, but who measure market share in terms of volume sales, may be deluding themselves in that volume can be bought at the expense of profit. The only market share measure that counts in the long run is the *sterling share* of the market. In other words, what percentage of the total expenditure made by customers in this market ends up as sales revenue?

Because market share is an 'after the event' measure, we need to utilize continuing indicators of competitive performance; this will highlight areas where improvements in the marketing mix can be made.

In recent years, a number of companies have developed a technique for assessing relative market place performance, which has come to be known as 'competitive benchmarking'. Originally, the idea of competitive benchmarking was literally to take apart a competitor's product, component by component, and to compare its performance in a value engineering sense with the company's own product. This approach has often been attributed to the Japanese, but many Western companies have also found the value of such detailed comparisons.

However, the idea of benchmarking is capable of extension beyond this simple comparison of technology and cost-effectiveness. Because the battle in the market place for the 'share of mind' that we referred to earlier is essentially concerned with perceptions, it is perceptions that that we must measure.

Companies such as IBM have led the way in conducting regular surveys among customers, in which they seek to measure exactly how their customers see them as suppliers, not just of a product, but of a total service. Not only does IBM measure the perceptions of customers concerning the relative performance of their products compared with those of competitors – it also seeks to measure the image that customers have of it compared with other groups in the 'office automation' field, such as Xerox, Hewlett Packard and Digital.

The measures that are used in this type of benchmarking programme include delivery reliability, ease of ordering, after-sales service, the quality of sales representation, and the accuracy of invoices and other documentation. These measures are not chosen at random, but are selected because of their importance to the customer. Market research, often based on in-depth interviews, would typically be employed to identify these 'key success factors'. The elements that customers identify as being the most important then form the basis for the benchmark questionnaire. This questionnaire is administered to a sample of customers on a regular basis – for example, British Telecommunications carries out a daily telephone survey of a random sample of their domestic and business customers to measure customers' perceptions of service. For most companies, an annual survey could suffice; in other cases, perhaps quarterly, particularly if market conditions are dynamic. The output of these surveys might typically be presented in the form of a competitive profile as in the example in Figure 5.6.

Summary

In the marketing environment at the time of writing, the ability to present customers with a total offer that is recognized as superior to competitive offerings has become the prime task of marketing. We have

Figure 5.6 Competitive benchmarking

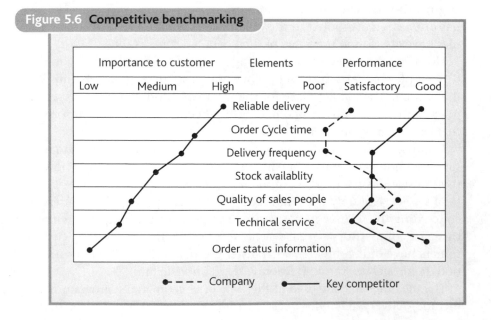

seen that it is possible to gain competitive advantage both through lower costs and through greater product and service differentiation.

Knowledge of the competition is as important as knowledge of customers. Increasingly, the leading companies are developing information systems that enable a continuing monitoring of competitive strategy and performance to be maintained (see Chapters 19 and 20).

These days, as the phrase 'competitive advantage' has become the rallying cry in so many organizations, it has become even more crucial to build marketing strategies that take account explicitly of competitive considerations.

Further reading

Kay, J. (1993) *Foundations of Corporate Success*, Oxford University Press.

Narver, J. and Slater, S. (1990) The effect of market orientation on business profitability. *Journal of Marketing*, **54(5)** (October) pp. 20–35.

Wensley, R. (1999) The basics of marketing strategy, in M. Baker (ed.), *The Marketing Book*, Butterworth Heinemann, Oxford.

Reference

Porter, M. E. (1980) *Competitive Strategy*, Free Press, New York.

Creating the value proposition

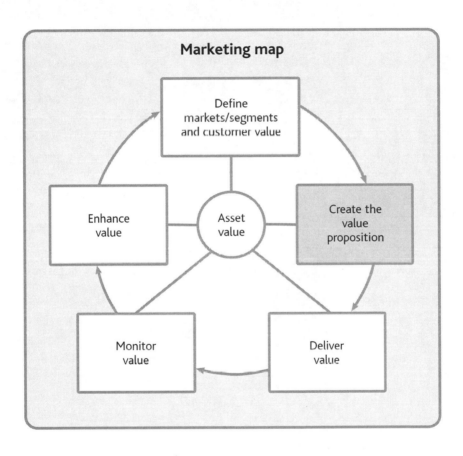

Marketing map

- Define markets/segments and customer value
- Create the value proposition
- Asset value
- Enhance value
- Deliver value
- Monitor value

6 Marketing planning

What is marketing planning?

The purpose of *marketing planning* and its principal focus are the identification and creation of competitive advantage. Marketing planning is the planned application of marketing resources to achieve marketing objectives. Given the increasing turbulence and complexity of the market place, and the rapid pace and impact of technological change, the need for a disciplined, systematic approach to the market has never been greater. Nor, it must be said, has the possibility of having one been so real.

The advent of computerized data collection and analysis, and the Internet with its time- and location-independent reach and interactive dialogue capability, has made previously remote marketing opportunities accessible. Our ability to share and act on information and ideas has also developed. Increasingly, we see functional silos replaced by cross-functional networks.

Marketing planning today is distinguished by the fact that all levels of management are involved, with the resulting intelligence coming from the market rather than from the heads of a remote group of planners with little or no operational involvement. The marketing axiom has taken an about-turn: nowadays 'you don't manage your customers, your customers manage you'.

The current trend in successful businesses is towards an emphasis on scanning the external environment, identifying at an early stage the forces emanating from it, and developing appropriate strategic responses. *Strategic marketing planning* is a management process leading to a marketing plan. It is a logical sequence and a series of activities leading to the setting of marketing objectives and formulation of plans for achieving them. (The precise steps in the strategic marketing planning process and the contents of a marketing plan are discussed later in the chapter.)

In small, undiversified companies this process is usually informal, whereas in larger, more diversified organizations, the process is often systematized. *Formalized marketing planning* by means of a planning system is, *per se*, little more than a structured way of identifying a range of options for the company, making them explicit in writing, formulating marketing objectives that are consistent with the company's overall objectives, and scheduling and costing the specific activities most likely to bring about the achievement of the objectives.

Although simple to grasp intellectually, strategic marketing planning is notoriously the most difficult of all marketing tasks. The reason why is that it involves bringing together into one coherent, realistic plan all the elements of marketing, and this 'coalescence' requires at least some degree of institutionalized procedures as well as an inevitable compromise between conflicting objectives. For example, consider these four typical business objectives: maximizing revenue; maximizing profits; maximizing return on investment; and minimizing costs. Each has its own special appeal to different managers within the organization, depending on their particular function. To achieve a kind of 'optimum compromise' demands accurate and collaborative understanding of how these variables interact, and steadfast rationality in decision-making.

Commercial success is, of course, influenced by many factors apart from just planning procedures. A myriad of contextual issues adds to the complexity of the marketing planning process. These include: company size; degree of internationalization; management style; degree of business environmental turbulence and competitive hostility; marketing growth rate; market share; technological developments and so on. However, irrespective of the size or complexity of the organization, some kind of structured approach to situation analysis is necessary in order that meaningful and realistic marketing objectives can be set.

Issues to be considered in marketing planning are:

- ► When should it be done; how often; by whom; and how?
- ► Is it different in large and small companies?
- ► Is it different in diversified and undiversified companies?
- ► Is it different in international and domestic companies?
- ► What is the role of the chief executive?
- ► What is the role of the planning department?
- ► Should marketing planning be 'top down' or 'bottom up'?
- ► What is the relationship between operational (one year) and strategic (longer-term) planning?

The benefits of a marketing plan

In one study, 90 per cent of the industrial goods companies involved did not, by their own admission, produce anything approximating to an integrated, co-ordinated and internally consistent plan for their marketing activities. This included a substantial number of companies that had highly elaborate procedures for marketing planning. Certainly, few of these companies enjoyed the advantages of formalized marketing planning and its output, an effective marketing plan.

The benefits to an organization of having a marketing plan are that it:

- ► achieves better co-ordination of activities;
- ► identifies expected developments;
- ► increases organizational preparedness to change;
- ► minimizes non-rational responses to the unexpected;
- ► reduces conflicts about where the organization should be going;
- ► improves communications;
- ► forces management to think ahead systematically;
- ► enhances the matching of available resources to selected opportunities;
- ► provides a framework for the continuing review of operations; and
- ► demands a systematic approach to strategy formulation, which leads to a higher return on investment.

Strategic and tactical marketing planning

The crux of marketing planning lies in knowing the difference between strategy and tactics. All organizations need to a have longer-term (strategic) marketing view as well as a short-term (tactical) marketing operation. Much of the difficulty surrounding marketing planning derives predominantly from not understanding the real significance of a strategic marketing plan as opposed to a tactical, or operational, marketing plan. A strategic marketing plan is for a period that extends beyond the following fiscal year, and usually covers three to five years. It is the backdrop against which operational decisions are taken, determining where the company is, where it wants to go, and how it can get there. A tactical plan is for a shorter period, normally for one year or less. While similar in content, its level of detail is much greater as it contains the scheduling and costing out of the specific actions necessary for the achievement of the first year of the strategic plan.

The pragmatic, profit-related reasons for needing to develop a strategic marketing plan, and for doing so before deciding operational courses of action, are illustrated by the 'survival matrix' shown in Figure 6.1.

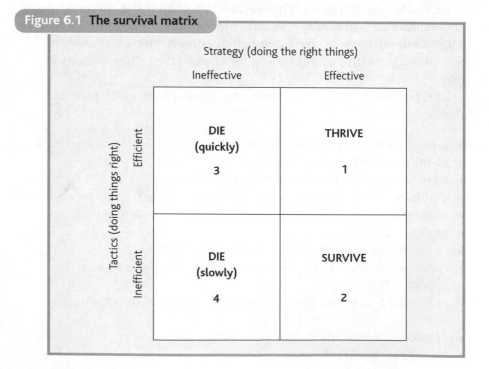

Figure 6.1 The survival matrix

The horizontal axis represents strategy as a continuum from ineffective to effective, while the vertical axis represents tactics on a continuum from inefficient to efficient. Those firms with an effective strategy and efficient tactics continue to thrive, while those with an effective strategy but inefficient tactics merely survive. Those firms to the left of the matrix are destined to die.

Tactical marketing plans should *never* be completed before strategic marketing plans. Most managers prefer selling the products they find easiest to sell to the customers that offer the least line of resistance. However, those who prepare tactical plans first and then extrapolate them merely succeed in extrapolating their own shortcomings. Such preoccupation with short-term plans is a typical mistake of companies that confuse sales forecasting and budgeting with strategic marketing planning.

Problems associated with marketing planning ignorance

Widespread ignorance about marketing planning, and confusion about the difference between strategic marketing planning, sales forecasting and budgeting, has curtailed or killed off many organizations with evident growth potential. Such agonizing outcomes can be avoided to a great extent by fully understanding what marketing planning is (and is not), and assimilating this understanding in practice.

A frequent complaint is marketing's preoccupation with short-term thinking, and an almost total lack of 'strategic thinking', or considering the longer-term implications of external and internal influences on the organization. Another complaint is that marketing plans consist largely of numbers, which bear little relationship to, and offer little insight into, current market position, key opportunities and threats, significant trends and issues, or indeed, how to meet sales targets. Financial objectives, while being essential measures of the desired performance of a company, are of scant practical help, since they say nothing about *how* the results are to be achieved. The same applies to sales forecasts and budgets, which are *not* marketing objectives and strategies. Basing company plans on a combination of forecasting and budgeting systems can only work if the future is going to be the same as the present or the past. As this is rarely the case, reliance on a forecasting and budgeting approach simply produces 'tunnel vision', and often leads to the following common problems:

- lost opportunities for profit;
- meaningless numbers in long-term plans;
- unrealistic objectives;
- lack of actionable market information;
- interfunctional strife;
- management frustration;
- proliferation of products and markets;
- wasted promotional expenditure;
- confusion over pricing;
- growing vulnerability to changes in the business environment; and
- Loss of control over the business.

These problems are symptomatic of a much deeper problem emanating from a lack of marketing planning. Marketing planning is about marketing objectives (*what* you want to achieve *vis-à-vis* products and markets) and marketing strategies (*how* you plan to achieve your marketing objectives). Case study 6.1 highlights the danger of relying on forecasts and budgets in the absence of a marketing planning system.

Case study 6.1 An example of marketing planning ignorance

The headquarters of a major multinational company, with a sophisticated budgeting system, used to receive plans from all over the world and co-ordinate them in quantitative and cross-functional terms (such as number of employees, units of sale, items of plant, and square feet of production area) together with the associated financial implications. The trouble was that this complicated edifice was built on initial sales forecasts, which were themselves little more than a time-consuming numbers game. The really key strategic issues relating to products and markets were lost in all the financial activity, which eventually resulted in grave operational and profitability problems.

The need for a marketing planning system

As companies are dynamically evolving entities operating within a dynamically evolving environment, some means of evaluation of the way in which the two interact has to be found to enable them to be better matched. As companies get larger, their operational problems become more complex. Written procedures are needed to make the marketing strategy explicit and the marketing concept understood. Thus, the bigger and more diversified the organization, the bigger the need for standardized and formalized procedures.

While the degree of formalization will change with organizational evolution, the need for a complete marketing system does not. The problems that companies suffer, then, are a function either of the degree to which they have a requisite marketing planning system, or the degree to which the formalization of their system grows with the situational complexities attendant on the size and diversity of operations.

Remarkably few companies have planning systems that possess these characteristics. Those that do have these characteristics succeed in coping with their environment more successfully than those that do not. They find it easier to set meaningful marketing objectives; are more confident about their future; enjoy greater control over their business; and react less on a piecemeal basis to ongoing events. In short, they incur fewer operational problems and as a result are more effective.

An organization with an effective marketing planning system is likely to have:

▶ widely understood objectives;
▶ highly motivated employees;
▶ high levels of actionable market information;
▶ greater interfunctional co-ordination;
▶ minimum wastage of resources;
▶ acceptance of the need for continuous change and a clear understanding of priorities;
▶ greater control over the business and less vulnerability to the unexpected;
▶ increased capacity/tendency to develop long-term, mutually beneficial relationships.

By contrast, organizations without effective marketing planning systems, while it is possible that they are profitable over a number of years, especially in high-growth markets, will tend to be less profitable over time and to experience problems that are the very opposite of the benefits referred to above. Furthermore, companies without effective marketing planning systems tend to suffer more serious commercial and organizational consequences when environmental and competitive conditions become hostile and unstable.

How marketing planning relates to corporate planning

Before turning our attention to the constituent steps in the strategic marketing planning process, it will be useful to discuss how marketing planning relates to corporate planning.

Marketing planning is the means by which an organization monitors and controls the many internal and external influences on its ability to achieve profitable sales, and communicates throughout its ranks the competitive stance it has chosen to achieve its objectives. It is therefore not possible to plan an organization's marketing activities in isolation from other business functions. Consequently, the marketing planning process should be based firmly on a corporate planning system.

A business starts at some time with resources and wants to use those resources to achieve something. This desired destination, or result, is a corporate objective. Most often corporate objectives are expressed in terms of profit, since profit is the means of satisfying shareholders or owners, and because it is one universally accepted criterion by which efficiency can be evaluated, which will in turn lead to efficient resource allocation, economic and technical progressiveness, and stability. The policies an organization adopts to pursue its profit objectives, such as to compete in a market, to manufacture themselves but to outsource distribution, to manage within cash flow and so on, are corporate strategies.

In practice, companies tend to operate by way of functional divisions, each with a separate identity, so that what is a strategy in the corporate plan becomes an objective within each department. For example, marketing strategies within the corporate plan become operating objectives within the marketing department, and strategies at the general level within the marketing department become operating objectives at the next level down (for example, advertising, sales promotion, personal selling). At a further level down, there would be, say, advertising objectives and advertising strategies, with the subsequent programmes and budgets for achieving the objectives. In this way, a hierarchy of objectives and strategies is formed, which can be traced back to the initial corporate objective.

The really important point, apart from clarifying the difference between objectives and strategies, is that the further down the hierarchical chain one goes, the less likely it is that a stated objective will make a cost-effective contribution to company profits, unless it derives logically and directly from an objective at a higher level.

Thus meaningful marketing objectives, concerning what is sold (products/ services) and to whom it is sold (its markets), will relate directly to corporate objectives, or the desired level of profit the organization seeks to achieve.

While marketing planning is based on markets, customers and products/services, business planning involves other corporate resources, which will have a bearing on the identified markets. It is therefore useful to understand how marketing planning relates to the corporate planning process. There are five steps in the corporate planning process, as outlined in Table 6.1.

Step 1 amounts to a statement of corporate financial objectives for the long-range planning period of the organization, which are often expressed in terms of turnover, profit before tax, and return on investment. Usually this planning horizon is five years, but the precise period should be determined by the nature of the markets in which the organization operates. A useful guideline is that there should be a

Table 6.1 Marketing planning within the corporate planning process

Step 1	Step 2	Step 3	Step 4	Step 5
Corporate financial objectives	Management audit	Objective and strategy setting	Plans	Corporate plans
	Marketing audit Marketing	Marketing objectives, strategies	Marketing plan	
	Other operational audits	Other operational objectives, strategies	Other operational plans	Issue of corporate plan, to include corporate objectives and strategies; operations objectives and strategies, etc.; long-range profit and loss accounts; balance sheets

market for the organization's products for long enough at least to amortize any capital investment associated with those products. It is advisable to keep the period down to three years, since beyond this period any detail in the strategic plan is likely to become pointless.

Step 2 is an audit, or systematic, critical and unbiased review and appraisal of the environment and the company's operations. In practice, the best way to carry out a management audit is to conduct a separate audit of each major management function. Thus the marketing audit (concerned with the marketing environment and marketing operations) is part of the larger management audit, in the same way that the operations audit is.

Step 3, objective and strategy setting, is undoubtedly the most important and most difficult of the corporate planning stages, since if this is not done properly everything that follows is of little value. This is the stage in the planning cycle when a compromise has to be reached between what is wanted by the several functional departments and what is practicable given the constraints within which any organization operates.

Step 4 involves producing detailed plans for one year, containing the responsibilities, timing and costs of carrying out the first year's objectives, and broad plans for the following years. It is important to include a *contingency plan* in the one-year marketing plan. This should consider what the financial consequences would be (that is, the effect on the operating income), if the planning assumptions did not come to pass; also what action the organization would take to mitigate any adverse financial effects of an unfulfilled assumption, so that the organization ends up with the same forecast profit at the end of the year.

Step 5 is an incorporation of these detailed plans into a corporate plan, which will contain long-range corporate objectives, strategies, plans, profit and loss accounts, and balance sheets. An important purpose of the corporate plan is to provide a long-term vision of what the company is, or is striving to become, taking account of shareholder expectations, both resource and consumption market trends, and the distinctive competence of the organization as revealed by the management audit.

What this means in practice is that the corporate plan will contain at least the following elements:

► Corporate objective, or the desired level of profitability;
► Corporate strategies, which denote business boundaries:
  what kinds of products will be sold to what kinds of markets (marketing);

- what kinds of facilities will be developed (operations and distribution);
- wthe size and character of the labour force (personnel);
- funding (finance); and

▶ Other corporate objectives, such as social responsibility, corporate/stock market/employer image, etc.

The relevance of the corporate plan to the marketing plan is immediately visible in that the first item to appear in the marketing plan is often a page outlining the corporate mission and objectives. It should consist of brief statements about the organization's role or contribution, business definition, distinctive competences, and indications for the future (that is, what the firm will do, might do, will never do). The mission statement should be followed by a section summarizing the organization's financial performance, and its financial projections for the three-year planning period. This will provide the person reading the marketing plan with an overview of the financial implications of the plan, including the organization's financial goals (revenue and profit targets), and how these will be achieved. The mission statement and financial summary represent the goal-setting phase of the marketing planning process, ensuring that the marketing plan is launched on a firm and realistic corporate footing.

The strategic marketing planning process

As mentioned earlier, the strategic marketing planning process is a series of logical steps that have to be worked through in order to arrive at a logical 'common format' for the implementation of strategy, or marketing plan. It is the systemization of this process that is distinctive, and that lies at the heart of the theory of strategic marketing planning.

Figure 6.2 outlines the constituent ten steps, highlighting the difference between the *process* of marketing planning and its output, the actual written marketing *plan*. A more comprehensive description of the components and procedure for producing a strategic marketing plan is provided at the end of this chapter.

Experience has shown that a strategic marketing plan should contain a mission statement; financial summary; market overview; SWOT analyses; assumptions; marketing objectives and strategies appropriately prioritized; and a budget containing details of timing,

Figure 6.2 The strategic marketing planning process

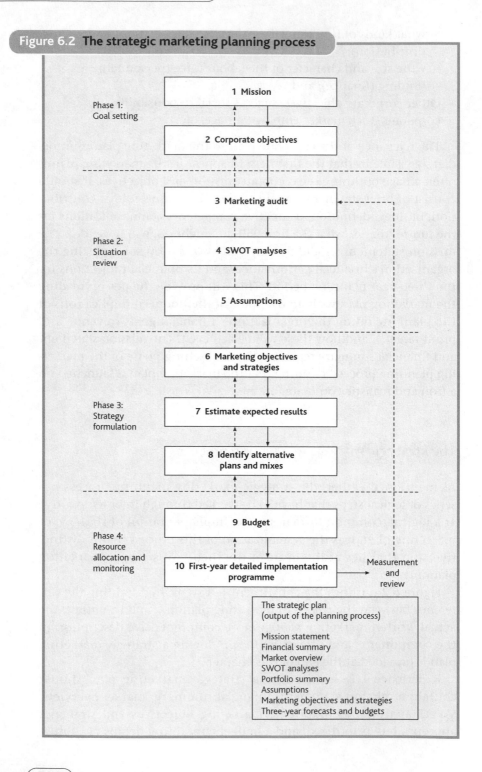

responsibilities and costs, with forecasts and financial outcomes. To ensure that these elements appear in the marketing plan, it is necessary to complete each of the first nine planning steps in succession before producing the detailed one-year plan. However, the dotted lines in Figure 6.2 indicate the reality of the marketing planning process; that is to say, it is likely that each of these steps will have to be gone through more than once before final marketing programmes can be written.

Although it is generally accepted that each of the marketing planning steps is applicable in most cases, the degree to which each of the separate steps in the diagram needs to be formalized depends to a large extent on the size and nature of the company. For example, an *undiversified* company generally uses less formalized procedures, since top management tends to have greater functional knowledge and expertise than subordinates, and because the lack of diversity of operations enables direct control to be exercised over most of the key determinants of success. Thus situation reviews or the setting of marketing objectives, for example, are not always made explicit in writing, although these steps still have to be considered.

In contrast, in a *diversified* company it is usually not possible for top management to have greater functional knowledge and expertise than subordinate management, hence the whole planning process tends to be formalized in order to provide a consistent discipline for those who have to make the decisions throughout the organization.

Marketing audit

As the marketing audit referred to in Step 2 of Table 6.1 is the primary mechanism for monitoring marketing performance in relation to the creation and delivery of customer value, it is dealt with in detail later in Chapter 19. However, for the purposes of proceeding with the strategic marketing planning process, let us explain briefly what this first step entails.

A marketing audit is a systematic, critical and unbiased appraisal of the organization's market environment and of its operations. It amounts to the collection and analysis of information to answer the question: 'Where is the company now?' Both the external and internal variables that impinge on the company's marketing performance are examined. The marketing audit is essentially a database of all market-related issues of the organization, which forms part of the organization-wide management audit. The marketing audit is sometimes referred to as PEST analysis (Political, Economic, Sociological and Technical), although this alternative name does not include competitor analysis.

SWOT analysis

To decide on marketing objectives and future strategy, it is necessary first to summarize the unit's *present* position in its market(s). The marketing audit must now be summarized in the form of a SWOT analysis. The acronym SWOT derives from the initial letters of the words *strengths*, *weaknesses*, *opportunities* and *threats*. In simple terms:

▶ What are the opportunities?
▶ What are the present and future threats to the unit's business in each of the segments that have been identified as being of importance?
▶ What are the unit's *differential* strengths and weaknesses *vis-à-vis* competitors? In other words, why should potential customers in the target markets prefer to deal with your company rather than with any of your competitors?

The SWOT should include reasons for good or poor performance. By identifying the critical success factors (CSFs) for the organization, and important outside influences and their implications, the key issues to be addressed will emerge.

Guidelines for completing the SWOT analysis

The marketing audit will have identified what are considered to be the key markets upon which the company should focus. For presentation purposes, it is helpful to prepare a SWOT for each of these key products. Each of these SWOTs should be brief and interesting to read.

Point 1 below indicates how the *opportunities* and *threats* section of the SWOT should be completed. Point 2 concerns *strengths* and *weaknesses*.

1 *Summary of outside influences and their implications.* This should include a brief statement about how important environmental influences, such as technology, government policies and regulations and the economy have affected this segment. There will obviously be some opportunities and some threats.
2 *Some important factors for success in this business.* How does a competitor wishing to provide products in the same segment succeed? Relatively few factors determine success: factors such as product performance, quality of software, breadth of services, speed of service and low costs are often the most important ones.

A brief statement should now be made about the company's strengths and weaknesses in relation to the most important factors for success that have been identified. To do this, it will probably be necessary to consider other specialist suppliers to the same segment in order to identify why your company can succeed, and what weaknesses must be addressed in the long-term plan.

A sample form for completing a SWOT analysis, leading to strategy formulation, is given in Figure 6.3. this form should be completed for each of the organization's market segments.

Planning assumptions

Having completed our marketing and SWOT analysis, assumptions now have to be made and written down explicitly. There are certain key determinants of success in all companies about which assumptions have to be made before the planning process can proceed. For example, it would be no good receiving plans from two product managers, one of whom believed the economy was about going into decline by 2 per cent, while the other believed the economy was about to grow by 10 per cent.

An example of presented assumptions might be:

With respect to the company's industrial climate, it is assumed that:

1 Industrial overcapacity will increase from 105 per cent to 115 per cent as new industrial plants come into operation;
2 price competition will force price levels down by 10 per cent across the board; and
3 a new product will be introduced by our major competitor before the end of the second quarter.

Assumptions should be few in number, and if a plan is robust – that is, possible irrespective of any assumption made – then so much the better.

Marketing objectives and strategies

The next step in marketing planning is the writing of marketing objectives and strategies, the key step in the whole process:

▶ *Objectives* are what you want to achieve; and
▶ *Strategies* are how you plan to achieve your objectives.

There can be objectives and strategies at all levels in marketing. For example, there can be advertising objectives and strategies, and

Figure 6.3 Sample form for SWOT analysis

SWOT analysis

(Note: This form should be completed for each product/market segment under consideration)

1 SBU description

Here, describe the market for which the SWOT is being done.

2 Critical success factors What are the few key things from the customer's point of view, that any competitor has to do right to succeed?

1
2
3
4
5

3 Weighting How important is each of these CSFs? Score out of 100.

Total 100

4 Strengths/Weaknesses analysis

Score yourself and each of your main competitors out of 10 on each of the CSFs. Then multiply the score by the weight.

Comp CSF	You	Competitor A	Competitor B	Competitor C	Competitor D
1					
2					
3					
4					
5					
Total (score weight)					

5 Opportunities/threats

What are the few key things outside your direct control that have had, and will continue to have, an impact on your business?

Opportunities

1
2
3
4
5

Threats

6 Key issues that need to be addressed

7 Key assumption for the planning period

1
2
3
4
5
6
7

8 Key objectives

9 Key strategies

Financial consequences

pricing objectives and strategies. However, it is important to remember that marketing objectives are about *products and markets only*. Common sense will confirm that it is only by selling something to someone that the company's financial goals can be achieved, and that advertising, pricing and service levels are the means (or strategies) by which we might succeed in doing this. Thus pricing objectives, sales-promotion objectives and advertising objectives should not be confused with marketing objectives. In other words, we can say that marketing objectives are about one or more of the following:

▶ Existing products in existing markets;
▶ New products for existing markets;
▶ Existing products for new markets; and
▶ New products for new markets.

They should be capable of measurement, otherwise they are not objectives. Directional terms such as 'maximize', 'minimize', 'penetrate' and 'increase' are only acceptable if quantitative measurement can be attached to them over the planning period. Measurement should be in terms of sales volume, money value (pounds, euros or dollars, for example), market share and percentage penetration of outlets.

Marketing strategies are the means by which marketing objectives will be achieved and are generally concerned with the four 'P's – that is, product, pricing, place and promotion decisions. Figure 6.4 highlights the need to plan and integrate the marketing mix elements against defined marketing objectives. The important process of defining marketing objectives and strategies is considered in Chapter 7.

Having completed this major planning task, it is normal at this stage to employ judgement, experience and field tests to assess the feasibility of the objectives and strategies in terms of market share, sales, costs and profits.

Programmes

The general marketing strategies are now deployed into specific 'sub-objectives', each supported by more detailed strategy and action statements, with timings and responsibilities clearly indicated.

Use of marketing plans

A written marketing plan is the background against which operational decisions are taken on an ongoing basis; consequently, too much detail

Figure 6.4 The marketing mix is defined against the marketing objectives

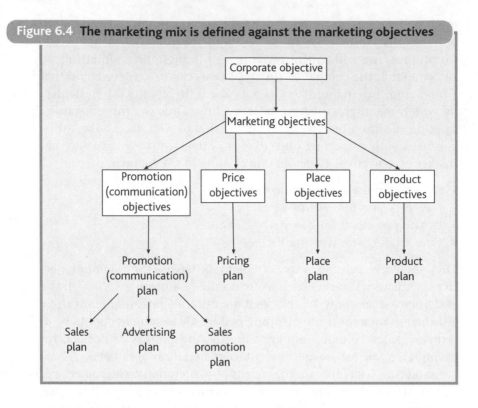

should not be included. We should remember that its major function is to determine where the company is *now*, where it wants to *go* and *how* to get there. This is central to the company's revenue-generating activities, and from it flow all other corporate activities, such as the timing of the cash flow, and the size and character of the labour force. Finally, the marketing plan should be distributed to those who need to know what is going on, since its purpose is an aid to effective management.

International marketing planning

The process of marketing planning outlined in this chapter is universally applicable, irrespective of company size and complexity. The only real difference concerns the degree of formality of the processes and procedures.

In the case of a company operating internationally, a more formalized approach is advisable in order to gain the economies of scale and scope that give international organizations their competitive edge. For example, in order to create a truly international brand such as Perrier or Castrol GTX, the key elements of global branding must be planned centrally. These issues are outlined in Chapter 9, where the following definition of a global brand is also given:

> A global brand is a product that bears the same name and logo and presents the same or similar message all over the world. Usually, the product is aimed at the same target market and is promoted and presented in much the same way.

Consequently, it is clear that the brand's positioning must be planned and controlled centrally. This will embrace the channels used to reach the target market, the price position within the market and, of course, the way it is promoted.

In many organizations, product planning needs to be controlled centrally in order to ensure a balanced global portfolio. This will entail an understanding of a product's position in its life-cycle in a country and region of the world in order to ensure that appropriate objectives and strategies are set for it, together with the decision of when and how to allocate R&D resources. The important issues in the process of international product planning itself are considered in Chapter 8.

Design and implementation of a marketing planning system

As a rule, formalized marketing planning procedures result in greater profitability and stability in the long term, and help to reduce friction and operational difficulties within organizations.

The really important issue in any system is the extent to which it enables control to be exercised over the key determinants of success and failure. Research has shown that certain conditions must be satisfied for a marketing planning system to work. There must be:

▶ *Openness* – any closed-loop planning system, especially if it based only on forecasting and budgeting, will deaden any creative response and eventually lead to failure. Therefore there has to be some mechanism to prevent inertia setting in through the over-bureaucratization of the system.
▶ *Integration* – marketing planning that is not integrated with other functional areas of the business at general management level will largely be ineffective.

▶ *Coherence* – separation of operational and strategic marketing planning will lead to a divergence of the short-term thrust of a business at the operational level from the long-term objectives of the enterprise as a whole, with the short-term viewpoint winning because it achieves quick results.

▶ *Leadership* – unless the CEO understands and takes an active role in strategic marketing planning, it will never be an effective system.

▶ *Time* – It can take three years to introduce marketing planning successfully.

As we have seen, a successful marketing planning system follows requisite, key steps:

▶ There will have to be guidance provided by the corporate objectives;
▶ A marketing audit must take place;
▶ A gap analysis must be completed;
▶ SWOT analyses must be drawn up;
▶ Assumptions and contingencies must be considered;
▶ Marketing objectives and strategies must be set;
▶ Individual marketing programmes must be established; and
▶ There must be a period of measurement and review.

All this work will take time, and will certainly require discussions with other functional departments, either to get information or to ensure collaboration. Thus it is important to schedule the tasks and timing, and to present the plans in a clear manner – for example, diagrammatically, as shown in Figure 6.5. The circle represents a calendar year and the time periods are given as examples to indicate the sequence of planning activities. As the company becomes more experienced in planning, the timetable can probably be tightened up and the whole planning period shortened. In the second planning year, months 11 and 12 could be used to evaluate the first year's plan and thereby prepare information for the next round of corporate planning. The planning process is an iterative one and a continual undercurrent throughout the year.

It is also clear from the planning cycle that key account planning must take place at the same time as, or even before, draft plans are prepared for a strategic business unit.

Significantly, there are two open loop points. These are the key times, or opportunities, in the planning process when a subordinate's views and findings should be subjected to the closest examination by a superior. By utilizing these 'oxygen valves', life can be breathed into marketing planning, transforming it into the critical and creative

Figure 6.5 Strategic and operational planning – timing

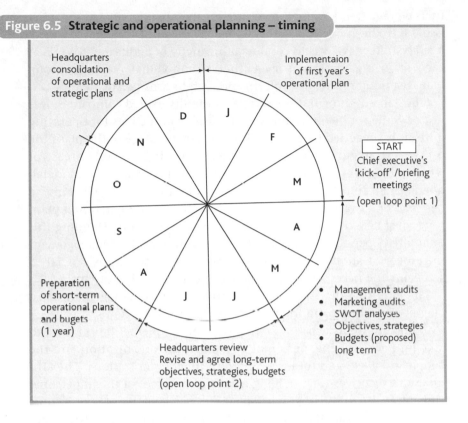

process it is supposed to be, rather than the dull, repetitive ritual it so often turns out to be.

There is a natural point of focus in the future beyond which it is pointless to plan for. Generally, small firms can use shorter horizons because they tend to be flexible in the way in which they can react to environmental turbulence in the short term. Larger firms need longer lead times in which to make changes in direction, and thus require longer planning horizons. While three and five years are commonly used, the planning horizon should reflect the nature of the markets in which the company operates, and the time needed to recover capital investment costs.

Remaining sensitive and responsive to the market place raises another question: Who should make marketing decisions? Top management who are remote from the scene, or those at 'the sharp end' who have intimate knowledge of the markets but less corporate authority? Location of marketing planning within the company is an important aspect of successful marketing planning. Marketing planning should take place as close to the market place as possible in the first instance, but the plans should then be reviewed at a high level within the organization to see what issues have been overlooked. One means of formulating an informed, overall strategic view is to conduct a hierarchy of audits and SWOTs at each main organizational level (that is, individual manager, group manager, profit centre, head office) and then to consolidate them.

Since, in anything but the smallest of undiversified companies, it is not possible for headquarters to set detailed objectives for operating units, it is suggested that at the situation review stage of the planning process, strategic guidelines be issued outlining possible areas for which objectives and strategies will be set (for example, financial, operational, human, organizational, marketing), or the CEO give a personal briefing at kick-off meetings. Strategic and operational planning must be a top-down and bottom-up process. Understanding this total interdependence between upper and lower levels of management in respect of audits and objective and strategy setting is crucial to achieving the necessary balance between control and creativity.

The vital role that the chief executive and top management *must* play in marketing planning underlines a key point. That is, it is *people* who make systems work, system design and implementation have to take into account the 'personality' of both the organization and the people involved, and these are different in all organizations. The attitudes of executives vary, ranging from the extremes of the impersonal and autocratic to the highly personal and participative. There is some evidence to indicate that CEOs who fail, first, to understand the essential role of marketing in generating profitable revenue in a business; and, second, to understand how marketing can be integrated into other functional areas of the business through marketing planning procedures, are a key contributory factor in poor economic performance.

The most common design and implementation problems with marketing planning systems are:

- ▶ Weak support from the chief executive and top management;
- ▶ Lack of a plan for planning;
- ▶ Lack of line management support:
  - Hostility;
  - Lack of skills;
  - Lack of information;
  - Lack of resources; and
  - Inadequate organizational structure;
- ▶ Confusion over planning terms;
- ▶ Numbers in lieu of written objectives and strategies;

- ▶ Too much detail, too far ahead;
- ▶ Once-a-year ritual;
- ▶ Separation of operational planning from strategic planning;
- ▶ Failure to integrate marketing planning into total corporate planning system; and
- ▶ Delegation of planning to a planner.

When marketing planning fails, it is generally because companies place too much emphasis on the procedures and the resulting paperwork, rather than on generating information useful to, and consumable by, management. Also, when companies relegate marketing planning to a 'planner' it invariably fails, for the simple reason that planning for line management cannot be delegated to a third party. The real role of the planner should be to help those responsible for implementation to plan. Equally, planning failures often result from companies trying too much too quickly and without training staff in the use of procedures or providing them with sufficient resources, as the following examples show.

One Swedish company selling batteries internationally tried four times, unsuccessfully, to introduce a marketing planning system, each one failing because management throughout the organization was confused about what was being asked of them. Furthermore, not only did they not understand the need for the new systems, they were also not provided with the necessary resources to make the system work effectively. Training of managers and careful thought about resource requirements would have overcome this particular company's problems to a great extent.

In contrast, a major multinational company, having suffered grave profitability and operational difficulties through not having an effective marketing planning system, introduced one over a three-year period. It included a training programme in the use of new procedures, and the provision of adequate resources to make them work effectively. This company is now firmly in control of its diverse activities and has recovered its confidence and profitability.

Summary

Effective marketing planning underpins the successful creation and delivery of the value proposition.

There is a process for marketing planning, the formalization of which is a function of size and product market complexity. This process is no different in an international context (see Chapter 8).

Marketing planning is a managerial process leading to a marketing plan. Strategic marketing plans should *always* be prepared before tactical marketing plans. A marketing plan should contain the following elements.

Contents of a strategic a marketing plan:

Mission statement
► A declaration of the *raison d'être* of the organization, covering its role, business definition, distinctive competence, and future indications.

Financial summary
► A brief outline of the financial implications over the full planning period.

SWOT analyses
► Only the SWOTs (not the audit) goes into a marketing plan.
► Summaries emanating from the marketing audit.
► A brief, interesting and concise commentary.
► Focus on *key* factors only.
► List *differential* strengths and weaknesses *vis-à-vis* competitors.
► List *key* external opportunities and threats.
► Identify and pin down the *real issues*; not a list of unrelated points.
► The reader should be able to grasp instantly the main thrust of the business; he or she should even be able to write down your marketing objectives.
► Follow the implied question, 'Which means that . . . ?' to get the real implications.
► Do not over-abbreviate.
► Spend time on the SWOT. It is worth it.

Assumptions
► Critical to the planned marketing objectives and strategies.
► Must be few in number.
► If a plan can happen irrespective of the assumption, the assumption is unnecessary.

Marketing objectives
► Goal statements about products/services and markets only.
► They articulate what the company is committing itself to, and the corresponding resource implications.
► They flow from the SWOT and must be compatible.

► They should be quantifiable and measurable. Avoid directional terms such as 'increase', 'improve' and so on.
► There will be hierarchy of objectives throughout the organization.
► Set priorities for the chosen marketing objectives.
► Do not confuse objectives and strategies (objectives – what we want to achieve; strategies – how we plan to achieve objectives).

Marketing strategies
► Product, pricing, place and promotion policies.
► Marketing strategies must eventually be transformed into detailed marketing actions, which are articulated in the product, price, place (distribution), and promotion (communications) plans.

Programmes
► Forecasts come last (not simple extrapolations); they are not objectives.
► Specific sub-objectives for products and segments, with detailed strategy and action statements (what, where, when, costs, and so on).
► Include budgets and forecasts, and a consolidated budget for the full planning period which details for each year the revenues and associated costs.
► Budgets and forecasts *must* reflect marketing objectives. Objectives, strategies and programmes *must* reflect agreed budgets and sales forecasts.

Adherence to a well-designed and well-implemented marketing planning system can do much to prevent marketing plan failure.

Further reading

Leppard, J. and McDonald, M. (1987) A reappraisal of the role of marketing planning. *Journal of Marketing Management*, 3(2).
McDonald, M. (1996) Strategic marketing planning: theory, practice; and research agendas. *Journal of Marketing Management*, 3(2).
Saunders, J. and Wong, V. (1993) Business orientations and corporate success. *Journal of Strategic Marketing*, 1(1) pp. 20–40.

Reference

McDonald, M. (2002) *Marketing Plans: How to Prepare Them – How to Use Them*, 5th edn, Butterworth-Heinemann, Oxford.

7 Defining marketing objectives and strategies

Strategic marketing and the value proposition

The definition of marketing objectives and strategies is a key step in the marketing planning process and the keystone locking the value proposition together. If we imagine the value proposition as an arched bridge connecting supplier and customer, we can ask ourselves 'Why would either party want to engage with the other, and what would entice them to act to do so?' This deceptively simple question raises a multitude of issues that combine to shape the 'give and take' of commercial relationships. Staying with this analogy, the top of a smooth and symmetrical arch would describe a value proposition of mutual and equal benefit, where both parties derive an acceptable level of satisfaction for an acceptable level of investment. The summit of a lopsided arch would indicate that one party was getting a better deal than the other from the interface, and that the structural integrity of the value proposition (and thus of any future relationship) was probably tenuous. The central role of marketing objectives and strategies in creating the value proposition is depicted in Figure 7.1.

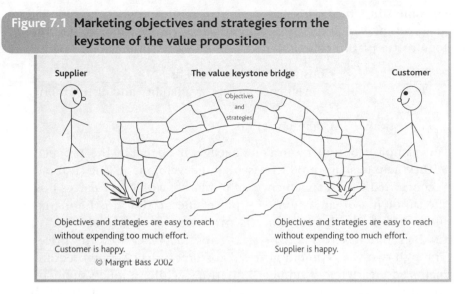

Figure 7.1 Marketing objectives and strategies form the keystone of the value proposition

Supplier   The value keystone bridge   Customer

Objectives and strategies

Objectives and strategies are easy to reach without expending too much effort. Customer is happy.

Objectives and strategies are easy to reach without expending too much effort. Supplier is happy.

© Margrit Bass 2002

Clearly, successful relationship development through strategic marketing depends on the construction of a manifestly strong and purposeful statement of value that respects the agendas of both parties. The creation of such a value proposition by the supplying organization depends first on choosing and prioritizing the markets and segments in which it wishes to operate. These decisions will be based on the analyses produced in the previous process (defining markets and customer value), and will take into account both the market's/segment's inherent attractiveness and the organization's actual and potential ability to meet those customers' needs and expectations. Target market selection will thus also be influenced by the corporate objectives.

The core of the value proposition to the customer will then be defined by the marketing objectives, or what the organization aims to achieve *vis-à-vis* its chosen market segments. The marketing objectives will be delivered by the marketing strategies.

Marketing objectives and strategies

Marketing objectives

Marketing objectives concern both what the organization hopes to receive from each segment in terms of, for example, market share, volume, value or contribution, and what it hopes to deliver to customers in return. This price/value proposition (what the supplier gives/gets and what the customer gives/gets) can be thought of as the four 'P's translating to four 'C's:

Product: Consumer wants and needs
Place: Convenience (access, availability and distribution)
Price: Cost
Promotion: Communication

For example, 'consumer wants and needs' will be met by the 'product', as they help to shape product design and development. The customer is concerned with 'convenience' of purchase, which influences how the supplying organization will 'place' the product in the market place. Similarly, the customer is interested in the total 'cost' of product purchase and ownership, not just the upfront 'price'. Through two-way 'communication' customers declare their requirements and learn about suppliers' offerings, while suppliers publicize their products and services, and gain customer knowledge through 'promotion'.

The important point about marketing objectives is that they are concerned solely with *products and markets*, as it is only by selling something to someone that the organization's financial goals can be achieved. If profits and cash flows are to be maximized, the organization must consider carefully how its current customer needs are changing, and how its products/services offered need to change accordingly. Further, they should be capable of measurement; otherwise they are not objectives. Marketing objectives are normally stated in standards of performance for a given operating period, or conditions to be achieved by a given date.

Marketing objectives are the nucleus of managerial action, providing direction to the marketing plans. An objective will ensure that a company knows what its strategies are expected to accomplish, and when a particular strategy has accomplished its purpose. Without objectives, strategy decisions and all that follows will take place in a vacuum.

All organizations serve a mix of different types of market, and marketing strategies enable them to select the customers, and hence the markets, with which they wish to deal. Marketing strategies are the routes by which an organization seeks to achieve its marketing objectives through the range of products/services it offers to its chosen markets. Marketing strategies are thus generally concerned with the four 'P's of the marketing mix:

- Product – the general policies for product deletions, modifications, additions, design, branding, positioning, packaging and so on;
- Price – the general pricing policies to be followed for product groups in market segments;
- Place – the general policies for channels and customer service levels; and
- Promotion – the general policies for communicating with customers under the relevant headings, such as advertising, sales force, sales promotion, public relations, exhibitions, direct mail, the Internet and so on.

The main components of marketing strategy are: the company, customers and competitors. When setting marketing strategies, it is important to know your company's position in the market, as well as the positions of your competitors, so that ideally you can meet customer needs by doing something your rivals are not expecting, and will find difficult to emulate or supersede. The point to remember about differentiation as a strategy is that your company must still be cost-effective.

Michael Porter's generic strategies matrix, shown in Figure 7.2, demonstrates that some markets are inherently more prone to lack of

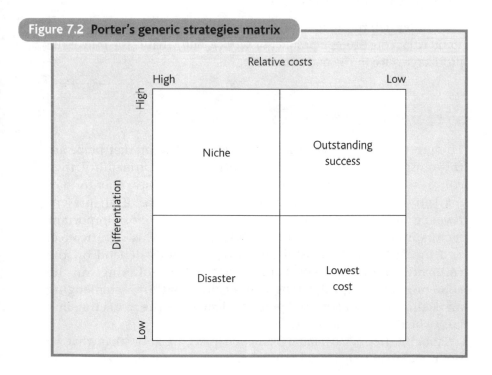

Figure 7.2 Porter's generic strategies matrix

differentiation in products and services. In such cases, the attainment of low costs must be a corporate goal if adequate margins are to be obtained. The ultimate strategy for commodity market situations, where there is no differentiation or cost advantage, is to move to either a cost leadership or a niche strategy. A niche position is achieved through offering added value, whereas in a cost leadership position, the values offered are cost competitive.

Some of the marketing strategies available to managers include:

1 Change product design, performance, quality or features.
2 Change advertising or promotion.
3 Change unit price.
4 Change delivery or distribution.
5 Change service levels.
6 Improve marketing productivity (for example, improve sales mix).
7 Improve administrative productivity.
8 Consolidate product line.
9 Withdraw from markets.
10 Consolidate distribution.
11 Standardize design.
12 Acquire markets, products, facilities.

In order determine marketing strategies it is necessary to understand what constitutes a product or service, and what is the role of the product/service in the marketing mix.

What is a product/service?

The products or services that are offered to the market place are the most visible signs of an enterprise. In all probability they convey to customers more about a company than any other form of marketing activity. Not only are they the source of all present revenue and profits, but they will also be the most important factors in terms of success in the future. Given this significance, and the fact that successful business operations depend on the company's ability to base its product or service offerings on the changing needs of a dynamic market place within a challenging marketing environment, the product element of the marketing mix has to be managed carefully.

From the ground covered in earlier chapters, we know that what we sell has to match up sufficiently with what the customer wants. The

Figure 7.3 Linking customer needs with corporate goals

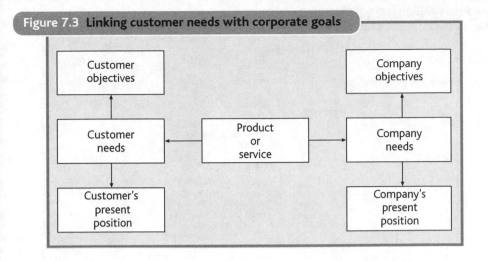

product or service links the customer to us, as shown in Figure 7.3. The customer should need our product or service, either to help solve some current problem being faced, or else to make a contribution in some way to corporate or personal objectives. For our part, we need a viable product or service to help us to improve our present position and meet our objectives.

While we should be clear about our own needs and objectives, those of the customers are not always quite so obvious. It is therefore helpful to look at the product or service we offer through our customers' eyes. Adopting the customers' viewpoint reveals that a product (or service product) is the total experience of the customer or consumer when dealing with the organization.

As illustrated in Figure 7.4, a product can be envisaged as a set of concentric circles. Functional features (such as components and performance) form the core. This is encircled by added values that enhance the basic features (such as reputation, corporate image, and style of service and support), known as the product or service surround (see Figure 7.5). Generally speaking, the product surround accounts for 80 per cent of a product's impact, while accounting for only 20 per cent of costs, while the reverse tends to be true for the core product. The importance attributed to the intangible elements, specifically brand name and value perceptions, is worth special consideration, and this is addressed in more depth in Chapter 9.

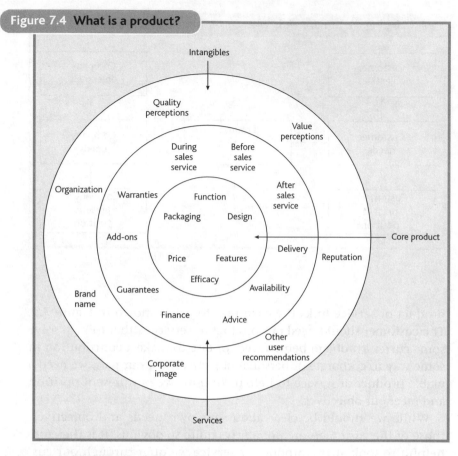

Figure 7.4 **What is a product?**

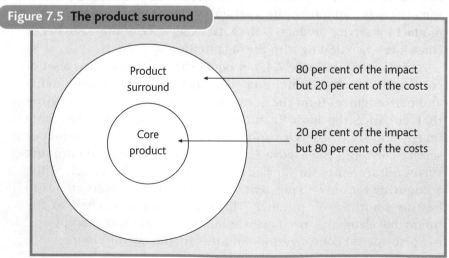

Figure 7.5 **The product surround**

Types of product/service benefits

In the customers' perception a product or service is more than just a physical entity, a sum of its component parts. When customers make a purchase, not only do they buy our product or service, but they also buy along with it a whole package, or 'bundle' of benefits. At the end of the day it will be their perception of these benefits that will influence their decision to buy, or not. Among the many different types of product/service benefits that people seek to satisfy their needs are:

► good value for money/competitive price;
► novelty;
► availability;
► good design;
► ease of use;
► fashionableness;
► safety;
► pride of ownership;
► economy in use;
► efficient performance/end results;
► ease of servicing;
► quality;
► packaging;
► prompt delivery;
► choice of colours, sizes and so on;
► reliability;
► validity – does what it promises;
► terms available;
► discount available;
► reputable image (of supplier);
► convenience/minimal disruption of normal routine;
► scarcity of value;
► ease of purchase;
► after-sales service;
► durability;
► shelf life – won't become obsolete too quickly;
► guarantee/warranty available;
► prestige or status;
► labour saving;
► 'storability';
► space saving;

- return on investment;
- availability of spares;
- range of accessories/peripherals;
- easy-to-follow instructions;
- made in the UK/made in a specific country;
- ecologically safe – won't harm the environment;
- freedom from artificial additives, or particular materials, e.g., non-allergenic; and
- Designer labelling.

The benefit analysis worksheet

The following process describes how we can arrive at a match between the benefits of our major products and selected market segments. Taking a specific market segment, look at the list of possible customer benefits mentioned earlier and:

1 Pick out the three major benefits for this customer segment. Identify these in some way on the list.
2 Next, select a further four benefits. Mark these in the same way.
3 Finally, identify all the other benefits on the list that are valued to a lesser extent by this key market segment.

Figure 7.6 Benefit analysis worksheet

	Major benefits			Secondary benefits				Lesser benefits										
Customer benefits / Products or services	1	2	3	4	5	6	7	8	9	10	11	12	13	14	15	Total	Ranking	Notes, comments, etc.
	Score max. 12 each			Score max. 6 each				Score max. 4 each										

Now make a list of all the products or services supplied to this market segment. Finally, combine the information just assembled by completing the benefit analysis worksheet (see Figure 7.6).

Notes on completing the worksheet

1 Write down the products or services offered in the spaces provided at the left side of the worksheet. There are six spaces. If more are needed, extend the worksheet on to another sheet of paper.
2 Write down the benefits identified above so that the three major benefits are put as headings to columns 1, 2 and 3 of the worksheet. The next four benefits are entered as headings for columns 4 to 7 inclusive. All other benefits are written as headings to column 8 and onwards.
3 Consider the first product or service listed on the worksheet. Score it according to how well it supplies the benefit at the end of each column. It will be noted that the first three benefits can score a maximum of 12 points, the next four a maximum of 6 points and the remainder a maximum of 3 points.
4 Repeat this process for the products and services.

Figure 7.7 is an example, provided here purely for illustration.

Interpretation of the worksheet
The 'total' score is an indicator of how many 'benefit points' each product is providing. In the example shown in Figure 7.7, Product A

Figure 7.7 Benefit analysis worksheet results

	Price	Performance	Safety	Design	Packaging	Durability	Discount	Delivery	After-sales	Instructions		Total	Rank	Comments
Product A	12	9	9	6	3	4	6	1	3	3		56	1	
B	6	10	7	4	3	6	6	1	1	2		46	3	
C	8	10	10	4	3	3	6	3	3	2		52	2	
D	4	8	12	6	3	6	6	3	1	3		52	2	

scores the most points and is ranked first, Products C and D come next to rank equal second, while Product B is ranked third.

Not only does this technique enable products or services to be compared and measured against the benefits they supply, it also gives rise to some very pertinent questions. For example:

▶ Why are Products B, C and D not competitively priced?
▶ Can the performance of the products, especially A and D, be improved?
▶ Why are the safety scores of B and A so low?
▶ Why is packaging so uniformly poor?
▶ Can the design of B and C be improved?
▶ What are the immediate steps that might be taken to improve the benefits provided to customers?
▶ Taking into account the ranking of the individual products or services (that is, their total benefit scores), is the correct allocation of energy and resources being made to each? Might their relative importance be reappraised?

Such questions asked of any company can only lead to a search for improvement. This will be just as true for our products or services as it was in the illustration given here. Moreover, since all such improvements are based on providing greater customer benefits, they hold every prospect of bringing about important changes. This process can be repeated for other market segments of our business.

The product/service life-cycle

The idea of benefit analysis that we have just explored is a very important one. It does have one drawback, however. It is like a 'snapshot' of the company's products or services at a given moment, and cannot portray what is happening over a period of time. Historians of technology have observed that all technical functions grow exponentially until they come up against some natural limiting factor, which causes them to slow down and eventually to decline as one technology is replaced by another. The same phenomenon applies to products, and is embodied in the product life-cycle (PLC).

The PLC is a conceptual tool that provides a means of describing the sales patterns of products, be they goods or services, over their time in the market. If absolute sales of a product within a market or segment are plotted on a period-by-period basis (usually annually),

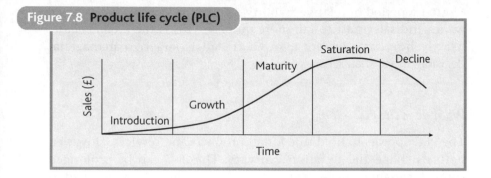

Figure 7.8 Product life cycle (PLC)

the 'standard' life-cycle approximates to an S-curve, as shown in Figure 7.8. In reality, product life-cycles adopt a number of different shapes and are never smooth, deviations from this norm being caused by the nature of the product and its patterns of consumption.

From a management perspective, the PLC concept is helpful in that it focuses attention on the likely future sales pattern if no corrective action is taken. Understanding the concept and the determinants of its shape can thus be a powerful aid to the development of marketing strategies. It is important to note that an organization is only concerned with the life-cycle trend of a total market or segment, and with the sales of its product within it.

Product life-cycles usually experience a number of successive stages. As depicted in Figure 7.8, the early part of the sales curve denotes a struggle to get the product or service known; sales are hard to come by and a lot of time and energy goes into developing contacts in order to create awareness and acceptance of it. It is aptly called the *introduction phase*.

Assuming that the product or service is acceptable to its target market, there then comes a time when it 'takes off'; everybody seems to want to buy it. This is the *growth phase*. But no market is infinitely expandable, and eventually the rate of growth slows as the product or service moves into the *maturity stage*.

Eventually a point is reached where there are too many firms in the market; price wars break out and some firms drop out of the market. Sales level off or decline gradually as demand has largely been satisfied, if not by our company, then by the many competitors who have been equally attracted by the growth potential of the market for this product/service. This is the *saturation phase*.

After a period of relative stability, interest in our product/service wanes and sales start to fall more quickly. This is the *decline phase*. Exactly how far sales are allowed to fall is largely a managerial decision, as we shall see.

What does the PLC tell us?

The PLC appears to hold true for all products and services. However, both its shape and duration can vary. The PLC can be prolonged through careful management and investment, or indeed hastened to an early demise by poor management at a cost of wasted of resources. For example, the life-cycle for fashion items and fad products can be steep, but short-lived, whereas the life-cycle of aircraft can run to many years, displaying a consistent sales pattern. There is a recognized propensity for life-cycles to become shorter as the rate of technological innovation increases and customers' expectations heighten. The mechanical typewriter, for example, may have enjoyed a life-cycle of decades while its latter-day equivalent, the word-processing program may have a life cycle measured in years.

The level of sales plotted on the vertical axis is usually given in unit or revenue terms. For marketing purposes, it is often of more value to measure sales against the growth in the market as this gives a better indication of the product's competitive ability and attractiveness to the customer. Of course, absolute sales volumes are also important as they determine revenue and current profitability.

The PLC can be used in a number of ways:

1 As a *predictive* device, forecasting how products may behave in the future and allowing corrective action to be taken. It can help us to understand how products relate to markets, and to appreciate where certain elements of the marketing mix may be more appropriate to particular PLC stages.
2 As a *comparative* device, warning of any significant deviations from the total market experience (see Figures 7.9 and 7.10), or enabling a strategic balance to be achieved among products within the same range.
3 As a *formative* device, assisting the design of future product/market strategies based on sales performance in combination with experience and additional analysis. It can provide clues about what are the most appropriate strategies to use at different stages of the life-cycle to best support and invest in our product or service.

Figure 7.9 Product/market strategy and the product life cycle (1)

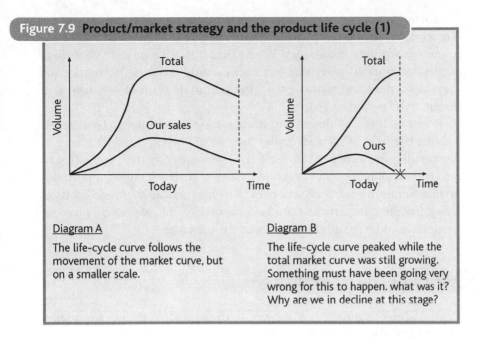

Diagram A

The life-cycle curve follows the movement of the market curve, but on a smaller scale.

Diagram B

The life-cycle curve peaked while the total market curve was still growing. Something must have been going very wrong for this to happen. what was it? Why are we in decline at this stage?

4 As a *manipulative* device, indicating when short-term strategies might be used to 'distort' the life-cycle to our advantage. For example, suppose this curve represented one of our products or services, as in Figure 7.9.

Figure 7.10 tells us that we have just passed through the growth phase and appear to be entering the maturity phase. If we take no action, we could expect the sales curve to level out and eventually decline.

Figure 7.10 Product/market strategy and the product life cycle (2)

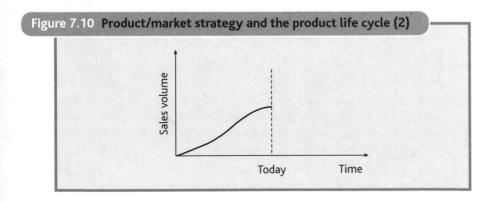

However, we could take steps to delay this process. We could, as Figure 7.11 shows, improve the product or extend the range and thereby stimulate more sales. When that initiative has run its course and sales start to level out again, we could extend the market or develop a new segment. Again, this stimulates the sales curve and extends the period of growth.

However, these actions all cost money and so they have to be weighed against the level of increased sales they would be expected to generate. Eventually, there comes a time when it becomes counter-productive to prop up an ailing product or service in this way. The section on portfolio management in Chapter 8 will help us in making the go/no-go decision about investing in particular products or services. But, for now, let us concentrate on understanding more about the life-cycle.

Life-cycle – costs and strategies

As the above example has shown, with respect to product management a company must be prepared to vary its strategies as the product or service moves through its life-cycle. But it is not only with respect to product management that alternative strategies should be considered. Pricing, distribution and promotional efforts also need to be

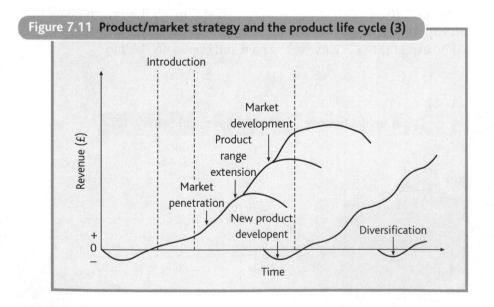

Figure 7.11 Product/market strategy and the product life cycle (3)

reviewed regularly. For example, early promotional efforts will almost certainly have to concentrate on creating awareness of the product, especially if it is a completely new product or service concept. Later in the life of the product, when awareness levels are high, it is likely that a company will need to spend more effort on positioning and imagery in what often turn out to be crowded markets during the growth phase. Similarly, distribution channels are likely to change, as is pricing. Clearly, it may prove fatal to refuse to bow to price pressures as the market reaches maturity, because if hard-won market share is lost at this crucial stage it could well affect profits adversely.

So, market circumstances change over the life of a product or service, and a company's policies should also change accordingly. Table 7.1 illustrates a set of guidelines used by one company in the electrical components market to help it determine appropriate marketing strategies at different stages of the life-cycle. In this case, the company combined the two stages of maturity and saturation.

Drawing a product life-cycle can be extremely difficult, even given the availability of some form of time-series analysis. This is connected with the complex question of market share measurement.

As was discussed briefly in Chapter 5, the firm needs to be concerned with its share (its proportion of volume or value) of an *actual* market. However, in order to measure an actual market, great care must be taken to ensure that a company is measuring the right things. Take the example of the company measuring the institutional markets for nylon carpet. It is clearly nonsense to include concrete in their measurement of the floor-covering market because concrete, although a floor covering, does not satisfy the needs that customers have for warmth and colour, and is therefore not part of their market. Neither, probably, should wool carpets or linoleum be included. To help with this, let us remind ourselves of the definitions given in Chapter 3:

▶ Product *class*; for example, carpets;
▶ Product *form*; for example, nylon rolls; and
▶ Product *brand*; for example, 'X'.

'X' as a brand, for the purpose of measuring market share, *is concerned only with the aggregate of all other brands that satisfy the same group of customer wants*. Nevertheless, the manufacturer of 'X' also needs to be aware of the sales trends of other kinds of carpets and floor covering in the institutional market, as well as of carpet sales overall.

Let us now broaden the discussion to a consideration of managing a range of products or services and the ways in which they satisfy market

Table 7.1 Life-cycle stages – characteristics and responses

	Introduction	Growth	Maturity/saturation	Decline
Costs	Can be high, because of inexperience in supplying and the cost of promotion.	Increasing due to increased volume and fighting off competition. High growth requires funding.	Stabilizing/reducing as experience and reduced competition take effect.	Can be high if not managed because of diseconomies of scale; for example, only small runs.
Demand	Unpredictable. Forecasts can vary widely.	Upper limits might be forecast but volatile situation sensitive to prices and competition.	Fairly well defined	Known and limited.
Competition	Largely unknown.	Many new entrants jump on 'bandwagon'. Competition fierce.	Marginal competitors leave. Remainder tend to specialize in particular segments.	New entrants are unlikely. Competition declines.
Customer loyalty	Trial usage, new relationship, little loyalty.	Some loyalty, but to ensure supplies many customers might have more than one supplier.	Well-established buying patterns with high customer loyalty.	Extremely stable. Customers are not motivated to seek new suppliers.

Table 7.1 *continued*

Ease of entry	Relatively easy because market leaders have not yet emerged. Customers feeling their way.	More difficult as some suppliers begin to establish market share and benefit from economies of scale.	Difficult because of established buying patterns. New business has tobe won.	Little incentive to enter.
Price	Price to capitalize on newness (high) or to penetrate the market (low).	Price competitively.	Price defensively.	Price according to perceived product life; for example, high for milk.
Promotion	Active and aggressive.	Active and aggressive.	Selective and specialized.	Minimal, if at all.
Product/ service range	Limited and specialized to meet the needs of early customers.	Rapid expansion in order tc capitalize on new opportunities.	Range expansion slows down or ceases.	Range narrows as unproductive items are dropped.

needs. The art of successful product management must be based on a clear view of just *how* the present and future product range will continue to meet the twin goals of customer and corporate objectives.

As a first stage in successful product management it is important to think of the 'product' as a variable in the marketing mix, in the same way that we consider price or promotion as a variable. The extent of freedom to manoeuvre on the product variable will depend largely on the internal resources of the firm and where its strengths are in relation to the competition as identified by the SWOT analysis (see Chapter 6). Answering the following questions can help us establish the appropriateness of current product strategy and provide a firm basis for developing future product/market strategy.

▶ What benefits do customers seek from this type of product?
▶ Does our product provide these benefits in a greater proportion than competitors' products?
▶ What competitive product advantages are causing us to lose market share?
▶ Does our product range still provide 'value-in-use' to the customers in relation to its cost to them?
▶ Does each product in our range still meet the corporate objectives set for it?

Product/market strategy

What is product/market strategy? Very simply, it is the totality of the decisions taken within the organization concerning its target markets and the products it offers to those markets. Strategy implies a chosen route to a defined goal and an element of long-term planning. Thus the product/market strategy of the firm represents its commitment to a particular direction in the future.

The effective company is one that plans for growth, and in terms of its product/market strategy seeks to plan its *product portfolio* well in advance – in terms required or determined by product policy. The company must plan for growth, and both product policy and product/market strategy must be growth orientated; but clearly the growth must have a purposeful direction if future profits and cash flows are to be maximized. This direction is provided through appropriate growth policies, indicating the *vectors* (variable directions) along which the firm is intended to move.

The Ansoff matrix

While the PLC is an effective aid to understanding how products behave in markets, it is not without its drawbacks. The PLC model is not especially adept at examining a range or portfolio of products, as the life-cycle may vary from one product to another. Also, the life-cycle has little/limited value as a predictive tool. Once the product has run its course, the PLC does not enlighten strategy for new products in new markets: it is relevant only to existing products within existing markets.

One helpful device for considering the product/market strategy is the so-called 'Ansoff' matrix, named after its developer, I. Ansoff. The Ansoff matrix shown in Figure 7.12 is a useful planning aid as it describes the four possible combinations of products and markets, or the four categories of marketing objectives. Marketing objectives consider the two main dimensions of commercial growth: product development and market development:

1 selling existing products to existing markets/segments (market penetration);
2 extending existing products to new markets/segments (market extension);
3 developing new products for existing markets/segments (product development); and
4 developing new products for new markets/segments (diversification).

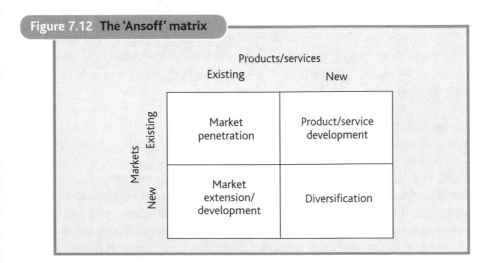

Figure 7.12 The 'Ansoff' matrix

Market penetration

This involves keeping existing customers and finding new ones in the same market, without changing the products/services offered. This implies that pricing and promotion will have to be very competitive, because other suppliers are not just going to sit back and let us take their business. However, there are fewer unknowns and therefore, in theory, fewer risks.

Market extension/development

This strategy involves finding new users in new markets for the existing product/service. It might mean going further afield geographically (or even exporting), opening up new market segments, or discovering new applications for the products/services. This strategy implies that the company has marketing strengths and the wherewithal to make inroads into new markets. Again, the element of dealing with the unknown makes this a slightly more risky strategy.

Product/service development

This strategy involves the modification of existing products/services to improve their quality, style or whatever characteristics are valued by customers. The ultimate goal would be to increase sales or profits, or even reduce costs, by taking advantage of new technology. This strategy implies that the company possesses the technical resources and skills to make it a viable proposition. Given the failure rate of new products/services and the element of the unknown associated with this strategy, it must be considered as slightly risky.

Diversification

This strategy involves developing new products/services for new markets/segments, and implies that new resources and skills will have to be developed. Since both products and markets will be new, it is a very high-risk strategy. Diversification is what has led many companies to become bankrupt, and why many of those that diversified through acquisition during periods of high economic growth have since divested themselves of businesses that were not basically compatible with their own distinctive competence.

There will different marketing responses to each permutation in the matrix, and the formulation of marketing objectives for each quadrant will be different for different companies. The term 'new products' infers a degree of technical innovation, and 'new markets' assumes an element of unfamiliarity in a market situation. The newness factor of the product/market combination corresponds to the level of risk that the company has to manage. Thus pursuing marketing objectives concerned with new products in new markets is the riskiest strategy of all because it takes the organization away from its known strengths and capabilities and further into the unknown.

The procedures described in Chapter 8 provide a means of determining the most appropriate product strategy to follow.

Gap analysis

As discussed in Chapter 6, corporate objectives lead to corporate strategies, which in turn suggest marketing objectives and strategies lower down the business hierarchy. Gap analysis is a technique used to explore the shortfall between the corporate objectives and what can be achieved by various strategies. As described in Figure 7.13, what it says is that if the corporate sales and financial objectives are greater than the current long-range trends and forecasts, then there is a gap to be filled. The operations gap can be filled by reducing costs, improving the sales mix and/or increasing market share. The strategy gap can be filled by finding new user groups, entering new segments, geographical expansion, new product development, and/or diversification. The marketing audit (see Chapter 19) should ensure that the method chosen to fill the gap is consistent with the company's capabilities and builds on its strengths.

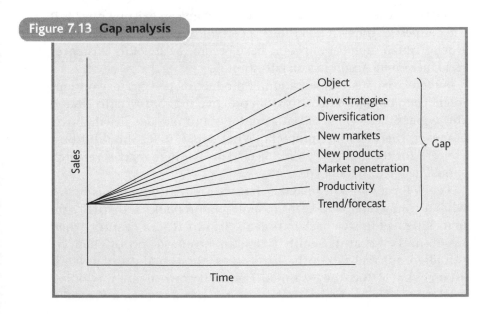

Figure 7.13 Gap analysis

Product revitalization versus new product development

The Ansoff matrix, referred to earlier in this chapter, has a useful simplicity because it strips marketing down to basics. It does none the less tend to over-simplify the issues surrounding product/ market strategy. The reason is that there are different kinds of new products and new markets. It is important that we are clear what these are.

There can be degrees of newness of the product:

▶ it can stay the same;
▶ it can be extended in some way – for example, new colours or sizes;
▶ it can be adapted (to address needs in other markets/segments), modified (to replace current models), or improved (to enhance performance or perceived value; the 'next generation'); or
▶ it can be a new product or concept entirely (revolutionary).

A similar analysis can be provided for markets:

▶ they can be the same;
▶ they can be broader in terms of how they are defined;
▶ they can include new coverage, but on related areas; or
▶ they can be totally new (unprecedented).

So, when exactly does a new product become an existing one? Is it after a specific time? When it is at a certain stage of its life-cycle? Or when a certain number of people have become aware of its existence? Here the simple Ansoff matrix falls short.

A more accurate representation of product/market strategy options might be to produce a matrix with more than four boxes, built around the degrees of newness of both products and markets listed above. However, there is still a problem. What comes first? Should it be a concern for technology? Or markets? This is where market research should help us … but does it?

Let us for a moment imagine that we are that ubiquitous buggy whip manufacturer who keeps cropping up in books and articles on marketing. Let us step back in time to the nineteenth century, when his business was at its zenith. Being an advanced sort of chap, he would go out and talk to his customers, the cab and cart drivers, asking what it was they wanted. Had he known it, he was doing market research, but at that time, of course, it hadn't been invented!

A few he talked to wanted better whips, but most of them were really fed up with horses. What with the price of hay and the smelly and unreliable nature of their charges, what they really wanted was to drive a car. Not any old car, but one with independent suspension and air conditioning. The problem was, like market research, the internal combustion engine had not yet been invented! This, of course, is a silly story, but it is not without value. First, it explodes the myth that marketing is all about asking people what they really want and then making it. Taking an extreme stance such as this is shown to be intellectually puerile. Second, it throws the nature of technological development into stark relief.

When it comes, technological development provides a quantum leap forward. Just think about the electronics industry. It really all stared with the invention of the thermionic valve. This gave way to the transistor, which was superseded by the miniaturized circuit, and most recently by the microchip. Each of these technological break-throughs spawned in their wake a multitude of technology-driven products that hitherto had been the stuff of science fiction stories.

Clearly, then, there are some markets that have a propensity to be supply-side driven. After the initial breaking of the innovative dam, which owes much to the 'R' of R&D, the new product eventually becomes modified and adapted. In other words, the 'D' of R&D becomes more important. It is in these kinds of businesses where there must be strong links between marketing and R&D.

There are, however, other markets that are fundamentally more stable and customer-driven. Here, marketers can keep their finger on the customer's pulse and respond to changing needs. Even then, it will be important to monitor the product in terms of its position in its life-cycle. Sooner or later, demand will become mature and the market will develop into a replacement market. Just look at what is happening to some of our famous companies at the time of writing. When it gets to this stage, there are really only three options open to the marketer:

▶ go for new technology and in effect shift the goal posts;
▶ do what marketers have always done – segment customers in a more creative way; or
▶ pray that you have the lowest costs in your field, otherwise you will not survive.

The question of how to manage the new product development process is dealt with in Chapter 8.

Summary

Ideally, the value proposition should be such that investment and benefit are 'mutual'. Marketing objectives and strategies form the keystone of the value proposition.

Marketing objectives are concerned solely with products and markets. Marketing strategies enable operating decisions to bring the supplying organization into the right relationship with the emerging pattern of market opportunities which previous analysis has shown to offer the highest prospect of success.

In managing products or services, the marketer must pay due regard to the benefits that customers seek as well as to the position in the product life-cycle. The appropriate marketing mix at the point of introduction will not be effective at the maturity stage, for example. The Ansoff matrix provides a useful framework for identifying the strategy options available to the organization as it seeks to develop its product/market base.

Further reading

Buzzell, R. and Gale, B. (1987) *The PIMS Principles: Linking Strategy to Performance*, Free Press, New York.

McDonald, M. (2002) *Marketing Plans: How to Prepare Them – How to Use Them*, 5th edn, Butterworth-Heinemann, Oxford.

References

Ansoff, I. (1965) *Corporate Strategy*, McGraw-Hill, Maidenhead.

Levitt, T. (1965) Exploit the product life cycle. *Harvard Business Review*, (November) pp. 81–94.

8   Product strategy

In this chapter we study the:

- ▶ successful product portfolio balances new and established products
- ▶ 'diffusion of innovation' curve
- ▶ Boston matrix and the directional policy matrix
- ▶ criteria that define market attractiveness
- ▶ risk/reward continuum
- ▶ methods for screening and testing products pre-launch
- ▶ difficulty of forecasting future sales

Portfolio management

The key to successful product strategy is a balanced portfolio of products that includes both established and new products. New products may result from pressures to customize, or from advancements in technological expertise. While technology-orientated companies may be especially prone to taking their eye off the customer ball, every organization should take care to maintain a market, rather than a product focus. It is important to remember that successful products are those that customers want to buy rather than those that companies want to sell.

The creation of sustainable customer value (achieving a mutually acceptable level of customer and shareholder/stakeholder satisfaction for a mutually acceptable level of customer and shareholder/stakeholder investment) requires a market-driven approach with a commercially-driven acumen. This means that we must not only recognize the behaviour of products, but also the behaviour of customers.

Diffusion of innovation

A useful extension of the PLC is what is termed 'diffusion of innovation'. Diffusion is the adoption of new products or services over time by consumers within social systems, as encouraged by marketing. It thus refers to the cumulative percentage of potential adopters of a new product or service over time. The 'diffusion of innovation' curve is shown in Figure 8.1.

The actual rate of diffusion has been found to be a function of a product's:

▶ Relative advantage (over existing products).
▶ Compatibility (with lifestyles, values and so on).
▶ Communicability (is it easy to communicate?).
▶ Complexity (is it complicated?).
▶ Divisibility (can it be tried out on a small scale before commitment?).

Diffusion is also a function of the newness of the product itself, which can be classified broadly under three headings:

▶ Continuous innovation (for example, the new miracle ingredient).
▶ Dynamically continuous innovation (for example, disposable lighter).
▶ Discontinuous (for example, microwave oven).

Figure 8.1 'Diffusion of innovation' curve

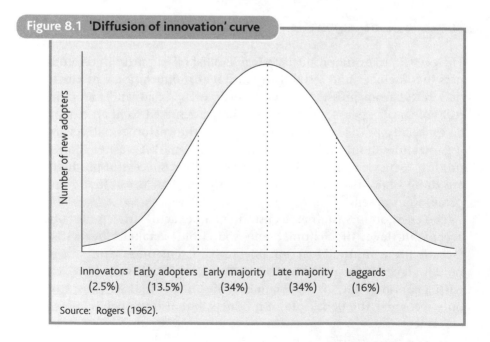

Source: Rogers (1962).

Discovering a typology for those who are prepared to buy and try new products ('innovators' and 'early adopters') can help considerably in the promotion of new products. If we can target early advertising and sales effort at winning over the trendsetters and opinion leaders in the market, then we can proactively increase our chances of also convincing the more conservative and sceptical customers to adopt our product.

At any point in time, a review of an organization's different products would reveal different stages of growth, maturity and decline. If the objective is to grow in profitability over an extended period, then the product portfolio should reveal a situation in which new product introductions are timed to ensure continuous sales growth. The idea of a product portfolio is for an organization to meet its objectives by balancing sales growth, cash flow and risk. Ideally, a company should have a portfolio of products whose life-cycles overlap, as Figure 8.2 demonstrates. This guarantees continuity of income and growth potential. It is therefore essential that the whole portfolio is reviewed regularly, and that an active policy towards new product development and divestment of old products is pursued.

A successful business would develop a portfolio more like that in Figure 8.2(b). In fact, over the years its growth could be attributed to a number of well-timed and profitable product/service launches like those shown in Figure 8.3. Therefore, in order to achieve a successful

Figure 8.2 A portfolio of several product life-cycles

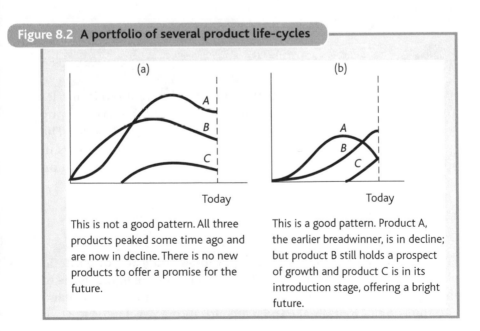

(a)

This is not a good pattern. All three products peaked some time ago and are now in decline. There is no new products to offer a promise for the future.

(b)

This is a good pattern. Product A, the earlier breadwinner, is in decline; but product B still holds a prospect of growth and product C is in its introduction stage, offering a bright future.

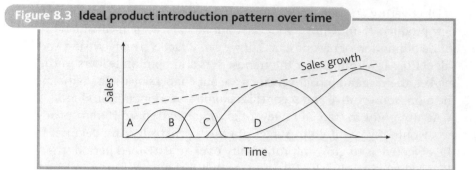

Figure 8.3 Ideal product introduction pattern over time

product/service portfolio, it will be necessary to manage our existing output and bring it into line with our longer-term objectives. At the same time, we shall have to be capable of generating not only profits but also sufficient funds to invest in new products and services.

In many respects, the idea of the product portfolio is similar to the investor's portfolio of stocks and shares. The investor, for example, may wish to achieve a balance between yield or income and capital growth; some shares might produce more of the latter and less of the former, and vice versa. Again, the investor might attempt to achieve a balance in terms of risk – some shares having a higher risk of capital loss attached, against which must be balanced the prospect of higher returns.

Cash management

All organizations have products that produce different levels of sales and profit margins. Profit occurs from the mix of products, ranging from low margin/high turnover to high margin/high turnover. The purpose of the marketing plan is to spell out at least three years in advance what the desired product combination is. RONA (return on net assets) can be portrayed as the business ratio:

$$\frac{\text{Net profit}}{\text{Net assets}} = \text{RONA}$$

Profits, however, are not always an appropriate indicator of portfolio performance, as they will often reflect changes in the liquid assets of the company, such as inventories, capital equipment, or receivables, and thus do not indicate the true scope for future development. Cash flow, on the other hand, is a key determinant of a company's ability to develop its product portfolio.

The Boston matrix

The Boston Consulting Group's simple matrix, given in Figure 8.4, is useful in product portfolio planning as it classifies a firm's products according to their cash usage and their cash generation along the two dimensions, relative market growth rate and market share. It shows graphically the positions of products in terms of their cash usage and cash generation, making it easier to see the relationship between multiple products. The Boston matrix is based on the principle that cash – not profits – drives a product from one quadrant to another. It is a valuable planning tool for considering the implications of different product/market strategies, and for formulating policies towards new product development, providing great care is taken over the 'market share' axis. The relationship of market share to cash generation is the higher the market share, the higher the output, and the lower the unit costs through economies of scale and the learning curve – thus a company can command higher margins and generate more revenue.

The measure of market share used is the product's share relative to the largest competitor. This is important because it reflects the degree of

Figure 8.4 The Boston matrix – cash-flow implications

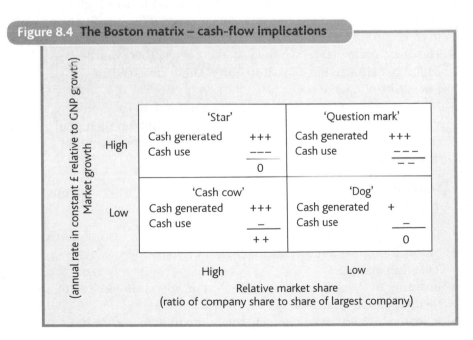

dominance enjoyed by the product in the market. For example, if Company A has 20 per cent market share, and its biggest competitor has 20 per cent market share also, this position is usually less favourable than if Company A had 20 per cent market share and its biggest competitor had only 10 per cent market share. The relative ratios would be 1:1 compared with 2:1. It is this ratio, or measure of market dominance, that the horizontal axis measures. The definition of high relative market share is generally taken to be a ratio of 1.5 or more.

The cut-off point for high as opposed to low market growth should be defined according to the prevailing circumstances in the industry, but this is often taken as 10 per cent. The somewhat picturesque labels attached to each of the four categories or products give some indication of the prospects for products in each quadrant.

The four quadrants, or categories of products, in the Boston matrix are sometimes labelled 'Star', 'Cash cow', 'Question mark' and 'Dog', to indicate their respective prospects:

▶ The *question mark* is a product that has not achieved a dominant market position and thus has a high cash flow; or perhaps it once had such a position and has slipped back. It will be a high user of cash because it is in a growth market. This is also sometimes referred to as a *wildcat*, or *problem child*.
▶ The *star* is probably a newish product that has achieved a high market share and is probably, on balance, more or less self-financing in cash terms.
▶ The *cash cows* are leaders in their markets where there is little additional growth, but a lot of stability. These are excellent generators of cash.
▶ *Dogs* have little future and are often a cash drain on the company. They are probably candidates for divestment, although such products often fall into a category aptly described by Peter Drucker as 'investments in managerial ego'.

Since the 'Cash cow' is the only quadrant that actually generates cash, some very clear messages come from the Boston matrix:

▶ To manage the product/service portfolio effectively the cash generated by the 'Cash cows' must be used to invest in 'Stars' and selected 'Question marks'.
▶ Investing in 'Question marks' with good prospects should lead to them developing into stars.
▶ Investing in 'Stars' should develop them into tomorrow's 'Cash cows'.

► The higher the relative market share of a 'Star', the better are its prospects as a 'Cash cow'.
► High investment in a 'Cash cow' should never be necessary.
► Investment in 'Dogs' is generally money wasted.

The Boston matrix can be used to forecast the market position of our products, say, five years from now if we continue to pursue our current policies. Figure 8.5 illustrates this process for a manufacturer of plastic valves. The area of each circle is proportional to each product's contribution to total company sales volume.

The directional policy matrix

There are, however, factors other than market growth and market share that determine profitability, so many companies use an expanded version of the Boston matrix known as the directional policy matrix (DPM). The DPM was developed by Shell, General Electric, McKinsey and others as a multi-factor approach to portfolio management. As shown in Figure 8.6, the axes become relative business strengths and market attractiveness, indicating the relative importance of each market to the business. So the same purpose is served as in the Boston matrix; that is, comparing investment opportunities among products or businesses. The difference is that multiple criteria are used. Although

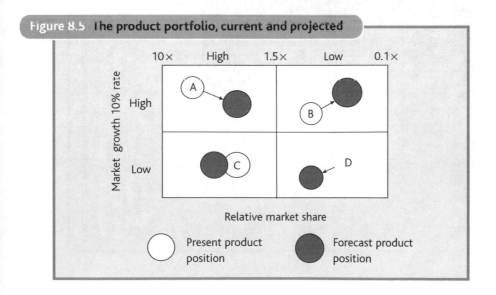

Figure 8.5 The product portfolio, current and projected

Figure 8.6 The directional policy matrix (DPM)

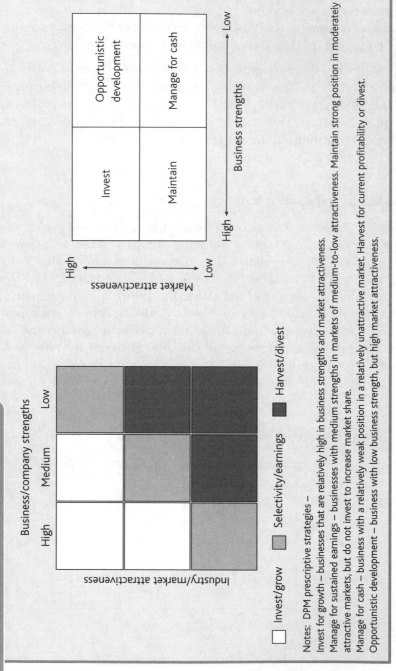

Notes: DPM prescriptive strategies –
Invest for growth – businesses that are relatively high in business strengths and market attractiveness.
Manage for sustained earnings – businesses with medium strengths in markets of medium-to-low attractiveness. Maintain strong position in moderately attractive markets, but do not invest to increase market share.
Manage for cash – business with a relatively weak position in a relatively unattractive market. Harvest for current profitability or divest.
Opportunistic development – business with low business strength, but high market attractiveness.

originally introduced as a 3 × 3 matrix rather than the conventional 2 × 2 matrix, the DPM is today used in either format. It is extremely important when using the DPM to define your markets clearly.

The vertical axis of a DPM represents the degree to which a market is attractive to an organization. The key determinant of market attractiveness is its potential to yield growth in sales and profits. Examples of market attractiveness criteria are given in Table 8.1. The most important are usually the first four.

The horizontal axis of the DPM is a measure of an organization's strengths, or potential strengths, in the market place. Ideally, judgements about business strength or position should be validated by independent research, and certainly, product proficiencies should be based on known customer requirements. Factors which might be considered when assessing business strengths are listed in Table 8.2.

Table 8.1 Criteria which might make a market attractive

Growth rate

Accessible market size

Competitive intensity

Profit margins

Differences between competitive offerings

Existence of technical standards

Compatible infrastructure

Ease of obtaining payment

Sensitivity to interest rates

General volatility

Degree of regulation

Barrier to entry

Rate of technological change

Likelihood of political stability

Potential for 'supply' partnerships

Availability of market intelligence

Note: This list is non-exclusive.

Table 8.2 Factors which might be considered, or which might yield, business strengths

Production capacity

Production flexibility

Product adaptability

Unit cost of production

Price position

R&D capabilities

Brands owned

Company image

Market share

Range of commercial contacts

Influence on regulatory bodies

Delivery performance

Service facilities

Channel access or distribution network

Size/quality of sales force

Note: This list is non-exclusive.

Case study 8.1 describes the use of the portfolio matrix.

Case study 8.1 Sealitt Ltd's portfolio matrix

Sealitt Ltd is a small company that makes various types of seals and gaskets. It's original product was the rubber used for fitting motor vehicle windows. These are supplied to motor factories, replacement window screen specialists and van/caravan converters.

The company then developed door trim rubber strips for draught and weather sealing, essentially for motor factories. This venture led to producing draught-excluder strips for DIY outlets. Its latest innovations are seals for double-glazing units and gaskets of all shapes, sizes and applications, mainly for engineering companies.

The company buys in most of its materials. Its strengths are the expertise it has developed for buying judiciously, and the ability to cut and shape materials economically while maintaining high standards. Its portfolio matrix looks like that shown in Figure 8.7.

Figure 8.7 **Portfolio matrix for Sealitt Ltd**

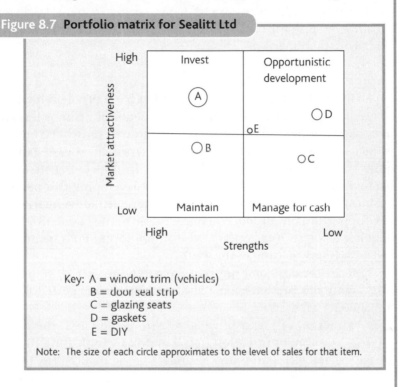

Key: A = window trim (vehicles)
B = door seal strip
C = glazing seats
D = gaskets
E = DIY

Note: The size of each circle approximates to the level of sales for that item.

The company's strengths are geared up to supply the 'motor trade'; and the demand for window trim makes it an attractive market. Similar strengths apply to door seals, but the market is less attractive since there is a smaller demand for replacements. (It would not have the capacity to supply the OEM – original equipment manufacturer – market, for example, Ford, Rover.)

Double-glazing seals looked on the surface a good proposition for Sealitt Ltd, but it was found that there was some new expertise to acquire; also, several customers went out of business without paying. The well-established double-glazing companies either produced their own seals or had approved suppliers. Thus, this item, which started as an 'opportunistic development', went almost immediately into the bottom right-hand quadrant.

Gaskets use the least of the company's business strengths but seem to be an attractive market. Sales are quite sizeable. DIY insulation is a small business and never seems to have taken off, mainly because the company has little experience in dealing with that particular market.

On analysis, it would seem that Sealitt Ltd has a problem looming in terms of future business prospects. At present door trim is less attractive than window trim, which has good growth prospects, but where is the next 'invest' product coming from? Since the sales of gaskets are quite good, should the company invest in improving its business strengths in this area and concentrate on developing this part of the business? Can the DIY insulation find more attractive markets? Is a new opportunistic product required with better 'credentials'? The double glazing sealing appears to be a flop, so should it be discontinued, as it is only getting in the way?

These are serious questions that have to be answered. To help with this, Figure 8.8 presents some strategy options suggested by directional policy analysis.

To extract more prescriptive advice from the DPM, the manager then added more information to the matrix by indicating the trends he expects for each part of the business (see Figure 8.9). His two-year-old forward projections are shown as dotted lines, and again the circles represent sales levels. We can see that overall the sales from the invest box are going to increase, but that the market growth will slow down slightly.

The 'maintain' product is planned to keep the same level of sales, but the market is certainly becoming less attractive and matches with fewer of the company's strengths.

Product C, the double-glazing seal, will be scrapped. The DIY insulation product E is seen to be fading away and is likely to be withdrawn. Gaskets (D) are planned to generate more sales, but the product is still short of being an invest product.

A new product, F, is scheduled to provide the lost revenue from C and E. This product, with the right investment, has the possibility of becoming a future opportunistic product. It certainly plays to more

Figure 8.8 Directional policy analysis for Sealitt Ltd

INVEST	OPPORTUNISTIC DEVELOPMENT	
Invest for growth: • penetrate market • accept moderate short-term profits • sell and promote aggressively • expand: geographically product line • differentiate product/service	Opportunistic development: • be critical of prospects • invest heavily in selective products/services	
MAINTAIN	SELECTIVE	MANAGE FOR CASH
Maintain market position and manage for earnings: • maintain market position with successful products/services • differentiate products/services to keep share of key segments • prune less successful products or services • stablize prices, except where temporary aggressive stance is required to deter competitors	• live with low growth • improve productivity • reduce costs • look for 'easy' growth segments	• prune aggressively • maximize cash flow • raise prices at expense of volume • minimize expenditure

of the company's strengths than the gaskets business. It is essential for the company to develop a new opportunistic product as the window trim sinks into the 'maintain' quadrant.

Figure 8.9 Portfolio matrix showing current and forecast positions

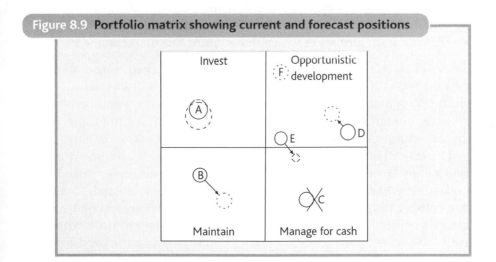

Programme guidelines suggested for different positioning on the DPM are provided in Figure 8.10.

Developing new products and services

Experience tells us that a significant proportion of most organization's revenue comes from products that have been introduced in the recent past. In practice, most new products and services emerge gradually from modifications of existing ideas and technology – from putting together familiar things in a slightly different way. It is this interplay between existing products or services and the search for improvement and innovation that provides the dynamism for the growth-orientated company.

However, the search for growth, prosperity and market opportunity is not without risk. New products are costly to develop or acquire, and are in grave danger of failure. As mentioned in Chapter 7, this danger is most poignant when new products are introduced into new markets. However, the chances of product failure can be reduced if marketing principles and personnel can be involved at every stage leading up to and including product launch.

It has been estimated that for every successful new product, between fifty and seventy new ideas have to be considered and that only one in four products that are test-marketed prove successful once launched nationally. Products that are successful tend to:

▶ deliver a significant differentiated benefit;
▶ possess a good technological fit with the supplying organization; or
▶ originate from businesses which 'have done their marketing well'.

These characteristics are more likely to be achieved where new product teams are created that comprise representatives from the organization's major management disciplines: operations, engineering, finance, human resources, and marketing. Good marketing input is crucial; without it, new products become a game of Russian roulette.

The essentiality of marketing knowledge in the development of new products and services stems from the fact that customer value is created when an organization's offer is 'faster, better, cheaper' than the competition. Achieving these superior qualities means getting closer to customers. The organization must understand fully what turns customers 'on' or 'off', and most importantly, must heed this insight in daily practice. We are all familiar with the increasingly

Figure 8.10 Programme guidelines suggested for different positioning on the DPM

Main thrust	Invest for growth	Manage for sustained earnings	Manage for cash	Opportunistic development
Market share	Maintain or increase dominance	Maintain or slightly milk for earnings	Forgo share for profit	Invest selectively in share
Products	Differentiation – line expansion	Prune less successful Differentiate for key segments	Prune aggressively	Differentiation – line expansion
Price	Lead – aggressive pricing for share	Stabilize prices / raise	Raise	Aggressive – price for share
Promotion	Aggressive Marketing	Limit	Minimize	Aggressive Marketing
Distribution	Broaden distribution	Hold wide distribution pattern	Gradually withdraw distribution	Limited coverage
Cost control	Tight control – go for scale economies	Emphasize cost-reduction, viz. variable costs	Reduce aggressively both fixed and variable	Tight – but not at expense of entrepreneurship
Production	Expand, invest (organic acquisition, joint venture)	Maximize capacity and utilization	Free up capacity	Invest
R&D	Expand – invest	Focus on specific projects	None	Invest
Personnel	Upgrade management in key functional areas	Maintain, reward efficiency, tighten organization	Cut back organization	Invest
Investment	Fund growth	Limit fixed investment	Minimize and divest opportunistically	Fund growth
Working capital	Reduce in process – extend credit	Tighten credit – reduce accounts receivable Increase inventory turn	Reduce aggressively	Invest

sophisticated customization programmes of companies intent on boosting our 'wallet share' and their profit share through targeted communications, and aggressive cross-selling and up-selling techniques. But how many companies know (demonstrably) where to draw the line between helping customers and harassing them?

The point is that sustainable growth is more about generating new solutions that offer value to customers, than about introducing new products and services to the market place. In other words, it is the response to changes in the business environment, and not change itself, that renders competitive advantage. The art of providing customers with solutions as well as products consistently and coherently in terms of organizational dynamics is considered in Chapters 21 and 22.

Strategy of minimal risk

The least risky way of dealing with the development of new products and services is not to innovate but to copy others. By taking this stance, the company avoids all the costs associated with developing new ideas and creating markets for them. Instead, it takes the ideas and modifies them according to its capacity. It then 'surfs' the wave in the market place created by the innovator.

The key to success with this strategy is *timing*. To get into the market too early, before the new idea becomes accepted, can put a company in the position of a trailblazer with all the attendant costs. But if a company arrives too late, the market for the idea may have been monopolized by others. Nevertheless, it does seem that a risk/reward 'rule' appears to operate along a continuum, as in Figure 8.11.

Although this may seem a little prescriptive, such a 'rule' is endorsed by proverbs and sayings such as: 'Luck favours the brave' and 'Who dares wins'. It will therefore be useful to look at other options towards the right-hand end of the risk/reward line.

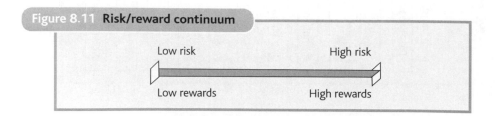

Figure 8.11 Risk/reward continuum

Low risk   High risk

Low rewards   High rewards

Creative ideas

The potential sources of new ideas for products and services are virtu-ally boundless. They can range from the sudden insight, the 'eureka' kind of invention, through to some very analytical techniques.

Here are just some sources of ideas for new products or services. There is no significance in the order in which they are placed:

▶ Brainstorming – a technique that involves a group of people 'free thinking' about the new uses to which a product or service can be put. The key to brainstorming is that *all* ideas are listed and judgement about their feasibility is suspended. Only when a large number of ideas has been generated are they considered in terms of feasibility.
▶ Talking and listening to customers or intermediaries.
▶ Monitoring technological developments.
▶ Monitoring new legislation (for example, that which has impact on safety, the environment or crime reduction). These can be potent sources for new products or services.
▶ Running an ideas scheme among staff.
▶ Attribute listing – this involves listing the attributes of a product or service and then modifying them in the search for an improved version.
▶ Carrying our market-gap analysis.
▶ Keeping in touch with what competitors are doing.
▶ Setting up a 'think tank' with staff and/or appropriate outsiders.
▶ Analysing past sales figures for significant trends.
▶ Making forced relationships – new ideas are listed and then worked at in pairs. Sometimes interesting products or services can emerge from this process. For example, separate gramophone, turntable, tape deck, amplifier and tuner were put together as a 'music centre'. More recently, a TV and video recorder have been integrated into a single unit.
▶ Conducting specific market research.
▶ Monitoring customer queries or complaints.
▶ Lateral thinking – looking at familiar ideas and turning them back to front. For example, a small company made glass-fibre boats but needed to diversify. It could have looked at other types of craft, but it decided that if its expertise was in making structures to 'keep water out' then it also had the expertise to 'keep water in'. By developing this line of thinking the company expanded into making storage tanks and reservoirs, essentially using its existing technology.

▶ Applying new ideas stemming from the availability or application of new materials. For example, new plastics materials are being developed that can make them ideal substitutes for more expensive metal products.

▶ Applying new ideas stemming from the availability or application of new technologies. For example, wireless application protocol (WAP) provides a platform 'gateway' for connecting mobile devices to the Internet, thus creating new services founded on wireless access to Internet-based content.

Irrespective of *how* we generate new ideas for products or services, there seem to be three universal 'laws' of which we should be aware:

▶ Successful innovators have a much better understanding of user-needs than their less successful contemporaries.

▶ The odds against a new product or service being successful are very high, in the order of 30 to 1 against. Therefore, to have one good idea it is likely that we would need to have considered about thirty; in other words, the quality ideas come from quantity.

▶ The key sources of new product/service ideas are likely to be based on research and development, and market research. Attractive though they might seem, successful ideas generated by creative-thinking techniques have been fairly limited, because they are likely to be product- rather than market-focused.

Other considerations

Perhaps generating the new idea for a product or service is the most difficult part of the process of innovation, but there are clearly many other factors to take into account before we rush to the market place:

▶ Is there a need for the new product or service?
▶ What sort of demand will there be?
▶ Are the customers likely to be new or existing ones?
▶ Can I reach the new customers?
▶ Will the new product/service fit in with the existing range?
▶ Do we have the resources and expertise to provide the necessary service?
▶ What does the competition provide? How does it compare?
▶ What will be the costs of providing this new product/service?
▶ What will be the result if we don't provide it?

▶ Will it make money?
▶ Is it what we want to make, or like making?
▶ Is it consistent with the image of our company?
▶ What life could we expect from the new product/service?

A screening procedure for ideas for new products or services

All the considerations we have just raised make it essential that new ideas for products or services are screened rigorously to ensure they will be viable. The screening procedure should look something like that shown in Figure 8.12.

We have seen that new products are the lifeblood of a company in its attempt to survive in a dynamic and competitive marketing environment. The search for viable and profitable new products must be a continuing task of marketing management, but it is a task that is fraught with risk.

For the majority of companies, the introduction of a new product involves a great deal of investment, both in the development process and in the initial introductory stage when market acceptance has to be won if the product is to succeed. This investment can represent a considerable slice of a company's resources, not only financial but also physical and managerial, yet there can be no fail-safe guarantee that the investment will yield the sort of return that the company would consider acceptable. In some cases, a single new product failure could bring disaster to a company, especially if it had pinned all its hopes on the new product only to find that the outcome fell far short of expectations.

Consider the case some years ago of the Rolls-Royce RB211 engine. Here the company had committed major resources to an engine that, while technically unimpeachable, did not match the wants of a large enough section of the market to recoup the tremendous development costs. Hindsight would suggest that this was an unwise step to take. As it was, it almost led to the collapse of the company.

Another example occurred in the consumer goods market, when a major food manufacturer invested heavily in developing a new dessert. Careful testing indicated that the product would be acceptable to potential customers. However, when the company proceeded to launch the product it found that retailers were unwilling to stock it, because the type of packaging developed for the product led to problems of stacking.

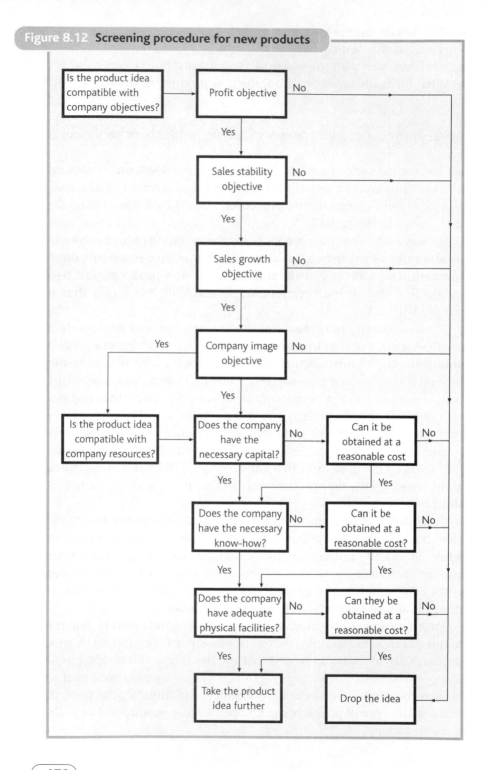

Figure 8.12 Screening procedure for new products

These examples can be matched with many others in the consumer, industrial and service markets. Research has indicated that, in some product areas, up to 80 per cent of all new products fail, in the sense that they do not meet marketing targets and are withdrawn soon after their introduction. Some product fields, such as grocery or cosmetics, are more prone to early failure than others, but, whatever the context, all the evidence seems to suggest a high rate of failure for new product introductions.

What, then, should marketing managers do to reduce the uncertainty that surrounds the new product launch? There are no crystal-ball revelations about prospects for success or failure in this area, but some procedures can be very helpful in quantifying the risks implicit in a new product launch. We shall now go on to explore some of these methods, but before we do so, we should first look more closely at some other factors involved in the new product-testing decision.

Testing procedures

Let us consider the means of testing available to a European manufacturer of sisal-based floor coverings who markets his products to the 'contract' market; that is, a market where an intermediary, often with an architect or a purchasing agent, buys the product for use in offices, hospitals and schools.

This is a fairly complex market where various types of floor coverings are available. It is a highly competitive market and, frequently, the floor covering is specified on the basis of some total, overall scheme for interior decoration.

On the advice of marketing consultants, this company was attempting to formalize its new product-testing procedures. Previously, they had tried to identify trends in styles and colours on the basis of past sales. There had always been an attempt to perform a 'break-even' analysis on the basis of projected costs and prices. Beyond this, new product testing was more a matter of technical assessment or product quality.

The consultants suggested a process of testing that involved several stages. (This process, which we shall examine in detail shortly, indicates activities that should take place, in one form or another, in all new product testing.) Each stage in the analysis provided the opportunity to pause and make one of three decisions: launch the product now; collect further information; or abandon the product now. The three decisions were given the shorthand of Go (launch the product),

Figure 8.13 Stages of new product development

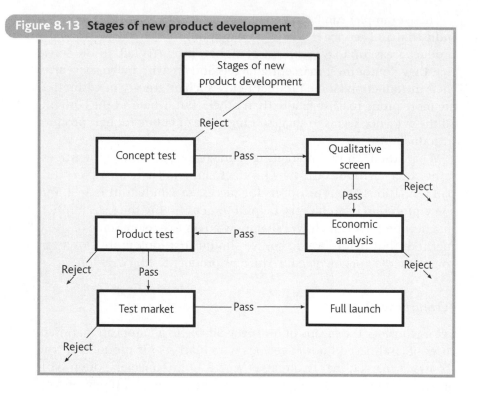

Go On (carry on testing), and No Go (reject) (see Figure 8.13). In the case of the floor-covering manufacturer, the sequence started with a test designed to give a broad picture of how acceptable the product concept was to its potential market. (This was accompanied by an initial appraisal of how the product might fit into the company's product portfolio.)

Concept test

This was administered by means of a dozen interviews conducted by trained interviewers, with architects and purchasing agents representative of the target market. The purpose of the test was to expose them to details of the technical specification, possible colour range and recommended uses of the product. Sometimes artists' impressions of designs and colours were shown. The results of this stage of the test sequence were entirely qualitative but they served to eliminate all those products that were complete non-starters. It was scarcely possible to make a decision to launch the product at this stage.

Qualitative screen

This was the next stage, and formed a screening process that posed two basic questions:

First, *is the product concept compatible with company objectives?* Issues involved were, for example:

▶ Does the concept complement our existing market offering?
▶ Is it compatible with the image that we seek and the segment of the market with which we identify?

Second, *is the product concept compatible with company resources?* Issues involved here were:

▶ Does the company have the capital to get this product to market and to develop an initial level of sales?
▶ Does the company have the necessary know-how and adequate physical facilities to handle the product successfully?

Economic analysis

If the product concept survived the screening process it was subjected to this next stage in the testing procedure. This analysis was designed to examine the economics of the project under differing assumptions of costs incurred and revenue achieved.

It was conducted at a fairly simple level as the company at that time had only a limited knowledge of how the market would react to products priced outside the narrow band with which the company was familiar. It was acknowledged that this stage of the testing sequence could be made considerably more sophisticated by applying methods of investment appraisal that were common in other companies.

Once this stage of the testing had been concluded successfully, the company might feel sufficiently confident of the viability of the concept to move ahead to a full-scale market launch. Such a decision would have to be based on some highly positive results from the initial stages of the test sequence, since the cost of setting up a promotional programme would be substantial. More often a decision would be taken to go on to the next, more expensive, stage of the analysis.

Product test

In this case, the product test was designed to gain impressions from a relatively large number of potential customers of how they would react to the physical product when it was compared with competing products. The expense of product testing lies in the fact that considerable quantities of the physical product must be provided. The aim of the test is to identify a representative sample of the target market and to interpret the reactions relative to the competing products. Aspects of the product tested at this stage would be physical characteristics, the range available, and the suggested usage, price and image connotations. This company recruited a panel of architects and purchasing agents who were invited to compare, according to a number of appropriate criteria, the proposed new products with selected competitive products. The analysis of these results enabled a picture to be built up of how the proposed new product compared with existing products in a number of key dimensions.

It was at this stage that the company normally made the final decision as to whether or not to launch the new product. Clearly there would still be some uncertainty about the new product's success, but the sequential testing had enabled this uncertainty to be reduced to an acceptable level. The company could have gone on, as many do, to the next test.

Test market

This, as the name implies, is an attempt to reproduce the conditions of a full-scale launch but on a much smaller scale. Often, a town or geographical area is chosen as representing the ultimate market; the product is launched in that town or area alone and its progress observed. As a test of this kind is very much an 'experiment', it is necessary to ensure that conditions within the test market would be such that they could be reproduced on a national scale. For example, no extra promotional effort should be expended other than an amount proportional to the total to be spent in the proposed full-scale launch.

It should be noted, however, that test markets can never be completely reliable indicators of ultimate market performance. Quite apart from the problems of 'grossing up' small-scale test-market results to provide a global picture, there is always the possibility of unusual competitive activities that distort the results.

Pilot projects

The use of pilot projects (small-scale versions of a larger undertaking taken in advance of a full-scale rollout) in testing products is becoming increasingly popular. Because such experiments are conducted in a real context, with every aspect of a true operation, they provide a realistic guide as to the potential outcome of a formal product launch. Valuable lessons can thus be learned at less cost, and with the opportunity for addressing inherent problems or revoking the product altogether, before the product is firmly introduced in the market place.

While we have portrayed these stages of testing as a sequence, it should be clear that some of the stages could be conducted concurrently, as with the qualitative screen and the economic analysis. Whatever the sequence, the purpose of new product testing remains the same: to reduce uncertainty surrounding the product to a level acceptable to the company while still enabling the launch to be made at the earliest possible time.

The methods of product testing might vary from marketing situation to marketing situation but, whether the product is a new airline service, a heavy-duty transformer or a vinyl wallpaper, the principles are universal and benefits considerable.

Forecasting future sales

The problem of estimating the level of future sales of any product, new or old, is ever-present and may be solved only imperfectly. Knowing in advance what levels of sales could be achieved, given a particular marketing mix and a particular marketing programme, would reduce considerably the complexity of the marketing decision. However, few people can claim the ability to predict the future accurately and in detail, and the marketing decision-maker has to fall back on other, less precise methods.

Even some of the most carefully prepared forecasts of future sales can be disproved by events. The wider environment in which the forecast is set changes in ways that are not always foreseen, and thus are not incorporated into the forecast. Energy crises, crop failures, droughts, revolutions – these are just a few of the major events that can upset the sales forecast. It could be suggested that, if the world is so dynamic, what is the purpose of forecasting in any case? The answer is quite simply that any attempt to reduce the uncertainty that surrounds the future will, if used as a flexible input to the planning process, make us question the appropriateness of what we are currently doing. It must be recognized, however, that forecasts are useful only of they are indeed used in a flexible way. Sales forecasts can too easily become straitjackets that inhibit the organization's activities, as when they are seen as targets, endowed with all the sanctity that numbers tend to assume in a management context.

Forecasts deal with contingencies, not certainties. The head of planning in a large multinational chemical company says, 'We have to have alternative plans that can deal with either/or eventualities'.

Establishing the nature of the 'either/or' is the task of the market fore-caster. Parallel to the need for flexibility is the need to recognize that the output of the forecast should be expressed in terms of a *range* of possible outcomes. Sales estimates share the imprecision of most fore-casting methods. Beyond this, however, it must be recognized that the process whereby any sales level is achieved is essentially *probabilistic*. In other words, chance has a central role in the outcome of any mar-keting process. Our forecasts can, and should, be made to incorporate the probabilities that are implicit in the marketing environment in which we operate.

The successful use of forecasting can be seen in the case of a manu-facturer of household durables. Prior to the start of each fiscal year they worked out three different forecasts: 'optimistic', 'pessimistic' and 'most likely'. If taxation levels changed, competitive activity became particularly aggressive, or if some other phenomenon occurred to alter the market, the manufacturer could adopt an alterna-tive plan without having to repeat the forecasting procedure. This approach enabled the company to react to market conditions with immediate flexibility.

But how do we start to grapple with the sales estimation problem?

Understanding market potential

The distinction between actual and potential customers is vital to suc-cessful sales estimation. Forecasters are concerned with establishing what proportion of the total market potential will be represented in their sales estimates. Market potential has been defined as the maximum possible sales opportunities for all sellers of a good or service. As such, it refers to the potential sales that could be achieved at a given time, in a given environment, by all the firms active in a specified product/market area or segment. Thus the concept of market potential extends our view of the market for our product, in that we see the product as competing against alternative means of satisfying the same need. Successful sales estimation will therefore depend on determining the proportion of the market that can be achieved, given a specific marketing mix and marketing pro-gramme. This situation is illustrated in Figure 8.14.

A presentation of this kind, of course, gives a static picture of actual and potential sales at a given time and in a given environment; it could be influenced both by environmental changes and by changes in marketing effort by any of the firms (including ourselves) in that product/market area.

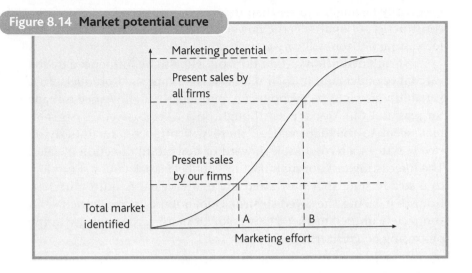

Figure 8.14 Market potential curve

Looking at the sales-estimation problem in this light, we see how it can be possible for estimates to become self-fulfilling prophecies, in that the estimate and the marketing mix/programme are dependent upon each other. In a sense, a given level of market achievement is predicated by what we believe to potentially achievable.

The forecasting horizon

Clearly, the time period we select for the forecasting exercise will influence our approach and our choice of estimation techniques. Most managers are accustomed to thinking in terms of short-, medium-and long-term forecasting, the actual length of these periods being determined by the organization's planning requirements. As an example, a manufacturer of wine bottles in Spain knows that its short-term forecasting requirements are based on its need to plan production schedules on a weekly basis. Its medium-term requirements are determined by the industry demand over the period of time it takes to install and make operational additional production capacity – in this case, a year. And the longer-term forecasting must take into account changing consumer requirements, such as easy-to-open bottles and changing technology in the bottling and packaging fields.

Precise definitions of what constitutes the short, medium and long term for any company will clearly vary, but should ultimately depend on the reaction time implicit in a company's activities and its organization. The reaction time for firms in ladies' fashion markets must necessarily be much shorter than for those companies engaged in the construction of hydroelectric power projects. Their definition of the forecasting horizon will vary considerably.

The firm's definition of that horizon will also be influenced by the variability of demand in their markets. For established products, that variability may not be pronounced, particularly if allowance is made for seasonal variations. Even though on a week-by-week basis sales may seem to fluctuate widely, there will often be an underlying steady-state or a recognizable upward or downward direction in sales. The forecasting task for manufacturers of beef stock cubes, a product in a steady state that has lasted for many years, is quite different from that facing the Swedish firm Uddeholm as they launch on a completely untried market a new grade of stainless steel for use in the processing of fertilizers.

The techniques of estimation

Two broad approaches to market estimation have been employed by market forecasters in their attempts to estimate future sales levels. These may be termed *macro* (or aggregate product-market) estimates and *micro* (or individual product) estimates. These approaches are not alternatives, but should complement each other in the information they provide. Both approaches can be qualitative and quantitative methods of estimation, depending on their objectives.

The macro level of estimation

Let us first consider the macro approaches to estimation. Here the emphasis is on observing the broad picture and, from that, deducing the implications for the product/market in which we are interested. Many business forecasters use leading indicators (that is, indices of related or even non-related activities) as aids in estimating changes in market conditions at the macro level. For example, in the UK, the *Financial Times* Ordinary Share Index has tended in recent years to signal changes in general economic conditions about six months in advance. Similar UK leading indicators, which would be classified as quantitative methods of estimation, are: new housing starts (a lead of about ten months), net acquisition of financial assets by companies (leading by about 12 months), and interest on three-month bank bills (with a lead of approximately 18 months).

Such indicators will only provide approximate pictures of general business conditions and cannot be guaranteed to offer consistent correlations. On the other hand, the forecaster may discern that there is a close fit between a seemingly unrelated activity and the sales performance of a particular product. One Danish manufacturer of garden furniture has established a satisfactory method of predicting sales on the basis of an apparent correlation between the rise in real wages in Denmark and the sale of their products, with a lag of 18 months. This does not necessarily imply any causal relationship – simply a statistical association – but it did seem to provide a useful aid to sales estimation.

There has been a considerable growth in recent years in the use of *marketing models* to provide a macro-type basis for sales estimation. Generally, these models are based on a number of statistically derived relationships drawn from empirical observations. Some of these can be relatively simple, embodying only a few relationships and requiring nothing more than a calculator to perform the manipulations. On the other hand, one Europe-wide oil company has recently developed a sophisticated energy model to guide it in formulating its strategy on synthetic fuels. The model covers all major energy forms, conversion technologies, transportation modes and demand. It also projects investment, financing and resource depletion to the year 2025, and even attempts to predict prices on the basis of supply and demand. A model of this kind attempts to *explain* the observed market behaviour in terms of marketing trends. This contrasts with the garden furniture example above, where the correlation is not explained, only accepted as an *observable* phenomenon.

Not everybody shares this enthusiasm for large-scale models, however, because of the problems of quantifying what are often qualitative and intangible relationships. Such relationships will often change considerably over time, thus making the model obsolete. Another factor weighing against the use of models is the considerable expense involved in collecting the necessary data. In many smaller markets, – it may be more cost-beneficial to employ less sophisticated estimation techniques.

An example of a qualitative macro estimation is the Delphi forecast (named after the Greek oracle who foretold the future). Here a group of experts discuss a problem, such as, 'What will be the major marketing features of the year 2010?', and provide a consensus of their opinions.

These macro approaches, it was suggested earlier, are particularly suited to forecasting that is intended, primarily, to depict broad market conditions. In themselves, though, they rarely provide a complete answer to the company's sales estimation problem. The micro-level approaches to estimation, which tackle the problem from the other direction, from the study of the sales prospects for an individual product, can often provide the missing pieces of the jigsaw.

The micro level of estimation

Micro approaches are based on building up, from an individual customer level, an estimate of what total sales of the product could be in a given period. Quantitative micro methods rely heavily on surveys of actual and/or potential customers of the sort discussed in Chapter 4.

Although the procedures involved may be very sophisticated, these studies basically rely on indications from respondents about their likely purchasing behaviour. For example, a German manufacturer of household electrical goods carries out a regular survey among a representative sample of actual and potential customers to ascertain the likelihood of their purchasing particular electrical appliances in the following 12 months. Using this device, they can track the way in which first-time sales will move, as well as the way that the replacement market is moving.

At the micro level, many companies rely on forecasts based solely on an analysis of past sales. In other words, past sales are charted with a view to identifying patterns and trends that enable projections to be made. The nature of projections must be clearly understood: they are extrapolations from past behaviour and are based on an assumption that what happened in the past will be a guide to what will happen in the future, but this might not be the case. One British firm in the building products market expanded its production facilities on the basis of a sharp upturn in the mid-1980s, only to find that by 1990 the market had collapsed. The collapse lasted long enough to damage the firm's profitability and cast doubt on its chances of long-term survival.

An example of a qualitative micro estimate would be an estimate based on the judgement of members of the sales force concerning future sales.

Successful marketing management must be based on reliable estimates of market demand. It would probably be true to say that companies pay rather less attention to this crucial input to marketing decisions than they should. Success in the markets of the future will almost certainly require a reversal of this neglect.

International product planning

Inadequate product planning is a major factor inhibiting successful international marketing operations. The stories of product failures once an organization steps outside its home territory are legion.

One of the better-known stories concerns Campbell's – the soup manufacturer, which tried to sell its US tomato soup formulation to the British, only to discover, after incurring considerable losses, that the British prefer a more bitter taste. Even the industry giant, Philip Morris, did not understand sufficiently well that Canadians prefer a Virginia tobacco, and failed with their blended tobacco.

In general, the three most important questions to be answered in the domain of international product planning are:

▶ Do I need to adapt my national products when I sell them abroad?
▶ What product line should I sell in world markets?
▶ How do I develop products for international markets?
▶ What are the implications if I sell online?

In many markets the product application is not universal. Additionally, there are legal/semi-legal requirements that must be satisfied. All of this, of course, is in addition to the normal needs/wants analysis by means of market research. Yet other obstacles to overcome, however, are those concerned with production and distribution complexities not encountered in home markets.

If a similar product or service already exists in the target country, there is likely to be a standard for it. So, under the product itself, we need to look for:

▶ legal requirements (such as environment/pollution legislation);
▶ mandatory standards (such as electrical safety standards);
▶ industry standards (such as light alloy wheels in Germany); and
▶ voluntary standards (such as paper size).

One major problem is that, whereas standards are always well defined, they tend to be:

▶ different by country;
▶ many in number and coverage (measurement, quality, material properties, performance, safety and so on); and
▶ different in legal backing/adherence and rationale (protectionism, tradition and so on).

Figure 8.15 shows some of the physical product characteristics that need to be researched most carefully in all target countries. For example, in respect of raw material input, paper size is different in photocopiers in different markets; and different flour quality affects the design of baking machinery. In the case of size, there are different generator sizes in different countries. In the case of application, tyre requirements differ significantly in hot countries, although the product is essentially the same. In the case of packaging, codes, symbols, languages, protective requirements and the like differ from country to country.

Figure 8.15 Product characteristics in respect of foreign markets

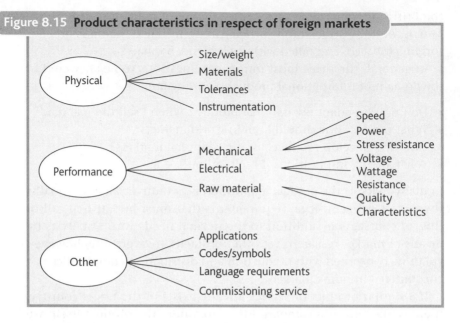

Not all of this, however, is bad. In the case of one boiler manufacturer, who discovered that the stainless steel lining became furred up because of the high chalk content of German water, and that copper piping suffered from a chemical reaction in Germany, changed the basic product design for the home market, as well as for the German market, saved 24 per cent on costs and opened up a much larger market for its boilers as a result.

Understanding market characteristics, then, involves several stages, as shown in Table 8.3. While it is tempting to stop at product/market

Table 8.3 Understanding market characteristics

Analysis	Seeking answers
Competitive product performance	*Why* is their product made the way it is?
Market usage patterns	*How* are the products used? *Where* will they be applied?
Consumer-specific expectations	*How* does the foreign customer's process differ from the home market? *What* do they expect from the product?
Product trials/tests	*Where* are the likely weaknesses of the product in use?

analysis, it is none the less prudent to consider product adaptation at a much broader company level. For example, do we have the design/technology capability, the labour know-how, the equipment/technical expertise, the correct production processes, such as special assembly versus batch assembly, and so on? For example, in the case of power cables, a European manufacturer had to switch machines and provide additional tooling. This in turn led to pressure on existing work-flows, resulting in a production plan change, with consequent capacity constraints, slower throughput, lower earnings for employees and, worst of all, increased production costs.

Issues such as these lead to the conclusion that the financial risks involved in entering overseas markets need to be evaluated most carefully. In particular, we are interested in the cost of adaptation, the resulting margins, the investment requirement and the likely ROI, leading to a preliminary assessment of the volume required in any particular foreign market, as shown in Figure 8.16.

The successful international company should be looking continuously for synergy and cost saving from any essential product adaptation. These are possible from the economies of scale in production, economies in product research and development, economies in marketing as a result of consumer mobility, and the impact of technology.

Figure 8.16 Specifications implications analysis

Product/product group	Country (note others where same specification for these products apply)	Current status of approvals in this product/market sector	Specific changes to meet specification	Time and cost to get approval					Total cost	Minimum volume required
				Technical changes	Production trials	Approval authority test	Cost of application	Ohter		

To summarize, international product planning involves the following:

▶ The product itself:
  – standardization; and
  – adaptation.
▶ Packaging and labelling:
  – protection/security;
  – promotional/channel aspects;
  – cultural factors;
  – package size;
  – language; and
  – government.
▶ Brands and trademarks:
  – global or national;
  – legal;
  – cultural; and
  – other marketing considerations.
▶ Warranty and service:
  – international customers;
  – safety;
  – varying quality control standards internationally;
  – varying use conditions;
  – promotion; and
  – service networks.

To achieve all these things successfully, the organization needs a marketing planning system that is consistent across each of the countries and regions in which it does business. While this will clearly be more difficult in the case of trading carried out through third parties, such as agents and distributors, it should, none the less still be the goal in order to exercise international control.

In summary, each management decision must resolve the following issues:

Whether to market abroad: geographical extension may be more desirable than product diversification, depending, of course, on circumstances. However, the decision to sell abroad should not be taken lightly.
Where to market abroad: this is one of the major decisions for international marketing. Choosing foreign markets on the basis merely of proximity and similarity is not necessarily the most profitable option.

What to market abroad: the degree to which products should be altered to suit foreign needs is a fundamental problem in international marketing, as can be seen from the section on international product management above.

How to market abroad: this is concerned not just with the issue of how to enter a foreign market, but also with the management of the four 'P's once a company arrives. Finally, there is the difficult question of how to co-ordinate the international effort in many foreign markets in order to gain competitive advantage.

Summary

The key to successful product strategy is a balanced portfolio of products that includes both established products and a steady flow of new products. The product portfolio can be analysed in terms of revenue-producing potential using the Boston matrix, and more comprehensively using the directional policy matrix (DPM).

The function of the Boston matrix is to aid forward planning by suggesting strategy for the future development of the product range: invest selectively in Question marks; invest in and grow Stars; maintain Cash cows; and examine Dogs critically and delete them as appropriate. 'Dog' products generate poor cash flow, and the costs of maintaining them can sometimes impede or destabilize overall business progress. While the axes of the Boston matrix consider *market growth rate* and *relative market share*, the axes of the DPM consider numerous variables under the headings *market attractiveness* and *business strengths*.

Because the chance of failure is high in new product launches, the use of formalized methods of appraisal is advocated, including market research as well as economic analysis.

Sales forecasting takes place against a background of uncertainty, and is therefore largely probabilistic. The task is influenced both by the forecasting horizon and by the stability of the markets in which we operate. Techniques include both macro and micro approaches.

The choice of product strategy in international markets is a function of three key factors:

▶ The product itself, defined in terms of the function or need it serves;
▶ The market, defined in terms of the conditions under which the product is used, including the preferences of potential customers and their ability to buy the products in question; and
▶ The costs of adaptation to the company.

Further reading

Meidan, A. and Moutinho, L. (1999) Quantitative methods in marketing, in M. Baker (ed.), *The Marketing Book*, Butterworth Heinemann, Oxford.

Morrison, A. and Wensley, R. (1981) Boxing up or boxed in? A short history of the Boston Consulting Group's share/growth matrix. *Journal of Marketing Management* **7** (2), pp. 105–30.

References

Day, G. (1975) A strategic perspective on product planning. *Journal of Contemporary Business*, (Spring) pp. 1–34.

Henderson, B. (1979) *Henderson on Corporate Strategy*, Abt Books, Cambridge, Mass.

Hichens, R. and Wade, D. (1978) The directional policy matrix: tool for strategic planning. *Long Range Planning*, 11 (June).

Rogers, E. (1962) *Diffusion of Innovations*, Free Press, New York.

Rogers, E. (1976) New product conception and diffusion. *Journal of Consumer Research*, 2 (March), pp. 220–30.

9 Brands

In this chapter we study the:

► notion of 'the augmented brand'
► difference between a brand and a commodity
► qualities of successful brands
► concept of brand management
► components of a brand
► positioning of corporate and global brands
► brand as a marketable asset

What is a brand?

Where a relationship with the customer develops, this is often personified either by the company's name or by the brand name on the product itself. ICI, IBM, BMW, Kodak and Cadbury are excellent examples of company brand names. Persil, Nescafé, Fosters, Dulux, and Castrol GTX are excellent examples of product brand names. A brand is a name, term or symbol (or combination of these) that identifies a product and differentiates it from those of competitors. A successful brand identifies a product as having a sustainable competitive advantage.

The distinction between a brand and a product can be demonstrated by revisiting Figure 7.1 briefly (repeated here as Figure 9.1). The two outer circles comprise the 'product surround', or the services and intangibles that circumscribe the core product elements. The concept of the 'brand' is embodied in the intangible elements. It is this wider, peripheral sphere that we shall examine in this chapter, with particular emphasis on brand name and value perceptions.

Figure 9.1 What is a product?

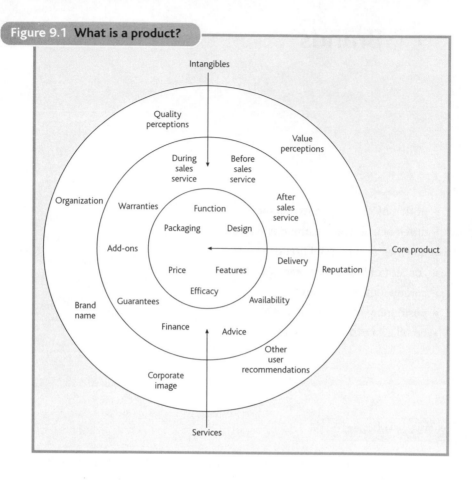

A brand name is not just a name on a product or service. It is an entity that offers customers (and other relevant parties) added values based on factors that extend beyond its functional performance. These added values, or brand values, differentiate products and help to determine customer preference, affinity and loyalty. While some might consider them to be 'intangible', for the purchaser or user, these additional attributes are very real. To illustrate the power of these added values, consider the result of a *blind* test (that is, where the brand identity is concealed), in which Diet Pepsi was compared to Diet Coke by a panel of consumers:

- ▶ Prefer Pepsi: 51 per cent
- ▶ Prefer Coke: 44 per cent
- ▶ Equal/can't say: 5 per cent

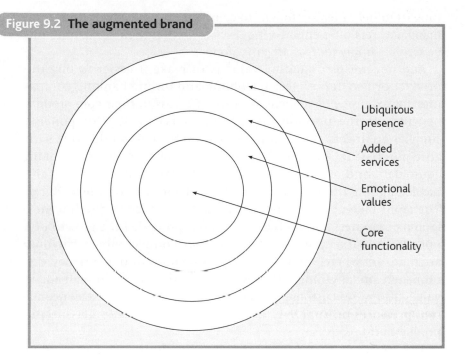

Figure 9.2 The augmented brand

Ubiquitous presence

Added services

Emotional values

Core functionality

When the same two drinks were given to a matched sample in an open test (that is, the true identity of the brands was revealed), the following results were produced:

- ▶ Prefer Pepsi: 23 per cent
- ▶ Prefer Coke: 65 per cent
- ▶ Equal/can't say: 12 per cent

How can this outcome be explained if not in terms of the added values that are aroused in the minds of consumers when they see the familiar Coke logo and pack? Here, the customer value is emotional and it has been consciously fostered over the years by successful Coca-Cola advertising.

It is not only in the area of emotional and psychological benefit that organizations create new forms of added value and differentiation for their brands. The notion of 'the augmented brand', as shown in Figure 9.2, illustrates this fact. Many companies now view added services as a major element of their brand offer. For example, some airlines provide their valued customers with transport to and from the airport, offering an end-to-end service. Freight forwarders provide logistics support to help their customers to complete cost effectively. Industrial manufacturers offer engineering services so that their companies can be seen to supply more than parts alone.

Another means of adding value is to make it easier to buy the product or use the service. Telephone and online banking companies, for example, have increased ease of access to their core product benefits via the provision of 24-hour services. RS Components supplies engineers and maintenance professionals world-wide with an e-purchasing solution that enables them to order and obtain equipment and office consumables at the last minute without the hassle of going through laborious internal authorization procedures. The rapid take-up of technological advances such as the Internet, laptop computers and mobile phones has propelled the growth of a ubiquitous market presence. We now have connectivity to 'anyone, anytime, anywhere' (and with the proliferation of network devices, ultimately on 'anything'). However, raising the stakes through added values also raises customers' expectations and, in turn, the concomitant pressures on suppliers to deliver ever more customer-specific products and services.

The unveiling of these value perceptions and their power to influence customer choice has given new impetus to the marketer's task and the host of tools at his or her disposal. When making a purchase decision, a customer is swayed by a complex range of factors associated with the complete product offer. The marketer's ability to identify those factors of greatest importance to the customer and to ensure that they are prominent in the offer will increase the likelihood of closing the sale. More significantly (if sustained), it will increase the probability that the customer will develop a sense of bonding and trust with the supplying organization, leading to future purchases as a repeat and loyal customer.

Despite its intangibility, a well-developed brand can exert influence on customers and competitors alike, and thus contribute to the way a product, company or whatever is positioned in the market place. It should be stressed that when we refer to the term 'brand' in this book we use it to encompass not only consumer products, but a whole host of offerings, including people (such as politicians and pop stars), places (such as Bangkok), ships (such as the *Queen Elizabeth*), companies, industrial products, service products and so on. The issues of brand perception and position surrounding 'added values' serve to further clarify the definition of a brand as compared to a commodity.

The difference between a brand and a commodity

Commodity markets are characterized typically by the lack of perceived differentiation by customers between competing offerings, and thus purchase decisions tend to be taken on the basis of price or availability and not on the brand or company name. In other words, one product offering in a particular category is much like another. While there may be quality differences, the suggestion is that, within a given specification, one carton of milk, for example, is similar to any other carton of milk.

In situations such as these, one finds that purchase decisions tend to be taken on the basis of price or availability, and not on the basis of the brand or the manufacturer's name. Thus one could argue that the purchase of petrol falls into the commodity category, and while the petrol companies do try to promote 'image', they inevitably end up relying on promotions such as free wine glasses and games to try to generate repeat purchase.

There are examples, however, of taking a commodity and making it a brand. A good example is provided by Perrier water: the contents of its bottles is naturally occurring spring water which at the end of the day, while possessing certain distinctive characteristics, is still spring water. Yet through packaging and, more particularly, promotion, an international brand has been created with high brand loyalty. Consequently, it sells for a price well in excess of the cost of the ingredients.

Conversely, one can also find examples of once-strong brands that have been allowed to decay and in effect become commodities. This process of decay is often brought about because the marketing asset value has been allowed to erode, perhaps through price-cutting or through a lack of attention to product improvement in the face of competition. This has happened in the UK fruit-squash drink market. In the 1960s and 1970s there were a number of very strong brands: Suncrush, Kia-Ora, Jaffa Juice, to name just a few. In this market the quality of the brand had traditionally been stressed, but a switch in promotional emphasis occurred in the 1960s towards promotional offers of one sort or another. Price cutting became prevalent and resources were transferred from advertising that promoted the values of the brand to so-called 'below the line' promotional activities. As a result, at the time of writing, the bottle of orange squash has been reduced to the level of a commodity to such an extent that the major brands are now retailers' own-label products.

Figure 9.3 depicts the process of decay from brand to commodity as the distinctive values of the brand become less clear over time, and the brand's ability to command a premium price therefore diminishes. So, today, we find a bottle of Perrier water selling at a premium over a bottle of orange squash!

The price of a brand is clearly not what customers pay for it. Rather, the price of a brand is the sum total of everything the customer has to do to realize its value. This includes the cost of ownership as well as of purchase. For example, customers spend time, energy and money searching for the right product and sales outlet. They also make an investment in related travel, purchasing, usage and eventual disposal of the product. Customers may also incur expenditure and perhaps inconvenience in the repair, replacement, relocation or upgrading of the product.

Savvy marketers have exploited this phenomenon and used brands as strategic marketing tools. Witness the rise in customer communications that expressly convey to customers more about brand values than product/service benefits, and that attempt to reach customers on every possible level: personal, financial, emotional, operational and relational. Marketers have also discovered the power of brand extensions, corporate endorsement and the company as brand. In the 1950s

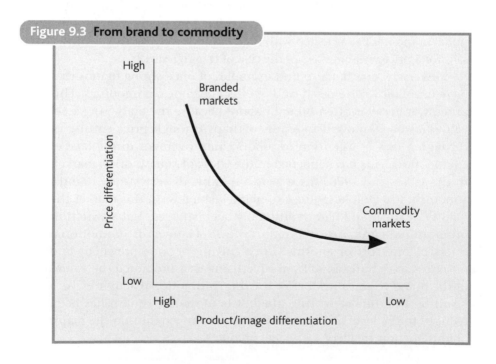

Figure 9.3 From brand to commodity

and 1960s brands embraced not just the activities of one company but also the combined activities of many companies through a prevalence of alliances and networks.

The difference between successful and unsuccessful brands

At the beginning of this chapter we said that a successful brand is one that identifies a product as having sustainable competitive advantage. The PIMS database (Profit Impact of Market Strategies), along with other databases, shows conclusively that strong, successful brands enable organizations to create stable, long-term demand, and to build and hold better margins than either commodity products or unsuccessful brands. (Brands, of course, can be either successful or unsuccessful. The once-great Marks & Spencer is a prime example of a premium brand becoming an unsuccessful one in the latter part of the twentieth century because of an obsessive focus on internal issues rather than on building superior customer value (though an upturn in its fortunes is being seen now).

Successful brands contribute profitability by adding values that entice customers to buy (and buy again and again), and encourage channel intermediaries, such as retailers, to stock them. They attract a high market share and a premium price. Typically, the brand leader obtains twice the market share of the number two brand, and the number two brand obtains twice the market share of the number three brand. The brand with the highest market share is always much more profitable, as a well-known PIMS study found: brands with a 40 per cent market share generate three times the ROI of those with a market share of only 10 per cent. Experience has also shown that the superior profitability generated by customer preferences can be self-perpetuating in terms of creating brand loyalty and customer referrals.

Successful brands also safeguard and strengthen their organizations. They provide a firm base for expansion into product improvements and variants, added services, new outlets and countries, and so on. In addition, they protect organizations against the threat posed by intermediaries, imitators and other competitors. And last, but not least, they help to transform organizations from being faceless bureaucracies to being dynamic businesses that are delightful to work for and deal with.

We must not, then, make the mistake of confusing successful brands and unsuccessful 'brands'. The world is full of products and services that have brand names, but they are not successful brands. They fail to fulfil several important criteria:

- ▶ A successful brand has a name, symbol or design (or some combination of these) that identifies the 'product' of an organization as having a sustainable competitive advantage; for example, Coca-Cola, IBM, Tesco.
- ▶ A successful brand invariably results in superior profit and market performance (PIMS).
- ▶ Brands are only assets if they have a sustainable competitive advantage.
- ▶ Like other assets, brands depreciate without further investment; for example, Hoover, Singer, MG, and so on.

There are many 'products' that pretend to be brands, but are not the genuine article. As the Director of Marketing at Tesco said: 'Pseudo brands are not brands. They are manufacturers' labels. They are 'me-toos' and have poor positioning, poor quality and poor support. Such manufacturers no longer understand the consumer and see retailers solely as a channel for distribution' (reported in *Marketing Globe*, 2 (10), 1992).

Seen in this light, pseudo brands can never be mistaken for the real thing because they lack the added brand values that define genuine brands. Generally speaking, an organization that is successful at branding has a customer orientation and culture that puts customers first. Moreover, this commitment to customer satisfaction and service excellence is reflected in the customers' belief that that the product:

- ▶ will be reliable;
- ▶ is the best;
- ▶ is something that will suit them better than Product X; and
- ▶ is designed with them in mind.

These beliefs are based not only on perceptions of the brand itself relative to other brands, but also on customers' perceptions of the supplying organization and opinions about its reputation and integrity. The key to prosperity is a 'win-win-win' strategy. Companies with successful brands study their customers and consumers, and provide them consistently with a product of excellent value, for which they are prepared to pay a premium and create demand pull through the retail chain. For their part, retailers are delighted with the gross margin return they get from their inventory investment in leading brands. This recipe ensures that customer, retailer and supplier all get what they seek from co-operating. There are no losers.

The point is that the title 'successful brand' has to be earned. The organization has to manage the reputation of its brands carefully so that customers will associate them uniquely with superior value. This means investing in every aspect of the company's operation so that the product delivers the added values it promises, and meets the physical, emotional, psychological (and even potential) needs of customers. The organization must provide concrete and rational benefits that are sustained by a marketing mix which is compatible, believable and relevant.

Brand management

The concept of brand management was created by Procter & Gamble (P&G), who in the 1930s encouraged two of its brands to compete and has since been reaping the rewards. P&G learned that a strong brand reassures the customer; it gives confidence in terms of the quality and satisfaction that can be anticipated from buying it. From all of this comes the possibility of long-term profits. Many brands are now household names, but the fascination with managing brands has moved beyond the household goods categories.

People with brand-management experience in fast-moving consumer goods companies are now in demand by financial institutions, service organizations, retailers and new technology-based companies and their marketing skills are being applied to 'own label' brands. For example, the HSBC Bank plc (previously the Midland) has introduced new brands of accounts, with names such as Vector and Orchard, which have been promoted strongly. Egg is already one of the most well-known brands in the UK financial services market.

Without a doubt, the concept of branding can fit very well with the idea of the corporate image. Take British Airways, for example. At one time the company was organized on the basis of a number of 'marketing centres', which were essentially geographical areas such as North America, Europe and Australia. With such an organization, it was very difficult to get a focus on customer service and to track down the real needs of customers.

There is now an 'umbrella' or 'master brand', which is British Airways itself. Under this are seven 'pillar' brands: Concorde, First Class, Club World, Club Europe, World Traveller, Eurotraveller, and Super Shuttle, each run by a brand manager and a group brand manager. Both customer service and profitability improved under the new system during the 1990s, but by the start of the twenty-first century, focus on cost-cutting instead of creating superior customer value eroded most of the progress made under Lord King. Since September 11th 2001, of course, the performance of weakened airlines such as British Airways has been disastrous.

Often brands are managed as mini businesses with brand managers acting like mini-CEOs competing for the company's resources in order to uphold the brand's distinctive advantage and grow market share. This has the positive effect of acknowledging that the money and effort spent on developing the brand's position is in fact an invest-ment in the generation of future benefits. Where category manage-ment is used as a basis for organizing consumer goods marketing, suppliers organize their brand portfolios to match their retail customers. They appoint category 'champions', whose focus is on maximizing profit from a category for the retailer rather than develop-ing brand franchises. Regardless of what form brand management takes, its function is to optimize the brand's potential through manag-ing its constituent parts carefully.

The components of a brand

The three principal components of a brand are: *brand strategy* (which stems from its position in the portfolio); *brand positioning* (what the brand actually does and with what it competes); and *brand personality* (its sensual, rational and emotional appeal).

Brand strategy

The first of these, *brand strategy*, stems from the position of the brand in the portfolio of the organization that owns the brand. Sometimes some poor brands are competing in high-growth markets, while others are competing in mature or declining markets. Thus the objectives for the brand could well call for differ-ent levels and types of investment (invest or harvest), innovation (relaunch, augment, cut costs), sales and distribution patterns (extension, reduction, broad, narrow), market share, usage aims (new, existing behaviour) and so on.

The first point to be made, then, is that an organization must be clear what the appropriate objectives are for a brand. As with product and marketing objectives generally, the brand objectives should reflect and reinforce the corporate objectives.

Brand positioning

The second component, *brand positioning*, is concerned with what the brand actually does and with what it competes. In other words, brand positioning starts with the physical or functional aspects of the product (the central circle in Figure 9.1). For example, Canada Dry is positioned in the UK as a mixer for brandies and whiskies, rather than as a soft drink competing with Coca-Cola, Pepsi-Cola and 7-Up. Similarly, Tide is presented as a tough, general-purpose laundry detergent, rather than a cleansing agent for woollens and delicates. Tesco is a high-quality superstore rather than a low-price supermarket. EasyJet.com purports to be the Web's favourite airline, distancing itself from the lumbering and higher-cost, longstanding carriers.

Positioning is usually performed against identifiable motivators in any market, only one or two of which are of real importance when developing a brand. These dimensions are best seen as bipolar scales along which brands can be positioned. Examples of these are provided in Table 9.1.

Because these dimensions are so obvious, they are easy to research in order to establish which are those that people regard as the most fundamental basis for buying. It will be obvious that not all consumers look for the same functional performance, so market segmentation becomes important at this stage. A useful starting point in this kind of

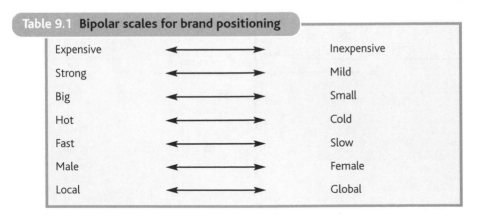

Table 9.1 Bipolar scales for brand positioning

Expensive	←——→	Inexpensive
Strong	←——→	Mild
Big	←——→	Small
Hot	←——→	Cold
Fast	←——→	Slow
Male	←——→	Female
Local	←——→	Global

primary market interpretation is to draw a bipolar map, as shown in Figure 9.4. Figure 9.5 shows an actual bipolar map for detergents.

Figure 9.4 A brand position map

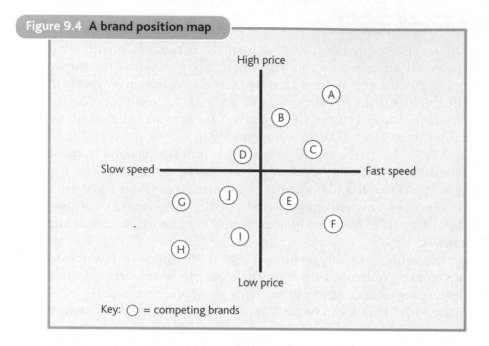

Figure 9.5 Bipolar map for detergents

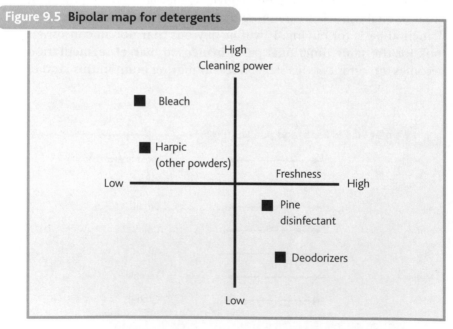

Clearly, the physical dimensions of any market will change over time, so this kind of basic research should be conducted on a regular basis to establish, first, what the main dimensions are, and second, whether the position of any competing product has changed. Competing products in commodity markets, because they are largely undifferentiated, are seen by the customer as occupying virtually identical positions, and thus to all intents and purposes are substitutable. The more distinctive a brand position, however, the less likelihood that a customer will accept a substitute.

In highly mature markets, brands are likely to be positioned close to one another. This indicates that the basic functional or physical characteristics are less likely to be the sole basis on which a product or service is selected.

This brings us to the final component, brand personality. Stephen King, when he was a brand specialist at J. Walter Thompson and a Visiting Professor of Cranfield School of Management, said that a product is something that is made in a factory; a brand is something that is bought by a consumer. A product can be copied, but a successful brand is *unique* and, particularly in mature markets, is a key discriminator in the market place.

Brand personality

Brand personality is a useful descriptor for the total impression that consumers have of brands, and in many ways brands are like people in that they have their own physical, emotional and attitudinal characteristics. Thus they are a complex blend of different characteristics that together create a brand identity. In this way, two brands can be very similar in terms of their functions, yet have very different personalities. For example, the Ford Fiesta, the Peugeot 205 and the Rover Metro all perform in a similar way in the functional dimensions of size, speed and price. Yet each has a totally different personality, the result of a blend of three sorts of appeal: sensual, rational and emotional.

Sensual appeal refers to the way the product or service looks, feels, sounds, smells or tastes. It is easy to imagine how this appeal can differ in the case of, say, cigarettes, beer or cars. In the service sector, Virgin Airlines have been very successful on this dimension.

Rational appeal concerns the way the product or service performs (what it contains, its relative costs and so on).

Emotional appeal is perhaps the most important aspect of a brand, and has a lot to do with the psychological rewards it offers, the moods it conjures up, the associations it evokes, and so on. It is easy to see the overt appeal of certain products as being, for example, particularly masculine, feminine, chic, or workmanlike, or 'flashy'.

As Stephen King says:

> The personality of the Ford Fiesta might be seen as that of a solid, respectable citizen, male, white collar, conscientious, hard working, not terribly ambitious, used to play football but now is more likely to spend Saturdays going on shopping expeditions, is proud to vote Conservative and reads the *Daily Mail*. The Renault 5, on the other hand, might be a tentatively dashing girl of 27, who wears what she thinks is the fashion of the moment, reads *Cosmopolitan*, drinks Campari, is a bit muddled about money and votes Liberal. The Fiat Panda might be a teenager, going to be good looking, but still a bit spotty, very uncertain about himself, under the bravado, but a good lad really. ('Brand-building in the 1990s', *Journal of Marketing Management*, 7 (1) 3–13).

Brand personality is also the result of a whole gamut of influences, such as the places where it is sold; the price charged; other brands from the same manufacturer; how it is used; the kinds of people who buy and use it; after-sales service; the name of the brand; advertising; point-of-sale material; PR; sponsorship; and many others.

However, for any brand to be successful, all these elements have to be consistent, since they will all affect the brand's personality, and it is this personality, above all else, that represents the brand's totality and which makes one brand more desirable than another. At its simplest, it is a brand's personality that converts a commodity into something unique and enables a higher price to be charged for it.

One of the present authors, in a book entitled *Creating Powerful Brands* (de Chernatony and McDonald, 1998), combines brand functionality and personality in a matrix. This matrix is shown in Figure 9.6. The vertical axis refers to a brand's ability to satisfy utilitarian needs, such as quality, reliability, effectiveness and so on, where the consumer's need for such benefits is high. The horizontal axis represents the brand's ability to help consumers to express something about themselves – for example, their mood, their membership of a particular social group, their status, and so on. Brands are chosen on the latter dimension because they have values that exist over and above their physical values. We call this dimension 'representationality'. For example, products such as Yves St Laurent neckties are effective brands for expressing particular personality types and roles, with functional attributes being secondary.

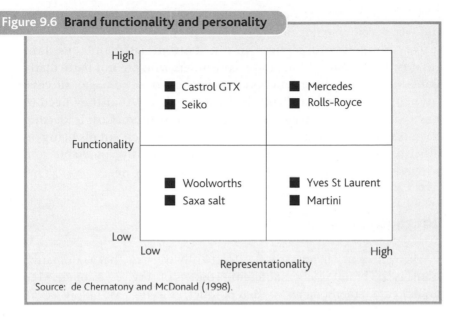

Figure 9.6 **Brand functionality and personality**

Source: de Chernatony and McDonald (1998).

It is possible, by means of market research, to identify the degree to which consumers perceive a brand as reflecting functionality and representationality, and then to plot these on a matrix. Having done this, it is then possible for the marketer to consider how best to use the resources available to support the brand.

For products and services in the top right-hand quadrant (that is, ones that both provide functional excellence and are good vehicles for non-verbal communication about themselves), a creative strategy that reinforces consumers' lifestyle requirements should be adopted, communicated through appropriate media channels. Additionally, the quality of the brand needs to be maintained through high standards of quality control and continuous product development. Also, strict control over channels of distribution should be exercised.

For products and services in the top left-hand quadrant (that is, ones bought by consumers because of a high utilitarian need rather than because of a need to say something about themselves), product superiority needs to be maintained continuously, as 'me-tooism' is a continuous threat to such brands. Also, heavy promotional support is important in communicating the functional benefits of the brand.

For products and services in the bottom right-hand quadrant (that is, ones that are less important for their functional attributes, but which are high as symbolic devices), it is clearly important to reinforce continuously the cultural and lifestyle aspects of the brand, and a heavy advertising presence is almost certainly more important than product-development issues.

For products and services in the bottom left-hand quadrant (that is, those that are bought by consumers who are not particularly concerned about either functional differences or self-image), successful branding is more difficult, because it is likely that they need to have wide distribution and be very price competitive. Cost leadership then becomes important to the brand owner, which entails being an efficient producer. Brands in this sector are obviously vulnerable, and to succeed an attractive price proposition is usually necessary.

The company as a brand

It will by now be obvious that it is frequently the case that a company's name is the brand used on different products or services, as opposed to an individual brand name for each product, as in the case of, say, Persil.

To present themselves in the most favourable way, firms develop a corporate identity programme, ensuring that all forms of external communication are co-ordinated and presented in the same way. Corporate identity can be a valuable asset, which, if effectively managed, can make a major contribution to brand success.

Classic examples of this include IBM, Virgin, Mercedes, Sony, Yamaha, JCB and countless others. It works well as a policy, given the prohibitive costs of building individual brands *ab initio*, provided the product or service in question is consistent with the corporate image. In this respect it is easy to see why Ford has been unable to compete effectively in the high-class car market, and was eventually forced to buy Jaguar in order to enter this segment. Equally, it can be seen why Mars was able to enter the ice-cream market using the Mars corporate brand name, but why it uses a totally different brand name, Pedigree, in the animal foodstuffs market.

While there is a 'halo' effect of using a famous corporate name on a new product or service, there are also risks to the total portfolio, should any one new product prove to be disastrous. For example, Levi Strauss was known and respected for jeans. Their extension into Levi tailored classic suits failed because of wrong associations. And adding the name Pierre Cardin to bathroom tiles in Spain did little for the value of this core brand!

Peter Doyle has developed a useful matrix for considering what an appropriate strategy might be towards corporate, as opposed to individual, product branding. This is given in Figure 9.7.

Figure 9.7 Corporate brand positioning

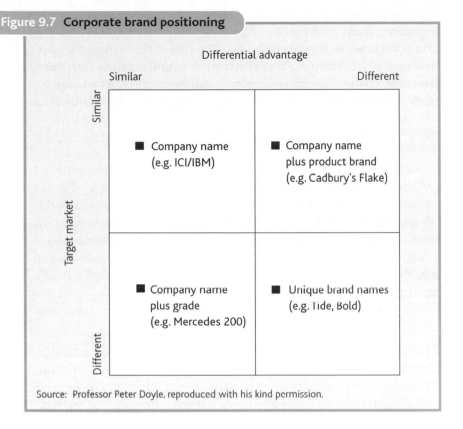

Differential advantage

Similar   Different

Target market — Similar / Different

■ Company name (e.g. ICI/IBM)

■ Company name plus product brand (e.g. Cadbury's Flake)

■ Company name plus grade (e.g. Mercedes 200)

■ Unique brand names (e.g. Tide, Bold)

Source: Professor Peter Doyle, reproduced with his kind permission.

Global versus local brands

So, if we can now distinguish between a brand and a pseudo brand, what is a global brand? Here is a definition: *a global brand is a product that bears the same name and logo and presents the same or a similar message all over the world.* The product is usually aimed at a similar target market, and is promoted and presented in much the same way.

A survey that encompassed 10 000 people in the USA, Japan and Europe established the ten most widely recognized brand names. Top was Coca-Cola, followed by Sony, Mercedes-Benz, Kodak, Disney, Nestlé, Toyota, McDonald's, IBM and Pepsi. There are probably few surprises here, but what are the alternative options to having a mass global brand?

There are only two broad options:

▶ develop a global brand, such as American Express or Coca-Cola; or
▶ have a local brand in each country or region of operation.

What fuels the decision-making regarding the choice of option? Clearly, it depends mainly on the types of customer. However, there are some other practical considerations to take into account, such as the cost of production, the distribution costs, promotion, competitive market structure, channels, legal constraints, and operational structures. Case study 9.1 recounts how an industry giant struggled with this question.

Case study 9.1 **Procter & Gamble test brandwidth in Europe**

> Procter & Gamble experienced major problems trying to get washing powders and liquids established under one brand name across Europe. For one thing, they had to try to accommodate different types of washing machine, different types of water, different washing habits, and different cultures. Then there was the business of getting to grips with market structures and competition, and finally but importantly (because it can be the greatest barrier of all), getting its own operating structure right.

Clearly, then, the benefits to be derived from economies of scale have to be weighed very carefully against the difficulty of setting up a global brand, as the following matrix, Figure 9.8, shows. Although three of the quadrants reduce to fairly obvious choices, the top right-hand quadrant is still something of a poser. Our own inclination is

Figure 9.8 **Global versus local brands**

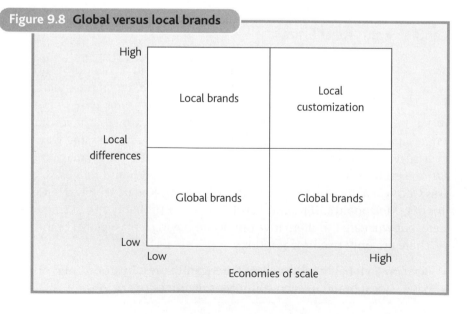

210

that, when faced with great difficulty, but high economies of scale, we would endeavour to establish global brands.

Of course, while the matrix only represents a concept, it is possible to develop concrete data for it in much the same way as the directional policy matrix, described in Chapter 8. For example, all the savings attributable to economies of scale could be calculated – manufacturing, R&D, purchasing, logistics, better management control and so on. Equally, local differences could be assessed, taking into account the infrastructure of markets, demand homogeneity, culture, political/legal framework, market structure, competition and the like.

By looking at international markets in this way, the odds come out very much higher in favour of global brands compared to local ones. Predictions about future trends only serve to reinforce this hypothesis. For example, in the European single market is has been predicted that:

- ▶ prices will tend to harmonize towards the lowest levels across Europe;
- ▶ purchasers will tend to buy on a Pan-European basis to gain maximum price advantage; and
- ▶ major distributors (especially importers) will operate transnationally and take advantage of remaining price differentials and low-cost suppliers.

There is already some evidence to confirm that these trends are already happening. The growth in global branding is a direct result of the explosion of media consumption amongst the young. In every country the data show that the younger consumers are significantly more aware of international brands, particularly in fields like TV, music, video and sports.' The most fundamental point of all this is that one day there will eventually be a Euro-market, and there may one day be Euro-consumers in the foreseeable future.' The recent launch of the euro and the disappearance of a number of major national currencies has significant implications for market competition and market segmentation across the so-called 'Eurozone', with consequent reverberations elsewhere.

The portents are clear. Already, large Pan-European retailing groups are appearing, and if an organization does not have a European brand, especially if it is in fast-moving consumer goods, it does not appear to have very good prospects. It is brand names that win customers, make a profit and create customer loyalty. A good brand, at the end of the day, is the company's best marketing asset. For that reason it is shortsighted not to invest in the brand. To allow it to slip and become a 'me-too' commodity is tantamount to commercial vandalism.

Brand valuation

The question of asset protection and development is, in a sense, what marketing is all about. As brands are arguably the most important of all marketing assets, it is vital to ensure that they are regarded and treated appropriately in terms of resource allocation, strategic priority and 'market value'. We touched on the first two of these issues earlier in the chapter, so let us now consider briefly the matter of brand value from the perspective of brand ownership.

Being an asset of definable proportions (summarized as the current and future potential to deliver and communicate benefit within the market context), it should be possible to measure and value a brand. Like any other item of property, be it a company, an item of equipment, or a piece of real estate, a brand has a worth in the market place. The decision to own or to acquire a brand therefore involves judgements about the role, robustness and 'rearability' of the brand. How does it factor in the company agenda? Will it be sustainable? Is it capable of being built up and cultivated?

Traditionally, brand value has been represented as the singular ability to generate profits. However, there is growing recognition that company brands can also work across multiple markets as a means of improving customer retention rates and long-term profits. This is evident in brand terminology. For example, we are increasingly concerned with 'brand awareness', 'brand association', 'brand image', 'brand equity', 'brand recognition', 'brand recall', 'brand loyalty', 'brand switching', 'brand extension', 'brand elasticity', and so on. As regards estimating a brand's financial, or sale, value ('brand valuation'), we use the criteria of brand 'width', 'length', 'depth', 'breadth' and 'weight'. Clearly, then, brands do possess a relative value determinable by those who own, operate and trade in them.

Buying a major brand nowadays often makes more sense to organizations than launching a new brand, with all the risk and uncertainty this entails. This is just one of the reasons why brand valuation has emerged as a major issue in recent times, and why brands are increasingly sought-after as assets. The trend towards acquisitions by brand-led businesses seeking to accelerate product ranges and pursue geographic expansion that characterized the 1990s looks set to continue.

Some of the more spectacular examples of the value of brands as assets can be seen in acquisitions in which colossal premiums were paid above the balance sheet asset value. Philip Morris, for example, bought

Kraft for US$1.29 billion, four times the value of Kraft's tangible assets. Grand Metropolitan bought Pilsbury for US$5.5 billion, a 50 per cent premium on Pilsbury's pre-bid value. AT&T paid a massive premium for the NCR brand. RHM, taking its cue from this trend, more than trebled its asset value when it voluntarily valued its own brands and incorporated them on the balance sheet. Nestlé paid £2.5 billion for Rowntree in the UK, which had a balance sheet value of £0.4 billion. While this premium does reflect the potential value of Rowntree's distribution, customer relationships and branding expertise, the largest share of the premium was undoubtedly for the confectionery brands the company had nurtured carefully for decades: Kit-Kat, After Eight and Polo mints.

The reason why brands may be valued at figures far in excess of their balance sheet value is that it is relationships with customers, not factories, that generate profits, and it is company and brand names that secure these relationships. When brand names are neglected, their distinctive values are eroded and they can no longer command a premium price. Consequently, they offer no unique added values and decay into commodities.

Behind the brand name, of course, lies a world of other relationships, between, for example:

▶ *people* – employees, shareholders, suppliers, alliance partners, industry colleagues, legislators and so on;
▶ *resources* – information, 'intelligence', expertise, experience, finance, plant, equipment, materials, time and so on; and
▶ *events* – political upheavals, economic upturns and downturns, technological developments, social and cultural trends, ecological catastrophes/discoveries and so on.

The role of brand is thus not confined solely to delivering and communicating value, but also extends to creating value. Consider the 'people' factor for a moment. It is an accepted rule in marketing that happy employees make for happy customers (and thus happy shareholders, suppliers, retailers and so on.) It is also a known fact that dynamic and successful businesses tend to attract dynamic and successful people. By recruiting a highly skilled, enthusiastic and committed workforce, a company endows itself with value creators who will generate the present and future customer value in which customers want to invest. It also confers upon itself the qualities that support membership in lucrative value chains and networks. Having superior resources, and the flexibility to respond successfully to threats and opportunities, has a similar effect in ensuring the company continues to achieve customer value excellence.

Given the significance of brands to building customer relationships and corporate profitability and sustainability, understanding the implications of brand value is fundamental to good marketing planning.

Summary

The following quotation is from *Creating Powerful Brands* (de Chernatony and McDonald, 1998) 'A successful brand is an identifiable product, service, person or place augmented in such a way that the buyer or user perceives relevant, unique added values which match their needs most closely. Its success results from being able to sustain these added values against competitors.' Being able to this on a global basis will bring great rewards, but it will not be easy.

The three key components of a brand are the brand strategy, the brand positioning and the brand personality. For a brand to succeed, it has to have sensual, rational and emotional appeal. The degree to which functionality and representationality are important to consumers will determine the brand strategy.

Global branding versus local branding as a strategy will depend ultimately upon the homogeneity of demand patterns in different countries and the concomitant economies of scale to be enjoyed from created global brands.

Brand success lies in its sustainability. By understanding how customer value is created, the offer can be branded and positioned to create customer preferences and continually enhance the value of the brand.

Further reading

The Economist (1988) The year of the Brand, 24 December.
Landor Associates (1991) *The World's Leading Brands*, Landor
   Associates London.

References

de Chernatony, L. and McDonald, M. (1998) *Creating Powerful Brands*,
   Butterworth-Heinemann, Oxford.
Doyle, P. (1999) Branding, in M. Baker (ed.), *The Marketing Book*
   Butterworth-Heinemann, Oxford.

10 Pricing strategy

The pricing decision

The pricing decision is one of the most important issues the marketing executive has to face. Its impact will usually be reflected in the quantity of the product sold, the contribution to profits that the product will make and, even more crucially, the strategic position of the product in the market place. In addition, in a multi-product company it is frequently the case that a decision taken on the price of one product will have implications for other products in the range. It is not surprising, therefore, that much has been written and discussed on the subject of pricing, and that it has created considerable controversy as to how the price decision should be made.

Frequently, this controversy has centred around the role that costs should play in determining price. Traditionally, the price of a product is based on the identification of the costs associated with manufacturing, marketing and distributing the product with the subsequent addition of a mark-up to reflect the desired profitability. Such an approach has been criticized on a number of counts. First, it can prove to be extremely difficult in practice to identify the true costs that can only be allocated to a specific product on an arbitrary basis. Second, such a cost-plus approach to pricing ignores the demand sensitivity of the market place. It may be that a price determined on a cost-plus basis is higher than the market can bear. Attempts have been made to overcome these problems by using a *marginal cost* approach rather than a *full cost* approach, so that the pricing decision becomes one of attempting to maximize the contribution the product will make – that is, the difference between the *price* and the direct and attributable *costs*.

The basic problem with any cost-based approach to pricing is that it assumes implicitly that the customers are interested in *the company's* costs, whereas in reality customers are only concerned with *their own* costs. This can be expressed another way – customers seeks to acquire benefits and it is in order to acquire those benefits that they are prepared to pay a certain price. Seen from this perspective, the company making the price decision is faced with the need to identify the value – in the customers' eyes – of the benefits inherent in its product. The costs of that product thus become irrelevant to the pricing decision even though they are highly pertinent to the profitability of that decision. In other words, *costs determine profits*, not price.

Benefits and price

Throughout this book we have suggested that in any purchase decision customers are seeking to acquire 'benefits'. A product must bring with it the promise of performing certain tasks, of solving identified problems, or even of providing specific gratifications. Thus the product is not bought for the particular components or materials that go into its manufacture *per se*, but rather it is bought for what, as an entity, it can do.

The implication of the benefit concept from a pricing point of view is that the company must first identify the benefits the customers perceive the product is offering, and then attempt to ascertain the value the customers place upon them. The key issue here is that it is customer *perception* that is important. It may be, for example, that two competing companies offer products that are, for all intents and purposes, technically identical, and yet one company can command a premium price. Why should this be so? It may be that additional benefits offered by one company in the way of technical advice or after-sales service are perceived to be superior to those offered by another. Or it may just be that the 'image' of that company is seen as being superior. Whatever the reason, there are many cases of this type of 'differential advantage' that cannot be explained simply in technical or quality terms.

Strong brands have always been able to command a price premium. For example, one study looked at the price advantage IBM has traditionally had in computers, and found that IBM machines are priced substantially above competing machines of equal performance; this price differential appears to be independent of machine size. Since a substantial percentage of users are still willing to buy IBM machines even though their relative price is high, the implication is that IBM offers customers something to induce them to pay a substantial premium for an IBM machine. The study identified that this price premium was achieved not through superior hardware or technology, but rather through the image that IBM had for quality, reliability and customer support.

Another way to look at this price advantage is to think of the maximum price at which the product could be sold as being the sum of two elements. First, there is the 'commodity price' element; this is the base price for the generic product, which would be determined by supply and demand in the market place. On top of this should be added the 'premium price differential', which reflects the totality of the benefits that customers perceive will be acquired through purchase of that product. Figure 10.1 shows this concept diagrammatically.

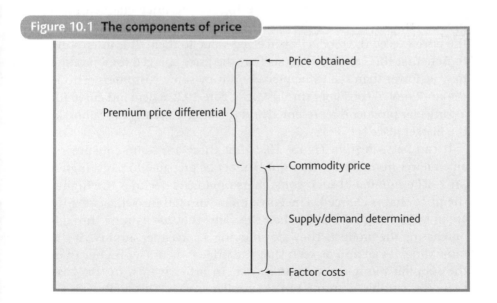

Figure 10.1 The components of price

The existence of this 'premium price differential' can only be explained in terms of perceived benefits. The task of the pricing decision-maker therefore becomes one of identifying these benefits and placing a customer value on them. It is really a 'bundle' of benefits, and so the first step in this suggested approach to pricing is to 'unbundle' the product and identify the individual benefit components that together constitute the totality.

Price and value

Every purchase by a customer is a 'trade-off'. The trade-off is between the value the customer places on the acquisition of the product versus the costs that are involved in that acquisition, plus any subsequent costs that might be involved – for example, maintenance or upgrading costs. (These costs represent 'the total cost of ownership'.)

There is nothing new in this idea. Economists have long talked about the concept of 'utility'. While some of their ideas on the relationship between price and demand may seem naïve there is nevertheless an important message for the pricing decision-maker in the recognition that price must be seen in terms of value.

The Victorian economist Alfred Marshall was the first to fully articulate the idea of price as a reflection of the value placed on a product or service by the consumer. He developed the concept of the *demand curve*, which simply stated that the higher the price charged for a product, the lower will be the demand for it as potential customers see the price exceed the product's perceived value to them. It is interesting to note that this concept suggests that the price charged for a product may be lower than the value placed on it by some customers. This is the notion of a 'consumer surplus'. In Figure 10.2, a demand curve for a particular product is represented and the price currently prevailing in the market place is P_1.

It can be seen from Figure 10.2 that there are some consumers, albeit fewer in number, who would in fact be prepared to pay a higher price. The number of such consumers obviously declines the higher the price that is charged. The consumers who fall into this category are in fact paying a price less than the value they are gaining through purchasing the product. They are enjoying a consumer surplus. At the same time, it can also be seen that the price P_1 is in fact higher than the supplier's long-run marginal cost. In other words, in this case there is a 'surplus' accruing to the supplier as well. This analysis is an

Figure 10.2 The demand curve

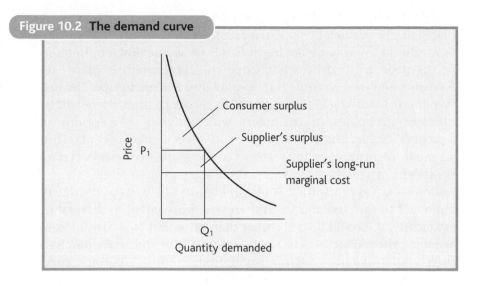

Figure 10.3 Consumer and supplier surplus

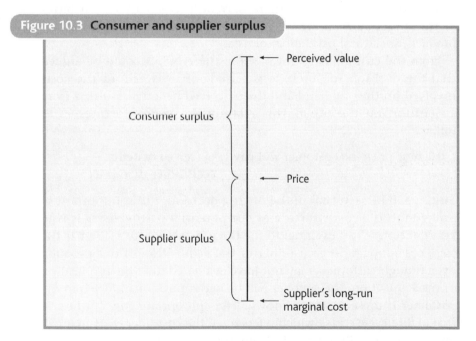

over-simplification of the real world, but it might be a useful focus for price decision-makers to think of their problem along the lines suggested by Figure 10.3.

The pricing problem can be seen in this way as an attempt by the supplier to achieve the greatest possible 'surplus' over long-run marginal cost while still pricing no higher than the perceived value placed on the product by potential customers.

An alternative way of looking at this is to see the problem in terms of the need to identify what value the target market places on a product and then to convert that value into a market price. The first step towards solving this problem is to recognize that there will be different groupings of customers with different perceptions of a product's value. These groupings are in effect *market segments*. Thus we might identify a specific segment of the market that seeks certain benefits from a product and values them at a particular level.

However, it is not sufficient just to identify the perceived value of a product to the customers and then set a price equal to that value. Frequently, there will be costs other than price that face customers in acquiring the product. These additional costs over and above purchase price could include freight, installation, training, maintenance, service, spares support and other 'life-cycle costs', as they are sometimes termed. In addition, there may be perceived costs in terms of risk of product failure or, particularly in the case of consumer products, social and psychological risk.

From the customers' point of view, therefore, it could be argued that the decision to purchase is a trade-off between all the costs involved on the one hand and the perceived benefits resulting from acquisition on the other. This relationship may be expressed as follows:

Highest price the customer will pay = perceived benefits −
costs other than price

Thus it can be seen that in the pricing decision it is as important to understand the cost structure of our potential customers as it is to know our own! It is essential to the pricing decision to recognize the total cost impact on a customer of the acquisition of our product. Even though customers may not have evaluated fully the implication of the acquisition, the supplier will be better positioned to sell to the customer if these costs are known. The appropriate concept here is that of 'life-cycle costs', which refers to all the customer costs that will be incurred by the customer from the acquisition of the product through to the end of its useful life. For example, in pricing a piece of numerical control equipment, the manufacturer should identify the effects that the equipment will have on the customer's manufacturing economics, its likely life, any maintenance and upgrading costs, and its disposal value, if any.

Given a full analysis of the life-cycle cost implications of the product, the pricing decision-maker can now focus attention on the identification and quantification of the product's perceived benefits.

Benefit evaluation

One of the first attempts to break loose from the constraints of cost-orientated pricing and to seek instead to incorporate some recognition of perceived value was the technique developed by the Glacier Metal Company, which it termed 'product-analysing pricing'. This attempted to build up a final price by identifying the physical features that go into the product, and then to value these features in customer terms. The method was based on a statistical analysis of previous prices obtained for similar products to provide quantified estimates of the relative contribution of each physical component to the final price. The analysis was limited as such to the physical attributes of the product and did not quantify non-physical benefits other than by talking loosely about the 'product surround'. Because of these limitations it did not provide the pricing decision-maker with the crucial information on customer evaluation of perceived product benefits – both physical and intangible. To do this we need to seek an alternative approach to benefit evaluation.

Trade-off analysis

In recent years a number of developments have taken place in the fields of mathematical psychology and psychometrics that have great value in quantifying the relative importance potential customers place on the various attributes of a product. These techniques are based on a type of trade-off analysis called 'conjoint measurement', a powerful device for quantifying the intangible as well as the physical benefits present in a product. The 'trade-off' approach to pricing follows a sequence of logical steps.

Step 1   Identification of benefit components

It is important to recognize that the potential customers for a product will have their own perceptions of the benefits contained within that product. To identify these perceived benefits it is necessary to conduct a limited, small-scale survey of potential and/or actual customers. The purpose of this study is to elicit the key features or benefits that are expected to be acquired as a result of using the product. Direct questioning can be used, such as, 'What is it that makes Brand X different from Brand Y?' More sophisticated procedures for elicitation of benefits exist, but essentially they all have the same purpose: to draw from customers their own perceptions of product features rather than the manufacturers'. So, in a study of customers for a new chemical compound, the following attributes might emerge:

▶ quality;
▶ availability;
▶ impact on customers' production economies;
▶ storage conditions necessary; and
▶ technical assistance.

The question is, then: 'What relative value is placed on each of these components?'

Step 2   Quantifying benefit values

Because a product is, in effect, the totality of its component attributes, a way must be found of separating these and measuring their individual value to the customer. It is here that conjoint analysis becomes particularly useful. Using the attributes identified in Step 1, the researcher presents to the sample of customers a variety of hypothetical products that contain different configurations of the previously identified attributes, each configuration having a different price. Thus, for the example of the chemical compound, the hypothetical product configurations in Table 10.1 might be constructed.

Clearly, there are many different combinations of attribute levels. Only two examples are given here but they will be sufficient to demonstrate the concept of a trade-off. The question put to the survey respondents is: 'Given that the two alternative products above are available, which would you prefer?' Both products have their advantages and their disadvantages, and the final choice will be based on the trade-off of the pluses and minuses. By extending the questioning to include other configurations of the same attributes it is possible, using conjoint analysis, to produce a numerical 'weight' for each attribute that reflects the relative importance attached to each of the attributes in question. More specifically, it enables the researcher to identify for each attribute the weight given to different *levels* of that

Table 10.1 Attribute levels

Attribute	Product 1	Product 2
Quality	Impurities less than one part per million	Impurities less than ten parts per million
Availability	Make to order	Available from stock
Impact on customer's production economies	No impact	Improves usable output by 10 per cent
Storage conditions	Stable product, long shelf life	Requires high level storage environment
Technical assistance	Manufacturer provides high-level technical advice	Weak
Price	£5 a pound	£5.50 a pound

attribute. Thus for 'quality' it will be possible to determine the extent by which 'impurities less than one part per million' is preferred over 'impurities less than ten parts per million' – or any level of impurity in the range under consideration.

However, the greatest advantage of using conjoint analysis in this context is that it also provides the researcher with *the relative utility of different price levels*. Thus we have a means of interpreting the price equivalence of differences in the perceived values of different combinations of product attributes. Step 3 describes this procedure.

Step 3   Determining the price equivalence of value

The output of the conjoint analysis of the data collected in Step 2 might typically appear as in Figure 10.4. For each level of each attribute a 'utility' is computed and this can be graphed to give a visual indication of the importance of that attribute. More importantly, though, it enables the value of this arbitrary 'utility' measure to be given a price equivalence. It will be seen from Table 10.1 that the difference in utility between a price of £5 and £5.50 is 0.25 (that is, $1.00 - 0.75$); thus the price equivalence of one unit of 'utility' is $(£5.50 - £5)/ 0.25$, that is, £2.

Using this information we can say, for example, that a 10 per cent improvement in saleable output is worth a price difference of £1 per pound ($£2 [1.00 - 0.5]$). Again, we can say that the benefit of a stable product with a long shelf life is worth an additional £0.5 per pound ($£2 [0.75 - 0.5]$) over a product requiring a high-level storage environment.

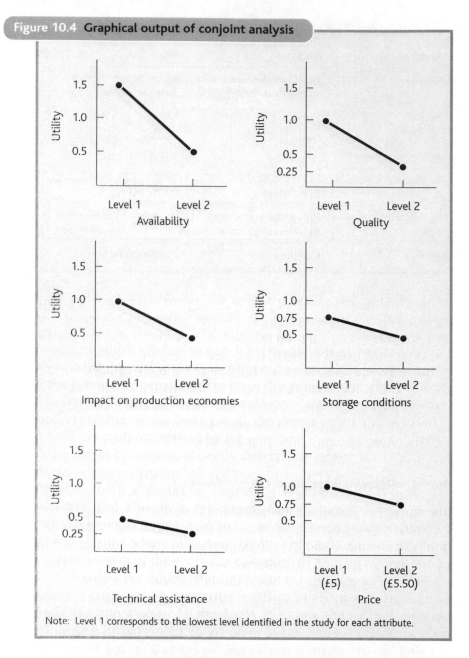

Figure 10.4 Graphical output of conjoint analysis

Note: Level 1 corresponds to the lowest level identified in the study for each attribute.

Given this information it is clear that the price decision-maker has a very powerful insight into the components of value in the customer's mind. The decision-maker can now also identify which product attributes have the biggest influence on value perception.

In the case examined here, for example, availability and quality are seen as the two major components of value. A change from Level 2 to Level 1 in availability brings an increase in utility of 1.0, and a change from Level 2 to Level 1 in quality produces an increase in utility of 0.75 (worth £2 and £1.50 per pound respectively).

This information on the 'price-equivalence' of customer values can provide a basis for price determination that reflects the worth the market places upon our offer. Perhaps one of the most important features of the value-in-use approach advocated here is that it focuses our attention on customer perceptions of product attributes and away from the narrower production orientation of suppliers' costs. In this sense it is very much a market-orientated approach to pricing.

There are also certain strategic issues raised by this approach to pricing, particularly with regard to marketing communications. It is well known that in many product/market fields there is a definite relationship between the price obtained and the perception of quality on the part of the customer. In other words, where there is a perception of 'added values', then the demand/price relationship can be altered radically. Where added values are perceived by the customer to exist, the demand curve is, in effect, shifted to the right, as in Figure 10.5.

Figure 10.5 The effect of perceived added values on the demand curve

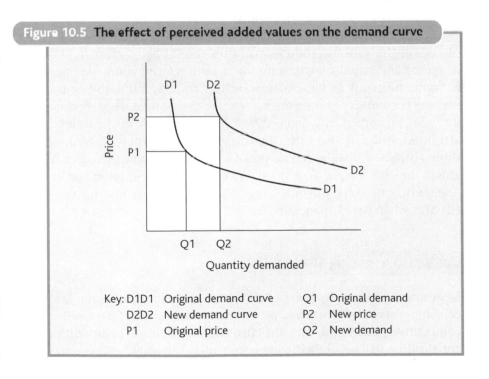

Key: D1D1 Original demand curve   Q1 Original demand
     D2D2 New demand curve   P2 New price
     P1   Original price   Q2 New demand

So, in this particular case, the effect of these heightened perceptions of customer values has been to stimulate greater demand but at a higher price.

To make use of this fundamental model for profit improvement we must recognize two basic factors:

▶ *Perception*: to what extent does the customer/potential customer perceive that our product embodies certain attributes?

▶ *Value/utility*: to what extent does the current/potential customer consider these attributes to be important in the purchase decision?

In the first case, if the perception of product performance falls below that of competitive products, what can be done? It may that the problem is largely one of communication. Perhaps we have not been forceful enough in our attempts to inform the market about the strengths of our product or, if we have, the message still has not come across. Alternatively, it may be that our product is deficient in these attributes and it may thus be desirable to institute a programme of product improvement.

If, on the other hand, we identify that our product scores highly, but on attributes that are perhaps given less weight by the customer (that is, their value/utility is lower), then we could downgrade the product on these attributes to improve overall profitability, or indeed reduce the price if appropriate. Similarly, recognizing the value/utility placed on the various product attributes should be of great help in designing and introducing new products, or in reformulating old ones.

From the point of view of marketing strategy, value-in-use can become the basis of a more effective segmentation strategy. Because different customers will have different perceptions of a product's attributes and will also differ in the value/utility they place upon those attributes, it will often be possible to target products to specific groups, or segments, in the market. Price is one of the simplest ways of segmenting markets, but price segmentation can become far more effective when based upon value-in-use.

Competitive pricing strategy

Most marketing activity takes place within the context of some level of competitive activity. Thus pricing decisions must clearly reflect competitive positioning, and the customers' perception of any differential values that are embodied in competitive offerings.

At one extreme is a market with one dominant supplier – say a 40 per cent market share to the nearest rival with 15 per cent – and where that dominant supplier has an offer that is high in perceived added values, then it is likely that a substantial price differential could be obtained. On the other hand, if there is no single dominant player in market share terms, and the market is effectively a 'commodity' market with no perceived product differences, then it is highly unlikely that any single supplier could command a higher price.

In any competitive market place the following relationship will normally hold:

$$\frac{\text{Perceived benefits (market leader)}}{\text{Price (market leader)}} \geq \frac{\text{Perceived benefits (competitor)}}{\text{Price (competitor)}}$$

In other words, to maintain a position of market share leadership, the ratio of price to perceived benefits must exceed that of the competition. Using this relationship it will be recognized that it is not enough to have a high level of perceived benefits if the competition has a substantially lower price. It will sometimes be the case that a supplier may develop an offer with substantial added values and sell it at a higher price, but in so doing will provide competitors with a price umbrella under which they can shelter while developing 'me too' products. The success of the so-called IBM–PC clones in the personal computer market provides a testament to this.

The position of the product in relation to the market life cycle will also be important in determining pricing strategy. Given the importance of maintaining or increasing market share in the early stages of the life-cycle as a means of increasing the speed of movement down the experience curve – to ensure both higher profitability and cash flow as the market matures – careful attention must be paid to the benefit/price ratio.

In the past, marketing authors have distinguished between *skimming* strategies and *penetration* strategies, particularly in the context of pricing new products. It has been suggested that a penetration strategy (that is, a low relative price) is a route to early gains in market share if:

▶ demand is price sensitive;
▶ economies of scale exist; and
▶ Competitive imitation is not difficult.

An example of such a pricing strategy might be the low price established initially for the sale of domestic TV satellite dishes.

Alternatively, it is argued that a skimming strategy (that is, a high relative price) could be appropriate, where:

► demand is not particularly price sensitive;
► there is a relatively flat cost curve (that is, unit costs at low volumes are not so much higher than unit costs at higher volumes); and
► There is limited danger of competitive imitation.

The pricing policy adopted by Rolex watches is perhaps an example of this skimming approach.

Figure 10.6 suggests the possible pricing strategies that may be appropriate given the opportunities for value enhancement or cost reduction. Value enhancement is a strategy based on building perceived benefits, while cost reduction can provide the basis for successful price competition. The rationale behind each of these options can be demonstrated by the use of the experience curve concept. As we have seen, it is usually the case that penetration strategies are more appropriate where the opportunity for cost reduction is greatest – that is, rapid movement down a steeply sloping experience curve can be achieved.

On the other hand, a skimming strategy is more likely to be appropriate where rapid cost reductions are unlikely – that is, the experience curve is less steep. Figure 10.7 outlines the logic of each of the four pricing options.

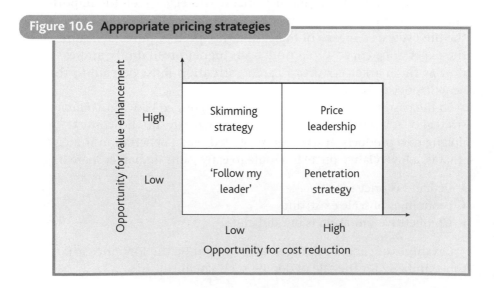

Figure 10.6 Appropriate pricing strategies

Figure 10.7 Price and the experience curve

(a) **Follow my leader**

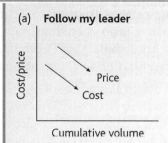

In this situation the industry price will follow costs and, in particular, the costs of the price leader

(b) **Penetration strategy**

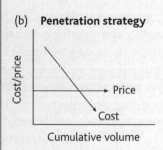

Here price is set low by the early entrant to gain advantage of the price-sensitive market and thus gain market share and hence lower costs

(c) **Skimming strategy**

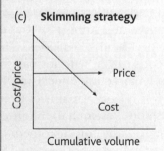

Under a skimming strategy it is assumed that the cost reduction opportunities are low, hence less steep experience curve

(d) **Price leadership**

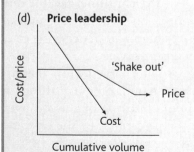

Through a combination of high added value plus low cost, these companies are able to bring down the price 'umbrella' and shake out the less innovative or higher-cost competitors

Note: All these charts assume logarithmic scales, hence the experience 'curve' is shown as a straight line.

Ultimately, however, neither a skimming nor a penetration policy will lead to a position of substantial market leadership unless the benefit price ratio is maintained at a higher level than that of the competition. The achievement of a favourite ratio is obviously not down to pricing strategy alone, but can only come about through a total focus of the marketing mix on differentiation while managing the operations of the business to provide a cost advantage.

Relationship pricing

It has sometimes been suggested that we have entered the era of the 'value driven' customer. This customer seeks even greater delivered benefits but at lower cost. Customers such as these can be found in every type of market, be it business-to-business or end-user. Price sensitivity seems to be as high as it has ever been, and customers are often quite willing to move from one supplier to another if the price/value equation does not appeal to them.

To counteract this tendency, companies such as Procter & Gamble have developed a philosophy of value-based pricing. Under value-based pricing, the customer (and the consumer) is offered a guaranteed lower price through the elimination of non-value-adding activities or strategies such as frequent promotions or brand extensions. The underpinning idea is that customers (or consumers) will not pay for non-value-adding activities or elements of a marketing offer. Thus, in the USA, Procter & Gamble used to offer over twenty variants of Crest toothpaste – different sizes, flavours and so on. Research highlighted that such variety did not create additional value for customers or consumers. In fact, the customers (the retailers) were not prepared to find shelf-space for such a range, and at the consumer level it only served to focus on the best selling variants. This meant that significant complexity was taken out of the supply chain and hence costs came down without any loss of customer or consumer value.

In ways such as these, lower prices can be charged while margins are maintained. Customer relationships are built on many things, as we have observed throughout this book, but one of the strongest drivers of an enduring relationship is the perception by the customer that this supplier delivers 'more for less'.

Value-based pricing, or 'everyday low price' (EDLP) as it has been termed, is not just applicable in retail markets. In business-to-business markets the quest for value on the part of customers is just as great.

Often this leads to 'deals' being offered by suppliers that are not based on cost reduction and are thus not sustainable. The key to 'everyday low price' in this environment is for both parties to collaborate in the search for genuine cost reduction through process improvement to enable prices to fall while margins are preserved. There is now a growing recognition in many industries that a partnership between buyer and supplier is a better way to achieve enduring cost reduction than the previous strategy of the customer playing one supplier off against another.

International pricing management

One of the most striking trends in recent years has been the rapid increase in the globalization of markets. Not only is this true in the case of well-established brands such as Coca-Cola, Marlboro and Gucci, but it is also apparent in markets as diverse as computing, motor cars and consumer electronics. Nor is the trend towards globalization confined only to products, we see similar transformations in services, whether it be banking, retailing or satellite TV.

At the same time, the corporations that have created and developed these global brands are refocusing their operations so that they too are global in their scope. What this means is that an electronics company, for example, may source some of its components in one country, sub-assemble in another, and with final assembly taking place in a third country. Managing these complex global networks becomes one of the prime challenges to the achievement of profitability.

The impact of this move towards the globalization of business on the pricing decision is substantial. First, there are implications for the cost of the product or service, and second, it is quite likely that there will be significant differences from country to country in the price sensitivity of demand. Let us consider both of these issues in turn.

Cost implications of global sourcing

As we have noted, there is an increasing tendency for organizations to source materials, and assemble and manufacture items offshore. The motivation for this is largely economic, based on the search for cost reductions. These lower costs may be available through lower labour rates, lower costs of material, lower taxes, lower costs of capital, or government assistance. At the same time, these organizations may also rationalize production so that individual country operations no longer produce a full range of products for their own national markets. Instead, the company may now focus production on fewer factories making a limited range of items, but for a regional or even global market. The opportunities for enhanced economies of scale in production through such strategies may be considerable. Companies such as Unilever, for example, which previously manufactured soaps and detergents in local factories for local markets, have now rationalised their production on a regional basis with fewer factories producing for wider markets.

While the advantages of such strategies seem to be readily apparent, there are a number of implications for pricing.

Exchange-rate fluctuations

Given the volatility of exchange rates between currencies, there is a considerable inherent risk in companies committing themselves to long-term offshore supply arrangements. Companies with the ability to switch production from one location to another at short notice clearly have an advantage. For example, Heinz can increase or decrease production of tomato ketchup in their regional plants with a high degree of flexibility in order to take advantage of exchange-rate fluctuations. Companies that lack this flexibility can often find themselves faced with substantial cost increases as a result of changes in exchange rates.

Changes in factor costs

Closely allied to the risk of exchange rate fluctuation is the problem of changes in factor costs such as labour, land or capital. Many companies decided to locate production in what were perceived to be low-labour-cost countries, often in South-East Asia, only to find that, with rapid economic development, the advantage proved to be transitory. Also to be taken into account is the way in which the costs of transport from the source of supply to the end market can change, in some instances eliminating any production cost advantage.

Transfer pricing

In complex, multi-level production and distribution systems within a single company, the issue of internal transfer pricing arises. In other words, at what internal price should products or supplies be 'sold' to the next stage in the chain? Sometimes these decisions will be determined by tax considerations, but often there will be other factors influencing the transfer price, such as internal accounting practices that might allocate overhead costs on some arbitrary basis, hence distorting the cost that is passed on down the chain. There are countless examples of companies that have been forced to charge higher prices in end markets because of an accumulated cost that reflects the real costs of supply.

Parallel imports

Often, identical products may be sold in different markets at different prices. This practice, known to economists as 'price discrimination', is made possible because of the different demand and supply characteristics in the different markets. However, once the price difference between markets exceeds the cost of acquiring and transporting those products from one market to another, then arbitrage or 'parallel imports' can become a serious problem for the company. This is a phenomenon that is encountered frequently in both consumer and industrial markets. One partial solution to this problem is to develop a unique brand for individual markets, but this may not allow economies of scale in sourcing, production and distribution to be achieved.

Global/regional purchasing

In the same way that suppliers are tending to operate on a global, or at least regional, basis, so too are their customers. If a major European retailer, for example, sees that a product is being sold by a manufacturer at a lower price in one market (because of supply/demand considerations), then that retailer may insist on buying that product at a price for the markets in which it operates. This will become more of a problem for suppliers as increasing numbers of customers band together into regional or global buying groups. Across Europe, a number of such groups already exist, particularly in grocery retailing.

A further challenge to international pricing management arises where the same brand may be positioned quite differently in different national markets. Stella Artois is a premium-priced lager in the UK, for example, whereas in its home country of Belgium it is seen as a 'regular' beer sold at standard prices.

Given these potential problems, what are the options for a company seeking to develop an international pricing strategy? The overriding consideration, as with pricing decisions generally, is that the price must reflect the value proposition that is presented to the customer in each market in which the product is offered. Based on this, the 'target cost' for the market can be identified – that is, the achievable price less the desired profit margin. Decisions on sourcing must be taken in the context of that target cost, taking into account total supply chain costs – preferably undistorted by transfer pricing manipulations. No pricing strategy will eliminate the risks we have identified above, but careful and continuous management of the pricing decision on a global basis will help to minimize them.

Summary

The pricing decision is one of the most important issues to be faced by the marketing manager. Almost every market is influenced to some extent by the relative price of the products competing in that market.

When customers buy products they are making choices based on their perception of the relative value of competing offers. The maximum price at which a product or service can be sold can be no greater than its perceived value.

It is proposed that price should be related to the value of benefits that our product or service delivers. Techniques such as trade-off analysis can be utilized to assist in the pricing decisions, particularly in the valuation of benefits.

Further reading

Diamantopoulos, A. (1991) Pricing: theory and evidence – a literature review, in M. Baker (ed.), *Perspectives on Marketing Management*, Vol. I, John Wiley, London.

Simon, H. (1992) Pricing opportunities – and how to exploit them. *Sloan Management Review* (Winter), pp. 55–65

References

Christopher, M. (1982) Value-in-use pricing. *European Journal of Marketing*, **16 (5)**, pp. 35–47.

11 Communication strategy

In this chapter we study the:

- ▶ The critical role of marketing communications
- ▶ The communications mix
- ▶ The difference between personal and impersonal communications
- ▶ The distinction between advertising and marketing objectives
- ▶ The implications of integrated marketing communications
- ▶ The corporate communications audit and the communication process
- ▶ The factors effecting media selection

Communications are critical

The role of marketing communications is to inform the market clearly and persuasively about the company, its products and services. As businesses compete in a progressively fiercer market place for a larger wallet share of an increasingly discerning and diverse customer base, they become ever more communication-dependent. The emergence of relationship marketing, customer relationship management, and various other marketing disciplines underline this point.

The field of marketing communications has seen dramatic changes since the 1980s, not least the unprecedented advances in marketing technologies. The ubiquitous Internet, ingenious smart cards, sophisticated customer databases, easily accessible data warehouses, and cost-effective direct mail have all contributed to a quantum leap in the quantity and quality of information exchanged between companies and their customers. Through information and communications technology (ICT), the pace of exchange has reached lightning speed and the costs of information processing have plummeted. The impact on the everyday lives of businesses and individuals has been profound.

While such developments afford tremendous opportunities for customizing product and service offerings and securing a competitive edge, they also spawn new challenges. Heightened customer and stakeholder expectations have raised the bar on industry benchmarks and standards of practice. Interactive dialogue has rendered market ignorance or complacency intolerable. Media bombardment and information overload has numbed individuals' receptivity to messages, and we are seriously at risk of 'throwing the baby out with the bath water'.

On the positive side, the shift from mass communications to individualized communications has seen greater customer involvement with particular goods and services, and better marketing use of a wider range of media channels and communication tools. Companies can now 'connect' with current and prospective customers in far more ways than was possible in the early 1990s. Consumer enthusiasm for new media, exemplified by the escalation in e-mail, discussion groups, data interchange and downloading, online advertisements and linked websites all provide new means for developing, strengthening and influencing relationships with customers, as well as other stakeholders and even competitors.

Given this climate of constant market change and growing market complexity, the need for marketers to convey information and ideas appropriately and evoke understanding is immense. There is no dispute: communications are critical.

The communications mix

In order to achieve its marketing objectives, an organization has to communicate with both existing and potential customers. It can do so in a variety of ways, either on an impersonal or a personal basis. Impersonal communication is accomplished indirectly, using advertising, sales promotion, point-of-sale displays and public relations, while personal communication is undertaken directly, in face-to-face meetings, generally using a sales force. (These represent the promotion 'P' in the marketing mix.)

The armoury of communication techniques at the organization's disposal, which might be used singly or in combination, can be blended together into an effective and persuasive *communications mix*. The choice of communications mix should be the most cost-effective solution for achieving the organization's communication objectives. These are derived from its marketing objectives, which in turn originated from its corporate objectives. Table 11.1 lists some common communication objectives.

Table 11.1 Common communication objectives

Educating and informing	Create awareness Promote understanding Inform Get enquiries	
Branding and image building	Get company name in file Create company image Reach personnel inaccessible to salespeople	The chosen communication objective(s) must contribute towards a total marketing programme, the objective of which is to achieve profitable sales
Affecting attitudes	Ease the selling task Get editorial Overcome prejudice Influence end users	
Encouraging loyalty/ affinity and reminding	Reduce selling costs Achieve sales (including repeat sales) Generate customer referrals	

Marketing-communication objectives should be concise statements of exactly what we wish to convey to the intended recipients. It will be seen that these objectives are highly specific, and are not expressed in terms of sales results, which are themselves influenced by the combined effects of the marketing mix and not just by the communications programme. The communication objectives (what we want to communicate) will then determine the communication strategy (how best to it). Figure 11.1 shows the correct position of communication strategy in the planning process.

From Figure 11.1 it is clear that the communication strategy is supported by a number of sub-objectives and strategies relating to the different communication tools employed. As the realm of personal communication (that is, word of mouth and use of the sales force – or 'personal selling') is covered in Chapters 13 and 15, respectively, this chapter will focus on impersonal communications. The two foremost methods of indirect marketing communication are *advertising* and *sales promotion*. It should come as no surprise, then, that the three components of the communications plan – the detailed articulation of the communication objectives and strategies – are the sales plan, the advertising plan, and the sales promotion plan (see Figure 6.4). Appropriately, the latter two are discussed here, while the sales plan is considered in Chapter 15.

Figure 11.1 Communication strategy in the planning process

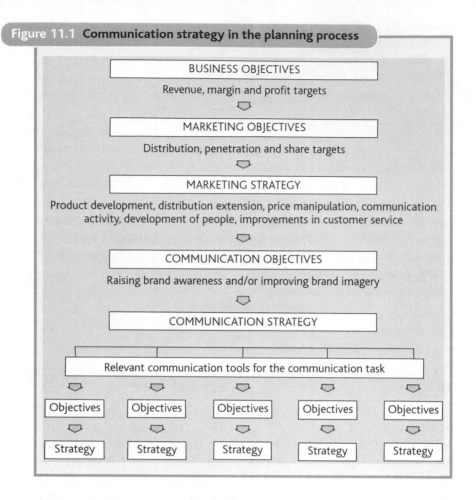

The figure contains:

BUSINESS OBJECTIVES
Revenue, margin and profit targets

MARKETING OBJECTIVES
Distribution, penetration and share targets

MARKETING STRATEGY
Product development, distribution extension, price manipulation, communication activity, development of people, improvements in customer service

COMMUNICATION OBJECTIVES
Raising brand awareness and/or improving brand imagery

COMMUNICATION STRATEGY

Relevant communication tools for the communication task

Objectives | Objectives | Objectives | Objectives | Objectives

Strategy | Strategy | Strategy | Strategy | Strategy

Advertising

Advertising (often referred to as 'above-the-line expenditure') uses measured media such as television, cinema, radio, print and electronic media (for example, banner advertising on websites). The usual assumption is that advertising is deployed in an aggressive way, and that all that changes over time is the creative content. But the role of advertising usually alters during the life-cycle of a product. For example, the process of persuasion (awareness, interest, attitude formation, decision to act) cannot normally start until there is some level of awareness about a product or service in the market place. Creating awareness is therefore one of the most important objectives of the company in the product life-cycle. If the offer has been matched correctly with customer needs and is perceived to be superior to competitors' offers, through the astute use of such vehicles as branding, pricing or customer-convenient distribution, then the customer will be persuaded to buy.

The 'diffusion of innovation' curve discussed in Chapter 8 is relevant here. Experience indicates that once the first 3 per cent of innovators have adopted the product, the early adopters will probably try it, and once the 8–10 per cent point is reached, the rest will be likely to follow suit. This pattern demonstrates the need for different kinds of advertising for each category of customer, and thus different sets of advertising objectives and strategies for different stages in a product's life-cycle. It is worth remembering too that, for optimum effect, advertising effort can be directed not only at consumers, but also at all those who influence commercial success, including channels, shareholders, media, employees, suppliers and government.

The acid test for confirming whether an objective is suitable as an advertising objective is to ask: 'Is it possible to achieve this objective by advertising alone?' If the answer is *no*, then it is not an objective for advertising.

A common misconception is that advertising objectives should be set in terms of sales increases. As advertising is one of a host of determinants of sales levels (which also includes product quality, price and customer service, for example), sales increases cannot be a direct objective of advertising. It is also important to be clear on the distinction between marketing objectives and advertising objectives. Marketing objectives are concerned with what products go to which markets, whereas advertising objectives are measurable targets concerned principally with changing attitudes and creating awareness.

There are two basic questions that advertising objectives should address: 'Who are the people we are trying to influence?' and 'What specific benefits or information are we trying to communicate to them?' Many companies use outside agencies to design their advertising. Advertising objectives, however, should *always* be set by the advertiser and *not* by an advertising agency.

There are many possible advertising objectives, such as to:

▶ convey information;
▶ alter perceptions;
▶ alter attitudes;
▶ create desires;
▶ establish connections (for example, the association of bacon with egg);

- direct actions;
- provide reassurance;
- remind;
- give reasons for buying;
- demonstrate; and
- generate enquiries.

Having defined and agreed the advertising objectives, all other steps in the process of assembling the advertising strategy then flow naturally from them. These subsequent steps address the following questions, which essentially form the process of producing the advertising plan:

WHO	... are the target audience(s)?
(*target*)	What do they already know, feel, believe about us and our product/service?
	What do they know, feel, believe about the competition?
	What sort of people are they? How do we describe/identify them?
WHAT	... response do we wish to evoke from the target audience(s)?
(*message-copy platform*)	... are these specific communications *objectives*?
	... do we want to 'say', make them 'feel', 'believe', 'understand', 'know', about buying/using our product/service
	... are we offering?
	... do we *not* want to convey?
	... are the priorities of importance of our objectives?
	... are the objectives whish are *written down* and *agreed* by the company and advertising agency?
HOW	... are our objectives to be embodied in an appealing form?
(*creative platform*)	What is our creative strategy/platform?
	What evidence do we have that this is acceptable and appropriate to our audience(s)?
WHERE (*media*)	... is/are the most cost-effective place(s) to expose our communications (in cost terms *vis-à-vis* our audience)?
	... is/are the most beneficial place(s) for our communications (in expected response terms *vis-à-vis* the 'quality' of the channels available)?

WHEN
(*timing*)
	... are our communications to be displayed/conveyed to our audience?
	What is the reasoning for our scheduling of advertisements/communications over time?
	What constraints limit our freedom of choice?
	Do we have to fit in with other promotional activity on:
	    other products/services supplied by our company?
	    competitors' products/services?
	    seasonal trends?
	    special events in the market?

RESULT (*performance success*)	What results do we expect? How would we measure results? Do we intend to measure results and, if so, do we need to do anything *beforehand*? If we cannot say how we would measure precise results, then perhaps our objectives are not sufficiently specific, or are not communication objectives? How are we going to judge the relative success of our communication activities (good/bad/indifferent)? Should we have action standards?
BUDGET (*investment*)	How much money do the intended activities need? How much money is going to be made available? How are we going to control expenditure?
SCHEDULE (*putting it all together*)	Who is to do what, and when? What is being spent on what, where and when?

There are three key points to remember about advertising:

1 *Advertising is an integral part of the marketing effort and must never be seen as an isolated activity*. Its effectiveness will depend not only upon the persuasiveness of the message being conveyed to customers and consumers, but also on the accuracy with which the target audience has been selected. Clearly, any product or service can offer several different benefits; for example, it can be newer, safer, cheaper, more efficient, or unique. Each of these benefits will have more, or less, appeal to different customer groups. Targeting the right message to the right people is the key to successful advertising.

2 *The most impressive, elaborate and indulgent campaign will not convince customers and consumers to buy again if the product or service, whose virtues the advertising extols, is non-competitive.* Advertising alone rarely produces long-lasting marketing success. While it will encourage, reinforce a message and perhaps even help to develop a loyalty to a particular product or service, it will be no substitute for an offering that fails to bestow the necessary benefits on a customer.

3 *Advertising can be subject to controls or constraints from one country to another.* For example, in the Netherlands, confectionery advertisements must be followed by exhortations to brush one's teeth. Cigarette advertising is banned in many countries. In the wake of AIDS, the advertising of condoms is only beginning to be allowed in some countries, and even so there are considerable differences in what is permissible. Cultural mores and sensitivities have a part to play concerning what is and what is not acceptable.

Sales promotion

Sales promotion (often referred to as 'below-the-line expenditure') is non-face-to-face activity concerned with the promotion of sales. It is essentially a problem-solving activity designed to encourage customers to behave more in line with the economic interests of the company – that is, to bring forward their decision to buy. Sales promotion involves the making of a featured offer to defined customers within a specific time limit. The offer must include benefits not inherent in the product or service, as opposed to the intangible benefits offered in advertising, such as adding value through appeals to imagery.

Typical tasks for sales promotion include controlling stock movement; counteracting competitive activity; encouraging repeat purchase; securing marginal buyers; getting bills paid on time; and inducing trial purchase. It is generally used as a short-term, tactical initiative, in contrast with the notion of advertising as a long-term, strategic activity that changes with the PLC. However, sales promotion does have a strategic role to play in helping to strengthen the bond between seller and buyer, and thus a sales promotion strategy is required to ensure that each promotion increases the effectiveness of the next in terms of impact and investment of resources. Further, it is possible to establish a style of sales promotion that, if applied consistently, will help to establish the objectives of a product over a long period of time, such objectives will be flexible and have staying power.

Confusion about what sales promotion is often results in expenditure not being properly recorded. Sales promotion expenditure is sometimes considered, for example, as advertising or sales force expenditure, or as a general marketing expense, while loss of revenue from special price reductions is often not recorded at all. Not surprisingly, sales promotion is notorious for being one of the most mismanaged of all marketing functions. In order to manage sales promotion expenditure effectively, it is essential that objectives for sales promotion be established, in the same way that objectives are developed for advertising, pricing or distribution. These will be dependent on the company's marketing objectives and may relate to any of the four 'P's.

Sales promotion seeks to influence:

Salespeople to sell

Customers to buy

Customers to use   more, earlier, faster, etc.

Users to buy

Users to use

Distributors to stock

In order to achieve these objectives, the promotion can take one of three forms. It can involve:

- money (price reductions, coupons, competitions);
- goods (free goods – for example, two for the price of one, trade-ins, free trials, redeemable coupons and so on); and
- services (guarantees, training, prizes for events, free services and so on).

When determining the nature of the sales promotion, the decision should be made first about which target group(s) need to be influenced most to make an impact on the sales problem, and, second, what type of promotion will have maximum appeal to that group. When considering the cost element, it must be remembered that the promotional costs have to be weighed against the benefits of reducing the sales problem – which the sales promotion is intended to solve. The cost-effectiveness of the sales promotion must be established and integrated into the overall marketing plan.

The objectives for each sales promotion should be stated clearly, such as trial, repeat purchase, distribution, a shift in buying peaks, combating competition, and so on. Then the strategy to implement the objectives must be worked out. Sales promotion strategy should follow the standard route of selecting the appropriate sales promotion technique; pre-testing; mounting the promotion; and, finally, evaluating in depth. Spending must be analysed and categorized by type of activity (for example, special packaging, special point-of-sale material, loss of revenue through price reductions, and so on).

As for the sales promotion plan itself, the objectives, strategy and brief details of timing and costs should be included. It is important that the sales promotion plan should not be too detailed, and only an outline of it should appear in the marketing plan. (Detailed promotional instructions will follow as the marketing plan unfurls.) It is also important to ensure that any sales promotion is well co-ordinated in terms of what happens before, during and after the promotion. At different stages, different people might be participating, and special resources might be required. Therefore the plan needs to be prepared in a simple way that all involved can follow. See Table 11.2 for what a sales promotion plan should contain.

Table 11.2 Sales promotion plan

Heading	Content
Introduction	Briefly summarize the problem on which the promotion is designed to make an impact
Objectives	Show how the objectives of the promotion are consistent with the marketing objectives
Background	Provide the relevant data or justification for the promotion
Promotional offer	Briefly, but precisely, provide details of the offer
Eligibility	Who is eligible? Where?
Timing	When is the offer available (opening and closing dates)
Date plan	The dates and responsibilities for all elements of promotion
Support	Special materials, samples, etc. required by the sales force, retailers and so on
Administration	Budgets, storage, invoicing, delivery and so on
Sales plan	Briefing meetings, targets, incentives and so on
Sales presentation	Points to be covered
Sales reporting	Any special information required
Assessment	How the promotion will be evaluated

Other communication tools and trends

There are a number of other indirect communication tools available to marketers. These range from conventional methods, such as point-of-sale displays, exhibitions and PR, to more contemporary techniques, such as direct mail, database marketing and interactive media.

Point-of-sale displays

Point-of-sale displays are sometimes called 'the silent salesman'. They can communicate valuable marketing information as well as contributing to sales. Attractively presented and placed in strategic locations, they can be a low-cost means of catching the eye of potential customers. However, the products on display must be suitably packaged, and the dispenser or showcase be designed for safety. It must also contain references to product price and how to obtain further information or advice.

Exhibitions

Exhibitions are becoming increasingly expensive to mount, and therefore companies have to ensure they going to get good value for their investment. While an exhibition offers the prospect of many potential customers making contact with a company without the sales team having to go out looking for them, this will not happen by chance. The stand will have to be designed to attract attention and interest. Stand staff will have to demonstrate high levels of skill and ask questions to ensure that they are using their valuable time with genuine prospects, and not with mere sightseers, or, as is often the case, staff from competing companies. There will have to be suitable sales aids and supporting material available, together with back-up systems to ensure that all prospects receive an appropriate follow-up.

Public relations

Public relations, or PR, is concerned with an organization's relationships with various groups, or 'publics', that affect its ability to achieve its goals and objectives. The aspects of these relationships that act as a focus for public relations are the image and information a market

245

holds about an organization (that is, its position in the market). At a simple level, this is achieved through publicity in various print and broadcast media. At a broader level, as encouraged by relationship marketing, this is achieved through activities that are more specific in their targeting and objectives.

PR includes the areas of: news generation, events, publications, sponsorships and donations, 'expert opinion' (individual endorsement by a knowledgeable representative of the organization), and 'visual identity' (identification or association through product design, logos, trademarks and so on). Increasingly, the PR function is becoming as much a means of personal communication as it is of impersonal communication. Many PR opportunities are used to stimulate personal contact with customers as well as to attract an impersonal response. While PR messages can be far more influential than advertising, PR is unlikely to replace advertising or other means of communication and promotion.

Internal marketing

Internal marketing is gaining credence as a vital communication tool as internal communications play an increasingly critical role in changing, reinforcing or questioning prevailing strategy and corporate culture. The perceptions held by management, staff, shareholders and partners about the organization throughout the value chain have a profound impact on the nature and future of relevant business relationships. It is therefore essential that all members of an organization's 'sphere of influence' are aware of the organization's intentions and actions, and are working towards common goals.

A seamless customer experience relies on the operation of a shared 'corporate memory' of the customer, which replicates the customer's own memory of encounters with the business. This means that all messages sent must be coherent and consistent, as well as customer-relevant, and that all incoming messages must lodged and responded to in a suitable, professional manner. The issue of messages that are conflicting or confusing, unnecessarily repetitive or outright inappropriate can do more harm than good. It is also important that all are invited to contribute constructive input through the appropriate processes. The role of internal 'people power' in corporate communications is developed later in this book.

Direct mail

Direct mail is much less haphazard than it once was, because of advances in technology and marketing thinking. However, a direct mail campaign has to be conceived carefully to stand any chance of being successful. Traditionally, direct approaches through the post have had very low response rates, but in recent times companies have become more adept at targeting their mailshots. One reason for this is the growth of, and access to, sophisticated techniques for analysing target prospects. Most prominent among these is database marketing.

Database marketing

Database marketing has gained popularity as access to technology has made it cheaper and easier to store and manipulate massive amounts of data. With the fragmentation of market segments on the increase, it is increasingly important for organizations to treat customers as individuals. Marketing information held about both the company's customers and competitor's customers is now a vital part of the marketer's toolbox. In the past, such information constituted mere mailing lists. Today, customers' names and addresses can be assimilated with other data, such as geo-demographics, and credit, lifestyle, smart card and transactional data to give marketers an in-depth insight into customers' behaviour patterns. Customer profiling is emerging as an important new approach in developing dialogue with individual customers. More about database marketing and related activities is given in Chapter 19.

Interactive media

The Internet as a marketing medium provides an ideal platform for one-to-one communication, enabling instantaneous and interactive exchange around the globe at relatively little cost. In addition to offering individualized benefits, such as convenience, 24/7 availability and self-service functions, the facilities of e-mail and discussion groups mean that self-nominated alliances and networks (of suppliers or customers) can grow rapidly. The use of on-screen computer prompts by customer service operatives optimizes the customer experience and allows further customer data to be captured and assimilated into future interactions.

The Internet can be used to promote and sell products/services, and to offer information, as well as to augment offerings through links to other websites. Some business-to-business companies have also used it to build close relationships with customers in technological markets. For instance, one manufacturer of highly complex controls for energy plants has created a virtual building site on its web page, which gives information on installation and safety regulations for recent purchasers. The Internet has proved itself to be a unique and effective tool for personalizing marketing communications.

Brand management

Brand management might reasonably be included here as a significant communication tool. As discussed in Chapter 9, branding is a powerful means of communicating the values of an organization as well as the value delivered by its products or services. Corporate and brand image is being recognized increasingly as a major influence on sales. In the commercial world, where it can be technically simple and financially tempting to duplicate a competitor's offering, the creation of a favourable or distinct/different image may give the company a competitive advantage. Truly effective brand management not only communicates existing value, but also works to create and communicate future value.

Having outlined some of the traditional and more recent tools found within the marketing communications toolbox, let us look at the development of integrated marketing communications (IMC) as a means of utilizing and managing these tools effectively.

Integrated marketing communications (IMC)

Ultimately, integrated marketing communications (IMC) is the strategic co-ordination of all marketing messages and the alignment of all methods of communicating with customers, be they consumers or other targeted, relevant (external and internal) audiences. IMC has evolved as marketers have moved away from traditional mass-media-based communications strategies towards those that are more personalized, customer-orientated and technology-driven.

Perhaps the most useful way to define integrated marketing communications is to illustrate what happens when a marketing campaign is not integrated. The marketing communications activities of the personal computer and software markets provide such an example. Companies such as Apple, Tiny and Microsoft spend millions of pounds on advertising and direct mail in order to increase consumer awareness of their brands. The point of sale, usually with a dealer, is full of sales promotion activities designed to persuade the customers to upgrade their equipment or purchase more powerful programs, and to benefit from improved software support and other ancillary services.

However, once the purchase transaction has been completed, the consumer soon realizes that the marketing messages they received prior to the purchase concerning customer service provision do not ring true. There have been many instances where customers have had to hold on a telephone helpline for more than two or three hours to speak with a service operator, only to learn there is no opportunity for dialogue or redress, despite advertising campaigns to the contrary. In this case, dialogue has been encouraged through promotion, but the company has failed to integrate its services and provide an effective feedback loop to deal with customer concerns and requests for help. The result is a seriously frustrated customer and a relationship heading for breakdown.

One of the main aims of IMC is to harmonize the promotional tools so that audiences receive a consistent and substantiated message. Integration within marketing communications works on two main levels: the creative and the strategic.

Creative Integration

The paradigm shift from a transaction to a customer focus acknowledges that *all* marketing is about communication, because people form their images of brands and companies from information provided by a variety of sources. One of the most important aspects of IMC is that it encourages a view of marketing communications from the customers' perspective, or as a flow of information from indistinguishable sources. Therefore the 'message', as opposed to the delivery, has to be the central focus of IMC. If different types of marketing communications are used to support brand positioning, they must work together in a synergistic fashion. Case study 11.1 provides an example of an IMC campaign that set out to achieve this integrated creativity.

Case study 11.1 BMW embraces creative integration

Companies that are confident about their marketing message have found that an integrated, creative approach to communicating it can bring real benefits. BMW employed an integrated marketing campaign in the launch of its Z3 roadster. By using its established agencies in a co-ordinated manner, BMW managed to explore a wider range of media opportunities than it had done previously. Central to the success of the campaign was ensuring that every agency understood the brand values of the car and the significance of the launch of the company's first smaller sports car.

Exploiting the car's product placement in the current James Bond movie, 'Goldeneye', three agencies worked together on a globally integrated marketing campaign that created a cult image of the product. Research had shown that targeted customers would be wary of any 'cheapening' or devaluing of the BMW brand, so it was essential that the feeling of exclusivity, quality and high status enveloped the vehicle's debut. The Bond link-up was seen as being perfect for the launch of the 'hottest new sports car of the decade', as the secret agent was associated all over the world with driving exciting cars and pursuing a thrilling, exotic and glamorous lifestyle.

The marketing campaign featured television advertisements and posters that delivered news of the coinciding launches of both the film and the car. In addition, customized dealer brochures were sent in electro-static bags marked 'Top Secret', which, when opened, gave off a green flash similar to that experienced by Bond in the film. The special brochures were also sent to existing BMW customers in recognition of their expressed affinity for the brand. The dealer network was involved in local premieres of the film, which included champagne receptions attended by local BMW customers. Combined with an effective local and national PR campaign, the 'Goldeneye' launch of the new BMW sports car achieved a high quality, consistent delivery of the marketing message.

Kate Wheaton at Evans Hunt Scott commented that a close alliance and working relationship with WCRS, the advertising agency, was possible because BMW is such a strong brand. There was no dissonance with any of the creative messages we all produced. Martin Runacles, BMW Marketing Director at that time, concluded that the integrated marketing strategy achieved a greater increase in brand awareness and customer retention levels among existing customers than a non-IMC campaign would have achieved. BMW's UK order books were quickly filled and, although the car was launched at the end of 1996, there was a six-month waiting list.

Strategic integration

As well as requiring creative synergy, there are also managerial implications for adopting an IMC strategy. Although IMC is now recognized as a distinct business process, the debate continues as to the role of IMC orchestrator. Should a client company place its entire marketing communications requirement with one agency, or should it instead engage a variety of specialists and retain control centrally?

The fact that agencies have been offering a range of communication services in-house is seen by many as a rush to diversify in order to retain profit margins as client spending shifts emphasis from advertising to 'below the line'. This trend has led some to argue that IMC is merely a repackaging of the full service agency ideal of the 1960s, similar to BBDO's 'seamless communications', or Young and Rubicam's 'whole egg' approach. But these were really more of a 'one-stop shopping' strategy by the agency suppliers, who understood that integration requires the overall marketing strategy, communication strategy and creative execution to be aligned.

Research has shown that the majority of marketers believe the orchestration of IMC should be undertaken by the marketers themselves. Success in this endeavour, however, is dependent on cross-functional collaboration in managing the marketing communications, preferably through the establishment of a functionally representative, dedicated team. It is also reliant on there being a 'corporate memory' of customer relationships, so that everyone in the organization has the same recollection and experience of the relationship as the customer, and no conflicting or repetitive messages are sent.

Whether or not the organization's marketing communications are integrated, or whatever the degree of integration in the organization's marketing communications, it is necessary to undertake a regular review of the communication strategy in relation to its performance and objectives in order to ensure that the marketing communications are coherent, consistent and most important, relevant.

Corporate communications audit

The corporate communications audit provides a system whereby the image of the supplying organization as perceived by its management can be compared with that held by the public or a specified target group. Often there is a divergence, and as a result of the audit detailed recommendations can be made for bringing the differing views more closely in line with each other.

The audit also produces secondary advantages. By interviewing a cross-section of staff within the organization, it soon becomes apparent if there are different perspectives on fundamental issues. Clearly, it is to the company's advantage to take corrective action to clear up any real or imagined misunderstandings. When it comes to analysing the views held about the organization by its external audiences, the divergencies of opinion are usually greater than internal differences. The audit therefore not only helps to identify inconsistencies, but, equally importantly, provides the clues for an improvement plan.

A powerful element in the corporate communications audit is the publications audit. This is a technique used to assess the effectiveness of printed and electronic (that is, website) material emanating from different parts of the company. Overall presentation and content, including text, graphics, frequency of issue and so on, are analysed in the light of their individual purposes and the overall communications strategies of the organization. Any recommendations for improvement or revision should, of course, be founded on a sound understanding of the communication process.

The communication process

The communication process can be illustrated simply by Figure 11.2. Essentially, the marketer is faced with similar communication problems to those experienced by any two people talking. The sender's message is determined largely by his or her values, knowledge, attitude and vocabulary; it could therefore be claimed to be worded in the

Figure 11.2 **The communication process**

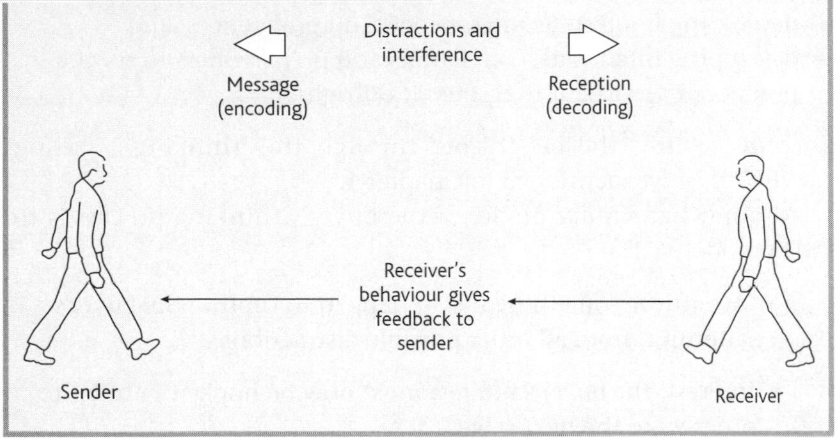

sender's personal code. If the receiver is 'tuned in' to the sender's code, because he or she shares similar values, attitudes and language, then the 'decoding' process is relatively straightforward. If he or she is not attuned to the sender's wavelength, then it is very difficult for the message to get through. The communication process is further complicated by the 'interference' that can come between the two parties. For the marketer, this may mean that the receiver is distracted, his or her attention being focused on other matters. Alternatively, the receiver may be confused by conflicting messages from competing suppliers of products or services, or may be suffering from message 'overload'.

The lessons for the marketer that stem from this simple communication model are fourfold:

► Keep the marketing message relatively simple.
► Word it in the receiver's language.
► Choose a medium/mechanism for transmitting the message that gives minimal distortion and interference.
► Know the target audience.

The important point is that, in order to design and achieve effective communication, the marketer must adopt the receiver's perspective. What types of media and messages appeal to the receiver? What mental processes take place in the receiver's mind on receipt of the message? There is evidence to suggest that the potential buyer goes through a thinking process something like this:

- becoming aware and developing understanding and knowledge (about the product or service and its supplier);
- developing interest, feelings, beliefs and preferences; and
- developing intentions, convictions and preparedness to try the product or service, or to dismiss it outright.

In other words, the buyer goes through the 'thinking', 'feeling', 'acting' cycle we mentioned in Chapter 1.

A somewhat similar model of the buyer's thinking process is the AIDA model:

A = Attention: something has to happen to capture the buyer's attention from all other possible distractions.

I = Interest: the buyer's interest must now be hooked in order to progress to the next stage.

D = Desire: a desire to own or use the product or service is generated in the buyer.

A = Action: action is required on the buyer's part to ensure that the desire becomes reality.

It is a relatively small step to combine these ideas and come up with a fairly comprehensive model that provides some useful clues about appropriate marketing communication methods. Figure 11.3 provides a generalized model of the communications and purchase decision process.

The changing nature of promotion and distribution

None the less, in spite of the somewhat traditional approach to communications outlined above, promotion and distribution are changing in a number of respects. New channels such as the Internet are emphasizing an already growing trend from mass media such as advertising, through addressable media such as direct mail, to interactive media such as call centres and the Web. Integrating these channels within a coherent strategy is not an easy task. Writers on the new field of IMC emphasize that, before engaging on detailed planning for each medium – writing sales plans or promotions plans, for example – it is necessary to choose which medium to use for which customer interaction. This is illustrated in Figure 11.4.

The choice of a channel/medium is generally a complex one, involving different media for different communications with the same

Figure 11.3 The purchase decision and marketing communications

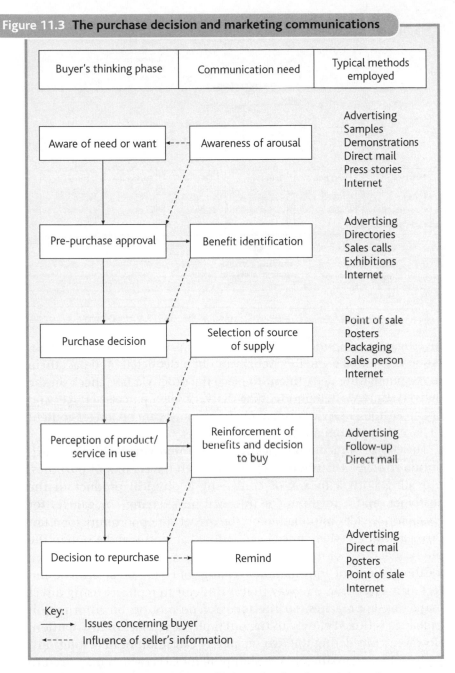

Buyer's thinking phase	Communication need	Typical methods employed
Aware of need or want	Awareness of arousal	Advertising Samples Demonstrations Direct mail Press stories Internet
Pre-purchase approval	Benefit identification	Advertising Directories Sales calls Exhibitions Internet
Purchase decision	Selection of source of supply	Point of sale Posters Packaging Sales person Internet
Perception of product/service in use	Reinforcement of benefits and decision to buy	Advertising Follow-up Direct mail
Decision to repurchase	Remind	Advertising Direct mail Posters Point of sale Internet

Key:
⎯⎯→ Issues concerning buyer
◄---- Influence of seller's information

customer. The organization will frequently also wish to leave some options in the hands of the customer. For example, a Dell customer may find out about Dell from colleagues or from press advertising;

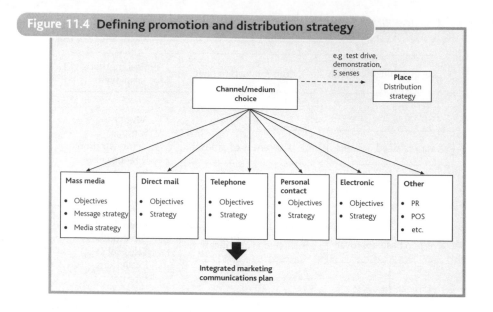

Figure 11.4 Defining promotion and distribution strategy

investigate which product to buy, what the price is and what configuration is required using the Web; print out order details and pass them to the purchasing department to place the order via fax; check on the delivery time via telephone; take delivery via a parcels service; and obtain customer service using e-mail. Customers are no longer content to have the medium dictated by the supplier.

The choice of medium is clearly closely intertwined with the distribution strategy. Distribution channels often have a mix of purposes, providing both a means of conveying a physical product to the customer, and a medium for information exchange. A garage, for example, provides information on the model, an opportunity for a test drive, a location where price negotiations can occur, and a step in the physical delivery of the car to the customer. A clothes shop provides a location where the information exchange of trying on a garment and feeling it can occur, in a way that is difficult to replicate using direct marketing approaches. So the focus of promotion on information exchange is linked closely to the often physical issues of distribution. However, considering the two separately can result in new solutions, such as direct banking or Web shopping for CDs (which may need to be sampled but won't need to be felt physically), and complementing the sales force with telemarketing and websites for minor transactions or less important customers in business-to-business markets.

Choosing the right medium for the right purpose, then, is not a trivial task. There is increasing recognition that this issue needs to be considered afresh, rather than simply following traditional practice in a given industry. But while writings on IMC explain the problem, there is little practical help for organizations on how to solve it.

A related problem is the changing nature of the sales process, which we shall turn to now.

Marketing operations and the new sales process

Once an overall marketing plan has been drawn up, including a plan for promotions, the plan must be implemented. This is the role of marketing operations – the delivery of the value to the customer that was specified in the planning process. But during the course of a year, plenty of finer-grained communications decisions need to be taken. To illustrate, we shall consider the map of the marketing operations process in Figure 11.5. (This is an expansion of the third subprocess in the marketing map, highlighted in Figure 11.6).

Figure 11.5 Delivering value – a map of marketing operations

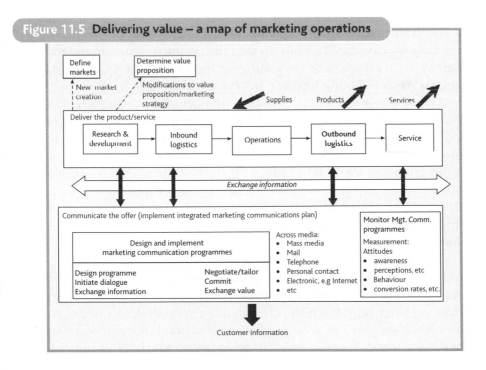

Figure 11.6 Marketing map

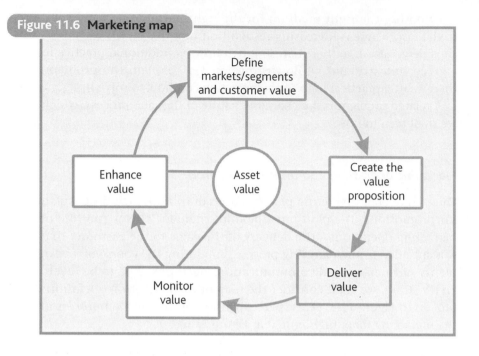

The starting point for our analysis of this 'Deliver value' process was Porter's value chain (see pp. 96, 290). (Porter, 1980). This is reflected in the tasks we have listed within 'Deliver the product/service' in the top half of Figure 11.5: R & D, leading to inbound logistics, through operations to outbound logistics, and finally to service.

However, we suggest that there are a number of marketing activities that shadow these value chain activities, under the general heading of 'communicate the offer'. Porter placed 'Marketing' after 'Operations' in the value chain, but in the-modern one-to-one world, these communications can occur in parallel with all the tasks involved in value delivery. One might, for example, check a product with customers at the R&D stage. The product may be tailored by the customer, resulting in different components being bought in, assembled and delivered, and so on.

Communicating the offer is managed typically by designing, implementing and monitoring a number of marketing communications programmes. A communication programme could be, for example, a direct mail campaign, an advertising campaign, a series of sales seminars, an in-store promotion and so on. We have also stretched the term 'marketing communication programme' to include management of such media as the sales force, which may be managed in a more continuous way, with annual targets broken down by quarter or month.

Whatever the medium, the campaign will be aiming to contribute to one or more of the tasks within the 'Design/implement marketing communication programmes' box. The tasks may have an unfamiliar look: in order to represent the interactive one-to-one nature of twenty-first-century marketing we have renamed the classic steps in the sales process. Figure 11.7 illustrates traditional views of the sales and purchasing processes, with this revised interaction perspective between the two.

Traditional 'push-based' models of marketing, in which, after the product is made, prospects are found and persuaded to buy the product, are illustrated on the left of the figure. The delivery and service that follow are operational functions with little relationship to marketing. Traditional models of buyer behaviour, illustrated on the right of the figure, assume more rationality on the part of buyers, but underplay the importance of what the buyer says back to the seller. The seller's offer is assumed to be predetermined, rather than developed in conjunction with the buyer.

The stages of the process of communicating value are therefore redescribed as follows:

Figure 11.7 Rethinking the sales process

Supplier perspective		Interaction perspective		Buyer perspective	
Advertising	Selling	Marketing activity	Interaction	Decision theory	Consumer behaviour
Brand awareness		Define mkt Understand value Create value proposition	Recognize exchange potential	Problem recognition	Category need
	Prospecting	Initiate dialogue		Information search	Awareness Attitude
Brand attitude • info re: benefits • brand image • feelings • peer influence	Provide information	Exchange information			Information gathering and judgement
	Persuade	Negotiate/tailor		Evaluation of alternatives	
Trial inducement					
	Close sale	Commit		Choice/purchase	Purchase process
	Deliver	Exchange value			
Reduce cognitive dissonance	Service	↓	Monitor	Post-purchase behaviour	Post-purchase experience

▶ 'Recognize exchange potential' replaces 'category need' or 'problem recognition'. Both sides need to recognize the potential for a mutual exchange of value.

▶ 'Initiate dialogue' replaces 'Create awareness' or 'Prospecting'. The dialogue with an individual customer may be begun by either party. One feature of the Internet, for example, is that, on many occasions, new customers will approach the supplier rather than vice versa.

▶ 'Exchange information' replaces 'Provide information'. If we are to serve the customer effectively, tailor our offerings and build a long-term relationship, we need to learn about the customer as much as the customer needs to learn about our products.

▶ 'Negotiate/tailor' replaces 'Persuade'. Negotiation is a two-way process which may involve us modifying our offer in order better to meet the customer's needs. Persuading the customer instead that the square peg we happen to have in stock will fit their round hole is not likely to lead to a long and profitable relationship.

▶ 'Commit' replaces 'Close sale'. Both sides need to commit to the transaction, or to a series of transactions, forming the next stage in a relationship, a decision with implications for both sides.

▶ 'Exchange value' replaces 'Deliver' and 'Post-sales service'. The 'post-sales service' may be an inherent part of the value being delivered, not simply a cost centre, as it is often still managed.

One-to-one communications and principles of relationship marketing, then, demand a radically different sales process from that traditionally practised. This point is far from academic, as the cited earlier will illustrate.

The company in question provides business-to-business financial services. Its marketing managers relayed to us their early experience with a website that was enabling them to reach new customers considerably more cost-effectively than their traditional sales force. When the website was first launched, potential customers were finding the company on the Internet, deciding the products were appropriate on the basis of the website, and sending an e-mail to ask to buy. So far, so good.

But stuck in a traditional model of the sales process, the company would allocate the 'lead' to a salesperson, who would telephone and make an appointment, for perhaps three weeks hence. The customer would by then probably have moved on to another online supplier who could sell the product on the day it was requested. Any customer that stayed was subjected to a sales pitch, complete with glossy materials, that was totally unnecessary, as the customer had already decided to buy. If a customer was not put off, he or she would proceed to be registered as able to buy over the Internet, but by then the company had lost the opportunity to improve its margins by using the sales force more judiciously.

In time, the company realized its mistake, and changed its sales model and reward systems to something close to our 'interaction perspective' model. Unlike those prospects that the company identified and contacted proactively, who might indeed need 'selling' to, many new Internet customers were initiating the dialogue themselves, and simply required the company to respond effectively and rapidly. The sales force were freed up increasingly to concentrate on major clients and on relationship building.

The changing nature of the sales process clearly raises questions for the design of marketing communications, such as: Who initiates the dialogue, and how is the effectiveness measured of attempts to do so across multiple channels? How is the effectiveness measured, not only of what we say to customers, but also what they say back? And how about the role of marketing communications as part of the value that is being delivered and paid for, not just as part of the sales cost?

The trend towards multi-channel communications strategies has been underpinned by developments in CRM technology, which we shall briefly consider next. (CRM is discussed in more detail in Chapter 13, while the use of information technology systems is dealt with in Chapter 19.)

The need for CRM systems to underpin tailored communications

The market for integrated CRM systems has arisen largely out of the frustration of many companies with their multiple customer databases developed for different tasks – as many as forty, in one recent case. Most major organizations are working towards a unified view of the customer, so that all aspects of the customer interface can be co-ordinated. In order to achieve this, systems need to manage customer data independently of the task being performed. For example, if customers enter their names and addresses on a website, they will not wish to be asked the same information via the telephone. This requires all tasks to be able to call on a single module that manages this customer data. Otherwise, the result is a spaghetti-like set of system interconnections. We term this the principle of *task independent data management*.

This point can be seen clearly in Figure 11.8. The 'task management' layer needs to be separate from the 'data management' layer,

Figure 11.8 Towards a viable CRM architecture

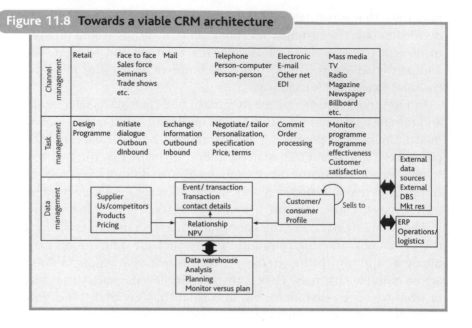

rather than different systems for each task endeavouring to manage parts of the customer data, as is still often the case.

Another point that is illustrated clearly by Figure 11.8 is the importance of *channel independent task management*. The 'channel management' layer of managing different channels or media is often bundled in with particular tasks. A 'direct mail system' will be *the* way in which the organization generates leads; an 'order processing system' will assume that orders come in to an order processing clerk (rather than, say, being made by a website), and so on. Such an architecture is inherently inflexible. An ideal architecture separates the issue of managing the medium from that of managing the task. That way, an order processing system could handle orders that originate via the Internet, in store and from field sales in exactly the same way, without needing three separate order processing systems.

It is all very well defining ideal architectures that facilitate integrated communications, but organizations are stuck more typically with a set of 'legacy' systems, which they can evolve but rarely replace in one project. Nevertheless, organizations need a sense of direction in their IT projects. From an IMC perspective, they need answers to such questions as: How can organizations find their way round the formidable array of personalization capabilities embedded in the latest technology for personalized websites, e-mail campaigns or mobile text messages? How can they decide when to use which, or when to stick with traditional one-to-many approaches? What methods are required to measure the effectiveness of communication strategies across different media, and how should data be collected and analysed to produce these metrics?

Two examples are given below (see Figures 11.9 and 11.10) regarding an attempt by a major global travel company to understand the information-seeking and purchasing processes of different segments. From these two examples covering seven different segments, it can be seen that the behaviour of each is totally different. Without such segmentation knowledge, an integrated communications plan would be impossible.

Selecting the right media

In choosing the most appropriate medium for the advertising message, the organization will need to consider four main factors.

1 *The characteristic of the medium.* This describes the geographical coverage the medium gives; the types of audience it reaches; the

Figure 11.9 The sun worshippers

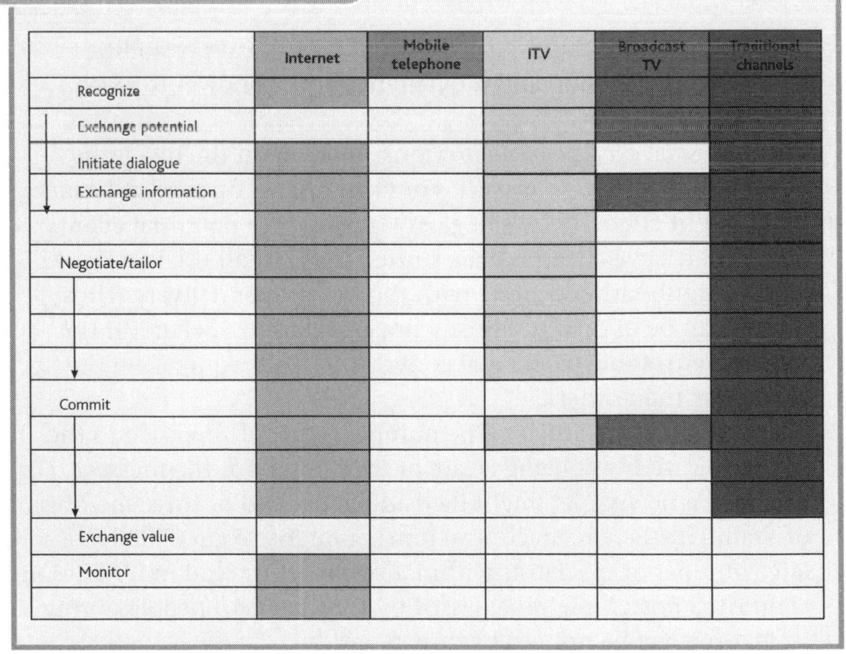

	Internet	Mobile telephone	ITV	Broadcast TV	Traditional channels
Recognize					
Exchange potential					
Initiate dialogue					
Exchange information					
Negotiate/tailor					
Commit					
Exchange value					
Monitor					

Figure 11.10 John and Mary Lively

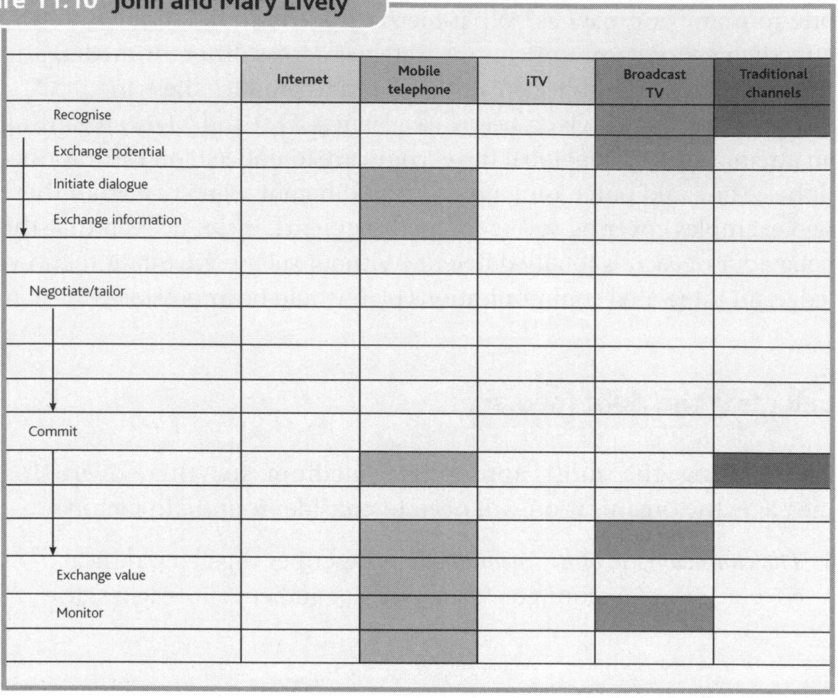

	Internet	Mobile telephone	iTV	Broadcast TV	Traditional channels
Recognise					
Exchange potential					
Initiate dialogue					
Exchange information					
Negotiate/tailor					
Commit					
Exchange value					
Monitor					

frequency of publication or screening; its physical possibilities (such as colour, sound and movement), and its power to reach special groups.

2 *The 'atmosphere' of the medium.* Consistency with the image an organization wishes to project. For example, an up-market beauty salon might choose to post a glossy brochure to potential clients rather than have cheap leaflets stuffed through all the letterboxes in the neighbourhood along with the newspaper delivery. Thus images can be of quality, elitism, popularity, fun – whatever the requirement, some media will convey the required image more effectively than others.

3 *The coverage of the medium.* The number of people exposed to the medium in terms of being aware of the content of the message. For example, a newspaper might be read by just two or three members of a family, whereas a technical journal might be circulated to a large number of specialists within a company or read in libraries. In contrast, a poster might be passed by thousands of people during its lifetime, yet be noticed by only a few.

4 *The comparative cost.* How much will it cost to reach a specific audience size? Cost per 1000 viewers/readers is often used as a comparative yardstick.

International and global communications

Extending the communication strategy across countries has an enormous appeal to most international companies because of the cost savings associated with this approach. There are two principal sources of potential savings. The first is to do with spreading the costs arising from producing copy, particularly with respect to advertising. For a company with world-wide operations, the cost of preparing separate print and TV/cinema films for each market would be enormous. The second derives from bulk purchasing; a phenomenon that will become increasingly important as media ownership and coverage becomes more international. Castrol GTX, Marlboro, Coca-Cola and the like are, of course, well-known examples of truly global brands with global communication strategies. Militating against these are the different functions and patterns of behaviour in different parts of the world, as well as differences in media make-up and availability, and access/usage in different countries. Whatever communication objectives and strategies are pursued, however, they must support the idea of 'mutual' value and trust.

Summary

The organization has an armoury of communication tools that it can 'blend' together into an effective and persuasive communications mix. Essentially, the communication strategy can be summed up in a short-list:

▶ What do we want to say?
▶ To whom do we want to say it?
▶ Why do we want to say it?
▶ How do we choose to say it?
▶ Where shall we communicate our message?
▶ When shall we say it?

These questions are deceptively simple, as answering than involves many important decisions affecting all levels of the organization.

Some communication tools might be more effective than others at conveying certain types of message to certain customers (or other stakeholders and competitors). Their appropriateness depends to a large extent on the potential purchasers' frame of mind and the stage they have reached in the buying decision process. The need to resolve any media conflict (that is, the sending or receiving of conflicting or confusing messages) and to pursue cost-effective communication strategies is a constant priority.

The role of advertising is never static. The recipient needs to receive new messages as his or her thought processes engage different phases of the buying sequence. Similarly, as the product or service moves through different stages in the life-cycle, so too must the advertising objectives reflect the change priorities.

The two-way dialogue afforded by interactive marketing communications offers tremendous scope to improve the design and delivery of communication strategy, for the benefit of all concerned. The emergence of integrated marketing communications (IMC) is a response to the growing need for strategic co-ordination and customization of marketing messages and methods.

Further reading

Crosier, K. (1999) Promotion, in M. Baker (ed.), *The Marketing Book*, Butterworth-Heinemann, Oxford.

Peattie, S. and Peattie, K. (1999) Sales promotion, in M. Baker (ed.), *The Marketing Book*, Butterworth-Heinemann, Oxford.

References

McDonald, M. (1987) *Effective Industrial Selling*, Butterworth-Heinemann, Oxford.

McDonald, M. and Wilson, H. (2002) *New Marketing*, Butterworth-Heinemann, Oxford.

Key account strategy

In this chapter we study the:

► five stages of KAM development

► use of focus teams at the Integrated KAM stage

► bases for defining and selecting key accounts

► significance of identifying the present position of KAM relationships

► development of key account objectives and strategies

► correlation between account relationship stage and account manager role

► factors that influence key account manager performance

Key account management

Key account management (KAM) is a natural development of customer focus and relationship marketing in business to business markets. It can offer critical benefits and opportunities for profit enhancement for both seller and buyer if it is managed with integrity and imagination. Even in non-global firms, and small and medium-sized enterprises (SMEs), attention to the key, or most valuable, business relationships can have a multiplier effect in creating sustainable competitive advantage.

The scope of KAM is widening constantly and at the same time becoming more complex. The skills of those involved at both a strategic and an operational level therefore need to be developed and updated continuously.

This chapter, based on unique research carried out at Cranfield School of Management, puts KAM relationships under the microscope. The Cranfield study tested and advanced some groundbreaking research carried out in 1994 by Professor Tony Millman and Dr Kevin Wilson, which found that the relationship between buyer and seller moved through observable phases. By conducting in-depth interviews with both suppliers and customers, Cranfield established the nature of the challenges faced by key account managers and their directors in their quest to maximize the full potential of the KAM business approach. These insights provide a practical framework for better understanding and practising key account management.

The chapter is in three sections. The first section describes how key accounts can develop over time; the second section discusses how key accounts should be selected and categorized for the purpose of setting objectives and strategies; and the third section recommends how people and material resources should be allocated to get the most out of key account relationships.

The origins of KAM

The roots of KAM can be found in various fields such as industrial marketing, sales management, purchasing management, the psychology of customer behaviour, and relationship marketing. These disciplines share a marked emphasis on relationship-building within a transactional context, a quality characteristic of and crucial to effective key account management. The development of KAM has been gradual and successive, evolving over time to meet changing needs and altered thinking. This evolution is reflected in the KAM process as a progression of five distinct stages of relationship maturity, as illustrated in Figure 12.1.

As the nature of the customer's relationship with the selling organization deepens from that of an 'anonymous buyer' to more of a 'business partner', the level of involvement between the two parties becomes correspondingly more complex. We have labelled the typical stages of relationship maturity as Exploratory KAM, Basic KAM, Co-operative KAM, Interdependent KAM and Integrated KAM. Our research showed that each stage of KAM is can be distinguished clearly by the issues having an impact on the relationship at the time.

Although Figure 12.1 shows an upward or positive development of the business relationship, a selling company should not always expect this to be the case. As with personal relationships, the business partnership can founder for a number of reasons, ranging from a relatively minor misunderstanding to a massive breach of trust. Additionally, the market position and priorities of the buying or

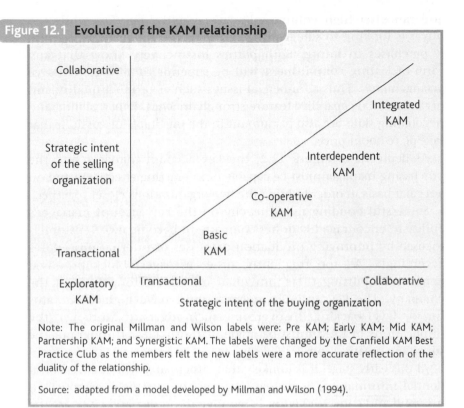

Figure 12.1 Evolution of the KAM relationship

Note: The original Millman and Wilson labels were: Pre KAM; Early KAM; Mid KAM; Partnership KAM; and Synergistic KAM. The labels were changed by the Cranfield KAM Best Practice Club as the members felt the new labels were a more accurate reflection of the duality of the relationship.

Source: adapted from a model developed by Millman and Wilson (1994).

selling company can change in ways that negate the strategic necessity for a close relationship.

Recognizing that the KAM relationship can break down at any time, Figure 12.1 none the less provides an overview of what can happen if all goes well. This model represents a useful tool for implementing KAM and is therefore worth studying in more detail.

Exploratory KAM

Exploratory KAM can be described as the 'scanning and attraction' stage. Like a spaceship seeking its mother craft, both seller and buyer are sending out signals and exchanging messages prior to taking the decision to get together.

Broadly speaking, the aim of both parties is to reduce costs. The supplier prefers customers who are leaders in their respective markets and can offer high volume sales over lengthy periods, while the buyer is looking to safeguard the quality and quantity of supplies it purchases in future. Both parties instinctively know that any form of lasting commitment will be superior to *ad hoc*, tentative arrangements. Thus commercial issues such as product quality and organizational capability feature strongly in KAM. Expert selling and negotiating skills are also paramount in the inevitable discussions that take place about price.

As depicted in Figure 12.2, the key account manager and the purchasing manager must be capable of interacting effectively and on a regular basis in order to bring the two organizations closer together.

Successful bonding relies heavily on the key account manager's ability to encourage his or her company to become more customer-focused by improving production processes or internal procedures accordingly. All too frequently, other managers block proposed changes by putting their individual interests before those of the company. The key account manager must have high-level status (or top-level backing) to overcome such adversity. Moreover, the implications of KAM must be made blatantly clear throughout the supplying organization.

At this early stage, it is unlikely that either party will disclose confidential information, as no basis of trust has yet been established. A careful and concerted effort is required to protect and cultivate the fragile relationship.

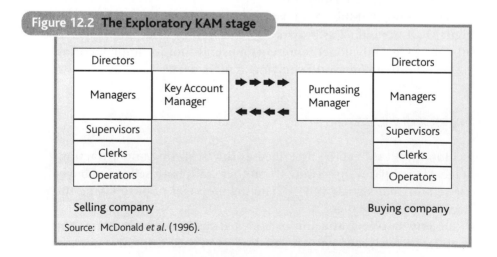

Figure 12.2 **The Exploratory KAM stage**

Selling company   Buying company

Source: McDonald *et al.* (1996).

Basic KAM

At the Basic KAM stage, transactions have begun and the supplier's emphasis shifts to identifying opportunities for account penetration. This means that the key account manager needs to have a greater understanding of the customer and the markets in which the customer competes.

The buying company, meanwhile, will continue market testing other suppliers for best price as it seeks value for money. It is therefore essential for the selling company to concentrate on packaging the core product or service and its surround into a customer-specific offer. Actions such as the simplification of 'paperwork' systems can contribute to a customer-friendly appearance.

At this primary stage, although there may still be a lack of trust, the relationship undergoes a subtle structural change. The key account manager and the customer's main contact are closer to each other, with their respective organizations aligned supportively behind them, as shown in Figure 12.3.

The single point of contact presented by the key account manager is a powerful benefit to the buying company in getting things done. To provide an effective customer interface, the key account manager

Figure 12.3 The Basic KAM stage

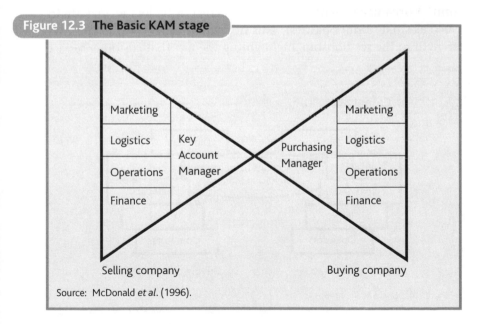

Source: McDonald *et al.* (1996).

must not only be highly skilled and approachable, but he or she must also have the status to demand and obtain speedy responses from the selling company whenever it becomes necessary. Without such status, the key account manager will be bypassed and, for example, a more senior figure will be sought who can deliver the buyer's requirements.

Co-operative KAM

By now, an element of trust has developed, and the selling company may be a 'preferred' supplier. However, the buying company is rarely prepared to put all its eggs into one basket, and will test the market periodically to check alternative sources of supply.

With increasing trust comes a greater preparedness to share information about markets, short-term plans and schedules, internal operating systems, and other issues. Employees of the selling company enter into discussions with their counterparts in the buying company and vice versa, forging links at all levels from operations to the board-room. This collaboration transforms the business relationship into a network with the key account manager and the purchasing manager at the core, as shown in Figure 12.4.

The multiple relationships portrayed in Figure 12.4 often extend beyond the workplace into the social arena. Interactions may take the form of organized events (such as golf days) or be less formal affairs (such as small dinner parties). This network arrangement brings new strength to the relationship, highlighting the fact that customer service

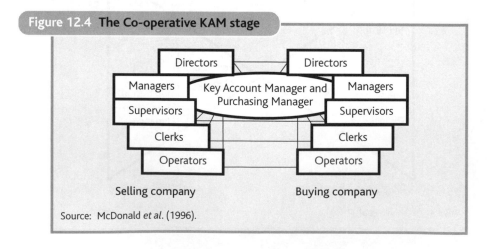

Figure 12.4 The Co-operative KAM stage

Directors — Directors

Managers | Key Account Manager and Purchasing Manager | Managers

Supervisors | | Supervisors

Clerks | | Clerks

Operators | | Operators

Selling company — Buying company

Source: McDonald *et al.* (1996).

operates on many levels and is driven by a desire not to disappoint personal contacts. It is this trust between people that gets results, rather than the somewhat patronizing statements of intent or customer charters favoured by many companies. However, as the willingness to co-operate is voluntary rather than contractual, the relationship is vulnerable to breakdown caused by staff turnover or random management.

Interdependent KAM

At this stage, the buying company regards the selling company as a strategic external resource. The two companies are sharing sensitive information and engaging in joint problem-solving. Such is the level of maturity of relations that each party allows the other to profit from the partnership. Consequently, pricing is long-term and stable; perhaps even fixed.

There also exists a tacit understanding that expertise will be shared. Collaborative programmes to improve products or to simplify the administrative systems that support the commercial transactions provide evidence of this interdependence. The selling and buying companies are now communicating jointly at all levels, as shown in Figure 12.5. It should be noted that the main customer contact is by now not necessarily the purchasing manager, but may be someone more senior.

Figure 12.5 The Interdependent KAM stage

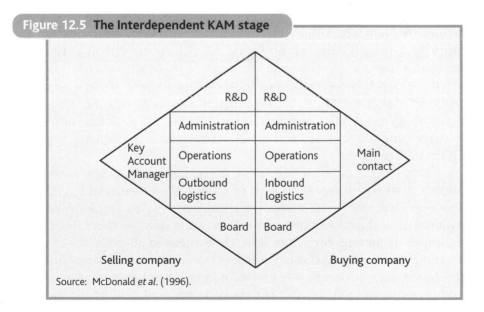

Source: McDonald et al. (1996).

At this stage, the corresponding organizational functions communicate directly. The key account manager and the customer main contact adopt a more supervisory role, ensuring that the various interfaces are effective, and that nothing deters or disrupts the working partnership.

The partnership agreement is long-term, extending to perhaps three or four years. Some buyers in our study asserted that in practice there is no limit. Even so, performance stipulations contained within partnership agreements may affect the longevity of commitment. The selling company will strive to uphold the 'spirit of partnership' by meeting all performance criteria consistently and to the highest possible standards. However, as there are no exit barriers in place at this stage, it is still possible for either party to end the relationship.

Integrated KAM

Integrated KAM refers to the companies relating so strongly and pervasively that they create a value in the market place over and above what either could achieve individually. In effect, the two companies operate as an integrated whole while still maintaining their separate identities.

At this stage, the key account manager's role changes fundamentally. The multiple linkages now function in a way that is largely independent of the key account manager. This is not to say that the role is redundant, but rather that the incumbent can take a much more strategic approach than before. Figure 12.6 illustrates arrival at the integrated stage.

The borders between buyer and seller become blurred. Focus teams made up of personnel from both companies assume responsibility for generating creative ideas and overcoming problems. The key account manager and the customer main contact merely co-ordinate the efforts of these teams.

The reason for constructing focus teams may be to tackle operational, market or project issues, or to introduce motivational forces. The respective teams will meet on a regular basis, setting their own agendas and objectives. Special project teams may be short-lived, existing only for long enough to serve their intended purpose.

At this advanced stage, the companies' electronic data systems are integrated, information flow is streamlined, business plans are linked, and the erstwhile unthinkable is now willingly explored. About the

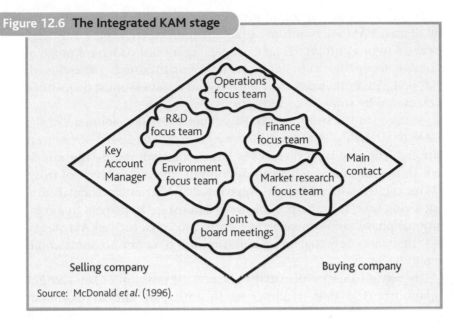

Figure 12.6 The Integrated KAM stage

Operations focus team

R&D focus team

Finance focus team

Key Account Manager

Environment focus team

Market research focus team

Main contact

Joint board meetings

Selling company

Buying company

Source: McDonald et al. (1996).

only issue that remains sacrosanct for the selling company is its brand. Any requests from the buying company that might undermine the brand should be rejected.

Determining the key account relationship

No one KAM stage is better than another; they are just different. The main question concerns the appropriateness of the relationship with a particular customer at a particular time. To illustrate this point, let us consider some of the relationships we experience in our personal lives.

Our relationship with passing acquaintances may not extend beyond an acknowledgement of familiarity such as nodding 'Good morning!', and at the other end of the scale are our close family and friends, with whom our relationship is warmer and stronger. The degree of intimacy in a relationship reflects the level of personal investment.

A reversal of our behaviour with these two groups would be seen as highly inappropriate, verging on the insane. Similarly, we do not seek intense friendships with everybody we meet. To do so would not only be unsuitable but also impossible, as we do not have unlimited emotional reserves.

In the same way, organizations do not possess the resources to have all of their KAM relationships at the integrated level, even if this were deemed to be appropriate. Like people, organizations have a range of relationships that can be intensified, maintained, or subdued. Naturally, investments of time, energy and resources must be justified and guided by strategic considerations.

As stated at the beginning of this chapter, the development of the KAM relationship is an evolutionary process. The speed of progress through the five typical stages is largely determined by the rate at which the buyer and seller can develop the necessary levels of trust. While some relationships may appear to 'stick' at one particular level for a long time, it is also possible for relationships to be held in a transitional phase, somewhere between any two consecutive KAM stages. It is therefore likely that an organization will have key accounts at different stages.

The significance of identifying the present position of key account relationships is that it allows us to anticipate the development requirements of individual accounts as well as the collective demands of the account portfolio. Such knowledge and understanding is intrinsic to the setting of key account objectives and strategies, as is explained in the next section of this chapter.

Developing key account objectives and strategies

A little thought will quickly expose the inadequacies of systems that classify key accounts into just three categories such as A, B and C.

As most companies are judged on the basis of profit, key accounts should be classified in accordance with their potential for growth in profits over, say, a three-year period. The Cranfield research showed that the criteria used by companies to measure potential profit growth are:

▶ available size of spend;
▶ available margins;
▶ growth rate; and
▶ purchasing policies and processes.

When each of these criteria are weighted and scored appropriately for each key account, the accounts can be evaluated in terms of profit growth potential on a 'thermometer' scale from low to high. There can be problems with this simple analysis – an obvious one being is that it does not consider the maturity or business strength of the key account relationship. As discussed earlier, the KAM relationship can be anywhere between the Exploratory stage and the Integrated stage.

In order to define and select target key accounts accurately, a full profile of each account must be obtained. This is achieved by measuring profit growth potential in combination with relationship maturity. A comparative guide using these two dimensions, as shown in Figure 12.7, is helpful in setting realistic objectives and strategies for key accounts.

Taking the boxes in each quadrant in Figure 12.7 in turn and starting with the bottom left quadrant Box 1, ('low potential/high strength'), it is possible to work out sensible objectives and strategies for each key account. Accounts meeting the profile of the bottom left quadrant are likely to continue to deliver excellent revenues for some considerable time, even though they may be in static or declining markets. Good relationships are already enjoyed and should be preserved. Retention strategies are therefore advisable, incorporating prudence, vigilance and motivation. More important, as the supplying company will be seeking a good return on previous investment, any further financial input here should be of the maintenance kind. In this way, it should be possible to free up cash and resources for investing in key accounts with greater growth potential.

The boxes in the top left quadrant (Box 2:'high potential/high strength') represent accounts with highest potential growth in sales

Figure 12.7 Identifying target key accounts, objectives and strategies

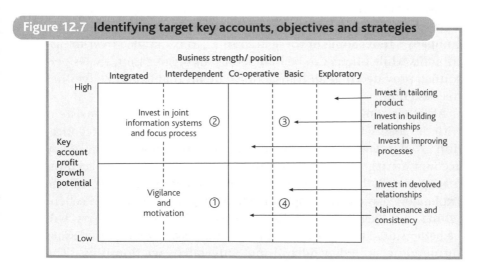

and profits. These warrant quite an aggressive investment approach, providing it is justified by returns. Net present value (NPV) calculations may be used as a basis for evaluating these returns, using a discount rate higher than the cost of capital to reflect the additional risks involved. Any investment here will probably be directed towards developing joint information systems and collaborative relationships.

Accounts situated in the boxes in the top right quadrant (Box 3: 'high potential/low strength') pose a problem, as few organizations have sufficient resources to invest in building better relationships with all of them. To determine which ones justify investment, net revenue streams should be forecast for each account for, say, three years, and discounted at the cost of capital (plus a considerable percentage to reflect the high risk involved). Having made these calculations and selected the promising accounts, under no circumstances should financial accounting measures such as NPV be used to control them within the budget year. To do so would be a bit like pulling up a new plant every few weeks to see whether it had grown! Achievement of objectives should instead be monitored using terms such as sales volume, value, 'share of wallet' and the quality of the relationship, enabling selected accounts to be moved gradually towards partnerships and in some cases towards integrated relationships. Only then will it become more appropriate to measure profitability as a control procedure. Accounts in which the company cannot afford to invest should be managed in a similar way to those residing in the final boxes to the bottom right.

Accounts found in the boxes in the bottom right quadrant Box 4 ('low potential/low strength') should not occupy too much of a company's time. Some of these accounts can be handed over to distributors while others can be handled by an organization's sales personnel, provided that all transactions are profitable and deliver net free cash flow.

All other company functions and activities should be consistent with the goals set for key accounts according to the general categorization given in Figure 12.7. This rule includes the appointment of key account managers to key accounts. For example, some key account managers will be extremely good at managing accounts in the Exploratory, Basic and Co-operative KAM stages, where their excellent selling and negotiating skills are essential, whereas others will be better suited to the more complex business and managerial issues surrounding interdependent and integrated relationships. The implications for key account managers are examined in the third section of this chapter.

Implications for the key account manager

The fundamental challenge of the KAM task is to succeed in a match-making exercise; that is, to marry the manager of most compatible and complementary qualities with a specific account in order to maximize the return on investment. The correlation between the development of the account relationship and the development of the account manager's role is summarized in Table 12.1. Of course, real life is not quite so pre-disposed to split conveniently into neat boxes and the table merely encapsulates what Cranfield found to be the general experience.

Clearly, the key account manager must be adept at balancing the growing expectations of both selling and buying companies. The roles and responsibilities of key account managers, and their ability to fulfil them, are critical to the success of any KAM strategy. So what is the personal specification of a key account manager?

As part of the Cranfield research, key account managers, their managers and their buying company contacts were all asked the same question, 'What essential skills/qualities does the key account manager need?' Surprisingly, there was little agreement among the three groups of respondents.

The selling companies involved in the study were unanimous in rating selling and negotiating skills as the chief essential attributes of successful key account managers. The buying companies, on the other hand, voted trustworthiness and strategic decision-making ability as the principal traits. Furthermore, the buyers disliked so intensely being sold to that they would not permit a salesperson to lead the key account team!

The disclosed discrepancy between the comments of managers or key account managers and those of customer contacts is particularly alarming, considering that these senior managers are responsible for appointing key account managers to valuable accounts.

The skill area that prompted most dramatic disagreement is that of 'selling/negotiating'. While selling companies put great store on these skills (62 per cent and 67 per cent, respectively), only 9 per cent of buying contacts rated them as important. In simply repeating old patterns, selling companies show their perspectives to be more outdated than perhaps they care to admit.

Table 12.1 Strategy, role and skills progression

	Exploratory KAM	Basic KAM	Co-operative KAM	Interdependent KAM	Integrated KAM
Selling company strategy	Invest in tailoring product	Invest in building relationship	Invest in improving administrative processes	Invest in sharing information and expertise	Invest in joint planning and development
Buying company concerns	Does supplier have product knowledge and industry expertise?	Does Key Account Manager demonstrate integrity?	Does Key Account Manager possess authority?	Does emphasis on key account teams mean loss of direct relationship?	Does autonomy of key account teams mean loss of direct control?
Key Account Manager's role	Identify prospective customers	Identify opportunities for account penetration	Facilitate formation of a network	Supervise relationship interactions and collaborations	Co-ordinate focus teams
Key Account Manager's skills	Technical knowledge, 'scouting' ability and communication skills	Product knowledge, selling and negotiation skills	Management skills, especially interpersonal skills	Full range of financial, marketing and consultancy skills	Full range of business skills, plus general management capability

Developing key account professionals

Training and development

The selling companies stated that they had encountered difficulties in designing appropriate training for key account managers, especially for those operating in global markets. Problems centred on the need to develop a range of competencies in traditionally specialist areas, such as:

► technical/product knowledge;
► relationship-building skills (interpersonal skills);
► finance;
► marketing/strategic thinking;
► business management;
► project management; and
► creative problem-solving.

According to respondents, the training of key account managers consists mainly of attending a number of short courses when deemed appropriate. On average, key account managers receive 5–10 days of training per year, excluding induction. Because recruits generally have a background in sales or marketing, training must deliberately set out to extend their skill bases in order to develop 'all-rounders' rather than better specialists. It seems unlikely that the *ad hoc* and limited approach to training identified here could ever create outstanding key account managers.

In terms of succession policy, selling companies do endeavour to ensure that the handover of a key account is managed with a sense of continuity. Where possible, new account managers are introduced to contacts by their predecessors, who then gradually pass over responsibility to the newcomers. Our study found that buying companies appreciate profoundly this smooth transition, and do not expect the new contact to be a clone of the old one. In fact, it was recognized that a new face can sometimes revitalize a flagging relationship.

Authority and status

'We don't want to be dealing with a postman who has to trot back [to the boss] every time we ask a question' was the graphic view offered by one buyer on the autonomy of key account managers. The perception of key account managers as lacking status and authority, especially in the early stages of the KAM relationship, was a recurring theme among the buying companies. Selling companies would be wise to address this concern. Key account managers, it seems, are well aware of expectations and feel the pressure to make decisions and commit their company, even when they do not have the authority to do so. Paradoxically, although the KAM relationship is intended to develop unique arrangements with the buying company, it is on decision-related matters that account managers most often have to refer back to their company.

It was generally agreed that the one area in which the key account manager has least room for manoeuvre is on prices and margins. Any discretion that is allowed constitutes a 'freedom' to operate within carefully defined bands.

When dealing with key accounts, it is important to remember that the position of the key account manager can easily be undermined if the buying company is allowed to gain the ear of someone higher up in the selling organization. Therefore, more senior managers and directors should always be seen to defer to the account manager.

Reporting and accountability

The Cranfield research revealed that 36 per cent of key account managers reported to directors within their companies. Reporting at a less senior level usually meant being accountable to a sales manager, sales and marketing manager, or business unit manager. All of the key account managers interviewed were, in effect, national account managers. Only four also held some global accounts, with responsibility for results achieved in other countries.

In most of the selling companies studied, key account managers did not have formal – or, for that matter, informal – teams assisting them. Working alone, they were expected to fulfil customer requirements solely by influencing their colleagues to mobilize the necessary resources, which would clearly make progression to interdependent or integrated stages extremely difficult, if not impossible.

Best practice key account management seeks to redress this operational weakness. As the KAM relationship matures, 'dotted line' project teams develop. Composed of functional staff, these teams report to the key account manager on specific matters of interest, while remaining responsible to their functional manager throughout the working day. Not surprisingly, this duality of duty can be a source of tension. However, problems are not normally about questions of loyalty, but about confusion over priorities. Where project teams are more formalized, team members are set specific objectives and time frames. In this team environment, it is imperative that the key account manager, as the main customer interface, keeps team members fully updated on all operational and strategic issues relating to their accounts.

Appraisal and reward

The majority of key account managers interviewed received a basic salary plus a bonus related to generated earnings, although a significant minority were employed on the basis of a straight salary. The level at which bonuses were set was a contentious issue.

Managers receiving 10–20 per cent of their income as a bonus felt that it was too low in relation to the importance placed on the volume of key account business. Other managers felt it to be unfair for bonuses to be linked closely to volume, since matters in the buying company such as market shifts over which the key account manager has no control could influence business volume.

In some of the selling companies, share options figured as a form of bonus, providing an incentive related to overall company performance. Many managers remained sales driven by a remuneration package based on 50 per cent salary and 50 per cent commission. Targets were set either by KAM directors or, more usually, were the outcome of negotiations between the director and the key account manager.

In addition to sales volume, the key account managers identified other performance criteria, including:

► customer satisfaction ratings;
► market share;
► account profitability;
► accuracy of forecasts;
► debt recovery;
► handling of complaints;
► number of new contacts; and
► new opportunities identified.

Where products were project based, key account managers were judged by the achievement of milestones and deadlines. In businesses marked by cyclical sales, such as capital equipment, the performance of key account managers was assessed against the total value of the selling company's product portfolio. This relative approach avoided the situation of having excessive bonuses one year and none the next.

Summary

The purpose of the Cranfield research was to advance understanding of key account management by finding out how selling companies operate, how their operations are perceived by buying companies, and where there may be scope for improvement. From the evidence gathered, the following conclusions can be drawn:

- business success depends upon excellent processes as well as excellent people and products;
- KAM is not a 'quick fix' management process, and thus companies need to think in terms of long-lasting, ongoing relationships;
- despite the attraction of KAM, businesses have difficulty in implementing it;
- the KAM relationship is particularly vulnerable in the early stages of development;
- not all accounts can be developed beyond Co-operative KAM (preferred supplier) even though sellers may aspire to interdependent or integrated relationships;
- higher level KAM relationships can only be achieved in customer-focused companies;
- organizing to meet the demands of global key accounts is particularly challenging;
- the key account manager is critical to the KAM relationship and requires skills considerably greater than those of a salesperson;
- the key account manager is likely to require ongoing training throughout his/her career as the role (and its inherent relationships) increase in complexity;
- in addition to training, selection, appraisal and remuneration policies influence the performance of key account managers;
- buying companies place a high value on the status and authority of key account managers and expect to deal with someone who can get things done; and

▶ account teams can enable a commitment to key accounts that transcends what key account managers can deliver working alone.

Our study has clarified many issues but has also raised some new and potentially far-reaching questions:

▶ If the KAM relationship is evolutionary, what is the next developmental stage likely to be?
▶ What is the best way to build key account teams?
▶ What are the special problems for key account managers who operate in complex supply chains or on a global basis?
▶ What are the organizational implications of global key account management?
▶ What kinds of decision support systems are required for key account management?
▶ How should the relationship between key accounts and non-key accounts be managed?
▶ How should the relationship between key accounts and non-key accounts be measured, particularly financially?
▶ At what level might the KAM relationship be seen to be a barrier to competition and fair trade?

While Cranfield's research provides a practical framework for understanding how key account management should progress, marketing professionals and business academics are not left unchallenged: the quest to maximize the potential of KAM is as long as the scope of KAM is wide.

Finally, it is clear that creating a value proposition for a key customer is just as crucial as it is for a market or a segment. Equally important, however, is to deliver the value proposition, once it has been agreed. This is the subject of Module 3.

Further reading

McDonald, M. and Woodburn, D. (1999) Key *Account Management – Learning from Supplier and Customer Perspectives*, Financial Times and Prentice-Hall, London.

Millman, A. and Wilson, K. (1996)Developing key account management competencies'. *Journal of Marketing Practice – Applied Marketing Science*, **2** (2), pp. 7–22.

References

McDonald, M., Millman, A. and Rogers, B. (1996) Key account management: learning from supplier and customer perspectives, *Cranfield University School of Management Report.*

Millman, A. F. and Wilson, K. J. (1994) From key account selling to key account management, Tenth Annual Conference on Industrial Marketing and Purchasing, University of Groningen, The Netherlands.

Delivering value

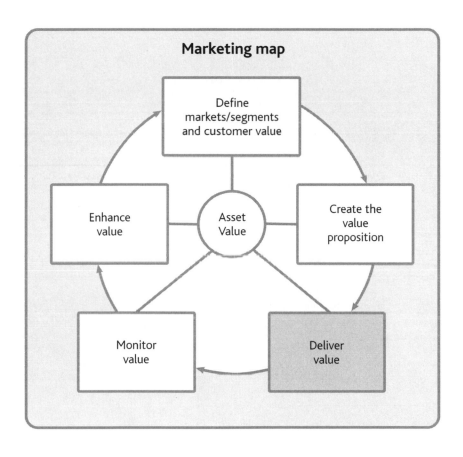

13 Managing marketing relationships

In this chapter we study the:

- ▶ trend towards adding value throughout the value chain
- ▶ emphases of a relationship marketing approach
- ▶ view of marketing as a cross-functional activity
- ▶ multiple markets model
- ▶ concept of partnership and the extended supply chain
- ▶ benefits of consumer involvement in building end user relationships
- ▶ considerations in a customer relationship management approach

The value chain

In Chapter 5 we saw that adding value through differentiation can be a powerful means of achieving a defensible advantage in the market place. The extent to which this can happen is maximized if value is added throughout the succession of supply relationships, or value chain. This is evident in the fact that logistics and wider supply chain issues have become key sources of competitive advantage. Increasingly, it is supply chains that are competing rather than individual organizations.

In the highly competitive field of consumer marketing, many suppliers and retailers are paying closer attention to the value chain at whose head they sit. These organizations have recognized that advantage can be gained by exerting influence across all those who affect their products and their ability to supply. These advantages include lower cost, higher quality, better availability, product innovation, speed to market, and a host of other important competitive factors.

In some industries, such as automotive manufacture, this management is sometimes delegated to a small group of key suppliers who are

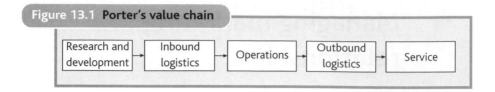

Figure 13.1 Porter's value chain

| Research and development | Inbound logistics | Operations | Outbound logistics | Service |

expected to influence and co-ordinate the other suppliers in the chain. In others, such as the computer supply industry, many businesses are working directly with suppliers right down to component level and beyond in seeking efficiency and innovation in order to deliver superior value.

The process of delivering the value proposition can be analysed using Porter's value chain (see pp. 96, 258), as shown in Figure 13.1. Although Porter placed 'Marketing' after 'Operations' in the value chain, we have removed it here, since in today's one-to-one world, marketing activities can occur in parallel with all the tasks involved in value delivery. For example, it is common practice to check a product with customers at the R&D stage, which may result in the use of different materials, or assembly and delivery methods, than was initially envisaged. What is clear is that delivering value successfully involves managing relationships effectively: relationships between people, processes and functions.

A relationship marketing approach

While it has long been acknowledged that the fundamental purpose of marketing is the 'getting and keeping of customers', the truth is that more attention has been paid, typically, to attracting customers than to keeping them. More recently there has emerged a recognition that marketing needs to encompass not only those activities necessary to capture business in the first place, but also to develop processes that will enhance long-term customer loyalty. This viewpoint is the foundation for the development of the concept of relationship marketing, which is based on the belief that the fundamental purpose of marketing is the creation and development of long-term profitable relationships with customers.

It should not be thought that relationship marketing is a replacement for marketing as it has been practised to date. Rather, it is an augmentation and a refocusing of the marketing concept with the emphasis placed on strategies to enhance customer retention and loyalty. Some of the major differences in emphasis between the traditional approach, which we label 'transactional', and the 'relationship' focus are summarized in Table 13.1. It will be seen from this table that the major difference between the relationship focus and the transactional focus is the emphasis on a continuous commitment to meeting the needs of individual customers, with particular stress on service and quality.

Many marketing practitioners might justifiably protest that they have been practising relationship marketing for years but did not realize it! In truth, however, many others have failed to recognize the importance of customer loyalty as a driver of profitability, and hence have tended to concentrate their efforts on a single-minded pursuit of growing sales. Relationship marketing as a philosophy is concerned with the 'quality' of market share, not just its absolute level: in other words, the minimization of customer defections and the building of long-term partnerships with customers who willingly become repeat purchasers.

In practice, this philosophy translates into maximizing customer value by maximizing the value of the relationships involved in creating and delivering that value. Here the word 'relationships' can be seen to extend beyond relationships between people (employees, customers, suppliers and so on) to include the relationships between the inputs and outputs of the five key marketing processes, which are represented as arrows in Figure 13.2.

Table 13.1 The shift to relationship marketing

Transactional focus	Relationship focus
Orientation to single sales	Orientation to customer retention
Discontinuous customer contact	Continuous customer contact
Focus on product features	Focus on customer value
Short time scale	Long time scale
Little emphasis on customer service	High customer service emphasis
Limited commitment to meeting customer exceptions	High commitments to meeting customer expectations
Quality is the concern of production staff	Quality is the concern of all staff

Figure 13.2 Marketing map

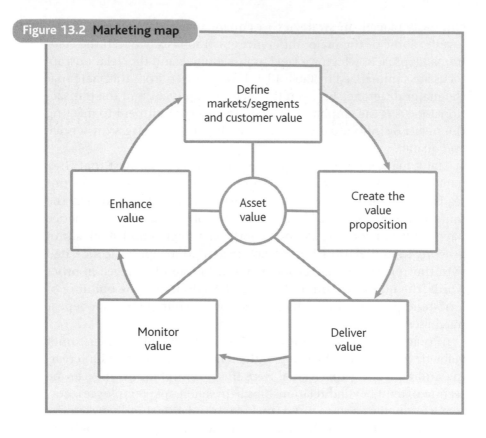

For example, in 'Deliver value', the marketing plans are the direct input and performance is the direct output. The closer the performance is to the plans, or how well the organization performs in the light of its careful planning, the higher the level of customer value. This outcome does, of course, also rely on the indirect inputs and outputs, such as how closely the marketing plans reflect the identified prospects.

Further, the extent to which the relationships between the organization's prospects, plans and performance can be maximized will be influenced by the information derived from the organization's monitoring activity, by its proven level of professionalism, and by its recognized future potential. In short, the marketing process can be seen to operate on a number of cross-related dimensions, and in so doing it draws on the involvement of various people and functional expertise from across the organization.

Marketing as a cross-functional activity

One of the distinguishing characteristics of the relationship marketing approach is that it places the emphasis on the need to take a cross-functional, business-wide approach to customer satisfaction. It sees marketing as a cross-functional, as opposed to a functional, activity. In other words, marketing is an integrated process, and not an isolated action. Figures 13.3 and 13.4 highlight this difference.

Clearly, there will always be a requirement for the marketing function to manage such tasks as advertising, market research, pricing and

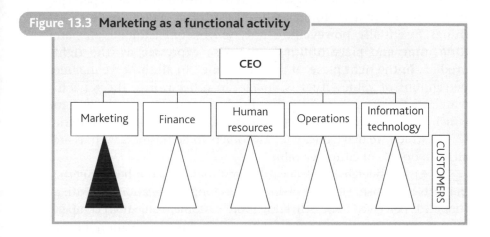

Figure 13.3 Marketing as a functional activity

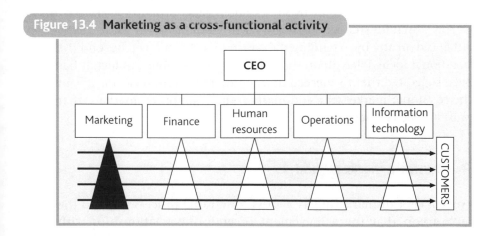

Figure 13.4 Marketing as a cross-functional activity

so on. However, overlaying the traditional vertical organization are a number of cross-functional processes that must be managed if the business is to be truly market-facing and value-driven.

These processes include such activities as new product development, order fulfilment (that is, the physical satisfaction of demand), marketing planning and the management of customer relationships. Obviously, this view of marketing has many implications for the organizational structure of the business, and these issues are addressed in Chapter 21.

As stressed throughout this book, a fundamental aspect of marketing processes is that they add customer value. What this means is the product or service on offer becomes more attractive to the customer because of the way things are done (and consequently more lucrative to the supplier, because it is selling well). Customer value is perceptual, and different customers will clearly place value on different things. Essentially, however, the only sources of customer value are form, time and place utilities, otherwise expressed as 'the right product, in the right place, at the right time'. In all three we include perceptions of value – that is, image. In other words, the ways in which we transform resources into products and services, the way in which we deliver them to meet the customers' requirements, and the way in which we make it easy for customers to do business with us are all components of customer value.

There is considerable evidence to suggest that there is inherent inertia in much buyer behaviour, implying that as long as a relationship with a supplier is perceived to be delivering more customer value than competitive offerings for the same price, there will be little motivation for the customer to seek another source of supply. Delivering superior customer value does not happen by chance, however – it requires a continuing focus on the processes whereby such value is generated.

This search for strategies that deliver superior customer value can be enhanced greatly by extending the concept of the 'market' beyond the traditional focus solely upon the end-users or customers. In fact, it has been suggested that to succeed in building long-term relationships in the consumer market (the end-market) there are other 'markets' that must also be considered.

The multiple markets model

The concept of marketing as a cross-functional process leads to the recognition that the achievement of enduring relationships with customers and consumers is dependent on other relationships too. For example, the relationships that organizations have with their suppliers and employees clearly have an impact on the relationships they have with their customers. This diversity of internal and external relationships can be described as identifiable 'markets' or 'market domains'. The thrust of the multiple markets model shown in Figure 13.4 is that organizations can best manage their network of relationships in different market domains by focusing on particular groups or market segments within them. There are, in effect, six main markets that must be addressed in a relationship marketing programme:

1. Customer markets;
2. Referral markets;
3. Internal markets;
4. Recruitment markets;
5. Influencer markets; and
6. Supplier and alliance markets.

Figure 13.5 The multiple markets model

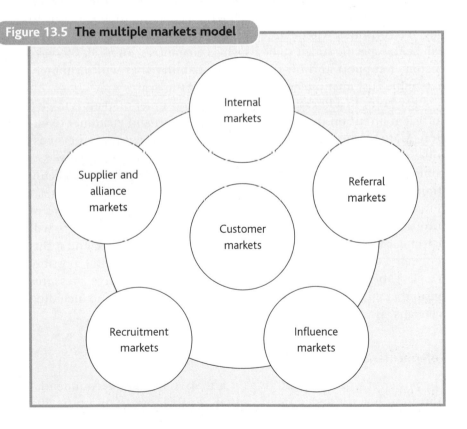

Customer markets

Customer markets are central to the multiple model, both because they remain the prime focus of marketing activity and because they are affected by the organization's success or failure in all the other markets. The customer market represents all the people or organizations that buy goods or services. It therefore includes intermediaries (retailers, distributors and so on) as well as end-users.

In this market, the impact of customer service can be profound. Often the only source of competitive differentiation is the quality of the service provided. This is particularly the case when dealing with intermediaries or distributors. For example, the amount of shelf-space a retailer is prepared to give to one brand over another brand in the same category will often be determined by the supplier's ability to operate a just-in-time (JIT) delivery system, or by the supplier's ability to receive orders electronically and to link information systems together.

Experience has shown that the service and quality dimension can be especially critical in the case of marketing to end consumers. When faced with the decision about which television set or mobile phone to buy, the consumer will be influenced partly by the brand name, but it will be the specific added values, such as guarantees, after-sales service, customer support and off-the-shelf availability that will ultimately determine customer preference and 'clinch' the deal.

A key point in addressing customer and consumer markets is to give sufficient attention to *both* customer acquisition and customer retention. Many companies concentrate too much on winning new customers at the expense of keeping existing customers. This is a common weakness among organizations that view marketing as being 'transactional'. Other companies place an emphasis on growing relationships with existing customers without nurturing new sources of future custom. The danger is that a proportion of customers will defect naturally to competitors, or leave the fold altogether, and if this represents key customers, the company will have lost a vital, possibly irreplaceable, asset. Either way, intensifying competitive pressures mean that all organizations need to achieve a customer base including 'veterans' as well as 'new recruits'.

Referral markets

The power of word of mouth is substantial. A purchase recommendation from a respected source is often worth more than any media advertisement. Referrals can come from sources of professional advice such as doctors, lawyers, bank managers and accountants as well as from existing satisfied customers.

Referral markets are often difficult to identify, but a start can be made by asking new customers what influenced their purchase decision. Referral markets must be researched carefully and the factors that influence their recommendations must be understood clearly. It is advisable to develop specific communication programmes that involve effective referral sources. For example, existing customers can be encouraged to act as 'recruiting agents' for the business. Often a small incentive is all that is needed to persuade a satisfied customer to encourage others to patronise the business. Once again, however, such strategies need to be planned and programmed so that they are not left to chance, but form a defined part of the overall relationship marketing plan.

Internal markets

There is now widespread recognition that one of the major determinants of marketing success is the existence of a strongly felt and unanimously accepted 'corporate culture' within the business. Sometimes this set of commonly held beliefs is termed 'shared values', reflecting the commitment to customers subscribed to by the entire workforce. The creation of such a culture requires vision and leadership, which is communicated at every level in the organization, and also open channels of internal communication. This is the realm of internal marketing.

Internal marketing involves regarding members of staff (and even shareholders and other stakeholders) as customers. In applying a customer focus internally, the needs, wants and desires of employees are identified, and programmes are constructed to encourage and enable them to engage in exchange activities with colleagues. The aim is to inform and motivate all the members of the organization towards defined goals of customer and corporate satisfaction. The resulting collaboration improves not only internal morale and operational efficiency, but also service levels to the external customer, thereby progressing the marketing campaign.

Seminars, workshops, team-building exercises, continuous and good two-way communication channels, newsletters, quality-improvement groups and, above all, a focus on the idea that everybody in the organization has and is a 'customer', are the ingredients of a successful internal marketing programme. In practical terms, however, internal marketing is limited in what it contributes to the wider issues of organizational culture, since it too often defaults to a communications exercise. Selling the need to value relationships with customers is a far more complex issue than just letting people know what is going on.

Recruitment markets

The scarcest resource for most organizations is no longer capital or raw materials: it is skilled people. An appropriately trained and experienced workforce is perhaps the most vital element in customer value delivery. But 'good people' are hard to find.

Global economics and the changing nature of employment have not helped to enlarge the recruitment pool, even if unemployment levels are climbing. The basic reason for the current lack of skilled workers is demographic trends. Most Western countries are experiencing a reduction in population growth, which means a relative shortage of new recruits entering employment. There is also the pressure constantly to seek economies and this has seen many Western industries rejecting domestic labour in favour of less expensive foreign labour, if only for partial operations, such as product assembly.

Because every organization is highly dependent on the quality of the people it employs, it is imperative that a high priority be given to recruiting and retaining employees who are likely to assist the company in achieving its overall marketing objectives. The aim should be to make the company into an organization that is attractive to people (both the job-seeking and the career-minded employed) who share the values the company espouses. For many businesses, appealing to newly-skilled workers is a key priority, whereas for others the focus may be on capturing specialists with years of experience.

Companies as diverse as Disney and the Ritz-Carlton chain of hotels have built up a reputation for service quality that owes a great deal to the care that is put into employee recruitment. Given the high costs of training new recruits in any business, it makes a lot of sense to ensure that the right people are recruited in the first place, and that, once in place, a strong emphasis is placed on minimizing employee turnover. Companies with higher than the industry average of staff turnover will often be poor performers in terms of customer service.

Figure 13.6 Employee satisfaction leads to customer loyalty

Evidence exists in many markets that a 'virtuous circle' can be created whereby committed and satisfied employees result in loyal and satisfied customers, which further encourages and reinforces customer orientation among the employees. This is illustrated in Figure 13.5. The issue of customer loyalty is covered in more depth in Chapter 14.

Influencer markets

Clearly, there are many sources of influence on buyer behaviour, and so the definition of an 'influencer market' is not straightforward. In the context of relationship marketing, an influencer is an organization, entity or individual that, directly or indirectly, might cause a customer to buy a product or service. A critical part of a relationship-marketing programme may therefore involve seeking to work more closely with the influencers. An example might be a margarine producer that seeks to encourage an interest in low-cholesterol diets by supporting research into heart disease. Another example might be manufacturers of domestic smoke alarms lobbying the government to invest in public-information programmes on fire protection.

Much of what we call 'public relations' is often focused on developing a positive attitude among critical influencer markets. The ultimate aim is to try to ensure that the environment in which we market our offer is as favourable as possible.

Still more sources of influence are the 'innovators', or 'early adopters' (see Chapter 8), who are often used by others as a point of reference or guidance. Drug companies, for example, have long recognized the importance of building close relationships with general practitioners (GPs), who have a position of influence among other doctors when it comes to prescribing practice.

Supplier and alliance markets

In the past, relationships with suppliers were often adversarial. It was thought to be good practice to have several suppliers for a single item and to 'play one off against the other'. Negotiation on price was the chief focus of the buyer–supplier contact and there was little appreciation of the connection between supplier relationships and success in the end market. Happily, this point of view is now changing, and the trend is towards increasingly collaborative relationships with suppliers.

Many companies have found that closer relationships with suppliers can lead to innovation in product design and functionality, quality improvements and lower purchasing costs. The move towards 'single sourcing' is also a part of this trend. The idea here is that the best way to gain the benefits of buyer–supplier collaboration is through working closely in a spirit of trust and long-term mutual commitment – a spirit that is unlikely to be engendered if the buyer insists on splitting his or her business between several competing suppliers.

This type of 'co-operative' relationship with supplier markets is known by various names. AT&T call it 'vendorship partnership', while the European electronics group, Philips, use the term 'co-makership'. In the USA it is referred to as 'reverse marketing'.

Alliance markets have emerged, as organizations have adopted increasingly strategic relationships with one another. Alliances are a potential source of supply of capital, managerial expertise, market position, global coverage, technological skills, and much more. The development of various forms of alliance (ranging from collaborative practice to joint working to joint ventures and, most comprehensively, merger) was a feature of the 1990s.

Relationships as partnerships

The basic philosophy underlying relationship marketing is that the goal of all marketing activity should be the establishment of mutually beneficial partnerships with customers. If customers perceive there is greater value in staying with a particular supplier than in moving to any other, then clearly they will stay. The challenge to management is to develop marketing strategies designed to create enduring customer partnerships, and to combat customer churn and switching behaviour.

Ideally, the concept of partnership should be applied to each of the markets contained in the multiple markets model. Hence partnerships with employees, with influencers, with suppliers, as well as with customers, will ensure greater long-term profitability for the business. Furthermore, it is worth remembering that partnership can operate between two or more parties, extending a 'win-win' situation to one of a 'win-win-win'.

For example, many companies are benefiting from closer relationships with suppliers. What these companies are discovering is that by working alongside suppliers they can find ways to take costs out of the supply chain by focusing on such things a just-in-time (JIT) delivery systems, linking ordering procedures through electronic data interchange (EDI), and eliminating the need for rework or error correction by quality improvement programmes. Such cost savings and cost reductions can then be passed on to customers, enhancing perceived added value. In addition, companies can build customer value by working together with suppliers *and* customers on product improvements and new product development. Indeed, some studies suggest that major sources of innovation are upstream suppliers and customers.

Supply chain management

What has emerged from this concept of 'proactive' partnership is the idea of the 'extended supply chain'. While traditionally companies have tended to see their strengths in terms of their own capabilities and resources, the notion of the extended supply chain looks beyond the legal boundaries of the company for new sources of competitive advantage. Supply-chain management can be defined as the management of upstream and downstream relationships with suppliers, distributors and customers in such as way that greater customer value-added is achieved at less total cost. The result of a successful supply-chain management programme should be enhanced profit for all the partners in the chain.

Many companies have already found considerable benefit in developing partnerships in the supply chain. The Rover Group has achieved a significant improvement in its competitive position through developing a strategy based on what it calls 'the extended enterprise'. The aim is to seek to develop a seamless pipeline that moves and converts materials and components cost effectively into customer-specific finished products in the shortest possible time. To achieve this requires close relationships with a reduced supplier base, JIT assembly and a responsive, centrally managed distribution system with online information links with dealers. The result is that customers can walk into a Rover outlet, sit down at a computer screen and literally 'design' the car they want from the options available. Once the decision to buy has been made, the order can be transmitted directly to Rover and the car delivered from a central distribution facility if available from stock, and, if not, the order can be included in the production schedule.

Rover's partnership strategy was inspired partly by the success of its alliance with Honda. In 1981 Rover signed an agreement with Honda to begin a number of collaborative programmes in research and development, production and joint sourcing. For Rover, this relationship led to significant benefits in terms of access to superior engine technology and exposure to Japanese manufacturing management methods.

The advantage to Honda of this collaboration was an accelerated entry into Western European markets, lower costs of purchased materials through joint procurement programmes, access to design and styling skills with a European focus, and a large and growing market for its engines. Other car manufacturers around the world are following similar strategies based on partnership and collaboration as they see the mutual advantages that can accrue.

The benefits of partnership arrangements are being discovered in other industries too. Laura Ashley, the fabric and clothing manufacturer and retailer, was losing money and customers as it encountered growing problems in managing its complex global network of material and product flows into and out of its factories. Customers in their retail outlets were frustrated as out-of-stock incidence increased and seasonal styles arrived late, if at all.

To overcome this loss of competitive advantage, Laura Ashley decided to focus on its strengths, which were essentially design and marketing, and to build a partnership with Federal Express to manage all its in-bound and out-bound logistics. Federal Express has expertise in managing time-sensitive deliveries world-wide and it has an advanced 'tracking and tracing' information system, which means that product flow can be managed against known requirements in the retail stores.

The Laura Ashley–Federal Express partnership provides a good illustration of the benefits to an organization of focusing on that part of the value chain where the firm has a competitive advantage and then seeking a partner(s) to manage the other parts of the chain where the partner(s) has (have) superior skills. Many airlines now outsource their catering requirements because of the focused skills of these outside specialists. One company that has been a consistent advocate of the 'strategic alliance' is the Japanese company Toshiba, (see Case study 13.1).

Case study 13.1 Toshiba advocates strategic alliance

Over the years Toshiba has sought out alliances through technology-licensing agreements, joint ventures and partnerships to complement its own internal strengths and resources. These alliances often involve a considerable financial commitment and are long-term in their intent. As a result, Toshiba has become a world leader in many technologies and markets. For example, through its joint venture with Motorola, Toshiba is now the biggest producer of large-scale memory chips. Its collaboration with IBM in flat-screen colour-monitor technology has given it a significant edge in this fast-growing market. Often in return for the technology it imports from its partners, Toshiba provides access to its manufacturing skills and its product-development capability, whereby technologies can be converted rapidly into marketable products.

Partnerships, whatever the type or the specific arrangements involved, lie at the heart of relationship marketing and in the complex business environment of the twenty-first century may often be the only means by which competitive advantage can be secured.

The stronger the relationship with a value chain partner, the greater the barrier to entry it presents to competitors.

Strengthening buyer–seller relationships

The traditional idea that buyers and sellers should maintain a distance from each other and only concern themselves with 'negotiating a deal' can no longer be sustained. Instead, the trend is increasingly towards a much wider, business-development-focused relationship, where the supplier takes a holistic view of the customer's needs. A good example of this is provided by recent developments in what is sometimes termed 'trade marketing'. While much of the emphasis in traditional marketing has been placed on end-users to 'pull' the product through the marketing channel, trade marketing is concerned with gaining access to the marketing channel and increasing the 'opportunities to buy' experienced by end users; in other words, to ensure maximum shelf-space, distribution and availability is achieved. Occasionally these strategies are referred to as 'push' strategies; however, such a term implies a production orientation, and it is probably better to talk simply in terms of a 'relationship strategy'.

Let us revisit briefly the subject of key account management, covered in Chapter 12. Figure 13.7 (which effectively repeats Figures 12.3 and 12.5) highlights the difference between the two approaches. The conventional buyer–seller interface is a fragile connection, easily

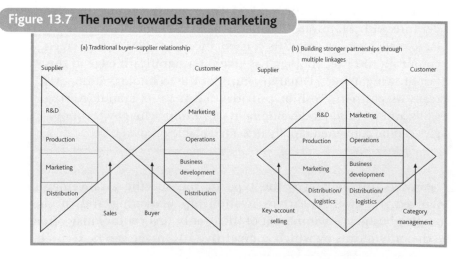

Figure 13.7 The move towards trade marketing

broken by competitors or the impact of market change. It is based on a motivation on the part of the buyer to maximize margin, and a motivation on the part of the seller to maximize volume.

In the relationship-based approach, the two 'triangles' are inverted to bring about a much stronger interface bond. Now there are multiple points of connection between the vendor and the customer. The objectives of the vendor are to develop the customer's business, to focus on the customer's return on investment and enhance the customer's own competitive capability. The benefit to the vendor if those objectives are achieved is the likelihood that it will be treated as a preferred supplier. At the same time, the costs of serving that customer should be lower as a result of a greater sharing of information, integrated logistics systems and so on.

Establishing such multiple 'connections' between the two parties clearly requires a mutual understanding of the benefits that can be achieved through partnership. In reality it will require a proactive approach from the vendor in which business solutions are presented to the customer; that is, a value proposition rather than a sales proposition. For example, many manufacturers marketing to the retail trade now seek to illustrate the impact of a proposed relationship in terms of a return on investment within the category in which the product in question competes. Thus the supplier must be able to demonstrate the impact that the relationship can have on shelf-space profitability, stock turnover and so on. For example, Johnson and Johnson in the personal healthcare market are category leaders for many major retailers. They undertake to optimize their returns for the retailer for a whole category of goods.

In the USA, these closer relationships between suppliers and retailers have led to the development of interlinked logistics and information systems known generically as 'quick-response' systems or 'efficient consumer response'. The underlying principle behind these systems is that information on sales is captured at the point of sale and transmitted directly to the supplier. The supplier can then schedule production and distribution on the basis of known demand rather than on order projections, which are unpredictable in volume and frequency. The benefits to the supplier are greatly reduced logistics costs and improved production efficiencies, while the retailer needs to carry less stock, and run out of stock less often. Such relationships have resulted in the supplier being awarded 'preferred supplier' status, thus gaining increased shelf-space. For example, within the first year of integrating their information and logistics system in this way with Wal-Mart (America's biggest retailer), Procter & Gamble's business with Wal-Mart grew by 40 per cent.

Marketing strategies which focus on optimizing channel relationships and the use of intermediaries are discussed further in Chapter 16.

Building end-user relationships

The ultimate business relationship is with the end-user. Even though the business may distribute its products through intermediaries, the challenge will always be to build an enduring relationship with the ultimate consumer. Meeting this challenge will never be easy. There will always be competitive offers that can match performance on the 'fundamentals'. Therefore, much more than customer satisfaction with the product or service is required to secure a long-term consumer relationship.

In Chapter 14 we shall discuss ways in which customer retention might be improved, but it is appropriate to stress here the importance of a two-way dialogue with consumers as a critical foundation for long-term, mutually profitable relationships. In many traditional marketing structures, a 'feedback loop' is not always available. Therefore opportunities for the consumer to respond to the experience of purchase and consumption should be created on a continuing basis. Customer 'hot lines', 0800 numbers and customer satisfaction surveys are just a few of the ways in which feedback can be obtained from the market place.

Consumer opinion should be involved at every step in the marketing process. For example, Boeing, the North American aircraft builder, has established extremely strong relationships with customers such as British Airways by involving them in the detailed design of aircraft from the drawing board onwards. Teams of engineers from British Airways worked alongside their counterparts at Boeing and General Electric (the engine manufacturers) to design the new 'Boeing 777' so that it would be both 'customer friendly' and 'end-user friendly'. Hence, British Airways engineering crews worked on improving the maintainability of the aircraft before it even left the drawing board. Similarly, luggage stowage in the cabin has been improved through close co-operation between Boeing and British Airways. It is largely because of the strength of this relationship that British Airways ordered fifteen 777s with General Electric engines with an option for a further fifteen at a price of £100 million each, in the face of stiff competition from Airbus and Rolls-Royce.

Barbour, the UK-based manufacturer of outdoor and sporting apparel, provides another example, albeit on a quite different scale, of how consumer involvement supports the building of end-user relationships. Purchasers of the various garments manufactured by Barbour are encouraged to return them to the factory when they need repair or reproofing and a free refurbishing service is provided at country fairs and exhibitions. Consumers' views on Barbour products are sought constantly, to help the company improve the product range. Advertising is also used to underline the theme of the relationship the Barbour user has with the product and, by implication, with the company. Small though the company is, it is highly profitable, with sales continuing to grow year by year.

Because the issue of improving customer relations and customer loyalty is so important, we have devoted Chapter 14 to customer retention strategy.

Customer relationship management

The term adopted at the time of writing for the philosophy outlined in this chapter is customer relationship management (CRM), in which the processes involved are underpinned by information technology. The exact definition of CRM varies according to whom you happen to be talking, or who is trying to sell it to you. This is because CRM is still in the formative stages of development and has yet to be given a universally agreed meaning. Following is a selection of the definitions of CRM being touted:

A continuous performance initiative to increase a company's knowledge of its customers.

CRM comprises the organization, processes and systems through which an organization manages its relationships with its customers.

Consistent high quality customer support across all communications channels and business functions, based on common information shared by employees, their customers and business partners.

A methodology, based on new information technology, that helps companies reach their long-held goals for improved customer satisfaction.

An integrated, multiple delivery channel strategy that allows companies to capture profitable new customers and improve service.

An emphasis on IT

It will be obvious from these descriptions that information technology (IT) forms the backbone of CRM. At the time of writing, CRM is being delivered as a method of combining one or more of the IT systems that exist or can be placed into an organization relating to the customer interface. Depending on the source of reference, the following are usually mentioned:

- ▶ Data warehouses;
- ▶ Customer service systems;
- ▶ Call centres;
- ▶ E-commerce;
- ▶ Web marketing;
- ▶ Operational systems (order entry, invoicing, payments, point-of-sale, and so on); and
- ▶ Sales systems (mobile representative communications, appointment making and so on).

The basic idea of CRM is to integrate these systems in such a way that the organization is able to manage its customers flawlessly. It goes without saying that operating different systems in the same organization which do not and cannot talk to each other is not conducive to efficiency. Nor does it allow for the delivery of a seamless customer experience. By integrating/cleansing/unifying diverse data and making it accessible in real time to those in the organization who need it, CRM can help the organization to develop and present a single view of customers. Such consistency and coherence in the treatment of customers contributes added value and, consequently, a competitive edge.

It will, however, be obvious that, no matter what particular definition is given for CRM, and no matter how much money is spent on databases and on systems for accessing and promulgating such data, unless there exists a deep understanding of the market and of the needs of customers within market segments, CRM will become merely the latest fad and will soon wane in importance.

The features of CRM

The promised benefits of adopting a CRM approach to managing customer relationships derive from the ability to reduce unpredictable customer behaviour to data that can be analysed, plotted, planned and categorized. Table 13.2 outlines the features of CRM.

Table 13.2 The features of CRM

- ► Customer analysis
- ► Market segmentation
- ► Manage target marketing activities
- ► Model customer behaviour (predictive)
- ► Customer service history
- ► Access self-service patterns
- ► Customer marketing history
- ► Measure customer retention
- ► Measure customer loyalty
- ► 'Single view' of the customer
- ► Revenue analysis
- ► Customer information (demographics and life cycle/lifestyle)
- ► Score customer responsiveness to different forms of communication and service
- ► Identify different forms of product/service in use

The question remains, however, will CRM deliver? If the answer is 'I don't care, let's give it a go', do you remember the last time you felt like this? When was it, about the time of business process re-engineering? Benchmarking? Customer service? Investors in People? Or was it even about the time of total quality management or 'Excellence'? None of these initiatives was a bad idea, but very few got anywhere near delivering the benefits that were promised.

Of course, executives hope CRM will be different. The problem is, this time we don't just risk messing up the back-office processes, now we are playing with customer relationships, and if we get CRM wrong, customers will leave, never to return.

What is CRM all about?

Ultimately, CRM has to be about *competitive advantage*. This is what organizations want and what the consultants can sell. There is also no doubt that CRM can be a major factor in achieving competitive advantage, but whether CRM is the whole answer is quite another question.

There are three legs to the CRM 'stool': strategy; marketing; and IT. Take just one of the legs away and it will fall over. Try to build CRM on just one leg alone and it won't stand up. The simple truth is, CRM projects will spill out enormous amounts of customer data. Whether the organization is able to make that data meaningful by turning it into information and then into knowledge depends on whether the organization knows what it wants to do with it. Imagine (and this is a real example) that you discover the most important fact (correlation) about the heaviest users of your communication service, is that they are likely to be cat owners. Then what? Joint promotions between telecoms and cat food? Too many companies believe that all they have to do is to collect large amounts of similarly pointless data and they will finally be able to meet those (ludicrous) cross-selling objectives. The power to annoy more customers, faster and at greater cost, is a distinct danger.

Appreciating the issues

All the CRM literature we have seen does (more or less clearly) state that the success of any CRM project depends on key strategic issues being agreed before any work is done. And, to be fair, those organizations marketing CRM solutions at the time of writing do mention the other things that need to be in place before (their version of) CRM will work. Unfortunately, these 'things' are neither small nor particularly easy to put in place. Of course, nobody writes this in red, or inserts health warnings at this point, but it needs to be done.

Perhaps it is time to learn from the pioneers of a previous technological age. Imagine CRM as the railway track. Lay the lines and it will get the train to its destination quickly and efficiently – you may have to knock down a few buildings standing in the way, but that is surely a small price to pay. The eighteenth-century entrepreneurs soon learned (sometimes the hard way) that success existed less in knowing how to lay the lines and more in knowing where people wanted the trains to go.

Pushing the image as far as (or even beyond where) it will go, imagine the company trying to build the first, fastest and best line to, well, anywhere really. Customers are taken along for the ride and arrive where none of them ever wanted to be. Exit the customers and exit the business – faster than if it had done nothing in the first place.

The point is that, in order to realize the benefits of CRM listed in Table 13.3, the organization must first be clear on where it is intending to go and how it is going to get there.

Table 13.3 The potential benefits of CRM

- ▶ Identify most profitable customers
- ▶ Serve most profitable customers better
- ▶ Manage less profitable situations better
- ▶ Identify the lifetime value of customers
- ▶ Reduce customer 'churn'
- ▶ Find profitable prospects
- ▶ Market the right products
- ▶ Reduce selling and marketing costs
- ▶ Improve effectiveness of marketing communications and direct marketing
- ▶ Improve customer service
- ▶ Focus Internet/e-commerce on the right customers
- ▶ Focus marketing to the right customers
- ▶ Refine marketing strategy
- ▶ Obtain competitive advantage
- ▶ Win!

So the questions that need to be answered are:

- ▶ Where are we now? (industry and market);
- ▶ What do our customers want? (benefits, not features);
- ▶ What will our customers want tomorrow? (company objective/future role);
- ▶ Do different customers want different things? (segmentation);
- ▶ Which customers should we be targeting? (strategic segmentation); and
- ▶ How do we differentiate our company/brand(s)? (differentiation/unique market position).

The investment involved in agreeing the organization's longer-term ambitions (and therefore the objectives for a CRM project) will be minute compared to the cost of the CRM project itself. Experience has shown that the IT and organizational costs of CRM are likely to run to many millions – and that is without the potential business costs of getting it wrong. Very few companies would embark on a major capital project without a feasibility study, or an acquisition without 'due diligence'. CRM should be treated no differently, and will therefore require a CRM audit.

What is a CRM audit? As the name implies, it is an unbiased assessment of an organization's current customer position and requirements from any CRM process, as described in Table 13.4. An audit such as this represents an investment that pays off in two directions: it reduces the downside risks of disaster and increases the upside benefits from success.

Taking the CRM decision

Any organization contemplating introducing CRM into its relationship management strategy should first ensure that it has given full consideration to the following key issues:

Customers: Customers are the name of the game. Without customers there is no business. Marketing guru, Theodore Levitt (1960) said: 'The purpose of a business is to create and keep customers'. Achieving that is not easy, especially as most customers make emotional rather than rational buying decisions and, more often than not, have no idea what they want.

Table 13.4 The CRM audit

▶ An identification of the market being served, answering 'What business are we in?'

▶ A quantification of the customer/process dynamics within this market

▶ An understanding of the competitive environment, including competitor positions and competitive dynamics

▶ An unbiased (*not* a priori!) segmentation of the market we are interested in serving

▶ An understanding of customer needs in each segment

▶ A realistic assessment of the organizational implications of introducing CRM

▶ An outline plan for the introduction of CRM

▶ An assessment of the likely costs and benefits of CRM for the organization

▶ An outline brief for CRM suppliers, especially IT

Relationships: How many 'relationships' does the firm have? How many of them are with commercial organizations? If the objective is simply to retain more customers for longer to make more money, this can probably be achieved by making fewer mistakes, so giving fewer excuses for customers to leave. Building a 'relationship' is quite another matter. Do customers want a 'relationship' in the first place? 'Please stop sending me birthday cards; just answer the phone when I ring' is a frequent customer complaint. Research indicates that supplier delusions about the state of the customer relationship have reached alarming proportions. It should also be remembered that, just as in our own personal lives the capacity to build close relationships with *all* our friends is limited, so too is it with major customers.

Management: Almost everything we read about CRM either talks about (or implies) the organization managing its customer relationships. Much as it might be the preferred route, it just does not work like that. As stated earlier in the book, 'You don't manage the customer; your customer manages you.' Most customers like to feel in control, so the organization helps them. Information flows, systems and processes designed from the customers' perspective might give the organization a better chance of achieving the desired results; happy customers spending more and more often.

Whether CRM is to become just another 'management fad', or whether it will achieve 'management solution' status depends on how well those who use it apply the concepts. In order of most frequent mention, these concepts are:

► A deep understanding of the market;
► Market segmentation (*not* 'your own database segmentation');
► Differentiation, positioning and branding; and
► Integrated marketing (marketing planning).

Because a CRM approach to managing customer relationships is based on the exploitation of meaningful customer data and identified customer behaviour, we have described CRM in more detail in Chapter 19, under the marketing subprocess, monitoring value.

Summary

As markets fragment and 'the competition' evolves, the traditional transaction-based approach to marketing is being replaced by a broader, relationship-based approach. Relationship marketing emphasizes that there must be at least as much attention placed on keeping customers as on getting them. This requires that marketing becomes a cross-functional rather than an isolated activity.

The development of successful relationship marketing strategies can be enhanced by a focus on multiple markets, namely: customer and consumer markets; referral markets; internal markets; recruitment markets; influencer markets; and supplier and alliance markets. Specific, but complementary, strategies should be designed for each of these markets, the ultimate goal being to create a partnership approach to marketing that embraces the entire supply chain to achieve greater customer value at every level in the chain.

The adoption of a CRM approach to managing the organization's relationships should be preceded by a serious consideration of whether the purpose for which it intended can be achieved through alternative routes, and whether the considerable investment that it is likely to entail is justifiable.

Further reading

Levitt, T. (1960) 'Marketing Myopia', *Harvard Business Review.* July–August, pp. 45–60.

Mattsson, L. (1997) Relationship marketing and the markets as networks approach – a comparative analysis of two evolving streams of research. *Journal of Marketing Management*, **13** pp. 447–61.

References

Christopher, M., Payne, A. and Ballantyne, D. (1991) *Relationship Marketing*, Butterworth-Heinemann, Oxford.

McDonald, M. (2001) On the right track. *Marketing Business* (June).

14 Customer retention strategy

In this chapter we study the:

- ► link between customer retention and profitability
- ► ladder of loyalty
- ► key elements of a customer retention strategy
- ► customer retention improvement process
- ► need to research the causes of customer defection and customer loyalty
- ► critical success factors and the critical failure factors
- ► importance of correct market segmentation for customer retention programmes

Customer retention alongside customer acquisition

It has been suggested that it costs up to five times as much to win a new customer as it does to retain an existing customer. The costs of capturing market share are not always easy to gauge, but there are many companies who now regret earlier strategies based on the blind pursuit of volume. While there is strong evidence for the link between market share and profitability, there is equally strong evidence to show that it is the *quality* of that market share that counts. In other words, does the customer base comprise, in the main, long-established, loyal customers, or is there a high degree of customer turnover, or 'churn'? If the latter is the case, then the chances are the company is not as profitable as it might be.

The international consulting company, Bain and Company, has suggested that even a relatively small improvement in the customer retention rate (measured as the percentage of retained business from one period to another) can have a marked impact on profitability. Their research indicates that, on average, an improvement of five percentage points in customer retention can lead to profit improvements of between 25 per cent and 95 per cent in the net present value of the future flow of earnings. Figure 14.1 shows how this profit impact varies across a range of industries.

Why should a retained customer be more profitable than a new one? First, because of the costs of acquiring new business in the first place, it might take time to bring a new customer into profit. Second, the more satisfied customers are with the relationship, the more likely they are to place a bigger proportion of their total purchase with the company, even to the extent of 'single sourcing' from it. Third, these retained customers become easier to sell to, with consequent lower costs; also, they are more likely to be willing to integrate their systems (for example, their planning, scheduling and ordering systems) with the company's, leading to further cost reductions. In some markets, satisfied customers may also refer others, leading to a further enhancement of profitability. Finally, Bain and Company suggested that loyal customers are often less price-sensitive and less inclined to switch

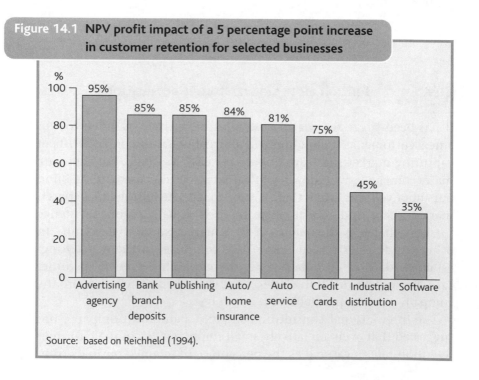

Figure 14.1 NPV profit impact of a 5 percentage point increase in customer retention for selected businesses

Source: based on Reichheld (1994).

suppliers because of price rises. All these elements combine to lead to the conclusion that retained customers generate considerably more profit than do new ones. Figure 14.2 summarizes this relationship.

A study of the North American car industry suggested that a satisfied customer is likely to stay with the same supplier for a further twelve years after the first satisfactory purchase, and during that period will buy four more cars of the same make. It is estimated that, to a car manufacturer, this level of customer retention is worth US $400 million in new car sales annually.

There is a direct linkage between the customer retention rate and the average duration of a customer relationship. For example, if the customer retention rate is 90 per cent per annum (meaning that 10 per cent of the existing customer base is lost each year) then the average customer lifetime will be ten years. If, on the other hand, the customer retention rate is improved to 95 per cent per annum (meaning that 5 per cent of the customers are lost each year), then the average customer lifetime will be twenty years. In other words, a doubling of the average customer lifetime is achieved for a relatively small improvement in the customer retention rate. Figure 14.3 illustrates the relationship between customer retention rate and customer lifetime.

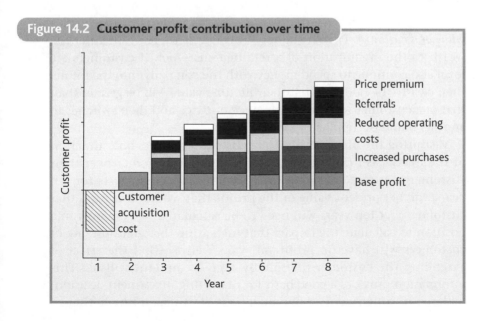

Figure 14.2 Customer profit contribution over time

Figure 14.3 Impact of customer retention rate on customer lifetime

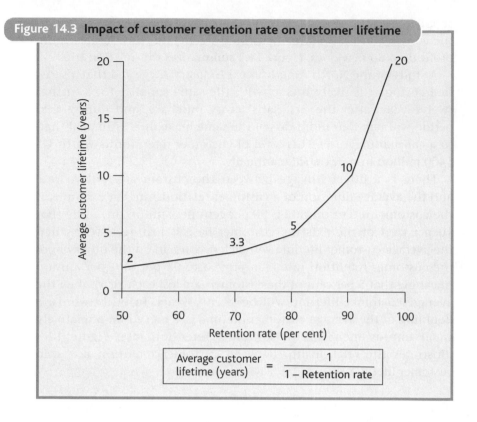

$$\text{Average customer lifetime (years)} = \frac{1}{1 - \text{Retention rate}}$$

An important statistic that is not always measured is the *lifetime value of a customer*. Put very simply, this is a measure of the financial worth to the organization of a retained customer. If customers are loyal and continue to spend money with the company into the future, then clearly the odds are that their lifetime value will be greater than that of a customer who buys only once or twice and then switches to another brand or supplier.

Measuring the lifetime value of a customer requires an estimation of the likely cash flow to be provided by that customer over their customer lifetime. That is to say, if a typical account lasts for ten years, the net present value of the profits that would flow from that customer over ten years will need to be calculated. We are now in a position to calculate the impact that increasing the retention rate of customers will have on profitability, as well as what the effect of extending the customer lifetime by a given amount will be. This information provides a good basis for marketing investment decision-making; in other words, how much is it worth spending, either to improve the customer retention rate or to extend the life of a customer relationship? This raises the complex issue of understanding, measuring and managing customer loyalty.

The ladder of loyalty

It will be apparent from the previous comments that customer loyalty must become one of the principal objectives of marketing strategy. Customer loyalty is defined as a commitment to continue to do business with a company on an ongoing basis. The aim should be to seek to create committed customers, not customers who are 'locked in'. A customer who is figuratively 'held prisoner' is unlikely to stay with their current supplier if an alternative supplier makes a satisfactory offer.

It is perhaps worth highlighting here that this notion of encouraging customers willingly and voluntarily to make repeat purchases with a particular supplier underpins a key marketing principle: customer choice. Having the option to choose, and options to choose from, is crucial to marketing dynamics. Without choice, suppliers would be unable to create a unique selling proposition (USP) and to target their most promising opportunities; and customers would be unable to express their needs and purchase preferences, settling for something less-than-acceptable, or not at all. As suppliers' promotional activities become increasingly aggressive and personalized, marketers test the fine line between exercising reasonable pressure and exerting excessive force. The most successful marketing, in terms of building long-term, profitable relationships with customers, has always been founded on a basis of mutual interest, trust and respect. This winning formula is unlikely to change in the foreseeable future.

When developing customer-loyalty-building strategies, it is helpful to think in terms of a supplier taking a customer up a 'ladder of loyalty', as portrayed in Figure 14.4. The bottom rung of the ladder represents the potential market for our product or service. At this stage we do not know the precise identity of these people (or companies) but we hope we know something of their characteristics – for example, their demographic profile, lifestyle and so on. The use of marketing databases (discussed in Chapter 19) can be a valuable means of distinguishing from among the 'suspects' any potential targets, or 'prospects' for our offer.

Figure 14.4 The ladder of loyalty

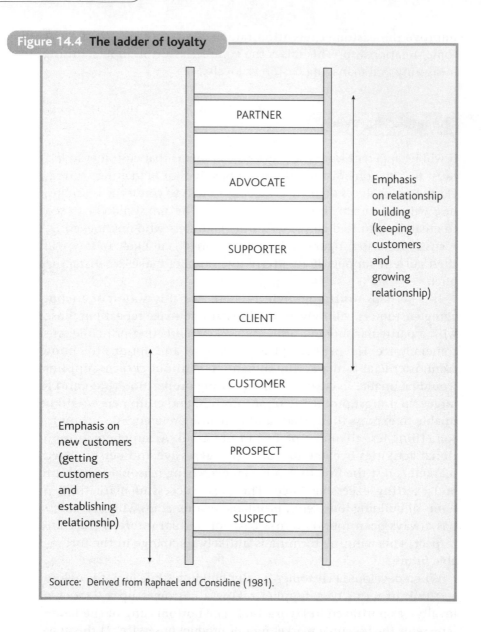

PARTNER

ADVOCATE

SUPPORTER

CLIENT

CUSTOMER

PROSPECT

SUSPECT

Emphasis on relationship building (keeping customers and growing relationship)

Emphasis on new customers (getting customers and establishing relationship)

Source: Derived from Raphael and Considine (1981).

Once prospects have been identified, the sales process proper begins. These prospects may first need to be 'qualified' to select those most likely to be in the market for our product or service, and to filter out those who are not. This can be achieved by a number of means, including direct mail, telephone interviews or even field sales visits, although the latter is usually reserved for use as a follow-up once enquiries have been received via other, more cost-effective means.

Only when a sale has been made, do we have a customer. For many companies, this closing of the sale is seen as the culmination of the marketing process. However, under the relationship marketing process, the conversion of a 'prospect' to a 'customer' should be seen as just the start of a journey of building customer loyalty.

To elevate the customer to 'client' status, we must establish a pattern of repeat buying by making it easy for the customer to do business with us. Being a client does not necessarily signal a *commitment*, however. Banks, for example, have regular customers who might be termed clients. Yet many of those clients may well express high levels of dissatisfaction with the service they receive, and if it were possible for them to move accounts easily, they would not hesitate to switch to another bank. In order to obtain seriously committed clients we must develop a customer-orientated approach that persuades our clients to become our 'supporters' – meaning that they are pleased with the service they receive and happy to provide continued custom.

If they are really impressed with the quality of service and if the relationship exceeds their expectations, they may turn into 'advocates' – meaning that they tell others about their satisfaction with our offer. Given the power of word of mouth, this type of advocacy can be worth more than any amount of advertising.

The final rung on the ladder of loyalty sees the customer as 'partner'. 'Partnership' is achieved where a mutually rewarding relationship exists, and neither party intends to leave the other. The concept of 'partnership' as a desirable goal of business relationships is fast gaining acceptance, particularly in industrial and business-to-business marketing. As stressed in Chapter 13, forging partnerships in the supply chain can yield considerable benefits.

The ladder of loyalty, while being a simple idea, can provide a practical framework around which to build specific customer retention strategies.

Developing a customer retention strategy

In the previous chapter we discussed the concept of relationship marketing, and suggested that the goal of marketing activity should be not only to win customers but also to keep them. This begs the question: 'What does it take to keep a customer?'

Customers continue to buy from a particular supplier because they perceive that the total 'value' they gain from the relationship is greater than the total cost that they incur. The challenge to the supplier, therefore, is to seek continually to improve the ratio between the perceived value the customer derives from the offer and the perceived cost. As mentioned in Chapters 9 and 10, the perceived cost includes not only price, but also switching costs and ongoing costs, such as maintenance, servicing and running costs.

If we wish to strengthen the relationship with our customers, it can be helpful to look more closely at *their* value chains. It is only by understanding their own processes that we can identify where in those processes it is possible for us as a supplier to have a positive impact. For example, if we identify that currently some customers are carrying high levels of inventory – say stocks of spares – then the implementation of a rapid-response logistics programme might enable them to carry less inventory, thus their costs will be reduced and they will run out of stock less often. Such an initiative could therefore both raise customers' value and lower their costs.

A similar approach can often be applied in marketing to end-users. For example, many modern consumers are 'time-sensitive' and products that can be augmented by a service dimension – for example, home delivery – can lead to a strengthened customer relationship. The North American company, Domino's Pizza, took a big share of the massive US market for pizza by basing its entire business philosophy around providing a reliable, speedy home-delivery service where customers receive their telephoned orders less than an hour after placing their call. Domino's expansion into the UK market is showing similar success. The key elements of a retention strategy are outlined in Table 14.1.

Table 14.1 Key elements of a customer retention strategy

► Retention strategy is based on clear and achievable retention objectives

► Retention objectives support and reinforce corporate and marketing objectives

► Visible leadership and commitment of senior management (personal enthusiasm and allocation of sufficient resources)

► Genuine empowerment of employees

► Valid endorsement of other stakeholders (shareholders, suppliers, legislators and so on)

Table 14.1 *continued*

- ▶ Relevant and accurate segmentation of customers (consider current and potential customer value)

- ▶ Meaningful and usable market information and intelligence

- ▶ Selective retention effort (grow most valuable customers/develop or drop least valuable customers)

- ▶ Design and development of proactive retention programmes (with goals of defection prevention and retention improvement)

- ▶ Organization-wide communication and implementation of retention programmes

- ▶ Continual monitoring of retention programmes performance and revision as necessary

- ▶ Regular review and reassessment of retention strategy

Developing a customer retention programme

Apart from striving continually to offer a superior product at a competitive price, with strong brand values (or corporate image), what else can a company do to stop its customers preferring to do business with the competition? Increasingly, organizations are realizing that they need to develop *active* customer retention strategies as opposed to the more conventional passive approach to retention. The market place of the twenty-first century – whether we are talking about consumer, service or industrial markets – is much more volatile than hitherto and is characterized by a greater willingness on the part of customers to switch brands or suppliers. Hence, the need to develop explicit programmes to improve customer retention has become a business imperative.

Figure 14.5 outlines an approach to developing a *proactive* customer retention programme based on understanding not only what motivates customers to stay with suppliers, but also what prompts them to leave suppliers. The average rate of customer retention that results from implementing the process represents the organization's customer retention level. The customer retention improvement process can be viewed as working from the top of the figure downwards, with the output of early warning and remedial action feeding back into customer retention level measurement. Let us review each of the steps in turn.

Figure 14.5 Customer retention improvement process

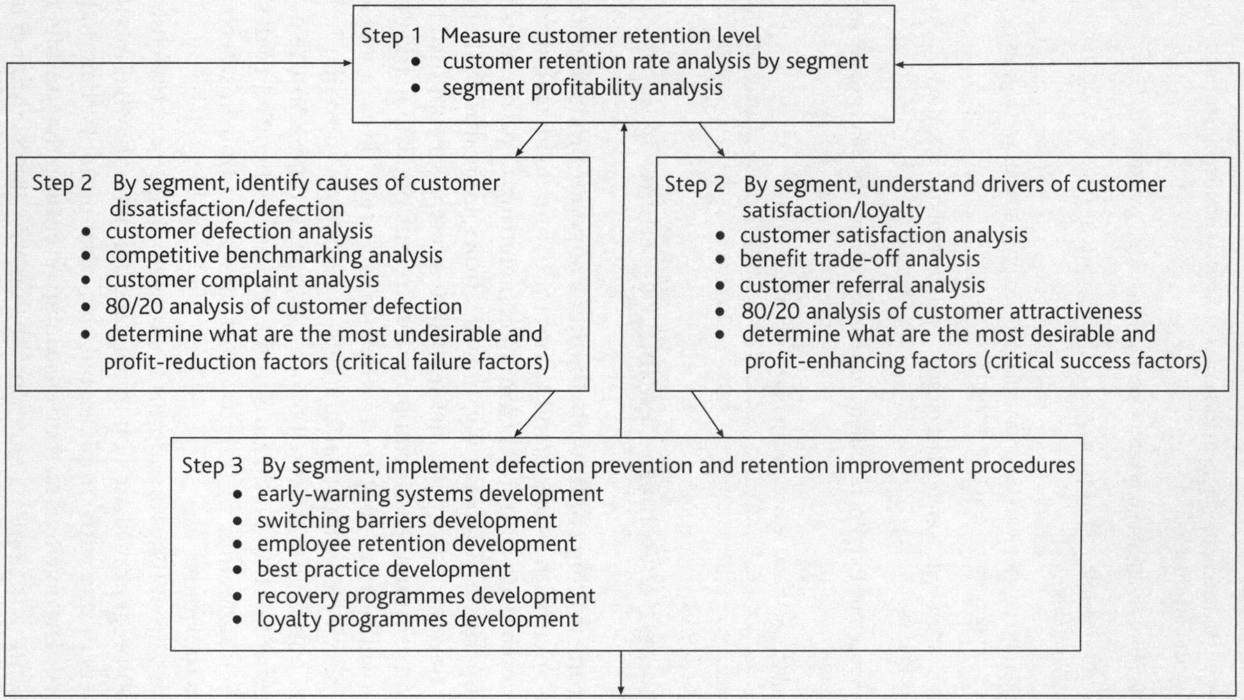

Step 1 Measure customer retention level
- customer retention rate analysis by segment
- segment profitability analysis

Step 2 By segment, identify causes of customer dissatisfaction/defection
- customer defection analysis
- competitive benchmarking analysis
- customer complaint analysis
- 80/20 analysis of customer defection
- determine what are the most undesirable and profit-reduction factors (critical failure factors)

Step 2 By segment, understand drivers of customer satisfaction/loyalty
- customer satisfaction analysis
- benefit trade-off analysis
- customer referral analysis
- 80/20 analysis of customer attractiveness
- determine what are the most desirable and profit-enhancing factors (critical success factors)

Step 3 By segment, implement defection prevention and retention improvement procedures
- early-warning systems development
- switching barriers development
- employee retention development
- best practice development
- recovery programmes development
- loyalty programmes development

Step 1   Measure customer retention level

Any effort towards customer retention improvement must be based on the current level of customer retention. Customer retention itself may be measured/defined in several different ways, depending on the circumstances. For example, in the case of long-term contracts such as insurance policies and bank accounts, retention is measured/defined by renewals. For more frequent transactions, retention is often used synonymously with customer loyalty, which may refer to customer attitudes, repeat purchase behaviour, or share of category requirements. Nevertheless, retention level measurement will necessarily take into account the customer retention rate, or percentage of customers at the beginning of the measurement period that remain at the end of the measurement period.

However, it is important to note that a single customer may be retained by more than one supplier within the same product or service category, and thus the retention rate being measured is 'non-exclusive'. For example, customers may hold savings or credit accounts with two or three different financial services providers concurrently in order to optimize their (personal or corporate) financial status. It is important to note also that a single customer might place the bulk of his/her business with one supplier, while still holding open less-used accounts. Thus the retention rate measured by the supplying organization that has the customer's major account will reflect a greater 'share of wallet' than the organizations that have the customer's minor accounts. For these reasons it is wise to track changes in individual and collective customer spending; that is, to monitor fluctuations in account spending and to identify any patterns of behaviour that digress from the customer norm.

Customer retention-level measurement must also consider the reality that some customer relationships are more precious to the supplying organization than others. As limited resources dictate that no organization 'can be all things to all people', it is vital that marketing strategies are selective and prioritizing. The aim should be to retain the most valuable customer relationships and to develop or drop the least valuable ones. This involves rewarding 'valuable customer relationship' behaviour visibly while actively dissuading customers who up to that point have not met (in the case of existing customers) or are unlikely to meet (in the case of potential customers) the 'valuable customer relationship' criteria. Such criteria form the basis of segment profitability analysis.

Segment profitability analysis is an examination of different customer segments in terms of their present and future profitability. Its purpose is to increase customer retention among the segments of highest 'attractiveness' to the supplying organization. What defines 'attractive' will vary from organization to organization, as each will be unique in its situation and goals. However, critical aspects of customer attractiveness for any supplier will be customer lifetime value and customer life-cycle position, as discussed earlier in the chapter.

Step 2   Identify defection causes/understand loyalty drivers

Measuring an organization's customer retention level is not an easy task, but it is a critical one. The customer retention level provides the springboard for launching improvements as well as the gauge for determining their effectiveness. Using the wrong measures, measuring the wrong things, or not monitoring customer retention sufficiently, can result in missing telling indicators of potential customer defection. It can also result in not recognizing potential opportunities for relationship growth. Let us consider more closely both sides of Step 2 in Figure 14.5, beginning with the left-hand box.

Identify causes of customer dissatisfaction/defection

Astonishingly, few organizations research thoroughly the underlying causes of customer dissatisfaction and defection. Those that do tend to conduct their marketing research solely on the basis of customer satisfaction, a criterion that does not always explain accurately *why* customers abandon one supplier for another. Poorly constructed satisfaction surveys and questionnaires are often the culprit. For example, a questionnaire used by one high street bank asked departing customers why they were closing their accounts. Among the available multiple-choice answers was 'the account is no longer required'. Not surprisingly, the vast majority of respondents ticked this box because it represented a safe and easy answer, and none of the alternative answers addressed the real reasons for defection.

Research into the loss of customer relationships can be carried out successfully through market investigation (telephone interviews, postal questionnaires and, where appropriate, in-depth interviews and focus groups), followed by careful data analysis and interpretation. The objective of such *defection analysis* is to dig as deeply as possible below the surface to identify the root causes of defection. For example, many business-to-business customers may cite 'price' as their reason for leaving a long-standing relationship, but that might be an 'umbrella' response harbouring dissatisfaction with customer service, lack of responsiveness, unreliability and so on.

Because the decision to change suppliers or brands is not taken lightly by most customers, it will usually be cumulative dissatisfaction that confirms the decision to leave. It follows, therefore, that, if we can pin down the causes of dissatisfaction, specific actions can be taken to redress, and ideally remove, them. Over the years, businesses have accumulated a wealth of experience in what works for customers and what does not. Organizations that not only survive, but also thrive, embody valuable clues about the causes of customer dissatisfaction and defection.

Thus, one popular method of identifying the root causes of customer dissatisfaction and defection is *competitive benchmarking*. This involves using accepted standards of performance as reference points for comparing an organization with its competitors. Checking an organization's performance on critical elements – for example, sales per unit, market share or customer churn – against that of established or emerging rivals, provides a 'relative' index of performance success. However, this comparison of performance to the best achieved by competitors has met with criticism in some industries, where the performance of even the leading competitor is considered to be poor. Many choose instead to use *best practice benchmarking*, which compares the performance of a process to the best universal performance standard. Where the organization matches recognized best practice, natural delight should be accompanied by a determination to take the lead and do even better. Where the organization exceeds best practice, the focus should be on working constantly to sustain this achievement and help to guide others in a similar direction. It is strongly advised, however, that competitive benchmarking and best practice benchmarking be used only in conjunction with in-house market research: there is little point in following a leader blindly whose direction may be misguided or, in the circumstances, inappropriate!

Customer complaint analysis is another way of revealing the features of customer discontent. Often customer complaints will provide an indication of the source of dissatisfaction, but it must be remembered that only a minority of customers complain – the rest just 'vote with their feet'. There is something to be said for actively seeking criticism from customers. Customer feedback, be it a constructive comment or a venting of frustration, provides a means for gaining insightful knowledge that can then be acted upon to deliver improvement and even innovation. It also provides a way of demonstrating to customers that they are valued for more than just the contents of their wallets. Research has shown that this 'feel-good factor' is a contributor to competitive differentiation and customer preference. Research has also shown that negative word of mouth can have a devastating effect. A customer may tell one or two other people about a good experience, but they will probably tell at least seven people about a bad one. Any retention programme should therefore welcome customer complaints and include procedures for dealing with them promptly and professionally as well as minimizing them as much as possible.

While there are many reasons why customers break off relationships with their suppliers, the 80/20, or Pareto, rule normally applies: that is, 80 per cent of customers leave for the same 20 per cent of reasons. A key component of the customer retention improvement process is therefore an *80/20 analysis of customer defection*. The negative aspects of performance that customers most frequently nominate as having the greatest bearing on their decision to leave suppliers are termed 'critical failure factors' (CFFs). Common CFFs include:

▶ a product that fails to perform as promised;
▶ poor service (for example, long queues/waiting times, untrained staff, unreliable delivery and so on); and
▶ price (for example, perceived value/perceived cost ratio is unacceptable).

Organizations that are dedicated to identifying the most prevalent reasons for defection and to redressing those causal factors within their control clearly have a leading edge over their competitors. Organizations that do not get to the bottom of customer switching behaviour are condemned to continue losing customers and achieving an unnecessarily poor (business and customer) performance.

Understand drivers of customer satisfaction/loyalty

The customer retention improvement process is, in a sense, a two-edged sword: it cuts both ways. On the one hand it aims to reduce or eliminate the propensity for customers to leave a company, while on the other it aims to reshape customer perception and cut out the competition to some degree so that customers stay with the company longer. Thus, in addition to and at the same time as identifying the causes of customer dissatisfaction and defection, we must also be seeking to understand the drivers of customer satisfaction and loyalty.

It is only by knowing what customers want that we can strive to meet their requirements better than do our competitors. (Simply knowing what they *don't* want doesn't tell us what they *do* want.)

Here, we use the term 'customer loyalty' in its broadest sense – encompassing customer affinity, or an inspired sense of empathy or association with a supplier, and customer 'stickiness', or a reluctance to break the bond with a supplier. Again, it is understood that a customer's loyalty is not the exclusive domain of one supplier, and that a customer may be 'loyal' to multiple suppliers simultaneously. One customer retention objective, therefore, is to shrink the customer's pool of preferred suppliers, while remaining firmly within it.

Effective *customer satisfaction analysis* requires organization-wide agreement about what exactly is meant by 'customer satisfaction'. For some suppliers, customers might be deemed to be 'satisfied' if they do not complain, while for others it might take a repeat purchase or two to be convinced. Yet others might adopt the stance that customers are *never* satisfied, and the best a supplier can do is to try not to *dis*satisfy them. So, the issue of measuring customer satisfaction levels is challenging, to say the least, especially as the factors that satisfy one segment may be inappropriate when applied to a different segment in the same market. Thus, great care is necessary in this crucial task, as can be seen from the case history at the end of this chapter.

The quest to identify the elements of performance that are most important to customers and that have the greatest influence on their relationship behaviour entails understanding customers from a customer perspective. *Benefit trade-off analysis*, or conjoint analysis (see Chapter 10) allows different product/service or brand benefits identified by the customer to be 'traded-off' against each other to reveal the customer's benefit priorities. The resulting information and insights can then be used to develop more customer-orientated and customer-specific marketing strategies.

Customers also offer valuable insights into what characteristics they deem important in a supplier by the recommendations they give to others about specific products, services or brands. Increasingly, supplying organizations are asking new customers how they found out about the company, and whether a friend, family member or colleague who had already tried the product or service had spurred their interest. By studying the nature of such customer 'advocacy' through *customer referral analysis*, suppliers can work out to some extent what drives customer opinion to the point where customers need to share 'a good thing' with people they respect.

Just as there are many reasons why customers are disappointed with the products and services they receive, there are also many reasons why customers are pleased, and even thrilled, with the outcome of their supplier relationship. These positive aspects, or critical success factors (CSFs), can be identified through an *80/20 analysis of customer attractiveness*. Studies to date have shown CSFs to include:

▶ a product that performs reliably and consistently every time;
▶ good customer service (for example, staff are well-trained and empowered to act, transactions are smooth, complaints are handled professionally, previous custom is remembered and rewarded, only relevant communications are received from the company and so on);
▶ availability (for example, no out-of-stock situations, convenient access to information and sales outlets and so on);
▶ an organization that is easy to communicate with, should the need arise;
▶ consistent messages across all points of customer contact;
▶ a product that appeals to the customer's image and lifestyle;
▶ a price that truly reflects the value offered; and
▶ other CSFs, depending on the product or service in question.

To summarize, understanding CSFs is the very lifeblood of marketing, because if we can outperform our competitors on some or all of these points, we shall truly know why our customers prefer to buy from us rather than from whomever else offers competitive goods or services. Also, knowing CSFs will enable us to strive continuously for improvement.

Step 3 Implement defection prevention and retention improvement procedures

The third step ensures customer retention improvement through taking both preventive and corrective action. Such measures are based on the knowledge and insights gleaned from the first two steps, and a commitment to do better.

A crucial feature of any retention improvement programme is *early warning systems development*. The value of an early warning system is that it recognizes a potential danger immediately and alerts those who need to know so that they are able to act promptly and responsibly either to remove the threat or to reduce its impact. As supplying organizations increasingly interact with customers through multiple touchpoints, it is increasingly important to have real-time, organization-wide performance feedback and procedures for processing effectively. Customer empowerment and technological advances mean that in many cases customers can depart or switch suppliers at the click of a mouse. It is also important that everyone in the organization is vigilant to emerging problems, is kept up to date on problem areas relevant to their responsibilities, and is invited to offer ideas for current and future problem-solving.

Customer defection prevention can also be obtained through *switching barriers development*. The idea here is proactively to dissuade the customer from leaving the relationship by erecting obstacles that make it especially undesirable or difficult to go. Strategic bundling, where groups of products or services are offered together as a package deal or 'bundle' of benefits, can prove irresistible to the determined bargain-hunter or convenience-orientated customer. Customer switching cost, or the cost to a customer of changing from using one product or service to using another can be an effective deterrent to customers who want to switch. However, it may also be a deterrent to potential customers who are wary that the cost of switching will be prohibitive if they find they are dissatisfied, so great care is needed here, and suppliers should adhere to a code of ethics that leaves them beyond reproach. (There is an in-depth discussion of this topic in Chapter 22.)

Team-based relationship management, or key account management (see Chapter 12), is a barrier often used in business-to-business marketing. It works on the basis that the more links that are forged between customers and supplier, the harder it will be for the customers to extricate themselves from the relationship. For example, a web of connections may be established between the supplier's production team and the customer's operations team, the supplier's marketing team and the customer's business development team, and so on. Any form of collaborative activity/investment can also be a 'tie that binds', providing a powerful disincentive to switch suppliers.

However, switching barriers should only be constructed if they serve the interests of both customers and supplier. If customers feel 'locked in' to an unsatisfactory relationship, or are offended by overt gestures that signal a degree of mistrust, this could lead to damaging publicity and greatly reduced profits.

Another major inhibitor to customer defection and dissatisfaction lies within the culture of the organization itself – *employee retention development*. We noted earlier that happy employees make for happy customers, and vice versa. This truism extends to employee and customer retention. Employees who are satisfied and motivated in their jobs, and based within an internal culture that they find exciting, challenging and worthwhile, are more likely to be retained than those who cannot claim to have such a positive work experience. Improved employee retention is likely to deliver improved internal and external service quality. This creates greater customer value, which in turn generates customer satisfaction and retention.

Best practice development within the organization also promotes customer retention. By comparing internal practices with those identified as superior through benchmarking (see Chapter 5), managers can seek to adopt better organizational and operational approaches where appropriate. Much guidance and benefit can be gained from learning from the experience of others. Situations where other departments or industries have achieved recognized excellence in customer satisfaction and retention can provide valuable sources of information and help.

In addition to implementing measures to prevent customer dissatisfaction and defection, it is important to take corrective action where necessary to rescue a failing customer relationship and remedy any damage caused. This is the area of *recovery programmes development*. Because it is inevitable that, even in the best-run businesses, things will go wrong from time to time, there needs to be a policy of rapid response to customers' problems. The response should be the result of laid-down procedures combined with a high level of employee empowerment to put things right. The procedures should be based on the assumption that the customer is 'innocent' and that it is the company that is at fault. Unfortunately, many organizations have this the wrong way round – they assume that the customer is 'guilty'.

Companies such as Marks & Spencer demonstrate that even though refunding the cost of purchases without question costs them money in the short term, in fact it makes them more money in the long term as customer satisfaction, and hence loyalty, is enhanced. British Airways has found that customers whose problems are resolved quickly and to their satisfaction are more likely to travel with British Airways the next time than those who had never experienced a problem with the airline. One car hire company also found that prompt response to customer complaints by front-line employees led to an increased probability that the customer would choose to use the company on the next occasion a car hire was required.

The key to encouraging customer loyalty where problems occur seems to be in the simple concept of employee 'empowerment'. Organizations that are prepared to let all their employees – and in particular their front-line people – have complete responsibility for sorting out customer problems reap exponential rewards. Removing the need to refer things to a supervisor or 'Head Office' allows employees to respond quickly and in a manner suitable to the specific situation. The result is a valued and satisfied customer, a valued and productive employee, and a professional and reputable company. The international hotel chain, Ritz-Carlton, has a policy that *any* employee can spend up to US $1000 without further authorization in order to solve a customer's problem. It is perhaps not coincidental that the Ritz-Carlton has an exceptionally high rate of customer retention, and incidentally commands premium room rates.

As well as seeking to resolve customers' problems, organizations should endeavour to exploit the absence of customer problems; that is, to build on customer satisfaction and loyalty. *Loyalty programmes development* is a growing trend as the challenge of retaining existing customers becomes ever more difficult and significant.

Like customer defection, customer loyalty can be hard to define and the criteria used must be carefully thought through. The mobile phone market provides a good example. A substantial number of mobile phone customers use 'pre-pay' services and have no contract, so loyalty must be measured in terms of 'dormancy'. Normally, account dormancy means that the customer does not have any outbound calls for between one and thirty days. However, if the customer is purchasing a certain amount of vouchers a month as a way of controlling their costs, they may be an active customer but 'invisible' to the dormancy measurement. If the service provider were then to launch a marketing campaign to promote, say, handset upgrades to all of its 'loyal' pre-pay customers, this customer might inadvertently be left off the target list, even though he/she would probably take up the offer readily.

It is also important to understand that defection does not necessarily imply *disloyalty*; it may just be that a competing supplier offers a better deal or bundle of benefits for a particular customer. Thus the design of any loyalty programme should recognize and respect customer choice, as well as recognize and reward loyal custom.

Many 'frequent flyer' programmes are based on a recognition of the existence of a small core of customers who travel the most miles, usually paying the full (undiscounted) fare. For these 'Gold' customers there will be red-carpet treatment, upgrades, personalized service and tailored promotions. While the aim is to improve retention rates among all groups of customers, it is inevitable that there will always be a core group of customers providing the greatest profit.

Rover, the car company, has developed a communications channel to its most important customers and seeks to maintain the closest possible contact with them. Its glossy magazine, *Catalyst*, is tailored to the specific interests of each recipient. Thus people who register their sporting interests as golf and fishing, for example, receive a version of the magazine that places greater emphasis on those sports and less on other things.

A traditional way of 'incentivizing' customers to stay loyal and to buy more is through discounts; in particular, volume-related and retrospective discounts. There is no point in a discount system that encourages 'forward buying' only; what the organization should seek is the increased volume that comes from several suppliers. Also, discounts should reward loyalty through retrospective bonuses and should be structured to encourage 'cross-buying' of other products from the supplier's range.

Structured programmes such as British Airways Executive Club encourage customers to aim for the next level of 'reward' through a three-tier membership: Blue, Silver and Gold, based on the number of miles travelled and the class of travel. General Motors enjoyed some success with its GM credit card – a card with a difference. Every time it was used to purchase goods or services, 5 per cent of the transaction value was awarded in the form of a rebate against the future purchase of a GM car.

It is worth emphasizing the important role played by senior management in taking the types of preventive and corrective action outlined here. Not only must top management approve any retention initiative, they must also be seen to endorse it actively though their enthusiastic commitment and support. Employees will only be inspired and encouraged to follow suit if strong leadership paves the way.

Customer retention improvement is an ongoing and iterative process, as the arrows in Figure 14.5 indicate. The consequence of implementing Step 3 will have an impact on the retention level measurement and thus require it to be reappraised and reviewed regularly. This in turn will influence efforts to identify the causes of customer dissatisfaction and defection, and to understand the drivers of customer satisfaction and loyalty, the results of which will feed into the development of any preventive and corrective procedures.

Case study 14.1 indicates clearly the crucial importance of correct market segmentation as a precursor to understanding CSFs leading to effective customer retention programmes.

Case study 14.1 Global Tech 'Service Segmentation'

This case history describes the use of market segmentation to assist in the development of a service product. Customer requirements were captured via qualitative research. The segmentation was completed through the use of quantitative research.

GlobalTech is the fictitious name of a real company marketing high-tech and service products globally. Customers are counted in hundreds of thousands. The markets are mainly business-to-business with a few very large customers buying thousands of items. Service is a major revenue stream measured in US $ billions.

The result was a set of segments that enabled the development of a new approach to delivering service while improving customer satisfaction. The process benefited from previous segmentations but was hampered by a changing market life-cycle and internal barriers.

The lessons learnt could be of interest to any organization having to care for large numbers of customers.

Background

A failed segmentation

GlobalTech tried to complete a marketing audit in the late 1990s. This including market definition, market segmentation and quantification. Each product division conducted their audit separately. They mainly used brainstorming techniques to define their markets and to produce the data required.

Lesson 1.

Markets transcend internally defined product divisions. Therefore it is best to understand the markets and monitor overall performance in those markets. To cut market information to meet the needs of internal reporting will lead to misinformation.

On completion, the results were compared across the divisions. It rapidly became apparent that each division addressed almost all the markets. However, the market definitions they produced were different, with significant bias to just the products they offered. Similarly, the segments each division identified where in conflict with the outputs from the other divisions.

On reflection it was agreed that the results were unreliable. They could not be used to help shape future strategies or marketing investments.

Market research decision

GlobalTech were now in the uncomfortable situation of being in a market information vacuum. Any confidence they had in their understanding of the market had been destroyed.

Consequently, the decision was taken that all future market analysis and understanding tasks would be supported by appropriate investments in market research.

> **Lesson 2.**
> **Do not** rely on the internally gathered opinions of Sales and Marketing staff to define markets and identify customer requirements and attitudes. **Do** invest in the necessary Market Research to provide a reliable segmentation and support for strategy and product development.

First market segmentation

The following year, the segmentation was redone, supported by extensive qualitative and quantitative market research. The objective was to understand and group into segments the product buyers in the overall market.

The qualitative study produced a very clear picture and definition of the markets addressed by GlobalTech. It also provided the customers' view of the benefits they sought from the products, and the differences in their attitudes towards their suppliers. The questionnaire for the quantitative study was based on the results of the qualitative study. The result was seven clearly defined product buyer segments.

This enhanced understanding of the market assisted with hardware and software product marketing but did not address service products or customer satisfaction and loyalty issues.

The need

As the twentieth century drew to a close, the market life-cycle had matured, and all but the more sophisticated products were perceived as commodities. Consequently, the opportunities for effective product differentiation had diminished. GlobalTech, in common with its competitors, was finding that customers were becoming increasingly disloyal.

For many years, product churns and upgrades from existing customers had accounted for some 70 per cent of GlobalTech's product revenues. Service and exhaust revenues (those revenues that follow on, almost automatically, from an initial product sale. These would normally include service plus training, consultancy, consumables, supplies and add-ons, and so on) almost equalled total product revenues. Service was perceived to be a key influencer of loyalty. But the costs of delivering service were becoming unacceptable. Concurrently, service pricing was coming under increasing competitive pressures.

The challenge was to increase loyalty while achieving a step function improvement in margins. Therefore it was decided to invest in a better understanding of the service market as an enabler to delivering cost-effective differentiation and loyalty. This case history covers the project from inception to implementation.

Service segmentation project overview

Process

The project was divided into three main phases: a qualitative market research study was followed by a quantitative market research study and finally the strategy development as illustrated below:

Case study 14.1 *continued*

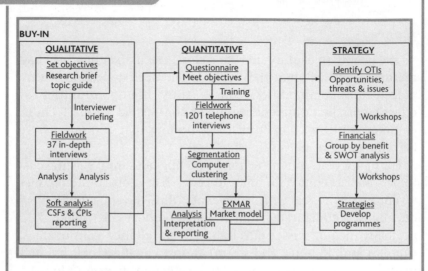

The GlobalTech main board director responsible for Customer Service sponsored the project. This was a critical prerequisite, as the outcome would have a significant impact on the organization, its processes and behaviours.

Similarly, the project team included key members of Service, Marketing and Finance to ensure buy-in. However, at that time, it was deemed inappropriate to include representatives from all but two of the countries because of travel implications, costs and resource impacts. In retrospect, this was not a good decision.

> **Lesson 3.**
> Try to anticipate the scale of organizational change that a major segmentation project may demand. Then ensure the buy-in planned from the start of the project embraces all those who will eventually have a say in the final implementation.

Business objectives

The project team agreed the overall business objectives:

▶ To develop strategies for profitable increase in market share and sustainable competitive advantage in the service markets for GlobalTech's products.

▶ To identify opportunities for new service products and for improving customer satisfaction within the context of a robust customer needs segmentation, which can be applied readily in the market place.

▶ To identify the key drivers of loyalty so that GlobalTech may take action to increase customer loyalty significantly.

▶ To provide the information required to help develop a new and innovative set of service products designed and tailored to meet differing customer requirements whilse reducing internal business process costs significantly.

Results from the Qualitative Study

The output from the qualitative study was a 93-page report documenting the results, in line with the desired research objectives. Some of the more surprising aspects were supported by verbatims. A key output was the polarization of very different attitudes towards service requirements that some buyers had in comparison with others. For example:

▶ Some wanted a response within a few hours, whereas many others would be equally happy with a response the next day.

▶ Some wanted their staff thoroughly trained to take remedial actions supported by a specialist on the telephone. Others did not want to know and would just wait for the service provider to fix the problem.

▶ Some wanted regular proactive communications and being kept up to date, while others wanted to be left alone.

▶ Some would willingly pay for a premium service, under a regular contract, whilse others would prefer to take the risk.

▶ The attitudes of professional buyers, procuring on behalf of user departments, were consistently different from those of the user departments.

Results from the Quantitative Study

The output from the quantitative study was extensive. It included a 168-page report and EXMAR, the software-based market model that provided an almost infinite number of views of the information. Much of the output was detailed demographic data, opportunities information and competitive positioning comparisons. However, the focus was on a fairly extensive executive summary for internal communications within GlobalTech. What follows are summarized extracts from those outputs.

The segments

Six market segments were identified as a result of iterative computer clusterings. Initially, the clustering routines had identified more segments, but by careful analysis this was reduced to what was decided to be the most manageable level. Some previously very small segments were merged with very similar larger segments.

Koala bears	Preserve their assets (however small) and use, say, an extended warranty to give them cover. Won't do anything themselves, prefer to curl-up and wait for someone to come and fix it. Small offices (in small and big companies). 28% of market
Teddy bears	Lots of account management and love required from a single preferred supplier. Will pay a premium for training and attention. If multi-site, will require supplier to cover these sites effectively. (Protect me.) Larger companies. 17% of market
Polar bears	Like Teddy Bears except colder! Will shop around for cheapest service supplier, whoever that may be. Full 3rd-party approach. Train me but don't expect to be paid. Will review annually (seriously). If multi-site, will require supplier effectively to cover these sites. Larger companies. 29% of market
Yogi bears	A 'wise'Teddy or Polar bear working long hours. Will use trained staff to fix if possible. Needs skilled product specialist at end of phone, not a bookings clerk. Wants different service levels to match the criticality of the product to their business process. Large and small companies. 11% of market
Grizzly bears	Trash them! Cheaper to replace than maintain. Besides, they re so reliable that they are probably obsolete when they bust. Expensive items will be fixed on a pay-as-when basis–if worth it. Won't pay for training. Not small companies. 6% of market
Andropov big bears	My business is totally dependant on your products. I know more about your products than you do! You will do as you are told. You will be here now! I will pay for the extra cover but you will ......! Not small or very large companies. 9% of market

Polarisations in attitude

The computer clustering generated the segments by grouping customers with like attitudes and requirements. This resulted in some marked differences in attitude between segments. As illustrated below, the Koalas really did not want to know about being trained and having a go. But the Teddies, Yogis and Polars had an almost opposite attitude.

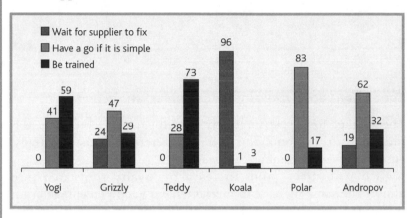

Satisfaction and loyalty

GlobalTech was measuring customer satisfaction for use locally, as a business process diagnostic tool, and globally, as a management performance measure. These satisfaction measurements were averaged across all customers, both by geographic Business Unit and by Product Division to meet internal management reporting requirements.

However, the outputs from the quantitative study showed clearly that these traditionally well-accepted measures were, in fact, almost meaningless. What delighted customers in one market segment would annoy customers in another, and visa versa. To make the metrics meaningful, they had to be split by key criteria and the market segments.

Loyalty was obviously highest where GlobalTech's 'one size fits all' service deliverable coincidently best matched a segment's requirement, as illustrated below:

Case study 14.1 *continued*

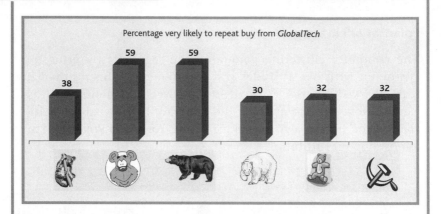

Percentage very likely to repeat buy from *GlobalTech*

Correlation between loyalty and customer satisfaction

The market life cycle for many of GlobalTech's products was moving into the commodity phase. Therefore, not surprisingly, customers were becoming less loyal.

Each percentage point increase in loyalty translated into almost the same increase in market share. Each percentage point in market share added many millions of dollars of gross revenues. The cost of reselling to a loyal customer was about a sixth of the cost of winning a new customer. Consequently, each percentage point increase in loyalty had a significant impact on the bottom line.

Because of this, the quantitative study included correlating the key drivers of satisfaction and loyalty within each market segment. The qualitative study identified some 28 key customer requirements of their service provider. The quantitative study prioritized these to provide a shorter list of 17 common requirements. The correlation exercise reduced this to only two requirements that drew a significant correlation between satisfaction and loyalty:

▶ Providing service levels that meet customers, needs; and
▶ Providing consistent performance over time.

Although GlobalTech was achieving the second, it was really only delivering the first in two of the market segments.

Case study 14.1 *continued*

Market attractiveness

As an aid to deciding where best to invest, a market attractiveness factors chart was produced using EXMAR, the market-modelling tool. Market demographic data from the quantitative study was combined with internal GlobalTech financial data. Each factor was weighted to reflect the relative importance to GlobalTech.

This highlighted quite a few issues and some opportunities. For example, the highest margins where coming from some of the least loyal segments.

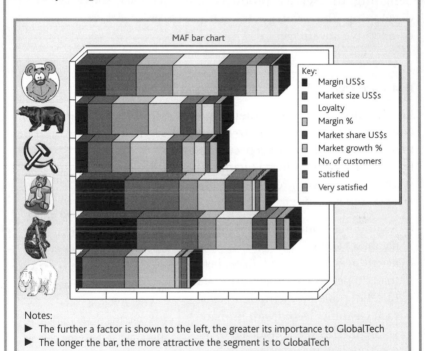

MAF bar chart

Key:
- Margin US$s
- Market size US$s
- Loyalty
- Margin %
- Market share US$s
- Market growth %
- No. of customers
- Satisfied
- Very satisfied

Notes:
▶ The further a factor is shown to the left, the greater its importance to GlobalTech
▶ The longer the bar, the more attractive the segment is to GlobalTech

Competitive positioning

Fortunately for GlobalTech, its competitors did not appear to have an appreciation of the market segments or the differing requirements of their customers. They were also mainly delivering a 'one size fits all' service offering. However, there were some noticeable differences in their offerings. These resulted in each major competitor being significantly stronger in just one or two market segments where their deliverable best matched the segment needs.

The quantitative study provided detailed rankings of the CPIs and CSFs for each market segment. These were to prove invaluable during the phase, designing the service products and developing the strategy to achieve competitive advantage.

> **CPIs** (critical purchase influencers) are the needs (benefits) buyers are seeking to have satisfied by their choice of product or service.
>
> **CSFs** (customer satisfaction factors) or **KDFs** (key discriminating features) are the buyer-perceived attributes by which the choice between suppliers is made.

Reachability

Key to GlobalTech implementing successfully any strategies or communications that were to be market-segment-based would be being able to identify each customer by segment. As part of the quantitative study, two statistical reachability tasks were completed:

► A sampling of internal GlobalTech databases showed that there was sufficient relevant data to achieve better than 70 per cent accuracy, using statistical imputation methods, to code each customer record with its market segment. This was considered to be good enough measurably to enhance marketing communications, but might not be sufficiently accurate to ensure always making the most appropriate offer.

► Statistical analysis identified four questions that would provide acceptable accuracy in segment

> **Lesson 4.**
> Understanding the different market segments helps in designing the required offers. But do not become fixated on reachability. It is not essential to code every customer to the right segment from day one.
>
> Where you are not really sure, let them see different offers and so position themselves.
>
> Similarly, be willing to accept that within a large organization some buyers may fall into slightly different, though normally similar, market segments.

identification. These questions could then be used during both in-bound and out-bound call centre conversations until such time as all customers had been coded.

The recommendation was to use both methods in parallel so that accuracy would improve over time. Also, the coding of larger customers should be given a priority.

Strategy development and implementation

Market understanding and strategy development

The challenge now was for the project team to absorb and understand all the outcomes from the two research studies. The team then had to turn that understanding into realizable strategies. To achieve this, a workshop process called OTIs (opportunities, threats and issues) was used.

Briefly, the process involved an extensive, but controlled, brainstorming session followed by a series of innovative strategy development workshops.

▶ A facilitator took the team systematically through every piece of relevant information available.
▶ Using brainstorming, the team tried to identify every conceivable opportunity, threat or internal issue associated with each item of information.
▶ The information was then also tested against a predetermined list of business behaviours and processes in an endeavour to entice additional and creative ideas out of the brainstorming.
▶ Using the CPIs and CSFs from the EXMAR market model, strengths and weaknesses were added, thus turning the process into a SWOT.
▶ Like ideas were merged.
▶ Each idea was given two scores in the range of 1–9. The first ranked the probable financial impact, where the second ranked the probability of success.
▶ The ideas were then grouped by like activity and where they had the same or an overlapping financial impact. This ensured

that double counting was eliminated, and that opportunities and threats were offset as appropriate. Any one group of ideas would take on the highest single financial impact score and a reassessed probability of a success score.

▶ If the resolution of an internal issue was a prerequisite for capturing an opportunity or overcoming a threat, then the issue plus associated costs and resources was included in the same group as the opportunity or threat. The norm was for a single issue to be attached to many groups.

▶ The groups were named and then ranked, both by financial impact and by probability of success. This provided a prioritized short list of imperatives that should deliver the maximum realizable benefits to both GlobalTech and its customers.

▶ Iterative discussions developed this into an overall strategy with a number of prioritized sub-strategies.

▶ Each sub-strategy was supported by a documented description of the opportunity. At this stage, encouragement was given to creating innovative, yet simple, implementation options that would maximize the chances of success. Each implementation option was supported by market, revenue and organizational impact data, associated issues, resources, costs, and required control metrics.

▶ Board members were involved in option selections and the investment approvals process.

▶ Finally, the implementation programmes and project plans were created.

The strategy

The overall recommendation was to create a set of service deliverables tailored to the individual needs of each segment. These would be complemented by a set of premium add-ons that could be offered to the appropriate segments. By focusing on business process simplification during the design of the offering for each segment it was hoped to eliminate redundancy.

The objective of each offering was to increase customer satisfaction significantly with an emphasis on those items that would have a most positive impact on loyalty. Some offerings were quite different from others, both in terms of the deliverable and the internal processes that made it possible. This differentiation was also intended to create a measurable competitive advantage in a number of the market segments.

A key to the implementation of the project was a recommended change to the customer satisfaction measurements, so that they became an effective diagnostic tool for tuning the ongoing deliverables for each market segment.

Implementation

Throughout the project, the same core team had been intimately involved with each stage of the project. They guided the work and took on board the results. They delved deeply into the analysis and did their best to understand the markets, their customer requirements and likely competitive impacts. Finally, they worked hard at developing the proposed strategies. They thought buy-in had been achieved by being sponsored by a main board director.

The implementation roll-out across country boundaries became difficult. Each country wanted their say. They had different views of their customer needs and how things should be done in their country. They did not understand easily or even accept the findings of the research and the meaning of the outputs.

The majority of these internal barriers were eventually overcome. Inevitably, there were compromises. These led the project team into believing that not all the market segments would be fully satisfied with the new offerings in all countries.

Summary

Retaining existing customers is more profitable than acquiring new customers, because:

► sales, marketing and set-up costs are amortized over a longer customer lifetime;

- customer expenditure increases over time;
- repeat customers often cost less to service;
- satisfied customers provide referrals; and
- satisfied customers may be prepared to pay a price premium.

The starting point for developing customer retention strategies and programmes is research. Encouraging customers not to leave the relationship, but to stay and buy more, requires an in-depth understanding of both what causes customers to depart and what motivates customers to buy from our company rather than from competitors. These critical failure factors (CFFs) and critical success factors (CSFs) will determine whether the organization can withstand any competitive comparison.

Clearly, there will normally be more than one determinant of supplier or brand choice, and they may well differ by customer. Indeed, a viable and often powerful means of market segmentation is to group customers according to their choice criteria.

It should also be noted that not every customer is equally attractive to the organization. With the 80/20 rule in evidence, it makes good sense to ensure that retention rates are highest among the 20 per cent of customers who provide the company with 80 per cent of total profit.

If customer retention strategies are to succeed, they should focus on the two related, but separate, issues of customer defection and customer loyalty. If these two parallel strands of the retention strategies can be managed successfully, then the probability of an improved customer retention rate will almost certainly increase.

The important point to remember about any loyalty programme is that it should not be designed to 'lock the customer in' – this leads inevitably to resentment on the part of the customer – but instead should be seen by the customer as a reward for loyalty.

Further reading

Christopher, M., Payne, A. and Ballantyne, D. (1991) *Relationship Marketing*, Butterworth Heinemann, Oxford.

References

Raphael, M. and Considine, R. (1981) *The Great Brain Robbery* (Pasadena, Texas: Business Tips).

Reichheld, F. A. (1994) Loyalty and the renaissance of marketing. *Marketing Management*, **2(2)**, pp. 10–21.

Reichheld, F. and Sasser, W. Jr (1990) Zero defections: quality comes to Services. *Harvard Business Review* (September/October), pp. 105–111.

15 Sales force strategy

The importance of personal selling

Most companies had an organized sales force long before they introduced formal marketing activities of the kind described in this book. In spite of this, sales force management traditionally has been a neglected area of marketing management.

There are several possible reasons for this. One is that not all marketing and product managers have had the experience in a personal selling or sales management role. Consequently, these managers often underestimate the importance of efficient personal selling.

Another reason for the neglect of sales force management is that sales personnel themselves sometimes encourage an unhelpful distinction between sales and marketing by depicting themselves as being at 'the sharp end'. After all, isn't there something slightly daring about dealing with real customers as opposed to sitting in an office surrounded by marketing surveys, charts and plans? Such reasoning is dangerous, because unless a good deal of careful marketing planning has taken place before the salesperson makes their effort to persuade the customer to place an order, the probability of a successful sale is much reduced.

The suggested distinction between marketing 'theory' and 'sales practice' is further invalidated when we consider that profitable sales depend not only on individual customers and individual products, but on groups of customers (that is, market segments) and on the supportive relationship of products to each other (that is, a carefully planned product portfolio).

A further factor to be taken into account in this context is the constant need for the organization to think in terms of where future sales will be coming from rather than to concentrate solely on present products, customers and problems.

Investigation of many European sales forces over the 1990s has revealed an alarming lack of planning and professionalism. Salespeople frequently have little idea of which products and which groups of customers to concentrate on, have too little knowledge about competitive activity, do not plan presentations well, rarely talk to customers in terms of *benefits*, make too little effort to close the sale, and make many calls without any clear objectives. Even worse, marketing management is rarely aware that this important and expensive element of the marketing mix is not being managed effectively. The fact that many organizations have separate departments and directors for the marketing and sales activities increases the likelihood of such failures of communication.

Although its importance varies according circumstances, in many businesses the sales force is the most important element in the marketing mix. In industrial goods companies, for example, it is not unusual to find very small sums being spent on other forms of communication and very large sums being spent on the sales force in the form of salaries, cars and associated costs.

Personal selling is also widely used in many service industries where customers are looking for very specific benefits. Insurance companies, for example, do use media advertising, but rely for most of their sales on personal selling. Customers for insurance policies almost always need to discuss which policy would best fit their particular needs and circumstances. It is the task of the insurance salesperson to explain the choices available, and to suggest the most appropriate policy.

Recent surveys show that companies devote greater expenditure to their sales forces than to advertising and sales promotion combined. Personal selling, then, is a vital and expensive element in the marketing mix, and every effort should be made to maximize the investment.

The solution to the problem of poor sales force management can only be found in the recognition that personal selling is indeed a crucial part of the marketing process, and that it must be planned and considered as carefully as any other element. Indeed, it is an excellent idea for the people responsible to go out into the territory for a few days each year and themselves attempt to persuade customers to place orders. It is a good way of finding out what customers really think of the organization's marketing policies!

The advantages of personal selling

As stated in Chapter 11, personal selling can be seen most usefully as part of the communications mix. (It will be remembered that 'personal selling' constitutes promotion via person-to-person conversation, be it at the customer's premises, by telephone, or elsewhere. Elements of the communications mix described as 'impersonal selling' include advertising, sales promotion, public relations and so on.)

Personal selling has several advantages over other elements of the communications mix:

► It is a two-way form of communication, giving the prospective purchaser the opportunity to ask questions of the salesperson about the product or service.
► Sales messages can be made more flexible and can therefore be tailored more closely to the needs of individual customers.
► Salespeople can use in-depth product knowledge to relate their sales messages to the perceived needs of the buyers and to deal with objections as they arise.
► Most important of all, salespeople can ask for an order and perhaps negotiate on price, delivery or special requirements.

Once an order has been obtained from a customer, and there is a high probability of a repeat purchase occurring, the salesperson's task changes from persuasion to reinforcement. All communications at this stage should contribute to underlining the wisdom of the purchase. Where existing customers wish to place further orders, the salesperson might use the opportunity to cross-sell or up-sell, thus strengthening the relationship by highlighting other relevant products and services in the company's portfolio.

Clearly, in different markets, different weighting is given to the various forms of communication available. In the grocery business, for example, advertising and sales promotion are extremely important elements in the communications process. However, the food manufacturer must maintain an active sales force that keeps in close contact with the retail buyers. This retail contact ensures vigorous promotional activity within the chain. In the wholesale hardware business, frequent and regular face-to-face contact with retail outlets through a sales force is the key determinant of success. In industries where there are few customers (such as capital goods and specialized process materials), an in-depth understanding of the customer's production processes has to be built up, and personal contact is of paramount importance.

Good salespeople can ascertain quickly the requirements of a particular customer, and identify to what extent these will be fulfilled by their company's offerings. Customers, for their part, can identify quickly whether the company understands their requirements fully, is a business of integrity and credibility, and is able to provide the necessary service support. To survive such scrutiny, salespeople must have sufficient background knowledge of the customer's purchase decision-making processes and the particular pressures and influences at play. They must also have a sound appreciation of the inherent implications for their own role and a confident plan of how to manage such implications successfully.

Key considerations for sales force strategy

The development and implementation of an effective sales force strategy is founded on several key considerations. These include: information needs; buy phases; buy classes; pressures on the buyer; and implications for the salesperson.

Information needs

Before attempting to produce a sales force strategy, it is necessary to establish what information customers will require from the sales force. Communication efficiency depends on achieving a match between the information required and the information given. The selling organization must therefore identify the major influencers in each purchase decision, and find out what information they are likely to need at different stages of the buying process. In the business-to-business context this may involve pinpointing relevant internal people as well as relevant members of the buying organization, in order to lay the groundwork for establishing links at multiple levels (see Chapter 12).

It will also need to know if the customer is buying for the first time, or contemplating a repeat order. Customer information needs may range from details about the product range and product performance, to price, running costs, guarantees, load sizes, competitor products, special offers, reordering and so on.

In order to source and supply the appropriate information for the appropriate people at the appropriate time, the selling organization must first be clear about the stages of the decision-making process that will need to be gone through; the types of purchase that will apply; the myriad of forces that will act upon the buyer; and how all these factors will affect the salesperson's role and the allocation of the sales portfolio.

Buy phases

The majority of salespeople operate in the field of industrial or trade marketing. However, the rapid growth in the services sector has enhanced the importance of personal selling in areas of consumer marketing. Whatever the arena, the tasks performed by the salesperson are essentially the same. The main difference is the added complexity of organizational buyer decision-making processes. For this reason, the focus here is predominantly on dealing with organizational purchasing as opposed to consumer purchasing.

The consumer purchase decision-making process (see Figure 1.5 on page 18) typically follows five buying stages, or 'buy phases': recognition of need; information search; evaluation of alternatives; purchase decision; and post-purchase behaviour. The organizational purchase decision-making process (DMP), in contrast, is more complex and usually entails eight stages. This is because most organizational purchase decisions involve a large number of people (DMU) and take an extensive amount of time and consideration. Table 2.1 from page 23 is repeated here slightly differently as Table 15.1.

In looking at the eight buy phases of the DMP it is clear that different people and different numbers of people will be involved in each buy phase. A useful way of identifying who is likely to be involved in the purchase decision, and at what stages, is to look at the purchase decision in terms of its 'unfamiliarity' to the buying organization. This 'unfamiliarity' can be broken down into two parts:

▶ The complexity of the product or service being proposed/ considered; and
▶ The degree of commercial risk or uncertainty surrounding the outcome of the purchase.

Table 15.1 The eight buy phases of the DMP

Buy phase	Characteristics
1 Problem recognition ↓	Changing business needs Supplier review Current product/service dissatisfactions
2 General need ↓	Innovation Cost savings Improved performance
3 Specification ↓	Buyer/supplier dialogue 'Qualifying' criteria 'Differentiating' criteria
4 Supplier search ↓	Risk profile of purchase Information gathering Consideration set
5 Proposals submission ↓	Qualification of suppliers Choice set Proposal solicitation
6 Supplier selection ↓	Proposals reviewed Buyer/supplier negotiations Selection and ratification
7 Order specification ↓	Blanket contract/order Order fulfilment procedures Relationship development
8 Performance review	Benchmark supplier performance Evaluation performance Endorse, modify or discontinue

Generally, the higher the 'unfamiliarity' in both these dimensions, the greater the number of people involved, and the higher their status. For salespeople, high unfamiliarity means that the majority of their activity will be concentrated at the beginning of the DMP. They will have to involve themselves at an early phase if they are to influence the outcome effectively. This is because a growing commitment operates throughout the DMP: early decisions are reinforced and become successively more and more difficult to change. Salespeople, therefore, will need to know the degree of unfamiliarity involved so that they can direct their efforts towards the appropriate people. If product complexity is high, but commercial uncertainty low, then the design engineers and technologists will have the more important role. If unfamiliarity is low in both dimensions, purchasing officers will tend to dominate the decision-making process.

Buy classes

In using this concept of unfamiliarity in the purchase decision, the salesperson can divide the DMP of his prospective customers into types of buying situation, or 'buy classes'. These were referred to in Chapter 2. Each buy class tends to require that certain phases in the DMP be followed. By understanding at the outset what these phases are likely to be, salespeople can manage their role in the process better and increase the chances of a favourable outcome.

New-task purchase

All eight phases of the DMP will normally be followed. Several functional departments of the buying organization will usually be involved: for example, manufacturing, design, finance, the company board and the purchasing department. People in all these departments can be influenced during the DMP, which, in the context of a new-task purchase, takes the longest time to reach a conclusion.

Straight re-buy

A limited application of the eight phases will be followed. Only one or two functional departments, such as the user and purchasing department, may be involved. All phases will apply in that they will have been followed in the initial purchase routine but, since the technical specification of the product is now known and unchanging, no further technical involvement is needed in the buying process. The only factors likely to worry the buyer, provided that quality is maintained, are price and delivery, and these therefore become important negotiating points.

Modified re-buy

Most of the phases will be followed. Changes in the product specification may be initiated by the salesperson (for example, an offer of improved performance or a reduction in price) or by the buying organization itself. The design and manufacturing functions may therefore become involved.

The industrial salesperson should always endeavour to change a straight re-buy situation into a modified re-buy situation, as this could serve to strengthen the existing customer relationship and open up new opportunities (through customer referrals or resulting innovations) for establishing other customer relationships.

In addition to understanding the customer's DMP, the salesperson must also appreciate the pressures on the buyer and on the members of the DMU.

Pressures on the buyer

Buyers are subjected to a number of *external pressures*, such as:

▶ *The economic situation*: Is it the best time for investment in new projects? What is the cost of credit? Can the company afford to proceed?
▶ *Political considerations*: Is it time to embark on new projects, when demand is perhaps being squeezed and government expenditure being cut back?
▶ *Technology*: Does the necessary technology exist for the project? Will the proposed product be overtaken by new technology in the foreseeable future?
▶ *Environmental considerations*: Will the new project be acceptable, or conservationists' interests or pollution controls prevent us from going ahead?
▶ *The business climate*: How will profit levels, interest rates and the cost of labour, for example, influence the decision of whether or not to proceed?

Buyers also have to contend with *internal pressures*, such as:

▶ *'Internal politics'*: Personal rivalries and vested interests will put pressure on the buyer.
▶ *Organizational culture*: Any natural resistance to change may be reinforced by a strong sense of 'this is way things are done around here'.
▶ *Conflicting objectives or priorities*: The buyer may have to try to reconcile conflicting advice and demands, and perhaps even act as referee in the final decision.
▶ *Time frame*: An element of urgency, imposed by related decisions on matters such as production deadlines and budget schedules, may exist. The buyer may have to judge between rushing the decision or risking serious upset to other activities.
▶ *Individual status within the organization*: The buyer's own level of authority and status will also affect the way in which the decision is reached and the degree to which other people in his company will influence the decision.

The buyer's own personality and past experience will present *individual pressures*, such as:

► *Historic prejudice*: Past purchases may bias the buyer's judgement. For example, good experiences may be used to justify staying with a particular supplier even if a salesperson can show that their product offers benefits which prove that a change of supplier makes good sense.
► *Embedded habits*: Patterns of routine and convention can act against the industrial salesperson who is trying to win a new order. Many buyers prefer to stay with known suppliers rather than risk the disruption of changing to other suppliers.
► *Perception barriers*: The buyer's perception of the purchase situation may be different from that of other people. Some managers may rate a particular feature of a new product very highly, but the buyer may be obsessed with price, for example, and may therefore resist change, whatever the evidence of its desirability.
► *Ignorance or lack of understanding*: Allied to the perception 'barrier', there may be the difficulty of persuading the buyer to change suppliers because they are not au fait with the issues and it thus takes a long time to absorb new information.

Implications for the salesperson

The way the purchase decision-making process operates in different circumstances has important implications for industrial salespeople. They have to:

► recognize the buying situation they face and the stage it is at, and determine how best to handle it;
► identify the DMU, or those people in the buying organization who are likely to be able to influence the purchase decision at that moment and during subsequent DMP phases;
► decide what benefits their product and their company can offer to each of these people, and what technical help they can give in an attempt to influence the decision; and
► attempt to convert straight re-buys into modified re-buys by demonstrating that their product has significant additional benefits over products used at present.

From the range of people they have to influence, the uniqueness of each sales situation and the extended amount time the purchase decision-making process might take, it is plain that industrial sales-people have a complex and demanding role to fulfil.

The role of the salesperson

The role of the salesperson is clearly about much more than just 'selling', and will vary according to the business concerned. A sales-person may be a consultant, a seller (in the purest sense of the word), a negotiator, an ambassador, a demonstrator, an order-taker or a composite of these and other roles. Let us consider for a moment the first four roles mentioned.

Consultant

Unlike in other forms of selling, the industrial salesperson is as much a consultant as a salesperson. In industry, selling is a focal point in the dissemination of information (unlike in the consumer field, where advertising plays the major role). Many industrial salespeople have technical qualifications in chemistry, engineering, electronics or management, and most have considerable product knowledge. Industrial salespeople are thus able to help their customers in many ways – in fact, they will find that some customers rely on them to solve problems for them to help keep them up to date technically. Without the advice and guidance of industrial salespeople, many manufacturing projects would run into severe difficulties and would be considerably delayed.

The key to a successful relationship between consultant and consulter is mutual trust and respect. To perform their role successfully, salespeople will have to show (perhaps over a period of time) that their advice is reliable and given in the best interests of the client. To do this effectively they need to listen to what the client wants, analyse the needs and recommend the best solution. They must be careful not to damage their company's reputation by giving bad advice just to gain a quick sale. Above all, they have to have an excellent understanding of their company's products.

However, this considerable product knowledge must be used correctly. Many industrial salespeople make the mistake of dulling the buyer's senses with sophisticated technical jargon. Years of training might have given the salesperson a deep understanding of his/her chosen subject, every word of which, they believe, must be used to impress and to demonstrate to the buyer their complete grasp of the subject. However, such displays can cause more problems than they solve. Buyers do not like to feel inferior in knowledge, even if they are, and when this happens they become at best bored and at worst annoyed. In either case, the sale is in danger.

Nevertheless, industrial salespeople can play an important part in helping their customers. They might work with design engineers to overcome problems associated with incorporating their product into the overall design, or with systems engineers in setting up procedures for using their product. In this way they are able to influence the decision-making process and build on the growing commitment that develops over time.

Seller

Industrial salespeople may believe that their value to buyers lies in their specialist knowledge rather than in their ability as a salesperson. If they think in this way, they are wrong. Only a few of today's sales-people will experience a seller's market; most will face a buyer's market where competition is rife. This is the golden rule of selling:

> When all things are equal, the orders usually go to the salesperson with the greatest SELLING skills.

Much of the rest of this chapter is concerned with selling skills, and these are indeed vital to the salesperson. However, selling ability is rarely enough to clinch a deal with the modern industrial buyer. Buyers today are better equipped than ever before. They are better educated and have information about the market that is as accurate as the supplier's own information; they also understand finance – margins, liquidity, cash flows and returns on investment capital. Armed with this 'intelligence', the buyer will be in a position to negotiate every aspect of the proposed deal. Furthermore, in times of recession, buyers have the power to back their demands.

Negotiator

Faced with such knowledgeable buyers, the industrial salesperson must actively understand the difference between negotiating and selling. A combination of sales ability and determination, without negotiating skills, can be a positive disadvantage. The too-eager sales-person, using closing techniques to clinch the sale, can be a disaster when it is negotiation that is required.

Negotiating is quite different from selling. Negotiating begins when each party realizes that the other has something they want. (Selling begins when the salesperson believes another party could benefit from purchasing their offering, whether or not they are in fact interested.) Negotiation is about the art of manoeuvre in order to secure the best possible deal for both parties. It involves mutual persuasion and mutual compromise. To be an effective negotiator, the salesperson needs a knowledge of costs, margins and the profitability of major customers; awareness of the impact of profit on minor variations in volume, price, costs and sales mix; and commitment to improving continually planning and performance.

Ambassador

In performing their various roles, salespeople are also a leading source and conduit of information. As their company's represen-tatives 'out in the field', they also serve as messengers for their customers, imparting their opinions, criticisms and ideas back to company headquarters. Their close access to customers and intimate understanding of their needs and operations makes them a valuable channel for gathering customer knowledge and passing on company communications.

Because the key role of the salesperson is to present the company's offer and to engage in two-way communications which negotiate the terms of a sale, it is essential that they have excellent relationship-building skills. The strength and longevity of the relationship will depend heavily on their success in gaining and maintaining the trust and respect of their customers, and of their company.

Identifying the buyer

Equipped with a sense of purpose and command of the task at hand, the salesperson can begin the process of organizing their sales approach. While all sales situations share similarities, their specific aspects will be unique and will therefore require careful preparation and planning. Chief among these planning issues is identifying the buyer accurately.

The industrial salesperson is faced immediately with two related problems. First, there is the problem of convincing a number of people or groups within the buying organization to behave in a certain way over an extended period. Second, there is the problem of finding out who in the buying organization in fact has the power to make or influence the purchase decision. It is very easy for the salesperson to waste their time attempting to achieve the impossible – selling to someone who cannot make a decision or who has no real influence on the decision-making process.

Reasons for this failure can only be poor preparation and fear. Once he/she has done the preparatory homework, the industrial salesperson can, or should, approach the task with confidence. Even so, many salespeople prefer to meet those in the buying organization with whom they are familiar and they count as friends, rather than risk meeting a buyer who holds an important position – such as a financial director, works director or managing director – even though they know that more senior executives have greater buying power.

These fears are groundless. Most senior managers are very reasonable people to deal with and few try to dominate the interview with questions to catch the salesperson out. In reality, it is sometimes the assistant – the junior buyer, the secretary or local manager – who makes life difficult for the salesperson. A buyer may be protected by a host of such people. It must be the salesperson's objective to bypass these gatekeepers and to see the person who can really make or influence the decision.

Managing the sales force

To optimize the sales force and obtain best value for money from personal selling, an organization must resolve three basic issues. It must decide the requisite number of salespeople, their precise role and how they are to be managed. Therefore, let us consider the methods for: determining the size of the sales force; establishing sales force objectives; and ensuring sales force motivation.

Determining the size of the sales force

Reviewing activities

The organization should begin its consideration of how many sales representatives it needs by finding out exactly how work is undertaken at the present time. It should start by listing all the things the current sales force in fact does. These might include opening new accounts, servicing existing accounts, demonstrating new products, taking repeat orders and debt collecting. This analysis should be utilized to explore if there are alternative ways of carrying out these responsibilities more cost-effectively.

For example, telephone selling has been shown to be a perfectly acceptable alternative to personal visits, particularly in respect of repeat business. The sales force can thus be freed for more complex work, which is not so susceptible to the telephone approach. Can debts be collected by mail, e-mail or by telephone? Can products be demonstrated in showrooms or at exhibitions? It is only by asking these kinds of questions that we can be certain we have not fallen into the common trap of committing the organization to a decision of how best to undertake selling responsibilities and then seeking data and reasons to justify the decision.

Measuring workload

Essentially, salespeople undertake three activities. They make calls, travel and carry out administration. These tasks comprise the *workload*. By analysing their current workload and considering alternative ways of undertaking these responsibilities, the organization can decide what constitutes a reasonable workload (that is, how many calls it is possible to make in a working day given the concomitant time values for clerical tasks and travel) and how territories can be allocated equitably. Equally, an assessment of existing and potential customers should be made and the annual total number of calls calculated, bearing in mind that different customer categories need different call rates. The following formula is helpful in ascertaining how many salespeople are needed:

$$\text{Number of salespeople} = \frac{\text{Annual total calls required}}{\text{Annual number of working days} \times \text{all salespeople's calls per day}}$$

There are, of course, several ways to measure workload. One major consumer goods company used its Work Study department to measure sales force effectiveness. The results of this study are summarized in Figure 15.1, which shows how salespeople's time was spent and approximately how much of their time was in fact available for selling. One immediate action taken by the company as a consequence was to initiate a training programme, which led to more time being spent on selling as a result of better planning. A separate initiative sought to improve the quality of sales performance in face-to-face situations with customers.

Figure 15.1 Breakdown of a salesperson's total daily activity

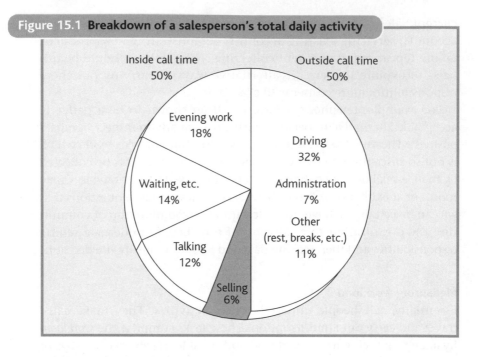

Another method involves getting sales representatives to measure their own workload. Research shows that salespeople carry out this measurement task diligently over the prescribed measurement period. The method involves recording their daily starting time and the miles or kilometres on the car clock, and repeating this throughout the working day for all calls. The only additional information required is the account category called on, and the time in and time out.

From this, it is possible to calculate over a two-month period, for example, the *average* time it takes to make a particular type of call (such as to a wholesaler, a chemist, a doctor, a hospital or a consultant). It is also possible to measure, given the type of territory (for example, town or country), how long it takes in travel to cover a given territory size. Finally, since administration is likely to be a fixed period of time for everyone, the organization has in its possession the vital information to measure, *territory by territory*, the precise workload of every salesperson. Territories can now be allocated equitably to all salespeople.

Sales force productivity

There are, of course, many methods of calculating workload, but there is one further factor that is worthy of consideration here: the 'productivity' factor. This is a subject we have researched over a number of years, and which has proved extremely valuable in helping companies to allocate their salespeople more effectively.

During the 1970s, again in the 1980s, and yet again in the 1990s, it was fashionable to predict the death of the salesperson as a key component in commercial success. Enthusiasts predicted that marketing methods would become so sophisticated and precisely targeted that the need for personal selling would vanish. This view became even stronger with the advent of the Internet. But salespeople are still around in abundance. Indeed, even now, many companies spend considerably more on personal selling than on all other forms of promotion put together.

The reason is not hard to find. Despite their very high costs, no one has yet discovered a more effective agency than the human being for communicating the full benefit of product offerings and for addressing customers' concerns. Despite the plethora of self-service options and automated information sources available, customers still seek to speak to a person in conjunction with or in preference to using other channels. Moreover, research shows that, even in industries that doubt the usefulness of the personal selling process, customers take a different line. For example – and one that confounds popular belief – a recent survey found that medical representatives are in fact welcomed by doctors and considered to be a most valuable source of information about developments in the pharmaceutical industry.

As the pendulum has swung back towards personal selling, companies have invested heavily to improve the productivity of their sales forces. Indeed, modern salespeople, for the most part, are significantly better than those at the end of the 1980s. But it is not the quality of the 'reps' themselves that has changed, so much as the quality of their direction and management.

Yet, given the extremely high costs of a sales force compared with other communication methods, increasing the productivity of a sales force remains a major challenge for the most enlightened and results-orientated sales manager, who is well aware that objectives such as increased sales are not the only yardsticks. Productivity at the time of writing calls for a combination of both quantitative and qualitative performance measures, particularly given the need for building long-term relationships with customers based on mutual trust.

One way of increasing productivity is to ensure that the requisite number of calls are made on different customer categories. This implies that not all customers are of the same importance to the supplier.

Different customer types

A firm's clientele normally consists of many types of customer, some large and some small. Some represent a high sales potential; others the opposite. Some clients are loyal to the point of folly; others are sufficiently cynical to change patronage at the slightest provocation. Yet others are almost phobic about the supplying company and need superhuman persuasion to change their attitude towards it. Sheer common sense demands that customers of different potential should have different amounts of sales time invested in them.

The trouble is that, understandably enough, the average salesperson enjoys calling on the loyal customer and dislikes the prospect of being constantly rebuffed by the hostile one. The result, also understandably, is that salespeople tend to concentrate on loyal customers, who will probably continue to buy from their company regardless. A simple analysis of call records can highlight the incestuous relationship developing between reps and buyers. Both sides are quite happy to fête each other at frequent intervals, although it is really a 'mutual admiration society' from which little additional commercial and marketing value can be derived.

The main difficulty is that if salespeople achieve their sales budget, little notice is normally taken of the fact that a lot of their time is directed unproductively – towards a customer who is literally 'in the bag'. Salespeople would no doubt reply that, if they were neglected, even loyal customers might lose 'affection' for their favourite supplier. This is obviously true. However, it is no less true that the main thrust of communication with very loyal customers should be quite different from that which takes place with hostile prospects. In the former case, the main purpose of the sales call is to maintain contact to reassure the customer that his/her loyalty is wise and to cement a happy relationship. In the latter case, the aim is to try to understand the reasons for the hostility, to attempt to remove them, and then 'sell' the product. These are totally different tasks; they call for different approaches and should yield different results.

This notion can be taken a stage further. A firm's clientele can be divided into three major groupings: those who love the supplier (the 'Philes'); those who are totally indifferent to the supplier as long as the offering is right (the 'Promiscuous' companies); and those who are hostile to the selling company and reluctant to buy from it at all (the 'Phobes'). The point is that each of the three groups needs to be addressed with different selling and communication techniques. In fact, there is a strong case for developing individual sales processes for each case.

The situation is further complicated by the need to distinguish between the level of sales effort directed towards large, medium and small customers. Since each of the three Phile, Promiscuous and Phobe groupings can represent a large, medium or small prospect, there are a nine possible customer types (see Figure 15.2). Obviously, some of the cells of the matrix shown in Figure 15.2 represent better opportunities than others. A small Phobe is probably not worth bothering about, since the results of even a successful resolution of the phobia will not justify the effort involved. A small Phile, on the other hand, will probably buy from the supplier in anycase. Since it only represents a small potential, however, the right approach is for the supplier to call infrequently, if at all, and then concentrate on assuring the customer that the affection is reciprocated. This can often be done by telephone. Spending any more time than the absolute minimum on such a client is unproductive.

Figure 15.2 'Philes', 'Promiscuous' and 'Phobes'

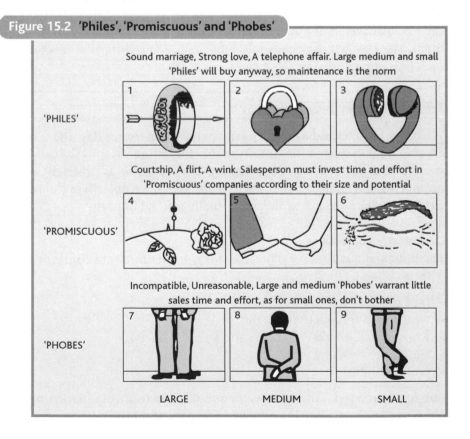

Large Philes are both loyal and important. They should be handled with a maintenance policy, under which a representative should do only what is necessary to maintain the business. In practice, this might consist of a personal telephone call once a week only. The frequency of personal visits is a matter of management judgement, since there is always an element of vulnerability to strong competitive moves. The medium Philes can be handled according to the same principles, although obviously the call frequency will have to be less.

The most promising pay-off for the time invested by the representative clearly comes from the company that is both large and 'Promiscuous'. The appropriate treatment here is an investment policy that might mean a much higher call frequency, with additional support from the company in whatever ways are thought necessary. The objective, if possible, is to move it up to the status of Phile. Medium and small Promiscuous customers can be handled in a similar way, but with a decreasing call frequency.

Large Phobes are an interesting challenge. The first thing to establish here is the reasons for the antipathy to the selling firm. If that can't be discovered, it may not be worth spending too much time on them. The characteristic personas and suggested selling postures for each type are outlined in Table 15.2.

Establishing sales force objectives

Whatever the method used to organize the salesperson's day, there is always comparatively little time available for selling. In these circumstances, it is vital that an organization should know as precisely as possible what it wants its sales force to do. Sales force objectives can be either *quantitative* or *qualitative*, and usually a blend of both.

Quantitative objectives
The principal quantitative objectives for the sales force are concerned with:

► how much to sell (volume);
► what to sell (product/service mix);
► where to sell (market segments and key customers);
► allowable costs; and
► profit margins.

The first three types of objective derive directly from the marketing objectives and constitute the principal components of the sales strategy.

Table 15.2 Customer types, their personas and selling postures

Customer type	Persona	Selling posture – main selling task consists of:	Key points about main selling task
Large/Phile (Box 1)	An important customer that has proved to be very loyal	(1) Maintaining contact – no more calls than absolutely necessary (2) Communicating details of all new developments (3) Responding to complaints (if any) (4) Collecting information about general developments pertaining to the use of the product and/or competitive practices	(4) It is important that the client receives a copy of the company's annual report – and that salespeople are authorized to spend an appropriate amount on maintaining and developing the relationship
Large/Promiscuous (Box 4)	A fairly difficult customer, apt to change allegiance at the slightest opportunity and very sensitive to price. However, it is a large potential user and the business is worth having	(1) Identifying the motivational stimuli of the members of the decision-making unit in such companies (what makes them tick?) (2) Planning sales presentations capable of demonstrating the cost/benefit and 'value-in-use' of the product (3) Maintaining a careful record of competitive pressures likely to affect sales (4) Demonstrating the selling company's ability and willingness to respond to problems and queries at all times	(5) Success in doing so will form part of the salesperson's performance appraisal system. Salespeople can be authorized to spend an appropriate amount on communicating with members of the client's decision-making unit provided they have identified the most appropriate people and can see a probability of a pay-off

369

Table 15.2 *continued*

(5) Endeavouring to change the attitude of the prospect from Promiscuous to Phile

Large/Phobe (Box 7) | A much more difficult customer to acquire and/or maintain. For some reason, known or unknown, it dislikes the supplying company to the point of phobia. It has large sales potential, but the amount of effort needed to convert the potential into results is probably prohibitive. This being so, the sales force should limit the time and effort it spends on such customers to the main tasks identified here

(1) Maintaining low-profile contact, if possible

(2) Endeavouring to diagnose the real reasons for the hostility and trying alternative solutions to any problems identified

(3) Monitoring changes in the company's ownership or personnel that might affect future relationships

(4) Keeping vigilant for serious let-downs or problems with other suppliers

(4) In general, salespeople must refrain from spending too much time or money on such unproductive clients until a change in attitude can be discerned

Medium/Phile (Box 2) | A loyal customer with a fairly good potential sales turnover. It is likely to buy without excessive sales effort

(1) Maintaining contact – no more than a few visits a year unless there are specific problems (strong telephone contact is preferred)

(2) Lavish expenditure should be discouraged, but customers in this category should be invited to fairs, exhibitions and other public

Table 15.2 continued

Medium/Promiscuous (Box 5)	An awkward, fickle customer, but one whose business is not insignificant. Beware of wasting too much time on penetrating such accounts. The main objective must be to 'flirt' with them in a fairly low-key attempt to persuade them to mend their ways	(1) Identify the motivations of the decision-making unit to find what incentive is likely to convert its members from 'promiscuity' to loyalty (2) Communicate at frequent intervals (although not through frequent personal visits) the great benefits of using the company's products
		(2) Communicating details of all new developments – mainly by means of letters and/or personalized mailshots celebrations and Christmas
Medium/Phobe (Box 8)	A hostile customer with only medium purchasing justification for wasting too much selling effort on it	(1) Trying to determine the reason for the company's hostility (2) Tracking and recording charges in the organization that might alleviate the phobia (3) If the hostility stems from past mistakes, ensuring that any corrective measures are brought to the notice of the client (4) Maintaining an up-to-date client dossier
		(As for Large Phobe – Box 7)
		(2) Emphasis here is to be through mailshots, telephone calls and literature. Correspondingly, expenses must be kept to an absolute minimum and should only be used in exceptional circumstances
		promotional events. They should also be given preference for promotional items planned for anniversary

371

Table 15.2 *continued*

Small/Phile (Box 3)	Although its loyalty is appreciated, the seller cannot reciprocate by giving it too much non-productive selling time	(1) Organizing an annual meeting to inform both all the small Philes of developments in the industry and the selling company (the meeting is a good opportunity for the small Philes and their friends in the sales force to demonstrate their mutual admiration) (2) Maintaining frequent (and less costly) telephone contact (3) Ensuring that the restricted contact does not make the small and loyal customers feel unwanted	(3) Happy communication can often be maintained through members of the sales administration team, who should be trained accordingly
Small/Promiscuous (Box 6)	This type of customer should mostly be ignored. They are small customers who feel that their limited purchasing power is sufficiently attractive to make selling organizations fight hard for their business. The only exceptions to this rule are when:	This type customer should mostly be ignored. They are small customers who feel that their limited purchasing power is sufficiently attractive to make selling organisations fight hard for their business. The only exceptions to this rule are when: (1) There are indications that the firm is likely to become big in the future; and (2) The customer is part of a larger organization that the selling company would like to penetrate	Very little time should be allocated to them. When they decide to become more loyal, they will receive more attention and affection.
Small/Phobe (Box 9)	Customers like these are more trouble than they are worth. Allow them to indulge their phobias in happy isolation.	Forget it!	

The sales plan is, in effect, a translation of these figures/products/ customers into individual targets for each sales representative, taking into account special factors such as their territory size, the size of customers within a particular territory, and so on. Additional quantitative objectives for the sales force are given in Table 15.3.

Qualitative objectives

Qualitative objectives should also be set. These will be related to the salespersons' skills in performing the job and can be appraised in terms of agreed standards of performance. The emphasis should be placed on measurable performance standards, such as expectations of work quality, efficiency, style and behaviour, rather than non-measurable factors, such as creativity, loyalty, interest and enthusiasm, which can easily be misconstrued as favouritism or unfairness.

Given such standards, it is not too difficult for a competent field sales manager to identify deficiencies; to get agreement on them; to coach in skills and techniques; to build attitudes of professionalism; to show how to self-train; to determine which training requirements cannot be tackled in the field; and to evaluate improvements in performance and the effect of any past training.

Table 15.3 Further quantitative objectives for a sales force

- ▶ Number of point-of-sale displays organized
- ▶ Number of letters written to prospects
- ▶ Number of telephone calls to prospects
- ▶ Number of reports turned in or not turned in
- ▶ Number of trade meetings held
- ▶ Number of sales aids used in presentations
- ▶ Number of service calls made
- ▶ Number of customer complaints
- ▶ Safety record
- ▶ Collections made
- ▶ Training meetings conducted
- ▶ Competitive activity reports submitted
- ▶ General market condition reports delivered

One consumer goods company with thirty field sales managers discovered that most of them were spending much of their day in their offices engaged in administrative work, most of it self-generated. The company proceeded to take their offices away and insisted that the sales managers spend most of their time in the field training their sales representatives. To assist them in this task they provided training on how to appraise and improve salespeople's performance in the field. As a result, there was a dramatic increase in sales, and consequently in the sales managers' own earnings. The sales managers quite rapidly overcame their resentment at losing their offices.

Ensuring sales force motivation

The key management activities involved in managing the sales force are summarised as:

▶ setting performance standards (both quantifiable and qualitative);
▶ monitoring achievements;
▶ helping/training those who are falling behind; and
▶ setting the right motivational climate.

While monitoring what salespeople do can be accomplished largely through reports, sales figures and so on, assessing *how* they do things usually requires observing them in action. As a rule, the higher the uncertainty surrounding the salesperson, the territory, the product range, the customer and so on, the more frequently should performance be monitored. Having measurable standards of performance enables managers to identify the area and nature of help that salespeople need, and to respond appropriately. For example, they may need more information about prices and products, more support in terms of administration or joint visits, or more training to improve their skills set.

Perhaps most crucial of all is creating the right motivational climate. To maximize sales force performance it is necessary to achieve the optimal balance between incentives and disincentives. While remuneration will always be a key determinant of motivation, sales managers can improve sales force performance by clarifying performance expectations; providing rewards consistent with performance; giving due praise and recognition; ensuring freedom from fear and worry; and encouraging in their sales team a sense of doing a job that is worthwhile and valued.

Moreover, attractive remuneration does not necessarily mean paying the most money, although clearly, unless there are significant financial

Table 15.4 Setting objectives for an individual sales representative

Task	Standard	How to set standards	How to measure performance	Performance shortfalls
1. To achieve personal sales target	Sales target per period of time for individual groups and/or products	Analysis of ▲ territory potential ▲ individual customers' potential. Discussions and agreement between salesman and manager	Comparison of individual sales persons product sales against targets	Significant shortfall between target and achievement over a meaningful period
2. To sell the required range and quantity to individual	The achievement of specified range and quantity of sales to a particular customer or group of customers within an agreed time period	Analysis of individual customer records of ▲ potential ▲ present sales. Discussion and agreement between manager and sales person	Scrutiny of ▲ individual customer records ▲ observation of selling in the field	Failure to achieve agreed objectives. Complacency with range of sales made to individual customers
3. To plan journeys and call frequencies to achieve minimum practicable selling cost	To achieve appropriate call frequency on individual customers. Number of live customer calls during a given time period	Analysis of individual customers' potential. Analysis of order/call ratios. Discussion and agreement between manager and sales person	Scrutiny of ▲ individual customer records Analysis of order/call ratio. Examination of call reports	High ratio of calls to individual customer relative to that customer's yield. Shortfall on agreed total number of calls made over an agreed time period

Table 15.4 *continued*

4. To acquire new customers	Number of prospect calls during time period. Selling new products to existing customers	Identify total number of potential and actual customers who could produce results. Identify opportunity areas for prospecting	Examination of ▲ call reports ▲ records of new accounts opened ▲ ratio of existing to potential customers	Shortfall in number of prospect calls from agreed standard. Low ratio of existing to potential customers
5. To make a sales approach of the required quality	To exercise the necessary skills and techniques to achieve the identified objective of each element of the sales approach	Standards to be agreed in discussion between manager and sales person related to company standards laid down	Regular observations of field selling using a systematic analysis of performance at each stage of the sales approach	Failure to identify ▲ objective of each stage of sales approach ▲ specific areas of skill/weakness ▲ use of support material

motivations within a company it is unlikely that people will stay. In drawing up a remuneration plan, which would normally include a basic salary plus some element for special effort such as bonus or commission, the following objectives should be considered:

▶ to attract and keep effective salespeople;
▶ to remain competitive;
▶ to reward salespeople in accordance with their individual performance;
▶ to provide a guaranteed income plus an orderly individual growth rate;
▶ to generate individual sales initiatives;
▶ to encourage teamwork;
▶ to encourage the performance of essential non-selling tasks; and
▶ to ensure that management can fairly administer and adjust compensation levels as a means of achieving sales objectives.

A central concept of sales force motivation is that the salespeople will exert more effort if they understand clearly what is expected of them, and what the concomitant rewards are for achieving their objectives.

Because of the uniqueness of each business situation and sales force make up, no two sales plans will be exactly the same. None the less, some general guidelines can be given. Table 15.4 is an example of setting objectives for an individual salesperson. These objectives will be the logical result of breaking down the marketing objectives into actual sales targets.

Summary

Sales and marketing are clearly linked, yet require separate attention. The marketing process is only completed when a sale is made. It is essential that a sales force strategy be developed that is integrated closely with the overall marketing strategy. Where sales departments act independently of marketing, they often attain their short-term sales goals but fail to achieve the mix of products and markets consistent with longer-term strategic marketing objectives.

Personal selling offers the benefits of two-way communication, which advertising and sales promotion cannot provide. Sales messages can be made more customer-specific, questions can be asked and answered, and the salesperson can ask for an order and perhaps negotiate on price, delivery or special requirements.

Such flexibility and personalization in communication can greatly enhance service levels and help to close sales, but at a high cost. When the total costs of recruiting, managing and providing salespeople with the necessary resources and support systems is considered, personal selling often accounts for more expenditure than do advertising and sales promotion combined. It is therefore important to plan how personal selling will be integrated into the 'communications mix', and then to organize the logistics to ensure that the right results are achieved cost-effectively.

The benefits to sales force management of following the strategic approach detailed in this chapter can be summarized as:

▶ Co-ordination of corporate and marketing objectives with actual sales effort.
▶ Establishment of a circular relationship between corporate objectives and customer wants that enriches the delivery of customer value.
▶ Improvement of sales effectiveness through an understanding of the corporate and marketing implications of sales decisions.

Further reading

Donaldson, B. (1999) Selling and sales force management, in M. Baker (ed.), *The Marketing Book*, Butterworth Heinemann, Oxford.
Jobber, D. (ed.) (1997) *The CIM Handbook of Selling and Sales Strategy* Butterworth-Heinemann, Oxford.

References

McDonald, M. (1987) *Effective Industrial Selling*, Butterworth-Heinemann, Oxford.
Robinson, P., Faris, C. and Wind, Y. (1967) *Industrial Buying and Creative Marketing*, Allyn & Bacon, Boston.

16 Channel strategy

In this chapter we study the:

► link between communication channels and distribution channels
► alternative channels of distribution
► role, selection and development of channel intermediaries
► options and techniques for determining channel strategy
► types of channel objectives that need to be considered
► impact of e-commerce on channel structure
► key elements of effective channel management

The link between channels of physical distribution and promotion

Let us start by emphasizing the close link between physical distribution channels and promotional channels, as outlined in Figure 16.1 (the same as Figure 11.4 on page 256). Promotion and distribution have been transformed by new channels such as the Internet. The choice of channel and medium is generally a complex one, and is closely intertwined with distribution strategy, as distribution channels often have a mix of purposes, providing both a means of conveying a physical product to the customer and a medium for exchange of information. A car showroom, for example, provides information on car models, an opportunity for a test drive, a location where price negotiations can occur, and a step in the physical delivery of the chosen car to the customer. A clothes shop provides a location where the information exchange of feeling a garment and trying it on can occur in a way that is difficult to replicate using direct marketing approaches. Similarly, the Internet can be both a promotional medium and a physical delivery outlet. So, the focus of promotion

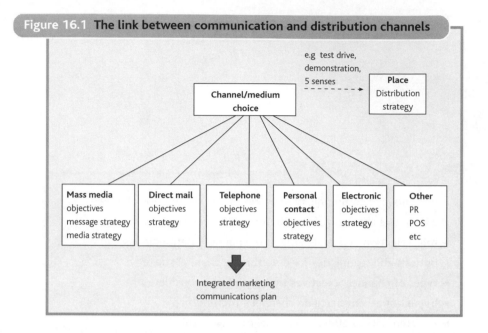

Figure 16.1 The link between communication and distribution channels

and information exchange is linked closely to the physical issues of distribution. None the less, in this chapter we focus exclusively on physical distribution channels, as this is still a major domain in marketing and needs in-depth consideration in its own right.

Channels of distribution

The fundamental role of a company's distribution function is to ensure that 'the right product is available at the right time'. This implies some organization of resources into channels through which the product moves to customers. A distribution channel may therefore be considered as the course taken in the transfer of the title of a product (or service) from its original source of supply to its ultimate consumer. It is necessary to consider both the route of exchange (and its administrative and financial control), and the physical movement of the product – as they may well be different.

As we have seen, distribution channels often have a mix of purposes, providing both a means of conveying a physical product to the customer and a means of exchanging information and ideas. For this reason, the selection, development and management of distribution channels is doubly important. When we consider that route-to-market decisions tend to be long-term as they are difficult to change once established, we see that channel strategy is a significant and enduring aspect of marketing strategy.

Typically, many companies will not pay too much attention to the question of channel choice, as it is not regarded as a variable in the marketing mix. (*Place* emphasizes the actual sales outlet; that is, the 'destination' rather than the 'journey'.) More often than not, the distribution channel will have taken its current form as a result of unplanned and haphazard development. Such a disregard for this vital area of marketing discretion means that many opportunities for profitable market potential are passed over. For example, an international chemical company selling into Europe, using their own sales force to sell direct to customers, found that by using a chemical merchant they could reduce their own sales costs and take advantage of a ready-made sales organization with a host of local contacts.

A British manufacturer of high-quality shoes found it possible to open up a new and profitable market segment through the catalogue of a national mail-order firm. This facility provided the company with an opportunity to reach a wider audience without compromising its traditional channels (upmarket, speciality shoe shops).

Another British company, a carpet manufacturer, was perplexed by its falling sales as total carpet sales in the UK remained at a high level. It was felt that the company had in some way got its quality or pricing levels wrong. In fact, a deeper examination of the company's situation showed that the culprit was its continued policy of selling through small, traditional, high-street carpet shops. The new growth outlets were clearly the edge-of-town carpet warehouses, which often offered discounts. These distributors now accounted for the lion's share of carpet sales, and the manufacturer had missed a wonderful opportunity by failing to recognize the change in distribution patterns and respond accordingly.

These three examples demonstrate the benefits of taking a fresh look at distribution channels. They each involved a reappraisal of the route by which the customer acquired the product, and a comparison of the costs and benefits of other distribution options.

Many companies do not rely on a single channel of distribution, but prefer instead to use multiple channels. They may choose different channels to reach different market segments, or they may approach a single market via a mix of channels. In such cases it is important to ensure that no conflicts exist between channels, particularly in terms of price competition. For example, an insurance company that is seeking to set up a direct, telephone-based sales channel will have to be careful that its established business using insurance brokers is not affected adversely.

Ultimately, the choice of channel(s) must be based on the long-term balance of the benefits and the costs of that choice. As Figure 16.2 shows, each channel can have distinctly different cost and revenue profiles. The channels of distribution available run the gamut from direct to indirect, and from traditional media to the Internet. The choice of channel(s) will have an impact on the organization's current and future levels of service effectiveness, customer closeness, operational efficiency, and corporate profitability. Any cost/benefit appraisal of channels therefore needs to be undertaken in the widest possible context. It needs to consider questions of marketing strategy, the appropriateness of the channel to the product, customer requirements, and the question of the comparative costs of selling and distribution. Marketing channel decisions, then, are *key* decisions, which involve the choice of an intermediary (or intermediaries) and detailed consideration of the physical distribution implications of the alternatives.

Figure 16.2 Alternative channels of distribution

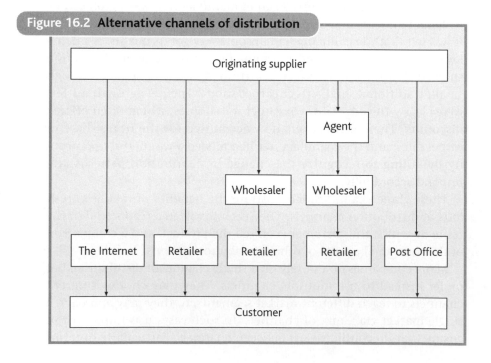

Channel intermediaries

The basic channel strategy decision is whether to sell direct to users, or to use some form of intermediary. The choice may be straightforward in that the costs incurred by selling direct may be just too high. When the decision is not so clear-cut, the choice will depend on an evaluation of the advantages and disadvantages of using intermediaries. The point is that the functions performed by intermediaries must be done by somebody in order that the final customer finds the overall offer worthwhile. Strategic decisions about channels are therefore concerned with who should perform these functions, and where they should be located.

The role of channel intermediaries

The role of an intermediary is to provide the means of achieving the widest possible market coverage at a lower unit cost than would be possible by supplying direct. Many intermediaries hold stock, and thereby share some of the financial risk with the principal or supplier. They may also use the same transport and storage facilities for a number of suppliers' products, thereby spreading the overheads and thus reducing the costs of distribution for each supplier. This important consolidation role is highlighted in Figure 16.3.

Apart from being more cost-effective, an intermediary should also complement the supplier's product range, pricing aspirations and

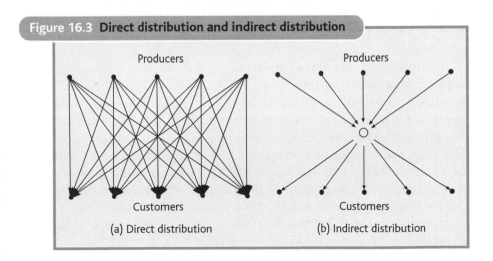

Figure 16.3 Direct distribution and indirect distribution

Producers   Producers

Customers   Customers
(a) Direct distribution   (b) Indirect distribution

service policies. Improved service response can be achieved by intermediaries who are closer to customers geographically, or who possess better local knowledge of the needs of customers in their area. In addition, intermediaries can enhance customer value through such means as one-stop shopping, systems integration, special packaging, or supplying in smaller, rather than bulk, quantities. This is the concept of a 'value-added distributor'.

The potential benefits of using intermediaries include:

► access to markets;
► economies of scale through consolidation;
► final product configuration;
► selling and promotion;
► provision of trade credit;
► holding inventory; and
► installation and customer training.

While using an intermediary carries benefits for the manufacturer, it also involves significant 'costs', the most important of which is the *loss of control* that accompanies such a channel strategy. As Figure 16.4 shows, there is no guarantee that an intermediary will present or position the supplier's products in the most appropriate way, or that priority will be given over other suppliers' products. There is also a *loss of customer contact* and a risk that an intermediary may withhold customer information, either because of the inconvenience of passing it on to the supplier, or the advantage it provides in relationship negotiations. Often, too, disparity exists between the respective objectives of the supplier and the intermediary, leading to conflict and suspicion in the relationship. Clearly, then, the use of intermediaries is accompanied by a possible *loss of opportunity*.

Intermediaries also represent a real and measurable cost to the supplier in terms of *margin forgone*. It is important to remember that any margin allowed to intermediaries should not be seen as a sharing of the supplier's profit. Rather, the margin should be regarded as a recompense for the transfer of cost from the supplier to the intermediary. Thus, for example, if a wholesaler carries an inventory on behalf of a manufacturer, then the wholesaler will incur a holding cost on that inventory. Since, presumably, this relieves the manufacturer of the need to carry that inventory, the wholesaler can be recompensed to the extent of the cost saved by the supplier. The concept of the *channel margin* is important in this context.

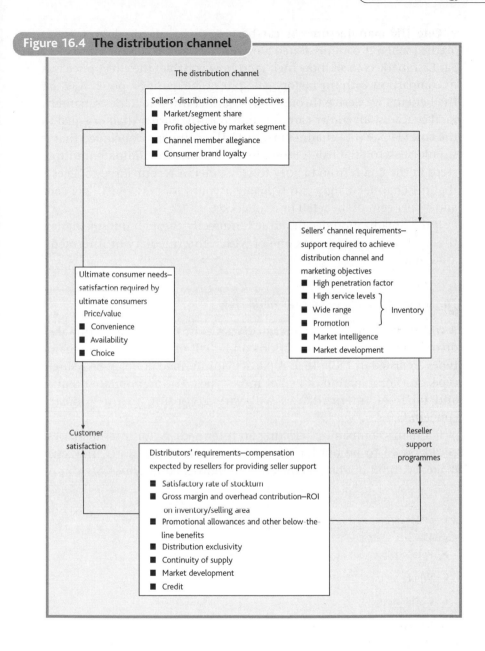

Figure 16.4 The distribution channel

The distribution channel

Sellers' distribution channel objectives
- Market/segment share
- Profit objective by market segment
- Channel member allegiance
- Consumer brand loyalty

Sellers' channel requirements—
support required to achieve
distribution channel and
marketing objectives
- High penetration factor
- High service levels ⎫
- Wide range   ⎬ Inventory
- Promotion   ⎭
- Market intelligence
- Market development

Ultimate consumer needs—
satisfaction required by
ultimate consumers
Price/value
- Convenience
- Availability
- Choice

Customer
satisfaction

Reseller
support
programmes

Distributors' requirements—compensation
expected by resellers for providing seller support
- Satisfactory rate of stockturn
- Gross margin and overhead contribution—ROI
  on inventory/selling area
- Promotional allowances and other below-the-
  line benefits
- Distribution exclusivity
- Continuity of supply
- Market development
- Credit

The channel margin can be defined as the difference between the price in the final market – the 'street price', and the price paid to the supplier – the 'factory gate price':

channel margin = street price – factory gate price

One UK manufacturer of car batteries was surprised by what it learned when it commissioned a market research study on some of its Far East markets to see how high (and how variable) the street price was in comparison with the factory gate price. The question posed was: are the benefits we derive through our channel intermediaries – namely, market access, inventory carrying and so forth, greater than or equal to the cost we pay (the channel margin)? The company concluded that it should seek to establish a more direct channel to eliminate multiple steps in the chain from factory to consumer. A recent survey suggests that the channel margin can typically account for between 15 per cent and 40 per cent of the retail price of goods.

If the organization decides to sell indirectly through intermediaries, the next decision becomes one of which intermediary or intermediaries to use.

The selection of channel intermediaries

A wide variety of channel intermediaries exist who will perform sales, distribution and service functions on behalf of a supplier. The major types are listed in Table 16.1. A particular intermediary may be a single type, or a combination of two or more types. The appropriate number and types of intermediaries will vary according to the industry concerned.

For many companies, selecting an intermediary (or intermediaries) could prove to be one of the most important decisions they ever make. Without doubt, an efficient and motivated intermediary can be

Table 16.1 Major types of intermediary

▶ Retailers in or out of town	▶ Direct mail retailers
▶ Wholesalers	▶ Franchised outlets
▶ Distributors	▶ Freight forwarders
▶ Dealers	▶ Merchandise clubs
▶ Agents	▶ Party sales organizers
▶ Value-added resellers	▶ Licensed manufacturers/service operators
▶ Original equipment manufacturers	▶ Websites
▶ Catalogue distributors	

a priceless asset; while a lacklustre one could ruin the company. A multitude of factors could influence the choice decision. Table 16.2 shows the results of a survey conducted of a sample of UK firms to discover the criteria used for selecting intermediaries. These factors are listed in order of rank, with the most important at the top of the list.

Clearly, these findings underline the fact that many of the key selection criteria relate to the intermediaries' marketing expertise and strength 'on the ground'. However, others would add the following considerations to this list, and suggest that they should also figure in any selection process:

▶ Is the intermediary creditworthy?
▶ Does the intermediary create the right image?
▶ Are their policies regarding inventory and customer service compatible with our company's?
▶ Are their total promotion activities and budgets what we would expect for success?
▶ Are their locations consistent with our overall distribution strategy?
▶ Does the intermediary carry competitor lines?

Table 16.2 Intermediary selection criteria

Criteria	UK ranking
Knowledge of the market	1
Market coverage	2
Enthusiasm for the product	3
Number and quality of sales personnel	4
Knowledge of product	5
Frequency of sales calls	6
Previous success/track record	7
Costs involved	8
Extent of dealing with competitors	9
Service and stocking facilities	10
Quality of service staff	11
Executives' career history	12

And perhaps the most important of all:

▶ Is the intermediary someone we can trust and with whom we could develop a good working relationship?

If the answer to the last question is negative, then all the other criteria are largely redundant, because the secret of success is to select intermediaries who, in effect, become business partners. Implicit in this is that the relationship between the parties be conducted in an open and mature manner. For channel relationships to succeed, they must be forged with clarity of purpose, and be fostered through mutual trust, commitment and gain.

The development of channel intermediaries

At a company conference, to which, for the first time, a manufacturer's overseas agents had been invited, discussion focused on communications. It is sad to report that the agents claimed unanimously that the only time they had ever had a visit from representatives of the company was 'when things went wrong'. Not only that, they also felt that they were kept 'in the dark' regarding future plans and new products.

The company in question was to be commended for taking such a bold step in organizing this conference as a means of integrating the agents more fully into the organization. The aim of the conference had been to learn how the agents perceived the company, and to use this knowledge to improve relationships. The company was surprised to find that, by seeming to focus on negative parts of the relationship, they had caused the agents to develop a defensive attitude: instead of trust, they had bred distrust.

The conference did, in fact, provide both the company and the agents with the opportunity to air difficult issues and to work through them amicably. Indeed, the event proved to be a watershed in the company's relationships with its overseas representatives.

So how can a supplier build a good relationship with an intermediary? Here are some tried and tested methods:

▶ *Understand the distributor's needs and problems.* This means getting out and talking to them regularly, not just when things go wrong. One company insists that its own sales representatives spend a set number of days per year 'working on the counter' in the distributors' premises.

▶ *Learn from distributors' experiences.* Monitor and feed back into internal knowledge management systems information about common problems, emerging opportunities, market trends and so on.

▶ *Conduct market research studies.* Encourage distributors to provide annual appraisals of the service they receive from supplier's, and make recommendations about improvements. Alternatively, conduct customer surveys and share the results with distributors. Positive results will enable them to increase sales, while negative results will allow them to help address evident weaknesses.

▶ *Create a distributor panel.* Have a small group of specially selected distributors meet at regular intervals to act as a sounding board for future policies and to get feedback on current issues.

▶ *Invite distributors' input in the development of the marketing plan.* This will encourage them to 'buy in' to those parts of the plan that make an impact upon distribution.

▶ *Establish two-way communications.* Ensure dialogue at many different levels – for example, director to director, salesperson to salesperson, clerk to clerk, and so on.

▶ *Demonstrate commitment to the distributor.* Refer customer enquiries and requests to the distributor and do not open up competing distributorships in their territory.

Later in the chapter we shall see how treating channel intermediaries as partners enhances channel management. First, however, let us consider the channel strategy options available, and understand that the use of intermediaries is not a forgone conclusion.

Channel strategy options

At first sight, the choice of channel strategy is deceptively easy. After all, there are basically only three options from which to choose:

1 To sell direct to the customer/user;
2 To sell to customers/users through intermediaries; or
3 To use a combination of 1 and 2 – that is, dual distribution.

However, the final choice of strategy will always be something of a compromise between the natural desire to keep control of the distribution of a supplier's products and the practical need to keep distribution costs to a bearable level. The distribution channel algorithm given in Figure 16.5 can be helpful in deciding channels of

Figure 16.5 Distribution channel algorithm

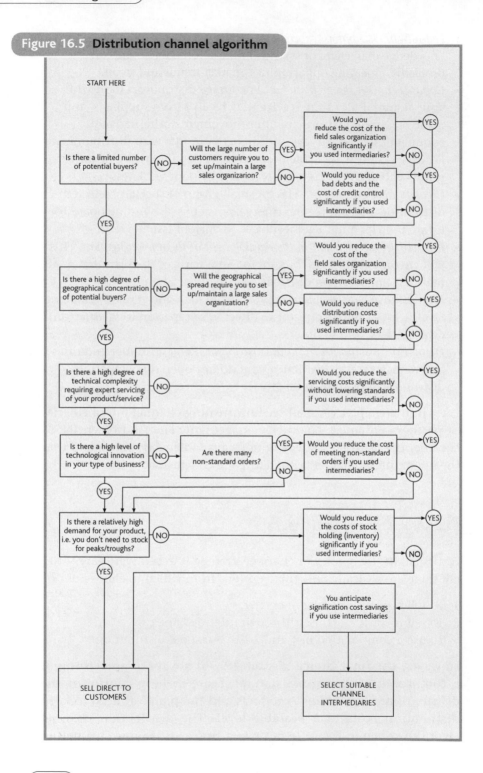

distribution, in particular in determining whether intermediaries are required.

Growth in the number, type and sophistication of distribution channels is mirrored in the range of strategy options available. The addition of the Internet and mobile devices to the more conventional channels has expanded the choice of individual as well as integrated routes to market. And with greater channel choice has come stiffer competition. Companies such as Direct Line, First Direct, EasyJet, eBay and Amazon all compete by exploiting IT-enabled remote channels to add value, reduce costs or both.

The opportunities these IT-enabled channels present for building profitable customer relationships are huge. Witness the rapid take-up of packages for sales force automation, direct mail, telemarketing, customer service, e-commerce and marketing analysis, which are available both separately and together as integrated CRM suites. But these packages, while providing an essential infrastructure, need to be supplemented by managerial processes to address such fundamental questions as which channels to use, and how best to use them to deliver customer value.

Our research suggests that companies can select from the following broad channel strategy options:

Single channel strategy The organization provides at least the bulk of the customer interaction through one channel. Direct Line and First Direct both started as primarily telephone operations, while in the Internet world the approach is referred to as 'pure play', represented by Amazon, eBay and so on.

Channel migration strategy The organization starts with one single channel, but is attempting to migrate its customer base on to another channel on the grounds of increased value or reduced cost. EasyJet initially sold tickets by telephone, but now provides financial incentives to its price-sensitive customers to buy online, most of whom now do so.

Integrated multi-channel strategy The organization offers different, interconnected channels to the customer without attempting to influence which one(s) the customer uses. A strategy based on the integration of multiple channels offers greater scope for respecting customers' channel preferences and propensities of use, thereby enhancing the organization's attractiveness and, ultimately, responsiveness to customers. It also works to ensure a 'seamless' customer experience, which will promote a stronger and longer customer relationship. Thomas Cook uses the Internet to generate leads and to take bookings, a direct sales force to sign up new major clients, a call centre to take orders, and its shops to do all these things. The point here is that Thomas Cook empowers its customers to choose how to access them. First Direct provides both telephone and Internet banking as an integrated service. While the Internet has much lower unit costs, and also has proved better for cross-selling, First Direct chooses to position itself on customer service and accept the higher costs from those customers who primarily use the telephone without penalizing them or rewarding Internet users.

Needs-based segmentation strategy The organization offers different channels to different customer groups to meet their varying needs. Each of these routes to market may use the same brand name, or different names. The insurer Zurich has multiple brands: Allied Dunbar, Zurich, Eagle Star and Threadneedle. Each brand has strengths in different routes to market – the direct sales force, independent financial advisers and company pension schemes – in order to serve customer groups with differing needs and attitudes.

Graduated customer value strategy The organization uses channels selectively according to the financial value of the customers. Many IT firms use account managers for high-value customers, and steer smaller customers to lower-cost channels such as the Internet, call centres or value-added resellers. The UK's clearing banks, however, are in danger of doing precisely the opposite; offering the high-cost branch network to the lower-value customers who prefer not to bank via telephone or the Internet.

The reason why channel strategy decisions are long-term is because each party will require commitment from the other, and the creation of any arrangement will involve considerable investment of both time and money. The decisions will be based on trade-offs between control, cost and marketing objectives.

Selecting the most appropriate channel strategy for any given market at any given time means ensuring it is aligned to and supportive of both the needs and expectations of customers, and the requirements and capabilities of the supplier.

Determining Channel Strategy

Value analysis

When deciding on a channel strategy, the starting point must be the customers themselves. If we do not offer them the channels they would prefer to use, a competitor will. But with new channels, how can we predict customer take-up in advance? Figure 16.6 shows a simple technique for doing this, called *value analysis*. It operates in a similar vein to benefit analysis (see Chapters 3 and 7). Value analysis amounts to plotting the relative strength of those factors that exert greatest influence on customer purchase preference for each type of channel used.

Value analysis begins with an identification of the customers' buying factors – the factors that determine which supplier gets their business. These are listed on the horizontal axis of Figure 16.6, along with weights out of 100, which represent their relative importance in the purchase decision. These factors will vary by customer segment, so the analysis must be done for each one. In the segment illustrated here, the customers are most interested in the cost they pay – the price plus any other charges such as delivery – but are also concerned with such factors as convenience of purchase and the ability to browse for the book they want.

The ability of each current or future channel to deliver against each factor is then assessed judgementally on a 1–10 basis. In this hypothetical example, the various means by which a book can be

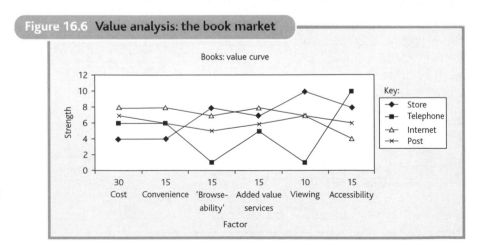

Figure 16.6 Value analysis: the book market

purchased are compared. It can be seen that taking all the factors together, the Internet and physical stores have the best matches to this particular segment. In reality, different segments of the book market are clearly best matched to different channels.

The score of a channel against price-related factors, such as 'cost' in this example, will be affected by the channel economics, which will determine the price that any competitor using the channel chain will be able to offer. One factor in assessing the channel economics is the transaction costs involved. The TPN Network business-to-business exchange set up by General Electric (GE), the first significant e-hub, saves GE 50–90 per cent on processing costs for each order. But acquisition and retention costs should not be forgotten. The dot.com arm of a retail chain recently discovered that customer acquisition through banner advertising was costing them £700 per customer, while the average sale was only £50. The good news for this bricks-and-clicks retailer in its competition with pure-play dot.coms was that it could leverage its physical stores for customer acquisition at a cost of just £13 per customer.

This example of physical stores and the Internet working together illustrates a complicating factor. In many markets, customers do not use a single channel. Rather, they use a number of channels in combination to meet their needs at different stages of their relationship with the supplier. To help define how this can best be done, we suggest using a tool termed *channel chain analysis*, which is portrayed in Figure 16.7.

Figure 16.7 Channel chain analysis: the PC market

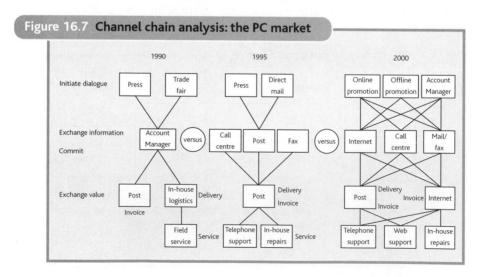

Channel chain analysis

Channel chain analysis involves describing which channels are used at which stages of the purchasing and value delivery process. The stages of the process are listed on the left of the diagram, and the channels used to accomplish the stage are listed against each stage. The channel used for one stage will often affect which channel is likely to be used at the next stage, so the relevant boxes are joined with a line.

In this example from the business-to-business PC market, three of the common channel chains being offered by the various competitors are illustrated. The channel chain on the left shows the traditional account management approach, as used by most competitors at the start of the 1990s, when the sales process was largely handled face-to-face by account managers. This model is still used for larger computers or major contracts, though it tends to be complemented by other channel chains that offer better channel economics for smaller deals.

One of these new channel chains was the direct model, illustrated in the centre of Figure 16.7 under the heading '1995'. Here, press advertising formed the dominant marketing tool, with further information being provided by product brochures and call centre staff. The actual order could be placed via a number of means – often a traditional fax or mail order placed by the accounts department.

More recently, many competitors have added the Internet to the channel mix, as illustrated on the right of the diagram. But most of these are far from pure-play Internet providers. Account managers might serve major accounts via building relationships and negotiating discount levels, while freeing themselves from the details of product configuration and pricing by the website, while the order itself is as likely to be placed by fax or post as it is on the Web.

Different channels, then, are needed at different points in the sales cycle, and different competitors may adopt different approaches. It is easy to imagine a fourth, pure-play Internet channel chain, which has a low-cost structure and is appropriate to certain price-sensitive segments. Indeed, there are competitors adopting this e-channel approach.

Having drawn the channel chains in current use, the next step is to consider possible future channel chains. This requires experimentation with channel chain diagrams to think through not only how the sale is to be made, but also how every other aspect of the customer's needs is to be satisfied. Will a mobile phone purchaser buying over the Internet be able to return a faulty phone to a nearby store? Will an e-hub be able to handle not just price negotiations, but also information flows on stock levels, complaints, returns and product development – and if not, what additional channels will be needed?

The trick is to offer a channel chain that is appropriate to the differing needs of a company's target segments. In other words, the acid test as to whether a channel chain will flourish is whether it represents a better value proposition to a specific group of customers. To test this, we recommend drawing the value curve we described earlier under value analysis, but comparing channel chains rather than the individual channels themselves.

There is a timing issue to be considered as well. Even if a channel chain offers a theoretically better proposition to customers, they may not yet be ready for it. A channel chain innovation, like a product innovation, is likely to proceed along the lines of Rogers' bell-shaped diffusion of innovation curve (see Figure 8.1 on page 158). For example, in order to encourage customers to purchase online, it is necessary to consider what proportion of the customer base has Internet access, and a preference and proficiency in using it to make purchases. We recall one department store that wasted millions on an aborted Internet service in the mid-1990s because it was simply too far ahead of its market.

Channel objectives

The underlying purpose of the distribution channel is to reach the customer in the most appropriate and cost-effective way. This means giving consideration to both the customer's buying objectives and the supplier's selling objectives, and achieving a productive balance of the two.

Customer objectives

While the requirements of the customer might vary from market to market, it is possible to generalize customer objectives relating to the decision of where to buy the product.

Price/Value This dimension is present to a greater or lesser extent in all markets. It implies that the customer is seeking a certain level of value or utility from the product or service, but there is an implicit trade-off between that value and the price charged. In this way, shoppers in the UK have a wide choice before them. At one end of the spectrum they can buy their groceries at Harrods; and at the other end they can choose the no-frills approach of Kwik-Save.

In industrial service markets the same principles of price/value optimisation apply; the only difference is that professional buyers are likely to use formalized evaluation techniques, such as value analysis, to help them to reach their purchase decision.

Convenience/availability It has long been recognized that these factors can play a key role in competitive markets. For example, in the UK, estate agents who traditionally played the role of 'marriage broker' between seller and buyer, now offer a range of ancillary services. Prospective property buyers can now complete their transactions through convenient 'one-stop shopping'. The recognition of this simple truth has led to some major financial service companies buying into estate agencies as distribution outlets for their products.

On the industrial front, manufacturers of high-density polyurethane foam plastic, which is used extensively in furniture upholstery, often set up plants where there is a high concentration of furniture manufacturers. Not only does this reduce the high transport costs of shipping 'bubbles of air' around the country, which would be the case if they were to move blocks of plastic foam great distances, but it also virtually guarantees supplies 'on tap' for the furniture companies.

Choice Choice of channel is, of course, a key component of competitive differentiation. The range of distribution channels made available to customers will not only determine how the supplier interacts with customers, and vice versa, but also how the supplier is perceived by customers. Customers who believe they are being valued in the treatment they receive, and their needs are being reflected in product or service offerings, are more likely to feel an affinity towards the supplier and to reward the supplier with their custom.

Issues underlying customer perception might include the following questions: Is it a 'customer-orientated' supplier, demonstrably aware of customer channel preferences and accessibility? Is it a 'technologically-current' supplier, dedicated to channel innovation and investing in the introduction of new or improved channels where relevant? Is it a 'future-thinking' supplier, actively planning for long-term sustainability rather than short-term gain? Is it a 'market-smart' supplier, visibly adept at exploiting the competitive environment in order to provide consistently superior customer value? Such concerns underline the significance for suppliers of appreciating and acting on manifestations of customer discernment.

Supplier objectives

The selection of distribution channels must fit the requirements and capabilities of the supplier in addition to meeting the objectives of the customer. Essentially, the supplier's channel objectives embrace *market*, *institutional* and *marketing* considerations.

Here is an example of how market considerations might influence the choice of channel. Suppose we were marketing financial services to individuals in the high tax bracket. It would not be appropriate to set up a network of door-to-door salespeople. Instead we would be likely to choose an indirect channel of distribution that might rely upon intermediaries such as accountants and bank managers to connect us with our target customers. Clearly, we would also be faced with making decisions regarding geographical coverage and penetration of our market, but these decisions are far less difficult to make once we are clear about our distribution channels.

Institutionally, the supplier should be concerned with issues such as image and appropriateness of the channel. For example, if we produced top-quality goods with a somewhat elitist image, then we will be wise to seek distribution channels that are consistent with this image. It would be counter-productive to do anything less.

Suppliers must also decide where to focus marketing efforts. They have two main marketing strategies open to them if they want to maximize the flow of their goods through the channel:

1 *Push strategy*. Here the supplier focuses attention on the distributor and uses an armoury of different approaches to 'sell-in' more of their products. They might use their field sales force, advertising and special promotions aimed at the distributor and their special incentive schemes. The use of 'trade marketing', whereby the supplier works closely with the distributor in developing joint marketing programmes, has become widespread since the 1990s.
2 *Pull strategy*. Here the focus of attention is the customer, and the objective of the strategy is to stimulate the level of demand so that the distributor is encouraged to stock the product. Marketing techniques used could include TV advertising, national press advertising and promotions, and in-store demonstrations and exhibitions.

In practice, most manufacturers would probably use a combination of push and pull strategies consistent with their marketing objectives and their capabilities.

The marketing strategy might also involve the development of different channels over time. For example, a direct sales force can help an organization to prove that a market exists through obtaining early market penetration, but is then replaced by dealers to obtain intensive distribution as a market grows. This may be followed by a move to exclusive distribution to create brand value in a mature market. Whatever the case, the decisions involved in determining channel strategy are not easy, but can influence success in the market significantly.

Channel management

Having devised a channel strategy, it must then be managed expertly if optimal return on investment is to be achieved. One element of good channel management is understanding the different contributions of customers (in terms of revenue streams, lifetime value, customer referrals and so on), and exploiting this individuality. Where indirect selling is used, suppliers have to develop appropriate relationships with their intermediaries so that working arrangements complement their marketing objectives, and minimize the problems of control and access to market information. Organizations can ensure effective channel management through attention to channel structure; channel motivation; channel partnership; channel conflict; and channel performance.

Channel structure

Until relatively recently there has been little innovation in the structure of distribution channels. Organizations have assumed that distribution channels are, by their nature, fixed and not easily changed. However, the phenomenal impact of the Internet and other technologies has challenged traditional thinking and paved the way for new ideas about how products and services should reach the market place.

The Internet, for example, has accelerated the trend towards 'disintermediation', or the removal of any intermediaries between the supplier and the consumer. This has caused the re-evaluation, and in some cases, redundancy, of certain employment roles. For example, now that customers can research and compare products online, and purchase tickets and holidays directly, travel agents are having to rethink their function and find new ways to provide value. Self-service banking has eroded the need for high-street branches, and telephone-based insurance companies have diminished the need for field sales representatives.

Organizations seeking to adopt new channels such as the Internet must redraw their market maps (see Chapter 3) and evaluate the implications of consequent changes in the value chain. There are five main ways in which the market map can be reconfigured, as outlined in Table 16.3.

Table 16.3 **Evaluating potential changes to the market map/value chain**

Ways to redraw market maps	Inherent questions	Examples
Product substitution/ reconfiguration: The underlying need for a product or service is replaced by a better option	Does an electronic channel enable the underlying customer need to be satisfied in a different way ('substitute products') or to be bundled into different product configurations ('reconfigured products'), which adds value?	A newspaper (bundled product) competes with web services that also provide news, job adverts, weather updates, etc.
Disintermediation: There is one less link in the chain by removing an intermediary whose primary function of information transfer can be performed more effectively by using the Internet	Does the removal of an intermediary improve physical flows? If so, can information flows or other value-adding services provided by the intermediary be handled as effectively by others in the chain?	Telephone and Internet banking
Re-intermediation: A previous intermediary is replaced by a new on-line intermediary, rather than bypassed	Does the replacement of an existing intermediary with a new on-line intermediary afford advantages in terms of cost-effectiveness and customer value? Do these advantages outweigh the negative implications of stopping one relationship and starting another?	On-line sites which search automatically for the cheapest car insurance compete with telephone-based car insurance brokers
Partial channel substitution: An intermediary's role may be reduced but not	Does the addition of an Internet communication channel improve information flows	Car manufacturers' websites build the brand and provide customer information while

Table 16.3 *continued*

Ways to redraw market maps	Inherent questions	Examples
eliminated, with some of its value being provided remotely by the supplier to the intermediary's customer	(e.g., faster, easier and cheaper communication with the customer)?	pointing customers to traditional outlets for their actual puchase
Media switching/addition: Links in the chain may remain the same, but communication between them may be partially or fully switched to the Internet from previous media	Within the current structure, can the Internet reduce costs or add value for some communications?	RS Components added a web channel to its dominant telephone sales model while still selling to the same customers

When reviewing or revising channel structure, an organization should consider whether alterations to channel structure are advisable in the light of existing relationships, and are sustainable given the inevitability of market and technological change. Which channel structure will be appropriate for the organization, for a particular channel type, will depend on which method can best attract end consumers in the target market/segment. This in turn will depend on the organization's ability to create and deliver value relevant to those customers' needs – and thus to the commercial requirements of intermediaries.

Channel motivation

The prime focus of intermediaries is satisfying their own customers, since they are their source of income. Intermediaries will also be concerned with issues of stock turnover and profit margin, and will tend to concentrate their efforts on the products that sell most easily. Suppliers must therefore actively encourage their intermediaries to give priority to their products and not those of competitors. Intermediaries can be motivated to act in the supplier's interests (as well as their own) through reducing prices or making the margin available more inviting. Suppliers should endeavour to minimize the risk of stock-outs on the part of the intermediaries, which may result from their reluctance to hold large inventories. At the same time, suppliers must stimulate intermediaries to promote their products rather than just wait for customers to turn up.

Perhaps the most important aspect of motivating intermediaries is to remember that they are, themselves, a market, and not just someone in the middle being paid to provide a service for the supplier. As a market, intermediaries' problems need to be solved in ways that recognize their perception of value. This will encourage them to be advocates for their suppliers. Areas of value to intermediaries include:

▶ sales support materials;
▶ market research about intermediaries' markets;
▶ advanced information about product development;
▶ fast responses to technical queries;
▶ the creation of market pull;
▶ rapid fault tracing; and
▶ product training.

Channel partnership

An organization's relationships with its intermediaries are often better managed if they can be formed into partnerships. Under a partnership arrangement, intermediaries are more likely to regard themselves as a meaningful part of their supplier's enterprise. The essence of 'partnership' will be *agreement* between supplier and intermediary about the supplier's general market policies, plus positive demonstrations of *commitment*. A significant signal of commitment to channel relationships is to devote a specific part of the supplier's marketing management structures to channel marketing.

This is not to say that channel partnerships cannot be changed, because they can be, and will often need to be. As a product matures through its life-cycle in the market, different arrangements may be required to match different market developments. As a simple example, mass markets need to be addressed in a different way from niche markets, and products that are tending towards commodity status do not require the same level of dealer sophistication in order to be competitive. Similarly, as the competitive status of a product improves through, for example, brand development, different types of intermediary may be required to maintain product positioning. In the early 1990s in the UK, both Nissan and Mazda made significant changes to their franchised dealer network; the former to gain better control, and the latter to upgrade the quality of its dealers in order to better complement the perceived quality and status of its newer models.

Channel conflict

Since channel members are normally independent organizations, there is always the potential for conflict, either between channel members themselves, or between an intermediary and its supplier. Resolution of such conflict is vital if intermediaries are to remain responsive to efforts to motivate them and a partnership relationship can be maintained.

Conflicts between channel members may be caused by supplier favouritism, or by the appointment of too many intermediaries within one geographical area, resulting in them fighting each other for a worthwhile portion of a finite business 'pie'. Alternatively, individual channel members may 'let the side down' through over-vigorous competitive activities or reductions in quality standards.

Conflicts between intermediaries and suppliers usually arise from supplier neglect or inconsistent channel management. Suppliers that make their products available through a number of competing intermediaries may even find themselves competing directly with their own intermediaries.

Conflict, and the resulting likelihood of a reduced return being experienced by all, can to a large extent be eliminated if someone within the distribution chain exercises a leadership role. It can therefore be in the manufacturer's interest to set out deliberately to take the initiative and strive for channel leadership, thereby bringing a sense of order and fairness to what could be a volatile and mutually destructive situation. However, leadership can only be sustained if suppliers can back up their stance with economic power, or with a unique, highly desirable product that is in great demand.

It is quite conceivable that channel leadership can pass to anyone else in the chain. Wholesalers, distributors or agents can, if they exploit their power according to their circumstances, influence the channel 'politics' to their advantage. An example of this can be found in the agricultural market in Western Europe, where some distributors have become more dominant and more powerful than their suppliers.

Channel performance

Since the success of manufacturers using indirect selling is heavily dependent on the effective performance of their intermediaries, it is necessary to have a general framework against which to assess channel performance. In recent years, marketers have used the concept increasingly of *performance auditing* of distributors. One way of doing this is to monitor outlets on a day-to-day basis, making a check on their sales, either in total or through the range. This information can be useful as a rough control mechanism for management, but a detailed performance audit will go further than this. Some of the elements that should be reviewed are:

► Sales performance:
  − current sales compared with historical sales;
  − sales compared with other channel members;
  − sales compared with target sales; and
  − sales growth trends.
► Inventory maintenance:
  − levels compared with contractual (if any) arrangements;
  − levels though the range;
  − levels compared with market trends;
  − number of 'stock-out' situations;
  − levels of competing stocks;
  − condition of inventory and facilities;
  − old stock on hand/attempts to shift it; and
  − stock-keeping records/control efficiency.
► Commitment:
  − enthusiasm/motivation of staff;
  − general housekeeping;
  − displays of products/sales material; and
  − number of suggestions/queries initiated by distributor.
► Competition:
  − competition from other intermediaries compared with sales figures; and
  − competition from other product lines stocked by the intermediary.
► General growth prospects:
  − Does the track record indicate future growth? Is it keeping pace with that projected for the region, trade area, and so on?
  − How does current performance compare with local yardsticks?
  − Is the intermediary's organization expanding/shrinking? Why?
  − What record of investment in their business does the intermediary have?
  − What are the qualifications/experience of their staff?

- What continuity is likely, for example, through management succession plans and health of key staff members?
- What evidence is there of adaptability to change?
- What are the intermediary's own business plans?

Having developed a set of criteria such as these, it ought to be possible to evaluate the performance and longer-term prospects of any distributor. More accurate assessment, for comparative purposes, can be attained by weighting the individual criteria according to their importance. Also 'point-scoring' techniques can be used in conjunction with the weighting if they serve a clear purpose.

The performance audit not only provides the marketer with valuable information about the current effectiveness of the distribution channel, it also establishes the basis upon which a distributor development strategy can be formed.

Too often, suppliers see themselves as *selling to* rather than *selling through* the intermediary. No small wonder then that, with this perception, suppliers are frequently dissatisfied with distributor performance. Four areas have been identified as being sources and symptoms of problems common among various types of intermediaries. These should be monitored closely by the supplier.

1 *Diversification.* The intermediary is spreading its limited resources over too wide a range of products or markets.
2 *Capitalization.* There is inadequate funding/cash flow to sustain the business unless tough management decisions are made.
3 *Market share.* Falling market share can be a valuable pointer to the fact that the intermediary is failing to be competitive.
4 *Attitude.* There is a negative attitude on the part of the intermediary towards the supplier company and its products.

In addition, field sales personnel should monitor the intermediary's performance in:

▶ financial management;
▶ sales personnel training;
▶ planning;
▶ network management;
▶ market development; and
▶ sales management.

It is in these areas that huge strides can be made in terms of enhancing channel performance. However, few suppliers have a sales force of sufficient calibre either to identify needs or to provide business counselling to intermediaries.

Some enlightened suppliers have set up separate specialist teams of advisers to fulfil such an intermediary development role, thereby overcoming what might be seen in some quarters as a dilution of the field sales activity. The results stemming from this type of investment indicate that distributors become more flexible, adaptive and successful, thus safeguarding the supplier's long-term strategic interests. In addition, considerable goodwill can be generated by this approach to intermediary development.

It must be remembered that the development of intermediaries can be costly, and the decisions regarding the depth and breadth of such improvement activities should not be taken lightly. However, there is an alternative approach to securing more effective control of a distribution channel and this is through a process called *vertical integration*. Vertical integration is also a common phenomenon in distribution channels. Such integration could involve a company merging with or absorbing those firms who are its sources of supply (*backward integration*), or taking similar steps to gain control of those intermediaries closer to its markets (*forward integration*). Such a movement, either forward or backward, can sometimes be accomplished without taking over the ownership of the firms involved.

Summary

Getting products or services to the market is a regulated dimension of the marketing mix. It is vital for the success of the supplier that customers should have access to the product or service through channels that meet their requirements as well as the supplier's.

In response to e-commerce, routes to market are being reconfigured in five main ways:

▶ product substitution/reconfiguration (such as e-mails instead of physical post);
▶ disintermediation (e-commerce can make intermediaries redundant);
▶ re-intermediation (a previous intermediary is replaced by a new on-line intermediary);
▶ partial channel substitution (an intermediary's role may be reduced, but not eliminated – as in the case of a car manufacturer

providing customer information, but pointing customers to particular outlets); and

▶ media switching/addition (the links in the chain may remain the same, but communication between them may be partially or fully switched to the Internet from the previous mechanisms).

Developing relationships with channel intermediaries based on partnership can be a powerful means of building competitive advantage. The aim should be to develop marketing programmes that are attractive to all members of the distribution channel and not just to end-users. In a *push strategy*, attention is concentrated on the intermediary to 'sell-in' more products, whereas in a *pull strategy*, the supplier emphasizes the creation of demand so that intermediaries are encouraged to deal in that product.

Case study 16.1, focusing on Allan-Bradley, shows how partnering with distributors can enable a supplier to build competitive advantage both for itself and its customers.

Case study 16.1 The benefits of partnering with distributors

Allen-Bradley, the world leader in automation control solutions, is a good example of a company that manages its portfolio of partners to achieve its goals. Naturally, it has partnerships with suppliers (as with Motorola for micro-processes), but even more interesting is its use of other partnerships. With its long-standing key distributors, for example, Allen-Bradley has steered away from traditional relationships towards *channel* partnerships.

Where once the company merely supplied its products to distributors of electrical/mechanical goods, it has now moved to strengthen the entire distribution chain. At the time of writing, it manufactures and ships more quickly to help reduce distributor inventory, works to build technical sophistication in distributor sales forces, and provides servicing for advanced software. In return, the distributors are not only selling more products, but they are also providing other value. For example, the distributors are beginning to supply more detailed and timely point-of-sale data that will support Allen-Bradley in its drive for manufacturing productivity and excellence in customer service.

As many of its customers' needs are broader and more complex than the company alone can satisfy, Allen-Bradley also manages a portfolio of more than eighty partnerships with *peer* companies. To fulfil its objective of solving customer problems, it has sought out and carefully selected companies that complement its product and service offering, even though some of them are direct competitors in certain applications. Annually, Allen-Bradley convenes its peer partners at its own trade show for customers. And, most important, through its relationships with these partners, the company is able to offer a complete portfolio of products to its distributors, negating the need for them to go to competing suppliers to fill out their product lines.

Through experience, Allen-Bradley has recognized the value of *customer* partnerships and has chosen a small number of global companies with which it can form close partnerships to develop new products, enter new markets, and build skill at creating and delivering customer value.

Source: Dull *et al.* (1995)

Further reading

Calantone, R. and Gassenheimer, J. (1991) Overcoming basic problems between manufacturers and distributors. *Industrial Marketing Management* (Winter) pp. 215–21.

Rosenbloom, B. (1999) Channel management, in M. Baker (ed.), *IEBM Encyclopaedia of Marketing*, Thomson International Press, London.

References

Christopher, M. and McDonald, M. (1991) *Marketing: An Introductory Text,* Macmillan, London.

Dull, S. F. *et al.* (1995) Partners. *McKinsey Quarterly,* **4.**

Distribution and logistics strategy

▶ expanding role of distribution and logistics

▶ concept of supply chain management

▶ connection between logistics and customer service

▶ logistics mix

▶ relationship between inventory and service levels

▶ trade-offs inherent in integrated logistics management

▶ distribution plan in relation to the marketing plan

The importance of distribution and logistics

For many businesses, distribution plays a small part in their marketing plans. When it *is* considered, the prime concern seems to focus on the physical aspects: the logistics of getting tangible products transported from the supplying company to the customer. The physical distribution function of an organization provides the time and place dimensions that represent *Place* in the marketing mix. This is depicted in Figure 17.1, in relation to the other utility-producing elements. The importance of 'place' is simple: if a product is not available when and where a customer wants it, it will surely fail in the market.

However, distribution embraces a much broader concept than just the delivery of goods. Chapter 16 emphasized how it takes into account the strategic importance of distribution channels and the potential value of channel intermediaries. The next chapter will highlight how it also ensures that 'customer service' is kept in the forefront of the company's deliberations about its marketing policies. Both channel strategy and customer service strategy are key sources of competitive advantage. What renders and releases this advantage is

Figure 17.1 Distribution provides time-and-place utility

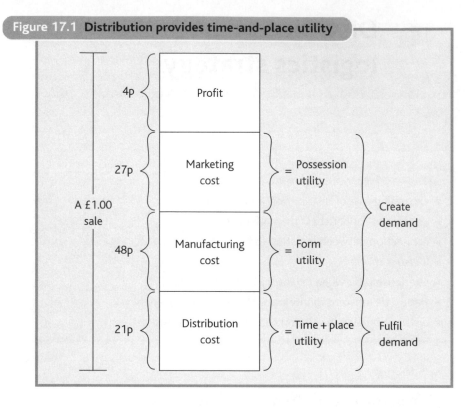

the distribution and logistics strategy that underpins them. The purpose of this chapter is to establish a sound understanding of the role of distribution and logistics, and how this role is evolving from the province of the supply chain to realm of the value chain.

Supply chain management

Logistics management is an integrative process that seeks to optimize the flow of materials and supplies through the organization and its operations to the customer. It is essentially a planning process, and an information-based activity. Requirements from the market place are translated into production requirements and then into material requirements through this planning process.

It is now being recognized that, for the real benefits of the logistics concept to be realized, there is a need to extend the logic of logistics upstream to suppliers, and downstream to final customers. This is the concept of *supply chain management*.

Supply chain management is a fundamentally different philosophy of business organization. It is based on the idea of partnership in the marketing channel, where a high degree of linkage exists between entities in that channel. Traditional models of business organization have been based on the notion that the interests of individual firms are best served by maximizing their revenues and minimizing their costs. If these goals are achieved by disadvantaging another entity in the channel, then so be it. Under the supply chain management model, the goal is to maximize profit through enhanced competitiveness in the final market; a competitiveness that is secured by a lower cost to serve, reached in the shortest time frame possible. Such goals are only attainable if the supply chain as a whole is co-ordinated closely in order to minimize total channel inventory; bottlenecks are removed; time frames are compressed; and quality problems are eliminated.

As companies struggle with new sources of global competition, it is clear that strong brands and innovative technologies are no longer enough; important though they are, even the strongest brands and ground-breaking products need to be supported by a supply chain. There are many new rules of competition, but the following are the most significant for supply chain management:

1 Companies compete through capabilities or 'the way they do things'.
2 As markets become increasingly 'commoditized', companies must find new ways of differentiation.
3 Mergers, acquisitions and organic growth are consolidating customer buying power.
4 To cope with these new challenges, suppliers need to leverage the strengths of their upstream and downstream partners in the 'extended enterprise'.

This new model of competition suggests that individual companies compete not as company against company, but rather as supply chain against supply chain. Thus the successful companies will be those whose supply chains are more cost-effective than their competitors'. So, what are the basic requirements for successful supply chain management? Figure 17.2 outlines the critical linkages that connect the market place to the supply chain. The key linkages are between supply management and manufacturing, and between manufacturing and distribution. Each of these three activities, while part of a continuous process, has a number of crucial elements.

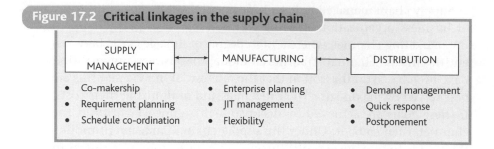

Figure 17.2 Critical linkages in the supply chain

SUPPLY MANAGEMENT	MANUFACTURING	DISTRIBUTION
• Co-makership	• Enterprise planning	• Demand management
• Requirement planning	• JIT management	• Quick response
• Schedule co-ordination	• Flexibility	• Postponement

Supply management

Historically, companies generally have paid scant attention to the management of supply. Even though the costs of purchases represent the largest single cost for most businesses, procurement has not been seen as a strategic task. That view is now changing as the realization grows that not only do procurement decisions and procedures have a dramatic impact on costs, but also that innovation and response-to-market capability are affected profoundly by supplier relationships.

The philosophy of *co-makership* is founded on the notion of a mutually beneficial relationship between supplier and buyer, rather than the more traditional adversarial encounter. With this partnership approach, companies will identify opportunities for taking costs out of the supply chain, instead of simply pushing them upstream or downstream. Paperwork can be eliminated, problems solved jointly, quality improved and information shared. By its very nature, co-makership will normally involve longer-term relationships based on single-sourcing, rather than multiple supply points. Xerox in Europe has adopted the co-makership philosophy, which has had the effect of reducing the company's supplier base from 5000 to 300.

A major benefit of working more closely with suppliers can be gained through involving them in the new product development process. A great deal of innovation now is supplier-originated, and closer partnerships with suppliers can often lead to significant opportunities for new product breakthroughs.

Manufacturing

The key word in manufacturing today is *flexibility*. The ability to produce any variant in any quantity, without a significant cost penalty, has to be the goal of all manufacturing strategies. In the past, and even now, much of the thinking in manufacturing has been dominated by the search for economies of scale. This type of reasoning has led to the formation of mega-plants, capable of producing vast quantities of a standardized product at incredibly low unit costs. It also has led many companies to opt for so-called 'focused factories', producing a limited range of products for global consumption.

The downside of adopting a flexible approach is that it can have the reverse effect by producing 'diseconomies of scale'. These diseconomies might take the form of a build-up of large inventories of finished products ahead of demand, an inability to respond rapidly to changed customer requirements, or a reduction in the variety of products that can be offered to the customer. Instead of pursuing economies of scale, the search is now on to identify strategies that will reduce total supply-chain costs, not just manufacturing costs, and that will offer maximum flexibility against changing customer requirements. The goal of manufacturing must be 'the economic batch quantity of one', meaning that, in the ideal world, we would make things one at a time in response to known customer demands.

Time has become a major competitive issue in most industries, and hence manufacturing and marketing strategies need to be closely coupled.

Distribution

The role of distribution in the supply chain management model has extended considerably from the conventional view that it is concerned solely with transport and warehousing. The critical task that underlies successful distribution today is *demand management.*

Demand management is the process of anticipating and fulfilling orders against defined customer service goals. Information is the key to demand management: information from the market place in the form of medium-term forecasts; information from customers, preferably based on actual usage and consumption; information on production schedules and inventory status; and information on marketing activities, such as promotions that may cause demand to deviate from the norm.

Clearly, while forecasting accuracy should always be sought, it must be recognized that it will only rarely be achieved. Instead, the aim of distribution should be to reduce dependence on the forecast by improving the quality and 'capture' of information about demand, and by creating systems that are capable of responding more rapidly to that known demand. The interlinking of logistics and information systems forms the underlying principle of *quick response* logistics.

Quick response logistics has become the aim of many organizations, enabling them to achieve the twin strategic goals of cost reduction and service enhancement. In essence, the idea of 'quick response' systems is based on a replenishment-driven model of demand management – as items are consumed or purchased, information is transmitted directly to the supplier and this immediately triggers an appropriate response. Often, high-speed, smaller-quantity deliveries will be made, the trade-off being that any increase in transport costs will be more than covered by reduced inventory in the pipeline and at either end of it, yet with improved service in terms of customer responsiveness. Certainly, information technology has been a major enabling factor in quick response logistics, linking instantaneously the point of sale or consumption with the point of supply.

In addition to quick response logistics, a further visible trend in distribution is the search for *postponement* opportunities. The principle of postponement dictates that the final configuration or form of the product should be delayed until the last possible moment. In this way, maximum flexibility is maintained, but inventory is minimized. The distribution function takes on a wider role as the provider of the final added value. For example, at Hewlett Packard, the objective is to minimize inventory held as finished product by carrying it instead as semi-finished, modular work-in-progress, awaiting final configuration once orders are received.

What is apparent is that distribution in the integrated supply chain has now become an information-based, value-added activity, providing a critical link between the market place and the factory. This closer connection with the market place not only makes the company more responsive to customer demand, and hence more agile, it can also reduce the cost of financing the supply chain. For example, at Cisco Systems, a leading provider of network routeing and switching equipment, nearly three-quarters of customers place their orders directly through the Internet. Suppliers are alerted immediately to the need for components, and contract equipment manufacturers, who also monitor the company's orders directly, then build uniquely configured products on a JIT basis. At the same time, the third-party logistics service provider is informed of the impending shipment requirements. As a result, customized products can be delivered and installed in much shorter time frames than previously. By linking suppliers and contract manufacturers through its 'digital value net' Cisco has been able to outsource 70 per cent of its production. This allowed it to quadruple output without adding capacity, and to shorten its time to market for new products by 66 per cent in just six months.

While IT and e-commerce certainly aid information-sharing processes, these linkages do not have to be based on advanced technology. More important is the willingness of all parties in the supply chain to act as partners, and to communicate openly and honestly. Some of the biggest improvements in supply chain agility have occurred through a change of attitude among the parties involved, where 'win-win-win' thinking has replaced the traditional adversarial approach. Table 17.1 summarizes the main differences between these old and new models of supply chain management.

The Impact of Logistics on Customer Value

The potential impact that logistics can have on customer value is considerable. As set out earlier in the book, customer value can be defined as the benefits the customer perceives to flow from the supplier relationship compared to the perceived costs. The benefits will typically comprise both tangible and intangible aspects. Tangible elements of the benefit 'bundle' might include product features and 'hard'

Table 17.1 Agile supply chain management versus traditional approach

Traditional approach	Agile approach
Stock is held at multiple echelons, often based on organizational and legal ownership considerations.	Stock is held at the fewest echelons, if at all, with finished goods sometimes being delivered direct from factory to customer.
Replenishment is driven sequentially by transfers from one stocking echelon to another.	Replenishment of all echelons is driven from actual sales/usage data collected at the customer interface.
Production is planned by discrete organizational units with batch feeds between discrete systems.	Production is planned across functional boundaries from vendor to customer, through highly integrated systems, with minimum lead times.
Majority of stock is fully finished goods, dispersed geographically, waiting to be sold.	Majority of stock is held as 'work in progress' awaiting build/configuration instructions.

service elements, such as on-time delivery. The intangible components of the offer might include the corporate image as well as 'soft' service elements, such as the helpfulness of the customer service call centre.

The cost that the customer incurs will be more than just the price charged for the product or service. Sometimes there can be significant transaction costs involved in placing orders, actioning progress, checking and remedying quality defects, checking invoices and making payments. There may also be ongoing costs, termed life-cycle costs, such as maintenance and running costs. It is the totality of these costs – often referred to as the total cost of ownership – that the customer evaluates against the perceived benefits.

Figure 17.3 draws these different ideas together and suggests that logistics, directly or indirectly, can have an impact on all the component elements of customer value. For example, to a retailer, product packaging can have a significant effect on in-bound distribution costs and shelf-space profitability. Suppliers who include logistics considerations in their product or pack design decisions can thus greatly improve customer value. A good example of this type of forward

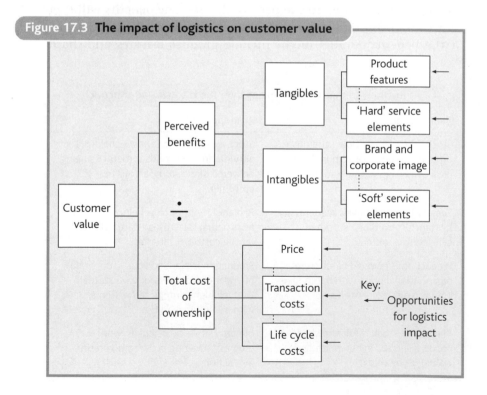

Figure 17.3 The impact of logistics on customer value

thinking is provided by Procter & Gamble (P&G), who redesigned the pack of their global shampoo brand, Head & Shoulders, and as a result, enabled 25 per cent more product to be moved and stored on a pallet. This initiative benefited P&G's retail customers as well as the company itself, with a further significant benefit accruing to the retailer through better shelf-space utilization.

Suppliers' logistics processes can also deliver enhanced customer value through ensuring more reliable delivery, thus reducing the customers' need to carry safety stocks. The supplier can provide further benefit to the customer by actively managing the customer's inventory – a concept known as vendor managed inventory (VMI). Under VMI, the supplier monitors the customer's inventory levels and, using this information, decides when to replenish stocks and in what quantities. The customer pays only when they use or sell the product. Large retail chains, for example, are increasingly forming partnerships with their suppliers to introduce these types of collaborative and mutually beneficial logistics arrangements.

From the standpoint of competitive advantage, this type of value-adding logistics activity can be very positive. The more the customer's processes become integrated with the supplier's processes, the greater the barrier to entry that is erected against competitors.

The connection between logistics processes and superior customer service is self-evident. This transparency has engendered an acceptance that customer service is much more than simply a question of motivating employees or producing generalized mission statements and slogans. Instead, the dimensions of service must to be understood in detail, and strategies need to be developed for effective service delivery.

The critical role of logistics service

The importance of logistics in marketing strategy is that it is the *process* that delivers customer service. As markets take on increasingly the characteristics of 'commodity markets', where customers perceive little difference between products at a functional or technical level, customer service can provide a powerful means of differentiation. In markets as disparate as industrial chemicals or personal computers, the struggle is to find ways to avoid the commodity trap. For many companies, the solution to this problem has come through enhanced service performance. Modern customers are service-sensitive, requiring availability of supply at short notice, for they often operate on a 'just-in-time' (JIT) basis, whether they are a manufacturing business, a retailer, or an end-user. The era of 'time-based competition' has arrived.

Customer satisfaction at a profit is the goal of any business organization, and the role of the logistics system is to achieve defined service goals in the most cost-effective manner. The establishment of these service goals is a prerequisite for the development of appropriate logistics strategies and structures. There is now widespread acceptance that customer service requirements can only be determined accurately through research and competitive benchmarking. Customer research may also reveal the presence of significant differences in service preferences among customers, thus indicating alternative bases for market segmentation in terms of service needs.

Tailoring customer service strategies to meet the precise needs of customers can be a powerful means of differentiation leading to enduring competitive advantage – service segmentation is a key means to achieving this end.

Understanding customers' service preferences is the starting point for re-engineering logistics processes to ensure greater cost-effectiveness; thus customers' service preferences should be the starting point for the development of logistics and supply chain strategies. The challenge to the organization then becomes one of how to re-engineer processes and to restructure conventional, functional systems to achieve these service goals at minimum cost.

Key to the achievement of these customer service goals is closer collaboration with downstream partners in the distribution channel. As discussed in Chapter 16, the way in which distribution channels are structured, and the relationships within them are managed, is crucial to competitive performance in any industry.

The logistics mix

The emphasis behind a logistics approach is to view the movement of products, as they pass through the manufacturing process and eventually to the customer, as a total system. Thus instead of marketing, production, distribution and purchasing – all working away oblivious to the others, and each trying to optimize its individual efforts – the logistics concept suggests that it may be necessary for some or all of these areas to operate suboptimally in order that the whole system may be more effective.

So, for example, the marketing manager might have to be prepared to accept a lower level of customer service than he/she would like; or the production manager might have to schedule shorter runs with more frequent tool changes if the overall effectiveness of the system is to be maximized.

In practice, there are five key decision areas that have to be addressed in logistics management: facilities, inventory, transport, communications and unitization. These variables constitute the *logistics mix*.

Facilities

Facility decisions are concerned with how many warehouses and plants a company should have, and with where they should be located in order to optimize the customer service/cost equation. For the majority of companies it is necessary to take the location of existing facilities as given in the short term. However, companies often have alternative options and opportunities opening up for them regarding how they plan their facilities. If the nature of demand and the location of major customers is forecast to change dramatically, then relocating manufacturing units and/or warehouses is an option that, in the long term, can lead to savings related to reduced distribution costs. However, increasing the number of field locations will result in an increase in trucking costs, and a reduction in retail distribution costs. So another marketing task is to determine the customer service levels that are likely to be required in order to be able to decide what constitutes optimal facilities.

Inventory

The cost of holding stock, whether by design or by accident, can be major element in a company's total distribution costs. It is often as high as 30 per cent of its value per annum. This is because of items such as interest charges, deterioration, shrinkage, insurance, administration and so on. Thus decisions about how much inventory to hold, where to hold it, in what quantities to order and so on become vital issues. Inventory levels are also instrumental in determining the level of service a company can offer its customers, and the kinds of arrangements it can establish with its intermediaries.

Transport

The important aspect of the transport decision concern such issues as what mode of transport should be used, whether to own vehicles or to lease them, how to schedule deliveries, how often to deliver and so on. Of the five distribution variables, transport has received perhaps the greatest attention in most companies, in that it is one of the more obvious facets of the distribution task. Certainly, in recent years, there have been many changes in this area, some of which are just gathering momentum. One of the most significant has been the growth of the specialist carrier, to replace the company's own transport service. However, we must remember that, taken in the total logistics context, transport might only account for a small proportion of the total logistics costs.

Communications

Logistics is not only about the flow of materials or products through the distribution system; it is also about the efficient flow of information in the form of orders, invoices, demand forecasts, delivery schedules and so on. Each of these 'communications' is likely to be an integral part of the customer service package, even if they were set up purely for administrative purposes. Without effective communications support, the logistics system will never be capable of sustaining a satisfactory customer service at an acceptable cost. It should be recognized that inefficiency here can lead to a build-up of costs in other areas of the business, such as, for example, in emergency deliveries, as well as in a permanent loss of sales through customers turning to alternative sources of supply.

Unitization

The way in which goods are individually packaged and subsequently accumulated in larger unit sizes can have major bearing on logistics economics. For example, the ability to stack goods on a pallet, which then becomes the unit load for movement and storage, can lead to considerable cost saving in terms of handling and warehousing. Similarly, the use of containers as the basic unit of movement has revolutionized international transport, and to a certain extent domestic transport as well. Mobile racking systems and front-end pricing by means of scanners are other unitization innovations that have had a dramatic effect on the way goods are marketed.

Together, these five variables of the logistics mix make up the total costs of physical distribution within a company. In some businesses, distribution costs can amount to 20 per cent of the selling price. This emphasizes the importance of considering distribution within the context of the entire marketing mix. Furthermore, it is frequently the case that a decision made in one area will have an effect on the other four. Thus it may be that a decision to open or close a depot will affect transport costs (longer or shorter travelling distances), inventory (stock levels at factory and other depots have to change), and possibly data-processing costs (for installing and operating new system requirements).

This is the idea of a *cost trade-off*. Managing the logistics function involves a continuous search for such trade-offs, the intention being to secure a reduction in total costs by changing the cost structure in one or more areas. Alternatively, investment in one of the logistic decision areas might be vindicated if it can be shown to differentiate the product from its competitors in a way that can bring increased sales revenue or improve the market share through better service.

The service-level decision

One of the fundamental cost trade-offs in logistics that has an impact on marketing performance is the question of *service levels*. The level of service is a measure of the extent to which the organization plans to make the product available and to support it in use; for example, with the provision of after-sales service.

The simplest measure of service is stock availability, usually measured as the percentage of demand that can be met from stock. Clearly, there is more to service than this, as we shall explore in Chapter 18. However, it can be regarded as the foundation of the service 'package'.

Naturally, the customer seeks maximum availability and the company will normally endeavour to supply it. However, the problem is that, as we increase the planned level of availability, the necessary investment in inventory rises more than proportionately. Figure 17.4 highlights the relationship between inventory and service levels. The reason the curve rises so steeply as the planned level of availability increases is that, even though the chance of running out of stock may be remote, additional safety stock must be held to cater for that eventuality.

Many companies frequently underestimate the true costs of holding stock. It is a fair estimate to account for a 25 per cent per annum holding cost for inventory (that is, 25 per cent of the book value of the stock) if we include the cost of capital, storage, obsolescence and insurance. Since most medium-to-large organizations carry millions of pounds worth of stock at any time, the annual cost at 25 per cent is clearly substantial.

Figure 17.4 **The cost of 'availability'**

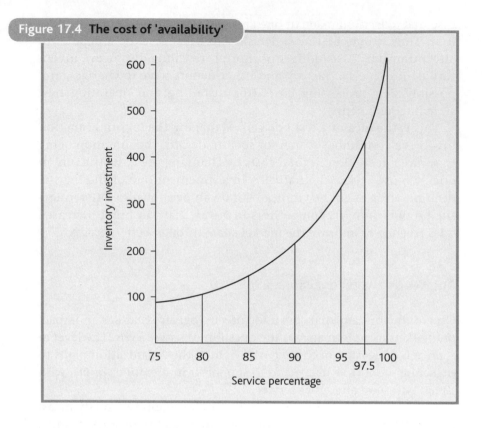

The trade-off that has to be considered, therefore, is: 'What is the cost of holding stock compared with the cost of running out?' If stock runs out too frequently, the outcome can be a substantial fall in sales revenue. At best, the company will forfeit the immediate contribution to its cash flow, while at the same time incurring some degree of customer hostility. At worst, the customer will not delay the purchase but will buy from a competitor instead. Clearly, the cost of running out of stock will vary from product to product, and will to some extent be dependent on the nature and availability of competing products.

Poor stock availability also antagonizes channel intermediaries. In a survey carried out in the USA, it was estimated that, if a supplier decreased stock availability by 5 per cent, nearly a quarter of intermediaries indicated that they would purchase elsewhere. Unaware of this reaction, supplying companies estimated that such a reduction of service would at worst lose them 'only about 9 per cent' of their outlets!

Profit Implications of Stock Management

Because we are dealing with aspects of human behaviour as well as economics when faced with an out-of-stock situation, there is no precise way of measuring the impact on profit. Instead, we have to evaluate the probabilities of stock-exhaustion consequences, estimate the frequency at which each of these consequences is likely to occur, and make a weighted judgement about the financial consequences. Below is an example of how this might be done:

Consequence of service	*Failure profit penalty*
► Loss of sale to competitor	► Gross margin of item
► Customer reordering	► Order-processing cost
► Loss of sale on related items	► Gross margin on all items
► Shipment of goods from other depots	► Expediting and transport cost
► Expediting of rush orders at factory	► Non-standard procedure cost
► Customer's ill-will	► Possible lost customer

Ideally, a market experiment should be conducted to measure more precisely the effect of non-availability on market share. There have been a number of reported studies suggesting that over a certain range of service improvement there can be a significant impact on sales. However, once 'saturation' level is reached the customer may find it difficult to distinguish small improvements in stock availability. Thus, as in Figure 17.5, it is suggested that there comes a point where diminishing returns to service improvement are encountered.

The task of marketing management when seeking to develop appropriate levels of stock availability is to balance the known cost of service against the estimated market response. Figure 17.6 depicts the basic trade-off between the cost function and the response function.

Integrated logistics management

One of the major problems with conventional approaches to distribution is that responsibility for it is spread over too many discrete functional areas; that is, there is a high degree of 'compartmentalization'.

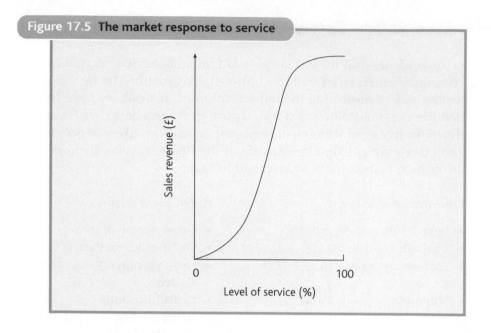

Figure 17.5 **The market response to service**

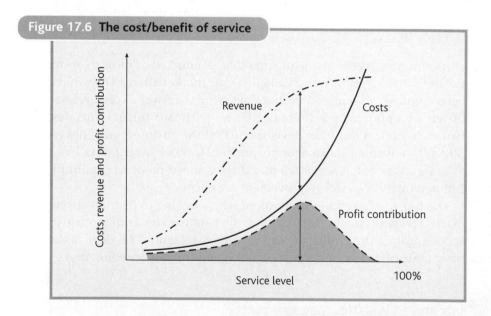

Figure 17.6 **The cost/benefit of service**

In one engineering company, responsibility for stock levels throughout the system was in the hands of the production department. Yet, *at the same time*, the purchasing manager was pursuing policies that conflicted with the production policy, and the distribution manager operated in an inflexible delivery system. Little wonder that the marketing manager was driven to despair by the erratic service levels customers received.

The acceptance of an integrated systems-based approach lies at the very heart of the logistics concept. This, together with the recognition that the interrelationship of the component parts of the mix makes them mutually dependent, should be the cornerstone of the marketer's philosophy.

Distribution planners must in some way unite the interlinked subsystems that together form the company. With their logistics orientation, they must be concerned with the flow of materials through the whole business process, from raw material through to the finished goods shipped to the customer. Figure 17.7 brings together those aspects of the company's operations involving flows – of either materials or information – which are the core concern of an integrated approach to logistics management.

In the traditional model, physical distribution management is concerned only with flows at the end of the production process – getting goods to the customer. In contrast, the integrated approach to logistics encompasses the total flow of materials and information into, through and out of the corporate system. Integrated logistics man-

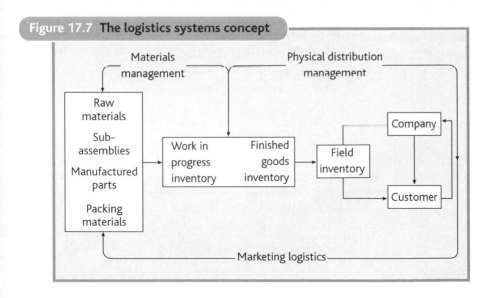

Figure 17.7 **The logistics systems concept**

agement views the supply chain as a value chain, specifying where customer value is to be created. This might involve recognizing that it is more appropriate for some elements of value to be created by other partners in the supply chain, as evidenced by the growth in outsourcing.

When taking an integrated logistics management approach, it is well to remember that there are a number of decisions/trade-offs which need to be specified in the distribution and logistics plan. These are depicted in Figure 17.8.

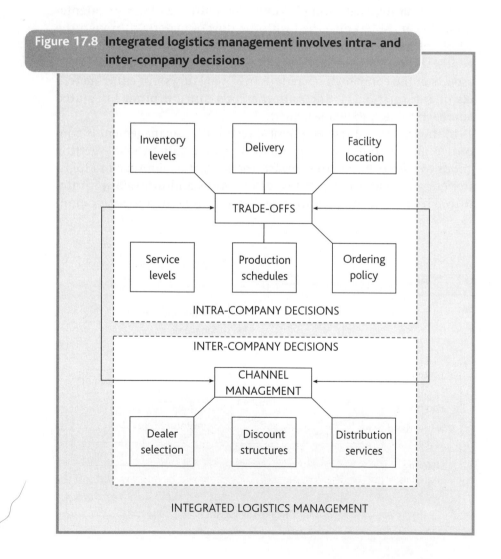

Figure 17.8 Integrated logistics management involves intra- and inter-company decisions

Distribution planning

As in the development of the other tactical plans, distribution planning should begin with the distribution audit (see Table 6.1), from which distribution objectives and strategies can be established. Distribution objectives can be many and varied, but the following are considered basic for marketing purposes:

▶ objectives related to outlet penetration by type of distribution;
▶ objectives related to inventory range and levels to be held;
▶ objectives related to distributor sales and sales promotion activities; and
▶ objectives related to other specific customer development programmes, for example, incentives for distributors.

A simple, iterative approach to distribution planning can be summarized as the steps listed below, the content of which will shape the distribution and logistics strategy:

1 Determine marketing objectives.
2 Evaluate changing conditions in distribution at all levels.
3 Determine the distribution task within overall marketing strategy.
4 Establish a distribution policy in terms of type, number and level of outlets to be used.
5 Set performance standards for distributors.
6 Obtain performance information.
7 Compare actual with anticipated performance.
8 Make improvements where necessary.

The interrelationship between developing the marketing plan and developing the distribution plan is usefully depicted in Figure 17.9.

Summary

Today there is a much greater recognition of the importance of distribution and logistics in the overall marketing strategy of businesses. Not only does the material flow through the firm attract substantial costs (for example, inventory holding charges, transport and storage) but the way in which the flow is managed can have a considerable impact on customer value as identified in customer service. More fundamentally, it provides the added value of 'time-and-place utility' to the product, without which the product is worthless.

Figure 17.9 The distribution plan in relation to the marketing plan

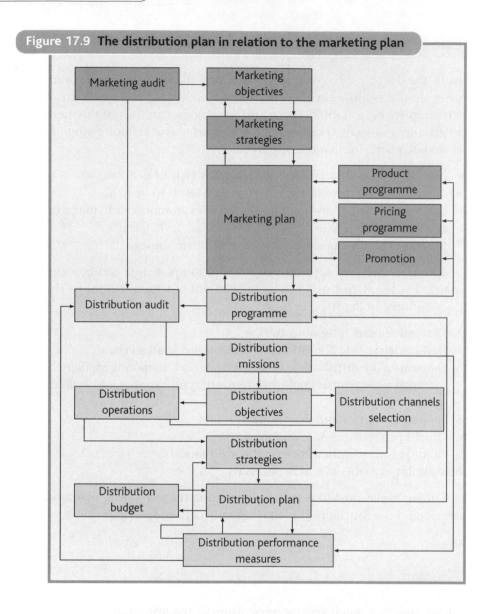

Unless there is a formalized distribution structure, distribution-related activities may be spread across production, marketing, procurement, finance and so on, leading to conflicts of interest between distribution decisions. A more centralized, interrelated distribution system, often referred to as 'logistics', will ensure that one distribution activity is traded off against another to arrive at the most efficient system overall.

The person responsible for distribution therefore has several variables to contend with in the search for trade-offs; taken together these constitute the *logistics mix*. There are five components to manage in the physical distribution of tangible products:

1 *Facilities* – the number, size and geographical location of storage and distribution depots.
2 *Inventory* – the stockholding levels throughout the distribution chain consistent with customers' service expectations.
3 *Communications* – the flow of information, for example, order processing, invoicing, forecasting and so on.
4 *Unitization* – the way in which goods are packaged and assembled into large units, for example, palletization, containerization and so on.
5 *Transport* – the modes of transport, delivery schedules and so on.

'Integrated logistics management' gives the logistics concept managerial application. It is an approach to distribution planning, implementation and control whereby two or more of the functions involved in moving goods from source to user are integrated and viewed as a coherent and cohesive system.

Further reading

Christopher, M. (1998) *Logistics and Supply Chain Management*, 2nd edn, *Financial Times*/Prentice-Hall, London.

References

Christopher, M., Payne, A. and Ballantyne, D. (1991) *Relationship Marketing*, Butterworth-Heinemann, Oxford.
Pine, J. (1993) *Mass Customization*, Harvard Business School Press, Cambridge, Mass.

18 Customer service strategy

In this chapter we study the:

- ▶ role and elements of customer service
- ▶ key steps for developing a customer service strategy
- ▶ importance of researching customers' service needs
- ▶ service level decision involves a cost–benefit analysis
- ▶ elements of a customer service package
- ▶ opportunity for tailor-made service offerings
- ▶ impact of corporate culture on customer service

Elevation of the customer service role

Three factors have perhaps contributed more than anything else to the growing importance of customer service as a competitive weapon. One is the continual development of customer expectations. Consumers are becoming increasingly demanding and sophisticated in their service requirements and expectations, and able to defend their bargaining stance/purchase position. Greater access to information, growth in self-assisted services, and the widespread change from a sellers' to a buyers' market, are just a few of the drivers of consumer empowerment. Similarly, in industrial purchasing situations, buyers are expecting higher levels of service from vendors, particularly as more manufacturers convert to JIT manufacturing systems.

The second factor is the inexorable transition towards 'commodity' markets, as the customer perceives little technical difference between competing offers. The power of the 'brand' is diminishing as the technologies of competing products converge, thus dulling or destroying product differentiation. Take, for example, the current state of the personal computer (PC) market. There are many competing models and these are substitutable as far as most would-be purchasers are concerned. Unless a buyer is particularly expert, it is difficult to use product features as the basis for choice. (This is also borne out by the fact that, as the mobile phone market has reached saturation point, industry competitors are turning to product 'fashionability' rather than product features to differentiate themselves.)

The third factor is the commercial realization that increases in customer satisfaction and retention levels can have a significant positive impact on corporate profitability and prosperity levels. It will be recalled from Chapter 14 that an improvement of five percentage points in customer retention can lead to profit improvements of between 25 per cent and 95 per cent in the net present value of the future flow of earnings. It will also be recalled that poor customer service can have a devastating effect on future opportunities in terms of negative publicity by word of mouth and unresolved problems through unregistered complaints.

Customer service is often seen as the focused handling of customer complaints, rather the holistic managing of customer relationships. Regrettably, such a perspective ignores the research finding that 98 per cent of dissatisfied customers never complain when they receive poor service and, more importantly, the accepted logic that reactive 'fire fighting' is much less productive than proactive 'fire prevention'. Experience has shown that companies that systematically attempt to improve customer satisfaction, through well-developed customer relationship management practices, reap the rewards of happy customers, employees and other stakeholders, and healthy profit margins.

This connection between good levels of customer service and good levels of customer satisfaction and retention underpins the common association of customer service with keeping, rather than winning, customers. Customer service therefore plays a pivotal role in relationship marketing. Getting this role right, and to a standard of expertise that is superior to that of competitors and sustainable in the longer term, requires an in-depth understanding of the nature and nuance of customer service.

What is customer service?

The output of an integrated distribution, or logistics, system is customer service. Customer service is a system organized to provide a continuing link between the first contact with the customer, through to the time that the order is received and the goods/services are delivered and used, with the objective of satisfying customer needs continuously. As customer service is increasingly a key determinant of competitive advantage, and it is likely that different customer segments will require different levels of customer service, managing customer service provision is a complex and critical activity.

It is also an expensive one. Operating service levels at 100 per cent can be crippling to the supplier, yet to drop below an acceptable level is to surrender one's market share to a competitor. Research has shown that once the service level (defined as the percentage of occasions the product is available to customers, when and where they want it) increases beyond the 70–80 per cent mark, the associated costs increase exponentially. In many cases, such high levels of customer service are not necessary.

The provision of high levels of customer service involves understanding what the customer buys and determining how additional value can be added to an offer to differentiate it from competing offers. Thus customer service can be seen as an activity that provides time-and-place utilities for the customer: in other words, there is no value in a product or service until it is in the hands of the customer or consumer. It follows, therefore, that making the product or service 'available' to the customer is a key ingredient in the provision of customer service.

Availability is, however, a complex concept, as it is affected by a range of factors that together constitute customer service. For example, availability may be influenced by delivery frequency and reliability, stock levels, and order cycle times. In fact, it could be said that customer service is determined ultimately by the interaction of all those factors that affect the process of making products and services available to the customer.

In practice, there are many definitions of customer service. One major study found the following range of descriptions of customer service among the industries surveyed:

▶ All activities required to accept, process, deliver and bill customer orders and to follow up on any activity that erred.
▶ Timeliness and reliability of getting materials to customers in accordance with the customer's expectations.
▶ A complex range of activities involving all areas of the business which combine to deliver and invoice the company's products in a

fashion that is perceived as satisfactory by the customer and which advances our company's objectives.

▶ Total order entry, all communications with customers, all shipping, all freight, all invoicing and total control of repair of products.

▶ Timely and accurate delivery of products ordered by customers with accurate follow-up and enquiry response, including timely delivery of invoice.

Clearly, while a variety of perspectives exist on the subject, what all definitions of customer service have in common is that they are concerned with relationships at the buyer/seller interface. Customer service may therefore be seen to be related to the building of relationships with customers and other markets or segments to ensure long-term relationships that are mutually trusting and profitable, and that reinforce the other elements of the marketing mix. It should be said that while some view customer service under *Place*, others advocate the extension of the four 'P's to seven 'P's, adding 'physical evidence', 'people' and 'processes', (Boom and Bitner, 1981) and regarding customer service as being synonymous with physical evidence.

The Elements of customer service

Given that customer service attends the buyer/seller interface, it can be examined under three headings:

▶ pre-transaction;
▶ transaction; and
▶ post-transaction.

The *pre-transaction* elements of customer service relate to corporate policies or programmes, involving written statements of service policy, and the planning of customer lifetime strategies and appropriate organizational structures and systems flexibility. *Transaction* elements comprise the customer service variables that are involved directly in performing the physical distribution function, such as product availability, order cycle times, order status information, and delivery reliability. *Post-transaction* elements work to support product usage and include product warranties, parts and repair services, and customer complaint procedure. It is at this post-transaction stage that cross-selling initiatives and managing the customer life-cycle become essential to the establishment of long-term customer relationships.

Figure 18.1 The elements of customer service

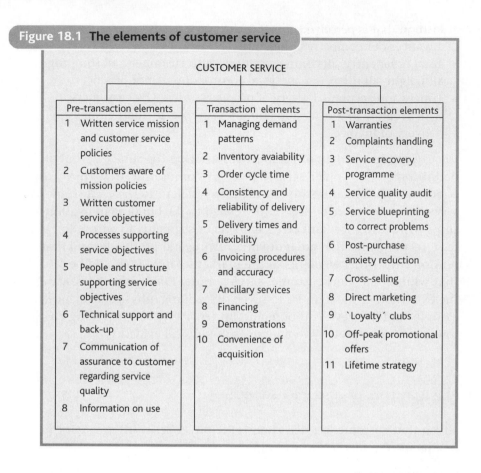

CUSTOMER SERVICE

Pre-transaction elements	Transaction elements	Post-transaction elements
1 Written service mission and customer service policies	1 Managing demand patterns	1 Warranties
	2 Inventory avaiability	2 Complaints handling
2 Customers aware of mission policies	3 Order cycle time	3 Service recovery programme
3 Written customer service objectives	4 Consistency and reliability of delivery	4 Service quality audit
4 Processes supporting service objectives	5 Delivery times and flexibility	5 Service blueprinting to correct problems
5 People and structure supporting service objectives	6 Invoicing procedures and accuracy	6 Post-purchase anxiety reduction
6 Technical support and back-up	7 Ancillary services	7 Cross-selling
7 Communication of assurance to customer regarding service quality	8 Financing	8 Direct marketing
	9 Demonstrations	9 `Loyalty` clubs
	10 Convenience of acquisition	10 Off-peak promotional offers
8 Information on use		11 Lifetime strategy

The key elements of customer service for each buying stage are outlined in Figure 18.1.

In any product/market situation, some of these elements will be more important than others, and there may be factors other than those listed that will feature significantly in particular markets. It is therefore imperative to understand customer service in terms of the differing requirements of different market segments, and to recognize that no universally appropriate list of customer service elements exists. A company may serve multiple markets, each with its own unique service requirements and priorities. A perfect example of this was illustrated in the case study of GlobalTech presented in Chapter 14 (see pp. 335–47).

The multivariate nature of customer service and market segments means that it is essential to have a clearly defined customer service strategy.

Developing a customer service strategy

There are four key steps to developing a customer service strategy, as outlined by Martin Christopher (1992).

1 *Identifying a service mission* – the company should articulate its service pledge and values within its corporate mission, and/or in a separate customer service mission statement. This declaration should focus on the unique and distinctive elements of the company's offer while reflecting the company's philosophy and commitment to customer service.

2 *Setting the customer service objectives* – the company's objectives, or goals, must be clearly defined and fully understood if effective strategies are to be developed. In terms of customer service, this involves answering questions such as:

▶ How important is customer service compared with the other marketing mix elements?
▶ With whom do we compete in the customer's mind?
▶ Which are the most important customer service elements – that contribute most to overall customer satisfaction and market share?
▶ What dimensions of service are seen as priorities by customers when they choose suppliers?
▶ How do we perform against the competition?

In considering levels of performance in setting these customer service objectives, service providers must consider the importance of service quality variables such as:

▶ Reliability – the ability to perform the promised service dependably, accurately and consistently over time;
▶ Responsiveness – prompt service and a willingness to help customers. Speed and flexibility are essential here;
▶ Assurance – knowledge and courtesy of staff and their ability to inspire trust and confidence;
▶ Empathy – caring, individualized attention to customers; and
▶ Tangibles – for example, physical facilities, equipment, and staff appearance.

3 *Customer service strategy* – most markets consist of market segments that seek different combinations of benefits. As all customers do not require the same level of service, segmentation can be a power- ful means of creating appropriate service packages for each relevant

435

market segment. Christopher's approach to developing a service-based strategy consists of four steps: identify the service segments and their specific requirements; identify the most important products and customers using Pareto analysis (see Chapter 3); prioritize the service targets; and develop the service package.

4 *Implementation programme* – once the most effective service package has been developed for each segment, the service package should then become part of an integrated marketing mix.

As with any other marketing strategy, for a customer service strategy to succeed, it must be well informed, well devised and well executed. What distinguishes customer service strategy from its marketing counterparts is the pervasive nature of its impact and importance. Customer service touches everyone and every aspect of an enterprise. Its influence extends from internal and external perceptions of the business to current and potential realities of commercial viability. Its role as the principal source of added value is confirmed by the growth of the 'service' sector in many Western economies. For example, over 50 per cent of the gross national product (GNP) of the UK is derived from the non-manufacturing sector and every year the percentage increases. Given the formidable responsibility attached to customer service, it is crucial that customer service strategy is based on meaningful market research, and suitable and sustainable service-level decisions.

Customer service research

There is a great premium to be placed on gaining an insight into the factors that influence buyer behaviour (see Chapters 1 and 2) and, in the context of customer service, which particular elements are seen by the customer to be the most important. The use of market research techniques in customer service has lagged behind their application in such areas as product testing and advertising research, yet the importance of researching the service needs of customers is just as great as, for example, the need to understand the market reaction to price. In fact, it is possible to apply standard, proven market research methods to gain considerable insight into the ways that customers will react to customer service.

The first step in research of this type is to identify the relative source of influence on the purchase decision. If we are selling components to a manufacturer, for example, who will make the decision on the source of supply? This is not always an easy question to answer as, in many cases, there will be several people involved. For example, the purchasing manager of the company to whom we are selling may only be acting as an agent for others within the firm. In other cases, the individual's influence will be much greater. Alternatively, if we are manufacturing products for sale through retail outlets, is the decision to stock made centrally by a retail chain or by individual store managers? The answers to these questions can often be supplied by the sales force (see Chapter 15).

With a clear indication of the source of decision-making power, the customer service researcher at least knows *who* to research. The question still remains, however: which elements of the vendor's total marketing offering have what effect on the purchase decision? Ideally, once the DMU in a specific market has been identified, an initial, small-scale research programme should be initiated, based on personal interviews with a representative sample of buyers. The purpose of these interviews is to elicit, *in the language of the customer*, first, the importance they attach to customer service vis-à-vis the other marketing mix elements such as price, product quality and promotion; and second, the specific importance they attach to the individual elements of customer service.

Assuming that through research we can identify the appropriate elements of the customer service mix for the specific market segments we are targeting, how do we decide on where to place this emphasis? Some kind of formalised logic needs to be adopted to guide the development and implementation of cost-effective service policies. This is the realm of the service-level decision.

The service-level decision

As stated at the beginning of the chapter, customer service is a system organized to provide a continuing link between the first contact with the customer, through to the time the order is received and the goods/services delivered and used, with the objective of satisfying customer needs continuously. Customer service thus encompasses every aspect of the relationship and is likely to involve the commitment of considerable resources.

In fact, as was explained in Chapter 17, once the level of service (defined here as the percentage of occasions the product is available to customers, when and where they want it) increases beyond the

70–80 per cent mark, the associated costs increase exponentially. Figure 17.4 on page 422 demonstrates the typical relationship between the level of availability and the cost of providing it. From the diagram it will be observed that the cost of increasing the service level by a small amount – say, from 95 per cent to 97.5 per cent – results in a sharp increase in inventory costs.

Significantly, many companies appear to be unaware of the level of customer service they are offering – that is, there is *no* customer service policy as such. Even where such a policy does exist, the levels are quite often set arbitrarily and are not the result of a careful market analysis. The question then arises: what level of availability *should* be offered? This question is relatively simple to answer in theory, but very difficult to quantify and achieve in practice, since different product groups in different market segments could well demand different levels of customer service.

In theory, at least, it is possible to say that service levels can continue to be improved so long as the marketing advantage that results continues to outrun the additional costs incurred. Conceptually, it is possible to draw an S-shaped curve, as shown in Figure 18.2, which suggests that, at very high levels of customer service, customers are unable to distinguish small changes in the service offered. When a company is operating in this region, it is quite possibly incurring more costs than are necessary for the level of sales being achieved. For example, marketing and sales managers who insist on offering maximum service to all customers, no matter what the profitability and location of those customers, are probably doing their company a disservice.

Figure 18.2 Customer response levels to increasing levels of availability

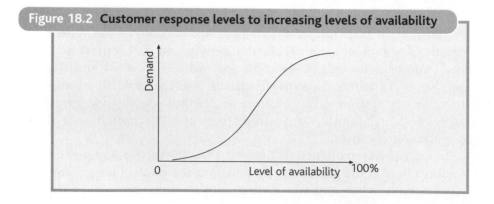

Cost–benefit analysis

By reviewing customer service policy carefully, and perhaps even introducing differential service levels for different products or different customers (at least on a trial basis), marketing can enhance its contribution to corporate profitability.

Somewhere between the costs and benefits involved in customer service, a balance has to be found. It will be at the point where the additional revenue returns for each increment of service are equal to the extra cost involved in providing that increment. To attempt to ascertain this point of balance, certain information is required. For example:

▶ How profitable is the product? What contribution to fixed costs and profits does this product make, and what is its sales turnover?
▶ What is the nature of the product? Is it a critical item as far as the customer is concerned, where stock-outs at the point of supply would result in a loss of sales? Does the product have characteristics that result in high stockholding costs?
▶ What is the nature of the market? Does the company operate in a sellers' or a buyers' market? How frequently is the product purchased? Are there ready substitutes? What are the stockholding practices of the purchasers? Which markets and customers are growing and which are declining?
▶ How profitable are the customers constituting each segment?
▶ What is the nature of the competition? How many companies are providing an alternative source of supply to customers? What sort of service levels do they offer?
▶ What is the nature of the channel of distribution though which the company sells? Does the company sell direct to the end-customer, or through intermediaries? To what extent does the company control the channel and the activities of its members, such as the stock levels and order policies?

This basic information is the raw material for the service level decision. To take an example, the level of service offered is less likely to have an effect on sales if, in fact, the company is the sole supplier of the product, and there are no substitutes. This is the case in some industrial markets, and from a short-term point of view to offer a higher level of service of, say, 90 per cent instead of 85 per cent, would probably have the effect of reducing the total profitability of the product.

The correlation between customer satisfaction, customer retention and customer profitability was discussed in Chapter 14. In financial terms, this link is explained by the fact that, as the relationship extends, the initial 'contact' costs, such as checking creditworthiness, no longer figure on the balance sheet. In addition, the more that is known about the customer as the relationship develops, the more offers can be tailored effectively to meet their needs. Thus the customer gets greater value, which in turn encourages more frequent and larger purchases. It follows, therefore, that when a company lowers its defection rate, average customer relationships last longer and profits climb. Viewed in this way, the costs of providing enhanced customer service could be seen as an investment in customer retention.

Customer service trade-offs

While, ideally, the customer would like to have the best of everything – for example, 100 per cent availability from stock, 24-hour delivery, reliable on-time deliveries and emergency ordering, it will probably not be cost-effective for the supplier to offer such a service. In the customer service decision, therefore, we are forced to make trade-offs. (The technique of trade-off analysis was introduced in Chapter 10.) At issue is which elements of service to trade off against each other? A simple analogy is the decision to buy a car. A customer might ideally like a car with the appearance of a Lamborghini and the performance of a Ferrari, but with the miles-per-gallon of a Fiat, the spaciousness of a Volvo estate and perhaps at the price of a Nissan! Clearly, not all these things are achievable in one car. The actual purchase decision can be viewed, therefore, as a reflection of the importance an individual attaches to each aspect of the purchase – that is, appearance, performance and price.

Thus, in the service-level decision, the marketer needs to research the service priorities of the company's target markets and to assemble a customer service package that is optimal for those markets and for the company.

Developing a customer service package

The key to developing a successful customer service 'package' (the customer's perception of logistics performance) is ensuring that it embraces product availability, with attractive order cycle times and mechanisms for minimizing customer inconvenience arising from order cycle times. This necessitates a dynamic knowledge of both customer needs and preferences, and the company's ability to satisfy them.

The starting point, then, is to establish those elements of the customer service mix that have the greatest impact on the buyer's perception of the supplier. This thinking needs to be carried right through into the design of the customer service package, because it will most probably contain more than one element. The following list contains the major elements of customer service that should be researched, (with reference to Figure 18.1, it will be noted that these elements span all three buying stages):

► frequency of delivery;
► time from order to delivery;
► reliability of delivery;
► emergency deliveries when required;
► stock availability and continuity of supply;
► orders filled completely;
► advice on non-availability;
► convenience of placing order;
► acknowledgement of order;
► accuracy of invoices;
► quality of sales representation;
► regular calls by sales representatives;
► manufacturer monitoring of retail stock levels;
► credit terms offered;
► customer query handling;
► quality of outer packaging;
► well-stacked pallets;
► easy-to-read use-by dates on outers;
► quality of inner package for in-store handling and display;
► consults on new product range regularly; and
► co-ordination between production, distribution and marketing.

This will almost certainly mean designing different customer packages for different market groups. At present, very few manufacturers/suppliers bother to do this. Basically, six steps are involved in this process:

1 Define the important service elements (and sub-elements).
2 Determine customers' viewpoints on these.
3 Design a competitive package (and several variations, if necessary).
4 Develop a promotional campaign to 'sell' the service package idea.

5 Pilot test a particular package and the promotional campaign being used.
6 Establish controls to monitor performance of the various service packages.

The design of the package will also need to take into account the differing needs of various market segments, so that the resources allocated to customer service can be used in the most cost-effective way. Too often, a uniform, blanket approach to service is adopted by companies, which does not distinguish between the real requirements of different customer types. This can lead to customers being offered too little customer service or too much.

The precise composition of the customer service package for any market segment should depend on the results of the market research described earlier. It will be determined by budgetary and cost constraints. If alternative packages can be identified that seem to be equally acceptable to the buyer, it makes sense to choose the least costly alternative. For example, it may be possible to identify a highly acceptable customer service package that enables the emphasis to be switched away from a high level of inventory availability towards improved customer communication. Once a cost-effective package has been identified in this way it should become a major part of the company's marketing mix – 'using service to sell' is the message here.

If the market segments we serve are sensitive to price, then the service package must be promoted actively. One way in which this can be achieved with great effect is by stressing the impact on the *customer's* costs of the improved service package, such as, for example, what improved reliability will do for their own stock planning; what shorter lead times will do for their inventory levels; and how improved ordering and invoicing systems will lead to fewer errors. All too often the customer will not appreciate the impact that improved service offered by the supplier can have on their own 'bottom line'.

Strategies for service

Beyond the simple presentation of a marketing message based around an improved customer service package lies the opportunity to develop tailor-made service offerings, particularly to key accounts, based on 'negotiated' service levels. The idea here is that no two customers are alike, whether in terms of their requirements or, specifically, in terms of their profitability to the supplier. One UK-based company in the consumer electronics field identified that while three of its major customers were roughly equivalent in terms of their annual sales value, there were considerable differences in the costs generated by each. For example, one customer required delivery to each of its 300-plus retail outlets, while the others took delivery at one central warehouse. Similarly, one company paid within 30 days of receiving the invoice, while the others took nearer to 40 days to pay. Again, one of the three was found to place twice as many 'emergency' orders as the others. Careful analysis of the true costs showed that the profitability of the three customers differed by more than 20 per cent. Yet each customer received the same levels of value-related discounts and customer service.

Conducting such a 'customer account profitability' analysis can provide the supplier not only with a basis on which to negotiate price, but also a basis for 'negotiating' service. While companies in the USA tend to be familiar with the importance of relating price discounts to customer-related costs, because of the Robinson–Patman legislation, it is rarely used elsewhere in a positive way. Thus, while the concept of paying more for an airmail letter than a surface mail letter is well established, it is less common to find a supplier offering different 'qualities' of service at different prices. Interestingly enough, business managers who accept the difference between First Class, Business Class and Tourist Class on the airline they fly with to see their customers, might never think of how that same principle could be applied to their own business!

Developing a customer service culture

In our eagerness to develop a customer service strategy it, would be a mistake to focus exclusively on the 'external' dimension of service; that is, customer perceptions. Of equal importance is the 'internal' dimension; that is, how do our people, our managers and work force, view service? What is their attitude to customers? Do they share the same concept and definition of service as our customers?

It would be a truism to suggest that ultimately a company's performance is limited more by the vision and the quality of its people than it is by market factors or competitive forces. However, it is perhaps only belatedly that we have come to recognize this.

Much has been written and spoken about 'corporate culture'. We have come to recognize that the shared values held throughout the organization can provide a powerful driving force and focus for all its actions. More often than not, though, we have to admit that most organizations lack a cohesive and communicated culture. Even if there is a defined philosophy of the business, it may be little understood. This lack of shared values can have an impact on the company in many ways, and particularly on its approach to customer service.

One viable way to assess the customer climate within the firm is to 'take its temperature' by means of an employee survey. One such method begins with identifying all personnel who have a direct or indirect impact on customer service. A useful device here is to consider all the points of customer contact, whether personal or impersonal, and to ensure that all the people involved in the different departments who influence the customers' perceptions have been identified. The focus of the survey should be on these key people's perceptions of service: what do they think is important to the customers? And how do they think the company performs, service-wise?

What quite often emerges from these internal surveys is that different employees hold quite different views as to what constitutes customer service. Similarly, they may often overrate the company's actual performance compared with the customer's own rating. Making such comparisons between customers' perceptions and employees' perceptions can provide a powerful means of identifying customer service problems and their sources.

This 'audit' of internal perceptions and attitudes towards service can form the basis of a programme of action aimed at developing a customer service culture. However, such a process, which almost inevitably will involve a major reorientation within the firm, cannot work without the total commitment of top management. The service culture must grow outwards from the boardroom, and the chief executive must be its greatest champion.

Within the customer service function, one very practical step is to set up the equivalent of a 'quality circle'. Such a scheme might involve looking at the total order-processing and invoicing cycle, and selecting individuals from all the sections involved. This group would meet at least once a week with the expressed objective of seeking improvements to customer service from whatever source. A further task that might usefully be given to this group is the handling of all customer complaints that relate to service.

Underpinning all these initiatives should be a company-wide education programme. Increasing numbers of organizations have come to recognize the key role that in-company education can have in developing a sense of shared values. Furthermore, because it is a basic tenet of psychology that attitude change must precede behavioural change, education can lead to a measurably improved performance. One of the best examples of this was the 1980s British Airways 'Putting People First' campaign, which resulted in a significant change in employee behaviour, and thus in the company's service performance in the market place. Alas, given the changed focus of senior management from the mid-1990s, this once great airline has seen a gradual decline in its perceived service levels, which are not entirely unrelated to a decline in staff morale.

Another technique used for measuring and improving service performance is competitive benchmarking. As discussed in Chapter 5, competitive benchmarking seeks to assess customers' perceptions of the company's performance against other suppliers from both within and outside the industry. Some financial services organizations, for example, benchmark themselves increasingly, not against other banks, but against companies such as Disney and Virgin who excel in customer service provision. These organizations believe that they can learn much more from comparing themselves with such companies, rather than from other companies in the financial services market. Figure 18.3 shows an example of competitive benchmarking for a manufacturing firm.

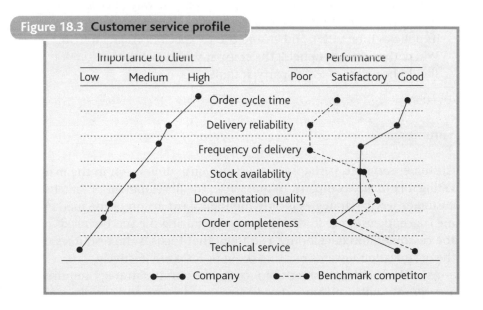

Figure 18.3 Customer service profile

It can be seen from the example that the elements of service that the client rates most highly are perceived to be delivered better, or better matched, by the company than by the competitor. The competitor's performance profile is poor in the areas that the customer values, and good in the areas that are not important to the customer. Companies that use competitive benchmarking find that it provides them with a clear guide for helping to develop business strategy, as it can often point to areas for improvement that have previously not been identified.

It is surprising, perhaps, that so few companies have defined policies on customer service – let alone an organization flexible enough to manage and control that service – when it is considered that customer service can be the most important component in the company's marketing mix. By way of addressing this weakness, it is suggested that three basic actions are required for the creation of a service culture and the management of customer service:

1 Define an overall company philosophy of customer service in terms of attitude, organization and responsibilities, and encourage everyone within the company to 'live and breathe' it.
2 Develop internal standards for customer service on careful studies that have explored the quantitative trade-offs between various levels of customer service and the costs of achieving such levels, so as to identify the most profitable policy for each customer segment.
3 Inform customers of what they might expect by way of customer service (perhaps in more general terms than the company defines its policies internally), and ensure these expectations are upheld. Where they are not upheld, the company, and not the customer, should be regarded as the party at fault.

Summary

Customer service is perhaps the most powerful dimension in the marketing mix of any company. In one sense, the development of targeted customer service strategies is only the logical extension of the marketing concept: customer service is about recognizing the specific needs of the customer and developing a strategy that focuses the resources of the organization towards meeting those needs cost-effectively.

As such, the development of a customer service strategy requires a corporate culture that extends beyond slogans and involves all levels of the organization in working together to ensure that, for customers, doing business with the company becomes a regular habit of choice.

To achieve the most effective deployment of corporate resources in developing a customer service policy, a number of prerequisites exist:

► the differing perceptions of the various parties to the purchasing decision in terms of customer service must be recognised;
► the trade-off potential between the various components of the customer service mix must be evaluated; and
► the unique customer service requirement of each product/channel/ market segment must be identified.

The choice of service level for a particular product should balance supplier costs and customer benefits, the point of balance being reached when the costs equal the extra revenue gained by the extra level of availability. Service level decisions will be tempered by other influential factors, such as:

► The contribution to fixed costs – for example, can it bear the cost of an upgraded service level?
► The nature of the market – for example, are there substitute products?
► The nature of the competition – for example, do they offer better service levels?
► The nature of the distribution channel – for example, does the company sell direct or through intermediaries?

The proven direct correlation between customer retention and profitability suggests that the costs of providing enhanced customer service could be seen as a justified investment in customer retention.

Further reading

Carson, D. (1999) Customer care and satisfaction, in M. Baker (ed.) *IEBM Encyclopaedia of Marketing*, International Thomson Press; London.

Stalk, G., Evans, P. and Shulman, L. (1992) Competing on capabilities: the new rules of corporate strategy. *Harvard Business Review*, **70**, pp. 57–70.

References

Berry, L. L. Parasuraman, A. and Zeithaml, V. A. (1988) The service quality puzzle. *Business Horizons*, **31(4)** (September/October), pp. 35–43.

Booms, B. H. and Bitner, M. J. (1981) Marketing strategies and organization structures for services firms, in J. Donnelly and W. R. George (eds), *Marketing of Services*, American Marketing Association, Chicago, pp. 47–51.

Christopher, M. G. (1992) *The Customer Service Planner*, Butterworth-Heinemann, Oxford.

Monitoring value

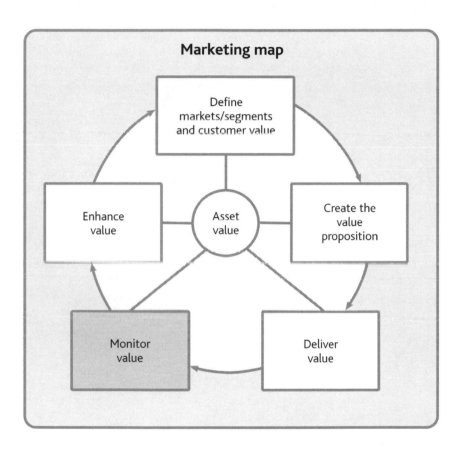

Marketing map

Define markets/segments and customer value

Create the value proposition

Asset value

Enhance value

Deliver value

Monitor value

19 Marketing information and control

In this chapter we study the:

► The main areas for monitoring value

► The marketing audit as a management information tool

► The importance of establishing a marketing information system

► The purpose of database marketing, data warehousing and data mining

► The 6'I's model of IT-enabled marketing

► The objectives of information management and control systems

► The marketing budget as a management control tool

The meaning of monitoring value

In the marketing map, the key marketing process of 'Monitor value' appropriately follows the output of 'Deliver value', or performance. The need to maintain regular surveillance over marketing performance is as important as that over any other aspect of business performance, and should not be underestimated. A laissez-faire attitude to management of customer value is not only dangerously irresponsible, it also ignores the central of pillar of the marketing concept: that marketing is a *matching process*. Achieving a match between the wants and needs of customers and the objectives and capabilities of the supplier cannot be left to chance if it is to be a commercially viable and sustainable aim. Instead, it must be a deliberate, concerted effort based on realism and commitment.

In Chapter 18 we emphasized the prominence of customer service as a competitive weapon, and the significance of developing a customer service culture to support its deployment. Clearly, neither the weapon nor the exercise of the weapon is of any use unless its construction and performance are relevant and reliable. (Obsolete armouries and considerable defence budgets attest to this fact!) Thus

451

the definition, creation and delivery of customer value through customer service and other sought-after benefits must reflect the profiles of both the customer and the supplier appropriately.

There are four main areas where monitoring can occur. These correspond to the main types of information dealt with in the strategic marketing planning processes of 'define value' and 'create value proposition', and derive from the implementation process of 'deliver value'. They may be summarized as:

1 *Value required* – (by customers at the latest indication) versus the expectations used in planning;
2 *Value delivered* – (to customers) versus the value proposition;
3 *Value received* – (by supplier) versus the corporate and marketing objectives; and
4 *Value perceived* – (by customers in terms of product/price/place/ promotion) versus the marketing plan.

Value required

First, the organization can monitor whether the value the customers require is consistent with the previous analysis of customer requirements carried out as part of 'Define markets/segments and Customer value'. The information for this may be obtained partly from the information gained in the 'Deliver value' process, or it may require special activity such as market research (see Chapter 4).

Value delivered

Second, the value delivered to customers can be monitored against the value proposition that was determined during the 'Create the value proposition' process. As all aspects of customer value delivery are measured by the customer's perception, this will again involve asking the customer by some means.

Value received

Third, the organization will also wish to monitor the value it receives against the marketing objectives established in the 'Create the value proposition' process. This is the area of regulation that most organizations are best at, through monthly analysis of sales by product, channel and so on (though analysis by segment or customer is often poorer than analysis by product, with customer profitability or lifetime value being generally difficult to obtain). But as the financial results are an indication of customer satisfaction, monitoring the value delivered to the customer is equally important and, for many organizations, one of the simplest ways of improving performance.

Value perceived

Finally, the overall effectiveness of the marketing strategies by which the value was delivered may be evaluated. The four 'P's of the marketing mix – product, price, place and promotion – provide the main criteria for gauging perception. The information on which such insight is acquired should be a synthesis of customer data, including customer purchase behaviour and customer feedback (both solicited and unsolicited), as well as trade press commentary and industry ratings in the case of industrial purchasing.

In practice, the predominant mechanism for monitoring these areas is the marketing audit. The marketing audit provides the basis on which performance can be appraised, so that the firm can seek further professionalization of its organization and operations in order to grow its competitive potential.

The marketing audit

Clearly, any marketing plan will only be as good as the information on which it is based, and the marketing audit is the means by which information for planning is organized. As stated in Chapter 6, a marketing audit is a systematic, critical and unbiased review and appraisal of all the external and internal factors that have affected an organization's commercial performance over a defined period. It answers the question: 'Where is the organization now?' By providing an understanding of how the organization relates to the environment in which it operates, the marketing audit enables management to select a position within that environment based on known factors.

The need to audit

Often the need for a marketing audit does not manifest itself until things start to go wrong for the organization, such as declining sales, falling margins, lost market share, under-utilized production capacity and so on.

However, without knowing the cause of these danger signs, management can easily treat the wrong symptoms and fail to address the root problems. For example, the introduction of new products, restructuring of the sales force, reduction of prices or cutting of costs are unlikely to be effective measures if more fundamental problems have not been identified. Of course, if the organization survived for long enough, it might eventually solve its problems though a process of elimination. Either way, the problems have first to be properly defined, and the marketing audit helps to define them by providing a structured approach to the collection and analysis of data and information on the complex business environment.

The form of the audit

Any organization carrying out an audit will be faced with two kinds of variable: those over which it has no direct control and those over which it has complete control. The former include economic and market factors, while the latter usually concern the organization's resources, or operational variables. This division suggests that the marketing audit should be structured in two parts:

▶ external audit – the uncontrollable variables (business and economic environment, the market and the competition); and
▶ internal audit – the controllable variables (organization's strengths and weaknesses, operations and resources *vis-à-vis* the environment and competitors).

The key areas that should be investigated under these two headings are outlined in Table 19.1.

Table 19.1 The marketing audit checklist

External audit (opportunities and threats)	Internal audit (strengths and weakness)
Business and economic environment	Marketing operational variables
economic	Own company
political/fiscal/legal	Sales (total, by geographical location,
social/cultural	industrial type, customer, by product)
technological	Market shares
intra-company	Profit margins/costs

Table 19.1 *continued*

The market	Marketing information/research
Total market, size, growth and trends	product management
(value/volume) Market characteristics,	price distribution
developments and trends	promotion
products	operations and resources
prices	
physical distribution	
channels	
customers/consumers	
communication	
industry practices	
Competition	
Major competitors	
Size	
Market share/coverage	
Market standing/reputation	
Production capabilities	
Distribution policies	
Marketing methods	
Extent of diversification	
Personal issues	
International links	
Profitability	
Key strengths and weaknesses	

Each of these headings should be examined with a view to isolating those factors that are considered critical to the organization's performance. It is important to omit at this stage any information that is unrelated to the organization's specific problems, so that the marketing plans that are eventually prepared are pertinent to the organization's future development. Inclusion of such things as brand-switching analyses or over-detailed sales-performance histories by company and product that lead to no logical actions whatever, only serve to cloud focus. The auditor's initial task, therefore, is to screen the enormous amount of information and data for validity and relevance, so that all extraneous information is removed. Some data and information will have to be reorganized into a more easily usable form, and judgement will have to be applied to decide what further data and information are necessary for a proper definition of the problem.

Thus there are basically two phases that comprise the auditing process:

1 Identification, measurement, collection and analysis of all the relevant facts and opinions that impinge on an organization's problems; and
2 The application of judgement to uncertain areas remaining after this analysis.

It will be recalled from Chapter 6 that the findings of the marketing audit then need to be formatted as a SWOT analysis in order to illuminate the business's key strengths, weaknesses, opportunities and threats. This 'information-turned-intelligence' will then provide the basis on which appropriate and realistic marketing objectives and strategies can be set.

Some of the principal points about the *marketing audit* are:

► A checklist of questions must be agreed and issued.
► Checklists need to be customized according to level in the organization to make them meaningful and relevant.
► It is essentially a database of all relevant company/market related issues.
► It should be continuous and dynamic.
► Do not hide behind vague terms, for example 'poor economic conditions'.
► Do incorporate product life cycles (PLCs) and portfolio matrices (see Chapter 7). Diagrams and corresponding words should match.
► It is a valuable 'transfer device' form incoming personnel.

'When' and 'who' considerations

As well as considering *what* the marketing audit should cover, *when* the audit should be undertaken and *who* should undertake it are also crucial to the effectiveness of the resulting marketing plan. Many people hold the mistaken belief that the marketing audit should be a last-ditch attempt to define an organization's marketing problems, or at best something done by an independent body from time to time to ensure that an organization is on the right track. However, since marketing is such a complex function, it seems illogical not to carry out a pretty thorough situation analysis at least once a year at the beginning of the planning cycle (see Figure 6.5). Many highly successful companies, in addition to using normal information and control procedures and marketing research throughout the year, also undertake an annual self-audit of everything that has had an important influence on marketing activities, as a discipline integrated into the management process. Such practice reinforces the role of the marketing audit as a planning as well as a monitoring tool.

This self-audit can be achieved, first, by institutionalizing procedures in as much detail as possible so that all managers involved in the audit, from the highest to the lowest levels, conform to a disciplined approach, and, second, by providing thorough training in the use of the procedures themselves.

A marketing information system

As mentioned in Chapter 5, a system to facilitate information flows needs to be developed so that there are appropriate inputs and correct data gets to the users in a sensible form. Sound marketing plans rely on sound marketing evidence, and this requires the organization of information into a coherent structure so that planners can match external facts about the market to internal facts and figures. In other words, good marketing centres on a marketing information, or intelligence, system (MIS).

Many companies have turned to technological innovation (for example, database technology) to extract vital information from often unwieldy and complex data. However, while computerized data collection and analysis can make marketing research easier by automating the reconciliation of internal and external audits, it can also conceal or divert attention from the reality of the situation. Companies are prone to collecting data that is readily available rather than that which is actually needed, and to accumulating data that they do not know how to use. There is also a common assumption that computerized analysis gives definitive results, where in fact, the data used for analysis may be incomplete, out of date, irrelevant, or flawed in some way. Thus the use of information, and the use of IT in managing information, must be guided by good judgement and a well-thought-through, systematic approach.

Information needs

Information is not the same as technology; nor is it information technology; and nor is it necessarily derived from information technology. There are many myths associated with the use of computers to hold marketing data, as Table 19.2 reveals.

As has already been established, information is not all hard, objective data; and companies will not necessarily become better informed by collecting more and more raw data, and storing it until it knows 'everything'. Accounting systems are often seen as a source of hard facts, since most accounting transactions have to be audited and therefore must be reasonably accurate. Yet most accounting data has little direct relevance to marketing strategy.

Table 19.2 Myths and realities about databases

Myth	Reality
The database collects what we need	We collect what is easily available
The database measures what matters	We measure what is least embarrassing
The database users understand what data they need	We know what we used last, what the textbooks say and what might be interesting on a rainy day
The database needs to hold more and more data	We feel safer with loadsadata, even when we haven't a clue how to use it
The database must integrate the data physically	We like neat solutions, whatever the cost
The database will save staff time	We need more and more staff to analyse data
The database will harmonize marketing, finance and sales	We all compete for scarce resources, and this involves fighting
The database is the one source of our market intelligence	We haven't thought through the business problems

Note: Thanks are due to Dr Robert Shaw for his contribution to this section.

Table 19.3 Examples of business objectives and segmentation methods

Business objective	Segmentation method	Information source
Market extension		
new locations	Geodemographics	Electoral roll (consumer)
new channels	Prospect profiles	Companies house (business)
new segments	Survey analysis	Prospect lists and surveys
Market development	Customer profiling	Sales ledger and added profile data
	Behavioural scoring	Models from internal data source
Product development	Factor analysis Surveys Qualitative methods Panels/discussion groups	

What information is needed to support marketing strategy? The answer to this question is something of a conundrum, since the information needs depend on the marketing objectives that form the strategy. Unlike accounting or manufacturing, which have fixed information needs, the information needs of marketing keep changing as a consequence of the evolution of the marketing strategy. Table 19.3 illustrates how different objectives require different supporting information.

Components of a marketing information system

For all the problems, there are, in practice, a limited number of basic underlying marketing issues with which all companies have to contend. Furthermore, the solutions usually adopted can be seen as variations on relatively few themes. The basic model of information flows to support a marketing system can be visualized as in Figure 19.1. The main components of an MIS are explained in Table 19.4.

The critical issue, then, when building such a system, is that it is not self-contained within marketing, but requires interface programmes that will alter the systems used by Finance, Sales and other internal departments, so that information can be produced that will be of direct relevance to Marketing department management. In addition, it will need to capture appropriate data-feeds from external sources to provide other supporting information.

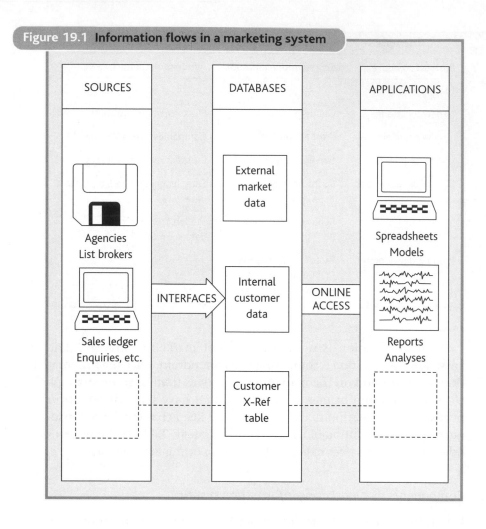

Figure 19.1 Information flows in a marketing system

The secrets of success in developing marketing information systems are:

▶ Understanding the information needs of marketing, and in particular how internal and external views of a market will be reconciled.
▶ Developing a strong cost – benefit case for the development of information systems, given that other systems, including financial ones, will have to be altered to accommodate the needs of marketing.
▶ Working continuously with internal IT staff until the system is built, while recognizing that they are/will be under pressure from other sources, especially Finance, and that unless marketing maintains momentum and direction, other priorities will inevitably win.

Table 19.4 The main components of a marketing information system

External market data: purchased from external agencies. These include governmental agencies, market research firms, list brokers and so on.

Internal customer data: collected from the sales ledger and other internal sources such as customer service, field sales, telesales, etc. It is coded and segmented in such a way that market-share figures can be created by comparison with external data.

Customer reference table: needed to make the system work effectively. It identifies customers (as defined by Marketing) and provides a cross-reference to sales ledger accounts. Whenever a new sales ledger account is created, the cross-reference table is used to determine the customer associated with that account. This avoids the need for costly manual matching or deduplication after the account is created. It is also used by marketing applications as a standard reference table for customers.

Databases: refer to all three of the above data types. They need to be structured using a technique known as *data modelling* which organizes the data into the component types that Marketing wants, and not the structure that Finance or anyone else provides. Usually, the data is held using *relational database* software, since this provides for maximum flexibility and choice of analysis tools.

Interfaces: refers to the computer programs that grab the data from the source systems and restructure it into the components to go on to the marketing database. These programs have to be written by the in-house IT staff, since they obtain and restructure data from the in-house sales ledger, and other in-house systems.

Applications: the software programs that the planners use to analyse the data and develop their plans. They include data-grabbing tools that grab the items of data from their storage locations; reporting tools that summarize the data according to categories that Marketing defines; spreadsheets that carry out calculations; and 'what-if' analyses on the reported summary data.

Source: Reproduced with the kind permission of Dr Robert Shaw of Shaw Consulting, London

Database marketing

Databases have traditionally been too large and expensive, and their performance to slow, for them to be cost-justifiable. Consequently, many of the marketing information systems in use at the time of writing are limited to summary sales-reporting systems. However, with the increased importance attached to direct marketing, telemarketing and sales performance management (using laptop computers), many companies are engaged actively in building customer databases. These

461

databases are then used to enhance the quality of the organization's relationship with its customers. ¡Good databases will enable: the personalization of communications; marketing managers to be alerted to needs automatically; and comprehensive customer records to be available 'at the touch of a button'. In addition, good databases can allow for micro segmentation based on criteria such as buying patterns, customer-initiated communications, fine-tuned demographics and other, normally difficult to discern characteristics.¡

One of the drawbacks to using databases is that they often represent a compromise between the strategic requirements of an organization's planners and the tactical requirements of other managers. Another problem for newcomers to the world of databases is that they sometimes fall prey to the pitfalls, and believe many of the myths, illustrated earlier in Table 19.2. The consequence of these problems is that databases often hold data that does not fit the purposes of the tacticians, far less the needs of strategic planners. The attempt to develop databases that serve both strategic and tactical purposes is often referred to as database marketing.

One of the most acute problems is that of reconciling the internal and external views of markets. The usual problem is that data retrieved from the sales ledger rarely possess the details needed to link customer records to market segments. Some of the problems are described in Table 19.5 against the key issues involved in identifying a market segment: what is bought, by whom, and for what reason?

Fusing together data from external sources and internal data, or 'data fusion', is becoming increasingly common as a solution to this internal – external problem. Where large volumes of data are involved, computer programmes, known as *deduplication routines*, are used to automate the matching of the data. However, automation rarely achieves more than 80 per cent accuracy in matching, and manual matching has to be applied to the remaining data.

The cost of matching external and internal market-coding schemes is driving some companies to collect customer profiles at source. This occurs either when they first enquire, or when their sales ledger records are first created. However, the cost of making changes to the sales ledger, and the fact that it is 'owned' by the Finance department, are often barriers to success. In the future, the Marketing department will need to work much more closely with Finance and IT departments if it is to develop databases successfully.

Table 19.5 Problems of reconciling internal and external market audits

External audit variable	Problem with internal audit
What is bought	Internal systems have rich detail on accounts and stock-keeping units. However, information about products such as colour, style, etc., can often be missing. Information on the outlets or channels through which they were sold is also very often lacking.
Who buys	Internal systems record who paid the invoice and who received delivery of the goods. They rarely record who made the buying decision or who influenced it. Even when buyer details are on the system, it is rarely easy to determine their characteristics such as age, sex, and so on.
Why	Internal sources of information on why people purchase is scarce. Enquiries can be qualified, using survey techniques, to provide some clues about why people respond to an advertising campaign. Customer satisfaction surveys may also yield clues. Call reports from field sales and telesales can also provide valuable clues, especially if survey disciplines can be observed by the sales staff.

Reconciling variables	Reconciling external with internal variables involves:
	    matching accounts to customers;
	    matching stock-keeping units to products;
	    matching external variables to internal records;
	    collecting data from sources other than the sales ledger
	    (e.g. from surveys of sales representatives).

Data warehousing

Data warehousing is way of combining and holding data from many corporate systems and external sources in a consolidated database, or data warehouse. The data can then be accessed by end users using online analytical processing (OLAP) tools. Thus a data warehouse is essentially an MIS that stores all external and internal information in a user-friendly, efficient and current format. Some key points about data warehouses are:

1. Data warehouses aim to integrate data from all operational systems, such as order processing and billing, into one database using a single data model. That is, there is a single consistent view of such things as customers and products. So, for example, a customer's name and address will only be stored once, and all the products

purchased by that customer can readily be ascertained. The data is refreshed regularly form the operational systems – typically overnight – to keep it up to date. So just as the operational systems at the customer interface are becoming better integrated, data warehousing represents the desire better to integrate information for purposes of management information and analysis.

2 Data warehouses typically hold historical information, not solely the current information needed for billing and so on. This has become possible because of the rapidly decreasing cost of computer power and data storage.

3 Similarly, increasing capacity allows the information to be held at a fine level of detail. Information can be stored about individual pur-chases, even for mass consumer markets, over substantial periods.

Taken together, these developments provide a rich store of informa-tion which, at least potentially, integrates the two key levels of data: customer/product level data; and aggregated data at the level of markets and product groups.

Data mining

Data mining is the process of discovering previously unknown infor-mation from the data held in data warehouses. Data mining software allows users to access the data warehouse to search for correlations between data that can be used in decision-making. Some of the analy-ses of particular relevance to marketing are:

1 *Segmentation*: subdividing markets using tools such as clustering analysis, a statistical technique which groups a large number of objects into few clusters with similar characteristics, where there are fewer differences within individual groups than among groups.

2 *Causal, econometric or predictive modelling*: predicting the effect on, say, future sales based on predictions of various 'independent variables' such as future price, advertising spend, competitors' prices and so on.

3 *Undirected searching for correlations*: asking the system to search for significant correlations between a large number of potentially connected variables, such as consumers' purchases of particular product lines. The revelation of patterns can be useful in strategy formation – for example, evident multi-purchase behaviour might suggest improvements in shelf management.

The 6 'I's model

Having reviewed the elements of a marketing information system and the range of IT systems used within marketing, both to support marketing operations and to provide information and analysis for planning purposes, one area in particular warrants further attention. This is the Internet.

The Internet is an important new way of interacting with customers, but it may not be considered in isolation. As discussed in Chapter 16, it forms just one of the channels by which the organization can conduct this interaction. In order to assess its potential contribution, we need a model for the role of IT in marketing more generally. Cranfield's 6'I's model, shown in Figure 19.2, summarizes the ways in which IT generally can add value to the customer and hence improve the organization's marketing effectiveness. Let us consider the Internet under these six headings.

Figure 19.2 The dimensions of IT-enabled marketing

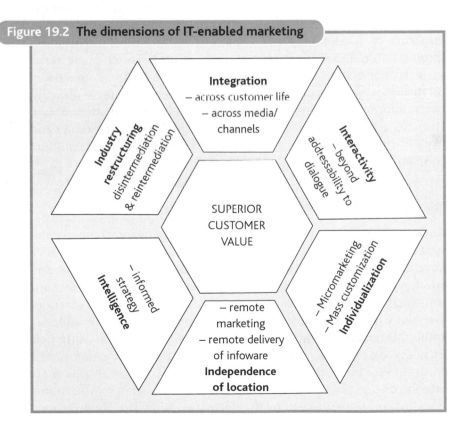

Integration – know your customer

For suppliers, building longer-term customer relationships means maintaining a dynamic knowledge of customers' requirements, preferences and expectations. While corner shop managers may be able to retain customer likes and dislikes in their heads, larger organizations need customer relationship management systems which manage data throughout the customer life-cycle, from initial contact, through information exchange and sales, to delivery and post-sales service. Enabling customers to reach the supplier through multiple channels means that this data must also be integrated across the various modes and mechanisms of communications in use. So, for example, a telephone salesperson knows about a service request that was sent the previous day by email, and a sales representative in the field can call on information about previous purchases and customer profitability to assist judgements about discount levels.

This interaction is as important with the Internet as with any other communication medium, a fact lost on companies who delegate the website to enthusiasts in an isolated corner of the organization, or outsource its development and operations with minimal provision for information transfer – hence repeating the mistakes often made in the early days of the call centre. As surveys continue to show, advertising products and services on the Internet is relatively easy; more difficult, but absolutely crucial, is to gather vital customer information, obtain customer feedback, utilize existing knowledge about the customer and exploit the Internet's interactive nature to add value though product configuration, online pricing, and so on.

Interactivity – beyond addressability to dialogue

Knowing customers means closing the loop between the messages sent to them and the messages they send back. Developments in IT have led to interactive communication tools such as the telephone and the Internet being used to complement less interactive mechanisms such as mail or media advertisements. Growing use of carefully targeted direct mail has characterized this as 'the age of addressability'. Interactive communication goes one step further – although in many cases the limited interactivity of the reply coupon will continue to be both sufficient and appropriate. Web channels offering online ordering, including searchable databases, order status tracking and hyperlinks to related websites, allow the organizations operating them to learn more about their customers as well as to leverage customer value.

Individualization – information-enabled tailoring

Gathering integrated information about a customer gives an organization the basis to individualize its products or services. The computer giant, Dell, provides a good example. The company's original strategy of selling personal computers 'off the page' in computer press, using mail and telephone to undercut its rivals, gave it the advantage of expanding easily to trading online. When the website was added as an alternative route to purchase, it was linked into the same databases so it could share the same information on products, customers and orders. Dell's website provides all the services that are available by telephone, plus value-added services such as online support, information on forthcoming releases, and user discussion forums. The fact that a high proportion of visitors to the site ultimately place their orders by other means, such as the telephone, highlights two important points: the impact of the Internet cannot be measured simply by measuring online sales; and, more generally, IT-enabled channels are often complementary.

Independence of location – the death of distance

Independence of location allows supplying organizations to achieve individualization economically. Niche products can serve their target markets even if those markets spread globally. The close connection between the distribution channel and the sales channel supports the argument that even physical products can, to an extent, become independent of location. For example, consider car dealerships or supermarkets. Exploiting the Internet's potential involves assessing whether the two are more effective together, separate, or in some new configuration.

Intelligence – informed strategy

Meaningful customer data can improve decisions on marketing strategy. For example, a UK bank is using intelligence from an integrated marketing database to inform its channel mix. Customer lifetime value informs decisions such as whether the bank should propose a face-to-face meeting with a financial adviser, and the bank uses geo-demographic data to profile customers of its Internet banking service in order to decide which of its other customers to contact about the service.

Industry restructuring – redrawing the market map

It is apparent that some industries are being restructured as organizations redefine themselves to take advantage of IT-enabled marketing, or are replaced by newcomers which operate according to the new rules imposed by such developments as 24/7 and mobile commerce. Use of the Internet threatens more traditional business practices by not only carrying out basic transactions, but also replacing human advice in product specification. For example, websites can be used to work out monthly mortgage payments, tax and so on: the user simply enters the required details into an online form which is then used to produce the calculation automatically. New electronic intermediaries will search for the best live quote from a range of life insurance companies.

To recap, the Internet can be used as part of a strategy for IT-enabled marketing:

▶ based on integration of customer data;
▶ providing interaction with the customer;
▶ allowing the product or surrounding services to be individualized;
▶ contributing to information needed for planning purposes; and
▶ reducing the constraints of location.

Decisions regarding whether and when it is appropriate to use the Internet should be guided by the nature of each customer segment, and in particular, the proportion of the target segment that has access to and usage of the Internet. The main question is, 'Do the features of the Internet match the needs of the interaction'?

Because all companies are in some ways unique, there are no easy, 'off-the-shelf' marketing information systems. However, there are few secrets of success in constructing a good one. These are:

▶ understanding what marketing needs, and in particular how internal and external views will be reconciled;
▶ developing a strong cost – benefit case for information systems, given that other systems, including financial ones, will have to be altered to accommodate the needs of marketing; and
▶ working continuously with internal IT staff until the system is built. They are under pressure from other sources, especially finance, and unless marketing maintains momentum and direction, other priorities will inevitably win.

Marketing should take place as close to the customer as possible. Marketing planners must therefore secure cross-functional understanding and co-operation if they are to develop the systems they require to ensure that the company's products meet present and future customer needs. They must build interdepartmental bridges to acquire data, information and knowledge on an ongoing basis. They must also ensure that such intelligence is meaningful and usable by management, for the chief purposes of measuring and improving performance, while upholding standards of quality, responsibility and accountability.

Information and control data objectives

Just as there is a hierarchy of corporate and marketing objectives, so there has to be a hierarchy of information and control data. For example, at the macro level in an organization, information will have to be generated to show overall sales volume, while at the micro level varying degrees of individual account detail will have to be generated according to the needs of the organization.

At the next level down, each department or function will need to generate its own specific control data, so that, for example, if an advertising objective is to achieve an attitude change over a given period, it will require an attitude survey in order to ascertain whether this particular objective has been achieved, and whether it possibly could, and should, be achieved better. Or, if the objective was to convey a particular piece of information to a specific target market, then again research would be necessary to establish whether this objective had been achieved and whether it could, in future, be maintained through a more cost-effective alternative strategy. The same principle would also apply to the sales function, which ideally will have a series of control data generated and distributed according to need, as well as establishing its own specialized control procedures when circumstances demand information that cannot be generated by the general company information and control system.

Any information system should be related closely to the company's organization and objectives so that relevant information for decision-making can be presented to each level of management. Thus the objective of a company's information and control system may include some of all of the following objectives:

- ▶ To provide a weekly guide to sales performance indicating any likely budget shortfalls.
- ▶ To review, each period, product/service performance in total and within each category of trade, providing comparison against the previous year, and against sales forecasts.
- ▶ To examine the contribution of each product/service to both sales and gross profit, and to assess the effect of the marketing mix on the overall profit percentage of each market.
- ▶ To provide for marketing management information that allows them to identify strengths and weaknesses by product/service, by market/segment and by geographical region.
- ▶ To provide sales-operating statements for senior management.
- ▶ To provide information by geographical unit for the use of sales and distribution management in restructuring territories and redefining distribution boundaries.
- ▶ To provide information by media and channel for the evaluation and improvement of communication and distribution strategies in respect of identified target markets.
- ▶ To enable sales management to review the trading situation of any customer in terms of profit and likely lifetime value.
- ▶ To encourage the development of profitable accounts not only through greater sales but also via increased delivery drop size and more relevant discounts and loyalty rewards.
- ▶ To enable sales management to monitor trading agreements and to extend, revise or revoke arrangements as necessary.
- ▶ To enable salespeople to schedule their work according to a predetermined, cost-efficient calling cycle.
- ▶ To ensure that, in the call, the salesperson is equipped with accurate and up-to-date information on the customer's order pattern, overall sales performance and sales mix, which will take account of expressed supply preferences and expectations.
- ▶ To analyse for sales management the productivity of salespeople in terms of calling rate and product placement.
- ▶ To identify, by type of outlet and product, the penetration achieved and the potential in existing accounts.

These, and many more, are the kinds of objectives that result in the detailed output a system will produce, such as brand performance. The important fact that emerges from any review of information and control procedures is that its purpose should be to provide management with the necessary information to enable it to monitor its progress towards its predetermined objectives, thus providing the necessary loop in the planning cycle.

None the less, the basic tool for controlling the marketing effort is the budget, which itself derives from the marketing plan.

The marketing budget

One of the most vexing questions for any marketing manager, or indeed, any marketing organization, is 'How much should we spend on marketing, and where?' The question is difficult because it requires an understanding of what should be included in a marketing budget, the way in which costs are generated, and the relationship between marketing expenditure and the results sought. Each of these areas is problematic and often requires sophisticated financial information and analytical tools for the development of effective programmes and budgets.

Budgeting practices

For many organizations, such information and tools are not readily available. In their absence, the most appealing approach is to use the previous year's figures as the base and to project forward. This, of course, takes into account inflation and prevailing market conditions, and adds on an amount that senior controllers will deduct at the budget review!

Zero-based budgeting
More preferable is an iterative zero-based approach which starts with marketing objectives and the programmes designed to achieve these objectives. Once activities have been identified, the incremental cost of these can be calculated and a budget established. If these are deemed to be too expensive, alternative activities or structures can be investigated. If these prove equally unacceptable, then a review of strategy is required, and so on. In this way, every item of expenditure can be tracked back to specific objectives, and indeed, the overall corporate objectives of the organization.

Variable cost budgeting
A less wide-ranging approach is to base the budget on variable costs, particularly for short-term budgeting, since certain costs, such as human resources and physical activities, can only be altered

significantly over the longer term. Periodically, however, this would require a zero-based approach to be used to review all products, markets and related activities. This would enable organizations to abandon obsolete and unnecessary features, and to make appropriate structural alterations. Many of the moves away from brand management towards category, or business process, management are a result of such reviews.

Life-cycle budgeting

Budgeting for marketing can also incorporate life-cycle costing. This involves assessments of the total costs involved in managing products over their life-time in the market (see Chapter 7). Such an approach requires marketing managers to plan ahead in terms of product upgrades, changing promotional activities, service and distribution support, and the way price is likely to alter over the life of a product. Long-term assessments of return on investment, payback and cash management can therefore be made, which will help both short-term budgeting control and organizational financial planning.

Operating and opportunity budgeting

A further approach to structuring a budget utilizes the notions of operating budgets versus opportunity budgets. Operating budgets cover those activities that are a continuation of existing programmes. The key issues here are in terms of efficiency and the maintenance of expected performance levels. This highlights the fact that marketing managers should be seeking constant cost-reduction and better ways of managing the marketing mix and obtaining marketing information, while at the same time countering adverse developments. An opportunities budget should be developed for unexpected circumstances that can yield financial and marketing benefits for the organization. One of the critical roles of marketing managers is to spot such opportunities and to feed them into the general management of their enterprises.

Human resources budgeting

Most budgets only provide for money, and specify where it should be spend. They do not contain the necessary provisions to make reasonably sure that the expected results can be obtained. They do not provide for the only resource that can produce results: accomplished people. This is particularly relevant to marketing managers, where skilled sales representatives, market researchers, advertising personnel and public relations executives are crucial to the survival of the company. Recruitment and training must be accounted for both in terms of time and money resources.

Sales budget

While the overall marketing commitment is the responsibility of any marketing manager, it may be that in smaller companies considerations such as product research and development, testing and extensive marketing research are not relevant in terms of a young or comparatively small operation. It may be that the sales budget will be central to the marketing manager's objectives.

Marketing costs

Since marketing management requires the development of an offer, which consists of various elements of the marketing mix, a marketing budget should, in theory, include all costs associated with operationalizing this mix. In practice, marketing managers do not, of course, have control over all these elements. In addition, the activities over which they do have control will vary from one organization to another.

For an organization that buys-in products that are then sold via a direct sales force, some form of catalogue or a direct mail activity, the marketing budget may be comprehensive and include selling costs; order processing; stockholding; merchandizing; packaging; and credit. For a manufacturing concern with complex logistics, selling via distributors or retailers and utilizing significant financial activities such as credit card or electronic data interchange (EDI) facilities, marketing may be more focused on the generation of demand and market forecasting.

The important point here is that marketing budgets need to be set in the context of organization-specific factors. This means distinguishing between controllable and uncontrollable costs, since combining the two inevitably invalidates the use of the budget as a planning and control mechanism. For example, in one European company, the largest component of the marketing budget was distributor commission; that is, the difference between sales value at list prices and revenues received from distributors. In fact, since commission rates were set by the Finance department and senior management, this was to a great extent an 'uncontrollable factor' for the Marketing department and Sales managers.

Another related problem is the danger of confusing overheads with direct or incremental costs. A product manager may plan sales promotions and construct a budget for them, but he or she is unlikely to be involved in determining the costs of administering the sales office and order processing system.

Even more difficult – yet essential if one is to improve the productivity of the sales effort – is to attempt to allocate costs right down to individual customer accounts in order to determine the true costs associated with dealing with specific outlets. Such an approach is based on the principle that the individual customer is the ultimate profit centre, and that costs incurred after production are related primarily to the customer and the unique factors associated with servicing the account, such as order size; sales discounts; returned goods; promotional items; and delivery costs.

Strictly speaking, a comprehensive marketing budget will include all direct and indirect costs of the marketing organization, such as:

- ▶ staff costs;
- ▶ office and equipment expenses;
- ▶ marketing mix costs:
  - product policy (for example, packaging, new product launches, modification launches, and so on);
  - pricing (for example, discounts given, price lists, commissions, and so on);
  - communications (advertising media and production costs, sales promotions, public relations, sales force and field costs, and so on); and
  - distribution (transport of finished goods, storage, warehousing, special deals with distributors, and so on).

The comprehensive budget implies a particular form of marketing organization and a particular type and degree of marketing management responsibility. Empirical studies have shown that it is all too easy to exaggerate the real responsibilities of the marketing manager. As marketing increasingly becomes a cross-functional activity, delineations of responsibility and the allocation of costs become even harder to define. At its simplest, for example, if the Marketing department has no responsibility for physical distribution, then physical distribution costs have no real place in the marketing budget. This highlights the question of what is, and what is not, a marketing cost.

It is important that each manager responsible for the marketing function should identify the costs and revenue for which he or she is accountable, considering the relevance of any fixed, variable, controllable and uncontrollable costs. It can be all too easy for the marketing function to find itself responsible for certain capital investment costs, depreciation of equipment costs, research and development expenditure, and public relations activity, when, in reality, the demarcation as to which item belongs to which department is a grey area because it has never been correctly allocated. Until this is clear, marketing objectives and strategies cannot be quantified in terms of expected results.

In an attempt to offer some guidance, distinguishing between order-filling and order-getting activities can help to identify marketing responsibilities and provide a basis for analysing the effectiveness of marketing activities. These may summarized as:

▶ order-filling activities – concentrated mainly on physical distribution costs such as transport, warehousing, order handling, credit and stocking; and
▶ order-getting activities – centred mainly on advertising, sales promotion and merchandizing.

Ultimately, however, the interweaving of a market orientation into all areas of operations, so that appropriate judgements can be made, will be most beneficial in directing and controlling marketing expenditure.

Summary

Marketing information is crucial to marketing planning and performance development. It can be seen to anchor marketing activities firmly in reality, while also giving marketing aims the wings to move beyond 'the acceptable' towards 'the exceptional'. The process of monitoring value, so that plans and performance can be evaluated and improved, focuses on four areas: value required; value delivered; value received; and value perceived. Each area can be examined using the distillation of key information and data provided by the marketing audit.

The marketing audit is a critical and unbiased appraisal of all the external and internal factors that have affected an organization's commercial performance over a defined period. As such, it offers a valuable management tool for the diagnosis and prognosis of problems facing the business to enable realistic solutions can be found. Dynamic information feeds and flows are best kept open via a marketing information system (MIS), which often benefits from exploiting the power of information technology. Any MIS should reflect the company's organization and objectives, and should not be self-contained within the Marketing department.

All budgets, no matter how they are constructed, enable managers to pull together their commitments, plans and projects, and all the costs involved, into one comprehensive document, thus providing a point of reference and control. A budget is a managerial tool, not just a financial device. While budgets are expressed mainly in monetary terms, these should be regarded as a kind of shorthand for the actual efforts needed. In other words, the marketing budget is an aid to thinking through the relationship between desired results and available means. The numbers can be worked out with comparative ease once the criteria for expected results has been explored fully and marketing management have a clear brief as to what they are accountable for, and what marketing objectives must be satisfied.

Further reading

McDonald, M. (1991) *The Marketing Audit*, Butterworth-Heinemann, Oxford.

Wilson, A. (1992) *Marketing Audit Checklists*, McGraw-Hill, London.

Wilson, A. (1999) The marketing audit, in M. Baker (ed.) *IEBM Encyclopaedia of Marketing*, Thomson International Press, London.

Reference

McDonald, M. and Wilson, H. (2002) *The New Marketing: Transforming the Corporate Future*, Butterworth-Heinemann, Oxford.

Evaluating marketing performance

Marketing measurement and accountability

A number of challenges facing management at the start of the twenty-first century have elevated the importance of issues related to marketing measurement and accountability. Business leaders are under intense pressure to deliver against stakeholder expectations; customers are demanding greater levels of customization, access, service and value; shareholders are expecting to see continuous growth in earnings per share and in the capital value of shares; and pressure groups are demanding exemplary corporate citizenship.

Meanwhile, the rules of competition have changed. The 'make and sell' model has been replaced by a new wave of entrepreneurial, technology-enabled competitors unfettered by the baggage of a legacy of bureaucracy, assets, cultures and behaviours. The processing of information about products has been separated from the products themselves, and customers can now search for and evaluate them independently of those who have a vested interest in selling to them. Customers have as much information about suppliers as they traditionally accumulated about them, which has created a new dimension of competition based on who acts in the customers' interests most effectively.

On top of all of these pressures, business metrics such as Share holder Value Added and Balanced Scorecards, together with pressure from institutional shareholders to report meaningful facts about corporate performance rather than the traditional, high-level financial reporting that appears every year in corporate accounts, are forcing business leaders to re-examine tired corporate behaviours such as cost-cutting, mergers and downsizing as routes to profitability.

Accounts are measured because it is a legal requirement. But the marketing budget is a discretionary spend and, historically, has never been measured according to any universally accepted and systematic rules. Consequently, the marketing budget is often the first to be cut the moment profits come under pressure. This unprofessional approach, however, is changing rapidly as senior management demands more accountability, hence measurability, from their marketing contingent.

Several principles should be followed when evaluating an organization's marketing performance and processes.

The need for objectivity

In marketing there are two basic kinds of data: hard data and judgemental data. Hard data measures outputs such as sales volume and value, market size, market share and profit margins. Judgemental data explains the reasons for the outputs. A SWOT analysis, for example, would normally seek to establish how well a particular organization meets the needs or requirements of a defined group of its customers (see Chapter 6). This presupposes that we in fact know what these needs are, and herein lies perhaps the biggest problem of marketing – how to be sure.

Hard data is relatively easy to gather from external databases, and most organizations have reasonably good measures of market size, and total sales by product or service type and by application. Those that do not can commission such data relatively easily and inexpensively from any good market research organization or consultancy. Figure 20.1 illustrates the types of data that all business leaders should ensure their organizations have.

But marketing departments should not rely on their own internal database for such information, as this will typically hold data only on current and possibly lapsed customers. The most important word

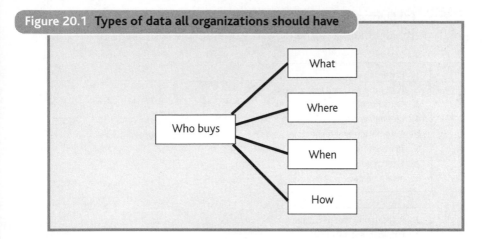

Figure 20.1 Types of data all organizations should have

missing from Figure 20.1 is 'why?'. Why do customers and consumers behave in the way they do? What motivates them to buy what they buy in the particular way they buy it?

Nearly every independent survey since the 1950s has indicated a substantial gap between the rational views of suppliers and the real reasons for their customers' behaviour. But organizations persist in relying on the views of their own managers – the sales force in particular. More recent evidence indicates that attitudes are not always linked to behaviour: many people approve of a product or an organization, but do not necessarily use it. For example, a recent survey of corporate good citizenship by the Consumers' Association in Britain showed that the three highest-rated companies were performing badly on profits, while the three lowest rated were exceptionally profitable. Another survey showed that Peugeot 106 drivers rated their cars far more highly than Ford Fiesta drivers, though the latter were far more likely to repeat purchase. So, organizations should be careful to ascertain how their marketers gather the motivational information they use, and how current it is.

The impact of the knowledge economy

In today's knowledge economy, the role of information processing (turning raw data and revolutionary insight into relevant knowledge) is increasingly critical to performance, and to the evaluation and improvement of performance. Knowledge is now popularly

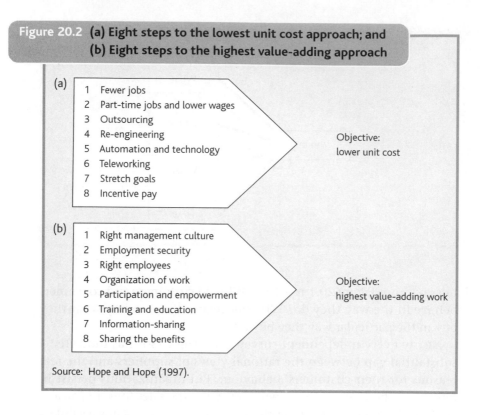

Figure 20.2 (a) Eight steps to the lowest unit cost approach; and (b) Eight steps to the highest value-adding approach

(a)
1 Fewer jobs
2 Part-time jobs and lower wages
3 Outsourcing
4 Re-engineering
5 Automation and technology
6 Teleworking
7 Stretch goals
8 Incentive pay

Objective:
lower unit cost

(b)
1 Right management culture
2 Employment security
3 Right employees
4 Organization of work
5 Participation and empowerment
6 Training and education
7 Information-sharing
8 Sharing the benefits

Objective:
highest value-adding work

Source: Hope and Hope (1997).

acknowledged as the *key* economic resource, and the extent to which organizations manage it effectively will determine their current and future success.

Being market-led is no longer enough; organizations need to be ideas-driven and market-informed. This has been an underlying theme throughout this book. As the workplace and market place have been transformed, so too has the character of business goals. Hope and Hope (1997) pin this change on an apparent shift in work objectives from 'lowest unit cost' to 'highest value-adding' work. The difference in approach is portrayed in Figure 20.2.

Productivity in the knowledge-orientated firm will be defined in terms of innovation, quality and relevance, or the generation of value through maximizing intellectual capital. Because investment in knowledge does not immediately or visibly translate into financial results, as do traditional, tangible outputs (return on investment or number of sales per employee, for instance), an organization needs new methods to measure and monitor performance. As Hope and Hope write, these measures will be less concerned with the volume of output (such as the number of orders processed) and more concerned with the value-adding content of work (whether orders are processed correctly the first time and without delay). The evaluation of performance therefore centres on customer service and satisfaction rather than on operational efficiency.

From 'cost' to 'value'

Case study 20.1 demonstrates how replacing a cost-based approach with a value-based approach to performance can promote business success.

Case study 20.1 Tesco's turnaround

In 1995, Tesco became the market leader in UK grocery retailing. Its arch-rival, Sainsbury's, had led the field since before supermarkets were introduced in the 1950s. Arguably, Sainsbury's was still the equal of Tesco in the four 'P's of Price, Product quality and range, Promotion, and Place. Yet consumers now considered Tesco's performance to be stronger, perceiving it to be the more progressive grocer of the two in its efforts to be genuinely innovative in meeting customer needs.

In the early 1990s, under the leadership of Sir Ian (now Lord) McLaurin, Tesco's senior management team began to concentrate on aspects of performance measurement beyond the four 'P's. Thus Tesco was the first to introduce value-added services, including loyalty cards, financial services, free Internet access and guaranteed shorter queues at the checkout. Until then, the corporate strategy had focused on margins, and management efforts were directed at extracting higher returns in a nation-wide cost-efficiency drive. Under the new value-based regime, the strategic goal was changed to 'delivering the best shopping trip to each and every customer'. In 1993, Tesco embarked on a series of initiatives designed to offer better value, improved stores and a higher level of customer service.

In order to manage the changes required to deliver better customer service throughout the shopping experience, Tesco broke down its customer service strategy into three areas:

1 *Culture*. This is the most difficult and intangible element of service delivery to manage effectively. With the launch of 'First class service' things began to change fast, as each of the 130 000

staff was given responsibility to look after customers in the way they thought best. Staff now perceive every customer as valuable, and understand that, over a lifetime, each individual has the potential to spend an average of £90 000 with the company.

2 *Standards*. By setting, measuring and managing service performance in store, such as the pledge to a 'One in front' policy at the checkout, the company was able to elevate service delivery from a level that individual store management deemed appropriate.

3 *Facilities*. Facilities were upgraded with the launch of the 'New look' initiative in 1993. The initiative was about introducing a series of tangible innovations, such as removing barriers at the entrance to the store and setting up more customer service desks, designed to improve the shopping experience.

The culture and climate created by these value-based initiatives was seen by the management as 'pure alchemy', which has allowed each individual store to develop stronger alliances with its own customers.

Tesco's success in satisfying customers has not gone unnoticed in other quarters. In 1997, the company's operating profits overtook Sainsbury's for the first time in its history, and the directors of Britain's 250 largest companies unanimously voted Tesco their 'Most admired company'.

As the Tesco experience illustrates, viewing business performance in terms of customer value can enable an organization to develop capabilities that will provide a basis for sustainable differentiation, and thus long-term competitive advantage. Empowering employees, elevating the customer service function and updating the work environment are just some of the actions that can have a resoundingly positive effect on internal morale and as well as an organization's asset value. (The topic of customer service culture is also developed in Chapters 18 and 21.)

This dramatic change in the way business performance is perceived, measured, analysed and interpreted (that is, less from the supplier's perspective and more from the customer's perspective), has given rise to a new form of performance evaluation known as 'marketing metrics'.

Marketing metrics

All organizations need to measure the effectiveness of their marketing efforts, and the means for doing so have evolved as the nature of marketing and technological capability have changed. In the 1980s, the rapid development of database technology followed the explosion in the desktop personal computers (PC) market. The 1990s saw the customer service movement, sales automation, brand valuation and the balanced scorecard. The twentieth century closed with the advent of 'marketing metrics', or agreed units of marketing measurement and their application. Marketing metrics were established partly because of a realization that marketing had never been truly accountable, and partly because technology now allowed senior managers to measure and evaluate customer relationships in a way that had not been possible previously.

The general rule of marketing metrics is: 'If you can't measure it, think carefully about whether you should do it.' Guidance is provided in the marketing metrics model shown in Figure 20.3.

Figure 20.3 Marketing metrics model

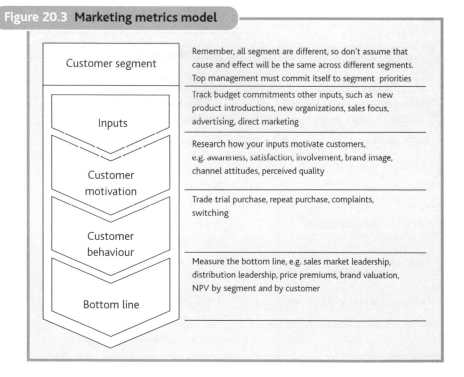

Customer segment	Remember, all segment are different, so don't assume that cause and effect will be the same across different segments. Top management must commit itself to segment priorities
Inputs	Track budget commitments other inputs, such as new product introductions, new organizations, sales focus, advertising, direct marketing
Customer motivation	Research how your inputs motivate customers, e.g. awareness, satisfaction, involvement, brand image, channel attitudes, perceived quality
Customer behaviour	Trade trial purchase, repeat purchase, complaints, switching
Bottom line	Measure the bottom line, e.g. sales market leadership, distribution leadership, price premiums, brand valuation, NPV by segment and by customer

In the case of strategic and tactical marketing plans, the major items listed in Table 20.1 need to be measured.

When selecting performance measures, it is important to check that they are:

▶ Aligned – do the measures reflect the corporate and marketing objectives and strategy, or are they disconnected?
▶ Actionable – are they directly actionable by someone?
▶ Predictive – can the measures provide early warning signals?
▶ Causal – do they indicate root causes, or are they merely symptoms?
▶ Necessary – will other measures suffice?
▶ Measurable – are they easy to measure and report?
▶ Meaningful – are they relevant, reliable and usable?
▶ Adjustable – are they flexible enough to be adapted to specific circumstances while still retaining integrity, or to be removed or replaced efficiently if deemed no longer appropriate?

The world's leading companies are committed to using marketing metrics. Those organizations that continue to ignore the legitimate demands of financial investors for better information about the return on marketing investments are doomed to failure. And those that do not respond to customers' calls for better information on product

Table 20.1 Major items to be measured in marketing plans

Marketing plans	Measurement
Market segment attractiveness	Track the important factors that make markets more, or less, attractive
SWOT analyses	Measure real strengths and weaknesses against properly researched customer attitudes and behaviour. Also measure key external indicators
Key issues to be addressed	Track whether key issues have been addressed
Assumptions	Record and track what actually happens
Strategic marketing objectives	Track key success indicators
Strategies, programmes and budgets	Track progress on strategies, programmes and their outcomes

availability, performance and manufacture (especially in the light of a growing universal conscience about environmental and social concerns), are destined never to achieve their full potential.

Summary

The pressure on businesses to reassess how marketing performance is measured, and how marketing is held accountable for its actions is mounting. At the same time, the demand for business leaders to reexamine embedded corporate behaviours and to contemplate change seriously is growing. Clearly, marketing performance evaluation is undergoing a transition.

The emergence of the knowledge economy has had a profound impact on the role of information, highlighting its importance in the evaluation and improvement of performance. This is evident in the trend towards a value-based rather than a cost-based approach to performance measurement.

Marketing metrics offer a viable means of self-assessment and comparative analysis. The selection of performance measures should be guided by specific attributes such as alignment to corporate and marketing objectives and strategies, and meaningfulness in terms of relevance, reliability and usability. As motivational data can be somewhat misleading, objectivity should be applied when measuring the effectiveness of marketing efforts.

Further reading

Ambler, T. (1999) The assessment of marketing performance, in M. Baker (ed.), *IEBM Encyclopaedia of Marketing*, International Thomson Press, London.

Ambler, T. and Kokkinaki, F. (1997) Measures of marketing success. *Journal of Marketing Management*, **13**, pp. 665–78.

Ward, K. (1999) Controlling marketing, in M. Baker (ed.), *The Marketing Book*, Butterworth-Heinemann, Oxford.

Reference

Hope, J. and Hope, T. (1997) *Competing in the Third Wave*, Harvard Business School Press, Boston, Mass.

Enhancing value

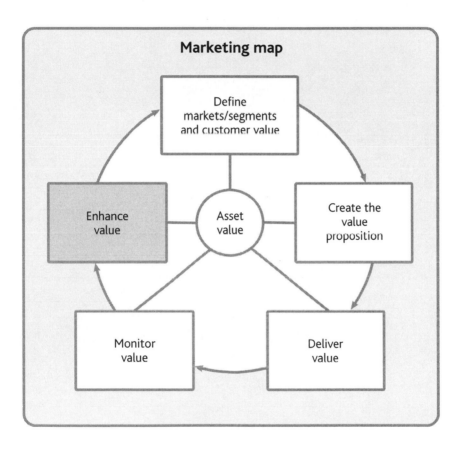

Organizational structure and culture

Growing professionalism to yield potential

The pursuit of superior professionalism in terms of building skills and competencies that distance competitors and drive innovation is shared by all organizations. However, the quest to 'professionalize' within the area of marketing does not take precedence on all business agendas, despite the fact marketing professionalism is the hallmark of commercial success. The reasons for this lie squarely with organization itself, and may be defined as the main organizational barriers to effective marketing planning. These are summarized as:

- ► *cognitive* – not knowing enough about marketing planning;
- ► *cultural* – the company culture is not orientated towards marketing planning;
- ► *political* – the culture 'carriers/leaders' feel threatened by marketing;
- ► *resources* – not enough resources are allocated to marketing;
- ► *structural* – lack of a plan and organization for planning; and
- ► lack of an effective MIS.

The difficulty in acknowledging and overcoming these barriers does not, however, mean that it cannot be done. Experience has shown that leadership and entrepreneurial skills, combined with well-honed marketing skills, is what characterizes the 'market leaders' from the 'wannabes' and 'has-beens'. Such professionalism, however, must be earned and embedded in organizational structure and culture.

Marketing professionalism requires the courage to question strategic priorities that do not appear to have been defined or refined adequately. It requires conventional wisdom to be challenged if it appears to be no longer relevant. It requires the discipline to follow the logical processes of strategic analysis and planning rather than jumping at the first good idea that comes along. But at its base, it also requires professional marketing skills and formal training in the underlying concepts, tools and techniques of marketing as a management discipline. The core professional curriculum comprises:

- ▶ market research;
- ▶ gap analysis;
- ▶ market segmentation/positioning;
- ▶ product life-cycle analysis;
- ▶ portfolio management;
- ▶ The marketing mix;
  - product management;
  - pricing;
  - place (channel management, customer service); and
  - promotion (selling, sales force management, advertising, sales promotion).

As has been emphasized throughout this book, marketing's role as a driver and deliverer of value emanates from the competitive stance adopted by the organization. If the organization is truly committed to acquiring and retaining mutually profitable long-term customer relationships, this will be reflected in all its activities, and not just those for which marketing is directly responsible. If the organization levies the bulk of expectation on the marketing function, in the absence of appropriate information and control systems, management practices and resource allocations, marketing will undoubtedly fail the test, and ultimately bring down the rest of organization with it. The point being reiterated here is that marketing forms an intrinsic part of organizational success. As such, it cannot be separated or isolated from other business activities, nor can it be seen to carry 'the hopes and dreams' of the organization without proper support and recognition.

This raises the fundamental issues of organizational structure and culture in the relentless pursuit of superior professionalism within marketing, and the organization as a whole. Thus a key step in the marketing process is 'Enhance value', where current levels of professionalism are strengthened and extended through assimilated learning to produce greater, *realizable* potential. This potential is then manifested in a myriad of ways throughout future iterations of the marketing process. Ideally, this process, which in this book has been depicted as a cycle, becomes an upward spiral, reaching ever-higher dimensions of value.

Organizational structure and marketing

Given all the principles of measurement outlined in the previous chapter, regarding the necessity and accuracy of monitoring value, it is none the less a fundamental truth that customers are indifferent to the ways in which suppliers are organized. The structure of suppliers' management and operations generally attracts little customer attention or interest; all customers want is the delivery of perfect products or services, on time, in full, whenever and wherever they want them, and preferably at the same price everywhere in the world where they operate.

Inconsequential though it may seem to the customer, the window of opportunity hinges firmly on matters of organizational structure. Chapter 17 endorsed the notion that, increasingly, it is supply chains, rather than the individual efforts of organizations, that compete in the market place. This transformation has profound implications for how companies organize to create and deliver customer value. Consider for a moment how difficult, if not impossible, it is to meet customers' expectations where the company organizes as follows:

1 Around 'production' units, such as factories. Each unit will endeavour to optimize its profitability, justifiably making its profit from production rather from action based on exploiting market forces.
2 Around 'functions'. With every function focused on achieving its own objectives, it is extremely difficult, if not impossible, for departments, individually or collectively, to take into account customer needs in any consistent or coherent way.
3 Around geographical groupings, such as the UK, France, Germany and so on. Here, country 'barons', each with their own profit and loss account, frequently relegate the needs of global customers and markets to their own narrow profit-maximizing motives.

There are, of course, many other possible combinations, none of which will be perfect.

Organization for effective marketing is a subject fraught with difficulty, largely because all companies and all markets are different. The complexities arising from the possible combinations of product, market, geography, function and size make it impossible to be prescriptive about the way a company should organize for marketing. None the less, there are some abiding general precepts that involve decisions at macro level about the centralization of management control, and at micro level about the structure of marketing activity.

Centralising and decentralising marketing activities

For organizations which have expanded so that they operate in several regions, the first choice is between centralizing or decentralizing their marketing activities. The point is that some method has to be found of planning and controlling the growth of the business in order to utilize effectively the evolving skills and emerging reputation of the firm, and so avoid an uncontrolled dissipation of energy and talent.

Centralized operations make co-ordination much easier and are better at avoiding duplication. From the depiction of centralized organization in Figure 21.1, it will be seen that there is no strategic level of management in the subsidiary units, particularly with respect to new product introductions. This kind of organizational form tends to lead to standardized strategies, especially with regard to product

Figure 21.1 A centralized company

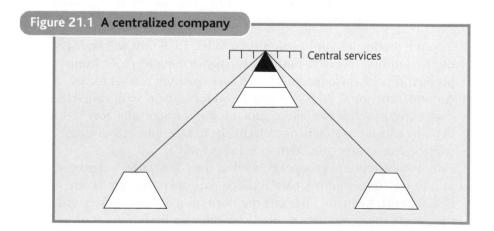

management. For example, when a new product is introduced, it is often designed at the outset with as many markets as possible in mind, while the benefits of market research in one area are passed on to other areas, and so on. The problem here, of course, is that unless great care is exercised, subsidiary units can easily become less sensitive to the needs of individual markets, and hence lose flexibility in reacting to competitive moves.

Decentralization allows for more flexibility and better exploitation of local opportunities. As Figure 21.2 shows, central services, such as market research and public relations, are repeated at subsidiary company level. It can also be seen that there is a strategic level of management at the subsidiary level, the acid test being whether subsidiary company/unit top management can introduce new products without reference to headquarters. The point about this kind of decentralized organizational structure is that it leads inevitably to duplication of effort and differentiation of strategies, with all the consequent problems, unless a major effort is made to get some synergy out of the various systems by means of a company-wide planning strategy.

In respect of achieving a flexible and enterprising organization, there are no 'right' or 'wrong' options. The choice will depend on the organization's product diversity, the need for local variations, and the management's ability to get a good balance between co-ordination and control. The latter is necessary to avoid fragmentation and to prevent managers feeling that they have no effective freedom of choice.

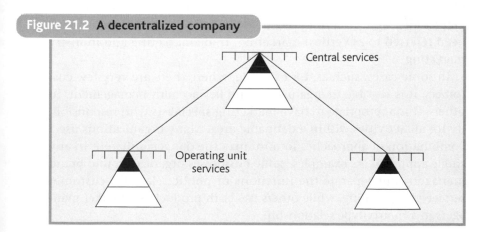

Figure 21.2 A decentralized company

Sadly, in many international organizations, it is not uncommon for local (that is, decentralized) marketing personnel to find themselves with no influence over product decisions, price or delivery, and they then become frustrated at having to manage a marketing mix over which they have little control.

An ideal arrangement, of course, is to organize around a combination of both in order to gain the benefits of each. This involves putting marketing as close to the customer as possible, while also having some kind of centralized marketing function. In this way, the potential for costly and unnecessary duplication is minimized, and the possibility of achieving economies of scale and effective knowledge transfer is optimized.

Structuring marketing department activities

For organizations with marketing departments, the second area of choice is the methodology for structuring the department's activities. The main decision is whether to organize around functions, products, markets, key accounts, geographical areas, channels, or some combination of two or more of these options. A functionally organized department would separate activities such as new product development; market research; customer service; advertising; market analysis; public relations; sales promotions and so on.

Alternatively, a marketing department could be organized around a series of product managers who would be responsible for the whole range of activities associated with their products or brands. This would include stimulating activity within the sales force and third-party resellers, as well as intra-company co-ordination. Organizing around markets would involve the creation of market managers, whether geographically, by sector, or by segment. Variations on this theme have been referred to as vertical marketing, trade marketing and industry marketing.

In some cases, such as, for example, where there are very few customers, it is sensible to organize around key account management. In others, it is appropriate to have marketing specialists with responsibility for all activities within a definable area. Many organizations use a combination of approaches to minimize the dangers inherent in any single approach. As examples, some businesses organize around brand managers, but separate the functions of public relations, customer service and planning, while others use both product and market managers in a matrix-type relationship.

Whatever organizational form is employed, it should be able to deal successfully with the spectrum of issues, including those surrounding marketing information, analysis and interpretation, and those regarding how best to organize for marketing planning and implementation. *How* the marketing process is managed must be congruent with the current level of organizational development. This is to say that marketing planning organization must reflect the organizational evolution of the company as it passes through characteristic life phases.

Organizational evolution

As depicted in Figure 21.3, organizational growth is propelled by reaction to crises. At start-up the firm is often organized around the owner, who tends to know more about customers and products than anyone else in the company (creative evolution). However, as the firm grows in size and complexity, and new products and markets are added, the organizational form breaks down and the owner must either sell up or allocate certain functional duties to specialized departments (directed evolution).

Eventually, these departments seek greater autonomy and a more delegative style of leadership prevails, which generates more autonomy at lower levels (delegated evolution). As growth continues, senior manage-

Figure 21.3 Organizational evolution

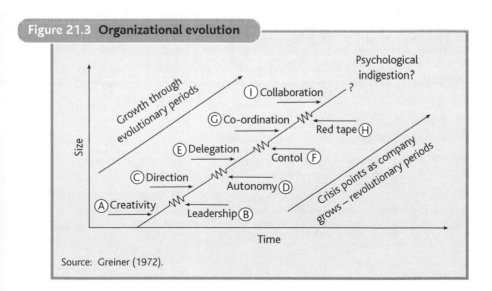

Source: Greiner (1972).

ment become concerned about the high levels of autonomy lower down in the organization and try to regain control by establishing better co-ordination between the various parts of the organization (co-ordinated evolution). Ultimately, these co-ordinated practices become institutionalized, and thus planning procedures become ritualized, and procedures seem to assume precedence over problem-solving. To redress the stifling effects of oppressive bureaucracy or 'red tape', the company strives towards a new phase of collaboration, with greater emphasis on teamwork, creativity and spontaneity (collaborative evolution).

Clearly, each solution to an organizational development problem gives rise to the next evolutionary phase. Since the key to successful marketing is to have a suitable organizational structure, understanding this pattern of structural change can indicate in a useful way appropriate organizational and planning frameworks. Figure 21.4 attempts to encapsulate the types of organizational structure as they relate to company size and complexity, and the associated

Figure 21.4 Types of organizational structure

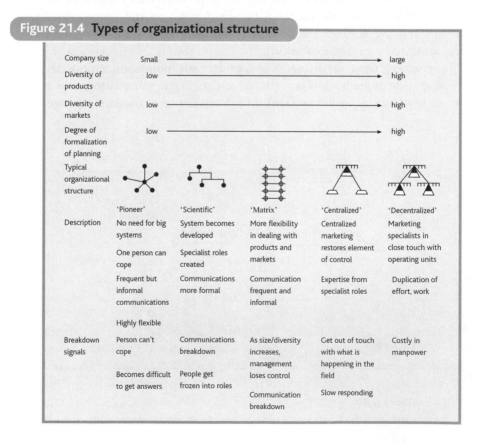

	'Pioneer'	'Scientific'	'Matrix'	'Centralized'	'Decentralized'
Company size	Small → large
Diversity of products	low → high
Diversity of markets	low → high
Degree of formalization of planning	low → high
Description	No need for big systems	System becomes developed	More flexibility in dealing with products and markets	Centralized marketing restores element of control	Marketing specialists in close touch with operating units
	One person can cope	Specialist roles created			
	Frequent but informal communications	Communications more formal	Communication frequent and informal	Expertise from specialist roles	Duplication of effort, work
	Highly flexible				
Breakdown signals	Person can't cope	Communications breakdown	As size/diversity increases, management loses control	Get out of touch with what is happening in the field	Costly in manpower
	Becomes difficult to get answers	People get frozen into roles		Slow responding	
			Communication breakdown		

degree of formality in the marketing planning process. (To evaluate the appropriateness of your own organizational structure, place an x on each of the four lines to indicate where your organization currently lies.)

Organizational traits and trends

No single organizational form can be recommended, as common sense and market needs are the final arbiters. However, the following factors always need to be considered:

▶ marketing 'centres of gravity';
▶ interface areas (for example, present/future; salespeople/drawing office and so on);
▶ authority, responsibility and accountability;
▶ ease of communication;
▶ co-ordination;
▶ flexibility; and
▶ human factors.

As these basic traits indicate, an organization's marketing planning effectiveness, (demonstrated through its performance and assessed through constant monitoring), is affected significantly by the way it organizes for marketing. The typical evolutionary pattern for an organization that has grown over time will lead it from being a 'one-man-band', where one person will perform all tasks, and where sales essentially involve order-taking with small amounts of prospecting or advertising, to the multi-functioning super-department incorporating a whole range of specialist activities, as illustrated in Figure 21.5. As an organization grows and becomes more sophisticated in its approach to marketing, it is faced with a number of options for structuring its range of marketing activities. Wherever practicable, it is sensible to organize around customer groups, or markets, rather than around products, functions or geography, so that personnel, accounting, production, distribution and sales policies are tailored to unique sets of market needs.

Increasingly, firms are organizing their operating units around customers or core processes, such as product development, order fulfilment and cost reduction. Quite a large 'industry', known as business process redesign (BPR), has grown up around this issue. Under BPR, each process is managed by a team that has responsibility for delivering efficiency in that area, and for meeting the objectives appropriate

Figure 21.5 Typical evolutionary pattern of marketing

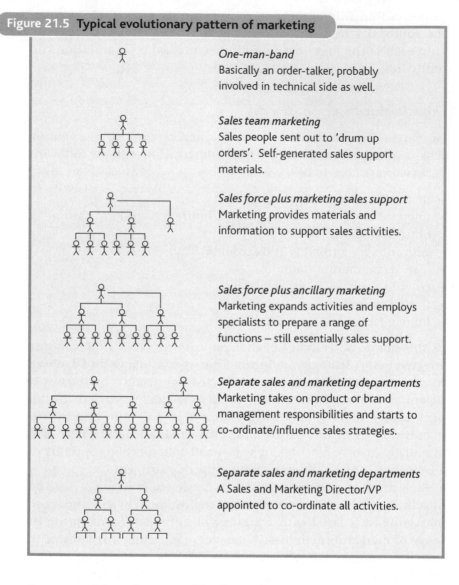

One-man-band
Basically an order-talker, probably involved in technical side as well.

Sales team marketing
Sales people sent out to 'drum up orders'. Self-generated sales support materials.

Sales force plus marketing sales support
Marketing provides materials and information to support sales activities.

Sales force plus ancillary marketing
Marketing expands activities and employs specialists to prepare a range of functions – still essentially sales support.

Separate sales and marketing departments
Marketing takes on product or brand management responsibilities and starts to co-ordinate/influence sales strategies.

Separate sales and marketing departments
A Sales and Marketing Director/VP appointed to co-ordinate all activities.

for competitive advantage. The key difference between conventional structures and a core process, team-based approach, is that the team becomes multifunctional with responsibility for, say, inbound logistics, production, sales and supply, rather than each activity stage being a distinct and separate operation. The Cranfield/Chartered Institute of Marketing research study into the future of marketing has demonstrated clearly that the world's front-running organizations now base their structures on customer groups and processes rather than on products. AT&T for example, organize around end-user markets, and appoint multi-disciplinary teams to focus attention on the specific needs of those markets.

It is also better to put sales and marketing under the supervision of one person, to ensure proper co-ordination of these distinct but inter-related functions, as shown in example (b) in Figure 21.6. Separation of sales and marketing at board level can cause a disparity between what marketing is planning and what sales is doing out in the field. Lack of a suitable organizational structure for an integrated marketing function, compounded by lack of meaningful information about market segments, means that marketing planning is unlikely to be successful.

Experience has shown that, above all, the very best marketing plans in terms of direction and performance emerge from an organization-ally *inclusive* process. Fundamentally, marketing planning is simply a process, with a set of underlying tools and techniques, for understand-ing markets and for quantifying the present and future value required by the different groups of customers within these markets – what mar-keters refer to as segments. It is a strictly specialist function – like accountancy or engineering – which is proscribed, researched, developed and examined by professional bodies such as the Chartered Institute of Marketing in Europe and Asia, and the American Marketing Association in the USA. Sometimes customer-facing activ-ities such as customer service, selling, product development and

Figure 21.6 **Organizing for marketing at board level**

public relations are controlled by the marketing function, but often they are not, even though many of them are included in the academic marketing curriculum.

In the model in Figure 21.7, representatives from appropriate functions are members of market planning teams, with the main body of work being done by the marketing representative, who has the professional skills to accomplish the more technical tasks of data and information gathering and market analysis. The team might also include a representative from product development, brand managers, key account managers and so on, depending on circumstances.

The advantages of this team-based approach to marketing planning are as follows:

1 Any plans emerging are based on a deep understanding of the organization's asset value (tangible and intangible assets) and capabilities.
2 Members of the team 'own' the plan, thus preventing implementation problems later on.
3 The marketing director, or whoever is responsible to the board for integrating and co-ordinating all the plans emanating from this process, can be sure that he or she is not foisting unwanted plans on to reluctant functional heads.
4 Any strategic functional plans, such as IT, logistics, purchasing, R&D and so on, will be genuinely market-driven or customer-needs-driven rather than production driven.
5 Any business or corporate plans that emerge at a higher level will also be market driven.

Figure 21.7 Organizing for marketing at operational level

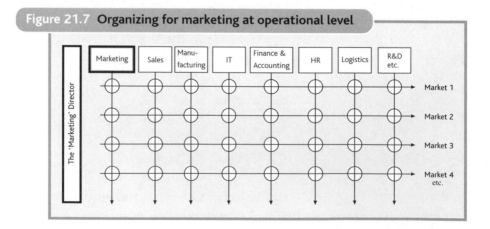

Organizational challenges for marketing

In addition to events such as the take-up of BPR, the position and struc-turing of marketing within organizations is being challenged and impacted by developments throughout the value chain. The first of these is the decline of traditional brand management as retailers become more powerful and, in some cases, substitute brands. Rather than a brand's franchise in the market influencing the choice of supplier, retailers are much more interested in costs, strategy alignment, and response to regional differences, as a basis for choosing suppliers (see Chapter 9).

The second development is the advancements being made in micro-marketing, which are encouraging marketing managers to look at differences between consumers in more elaborate ways, and to use sales promotion activities and database marketing for more accurate targeting (see Chapters 3, 11 and 19, respectively).

The third is the reduction in the effectiveness of mass advertising as media channels proliferate, and as it becomes harder to reach mass markets. These trends will support moves away from national and international brand management as a basis for organizing marketing, towards market-focused management structures, either as part of a process team, or as a framework based on relationships.

Fourth, the current popularity of category management as a basis for organizing consumer goods marketing is also affecting how suppliers organize their marketing activities. To match their retail customers, suppliers are organizing brand portfolios and appointing category managers, or 'champions', whose focus is on maximizing profit from a category for the retailer rather than developing brand franchises.

In the end, however, it must be remembered that structure is of only secondary importance in establishing marketing as an effective force within an organization. Of greater significance is the attitude of the managers working within the structures, and the ways in which they are able to influence other managers towards a market-orientated approach to their own responsibilities. If a market orientation is well embedded and stretches across its range of activities, it is almost possi-ble to argue that structure is irrelevant to marketing effectiveness.

Organizational culture and marketing

While the marketing process in terms of the five key subprocesses remains more or less consistent throughout, how that process is managed must be congruent with the current organizational culture. The alternative to this would be take steps to change the company culture and make it more amenable to a particular planning process.

Since culture tends to act to maintain the existing power structure and hence the status quo, marketing planning and implementation interventions in companies must be recognized as having a 'political' dimension; that is to say, the motivations behind them are not purely educational or commercial. Not least among the political issues is the question of whether or not a company's management style can adapt sufficiently to enable the marketing process to deliver the rewards it promises. For example, can managers who have led a company down a particular path suddenly change track? The iconoclastic books would claim that they can, because this is a much more optimistic message with which to sell copies. However, those who have carried out academic research, or are experienced consultants, would have some reservations.

We remain open-minded about this issue, believing that, if the business pressures on a company are sufficient, intelligent behaviour will win the day. We might be proved wrong, but in the meantime we reiterate the following messages as useful pointers for both marketing advisers and senior executives of companies.

Marketing's role in bringing the organization closer to customers, and thus in growing long-term and profitable customer relationships, is crucial to the success of the organization. This role is best fulfilled where marketing is treated as an integrated philosophy, discipline and function within the enterprise. It can, and should, both drive and support all other organizational activities in helping to achieve the overall corporate objectives. Thus, creating and maintaining a culture and climate within the organization that is conducive to value-based initiatives is the responsibility of marketing as much as, if not more than, any other aspect of the business.

In seeking to achieve the right organizational culture, the following five criteria are suggested as essential features of a good marketing organization. Its culture must be innovative; engaging; inclusive; rewarding; and empowering.

Innovative

As discussed in Chapter 8, resistance to change and discouragement of creativity are the foremost obstacles that face organizations seeking growth and prosperity. They can derive from a number of factors:

- the desire to maximise returns from existing capacity products and services;
- the desire to defend current patterns of behaviour, systems and procedures;
- the desire to minimize losses on existing plant and equipment (and people) through enforced obsolescence;
- the desire to protect status derived from past experience;
- the desire to avoid risk consequences; and
- fear of the unknown.

While sources of improvement and innovation (here defined as providing new solutions that offer value to customers) can be found almost anywhere in the organization, real change tends to come from the top. The visible enthusiasm and commitment of the chief executive and senior management towards exploring and implementing new ideas, be they situated in product, policy, management or operational development, is what promotes commercial vibrancy and adds customer value. Without such stewardship and affirmation, employees and other stakeholders are unlikely to mirror the direction and investment in innovation shown by their 'leaders'. In this way, the company can overcome fears and potential stagnation, and capitalize on its strengths by being able to respond to new situations. It is a flexible approach such as is that is the hidden strength of the small company. For example, the organizational culture in some enterprises acts as a damper and stifles initiatives which could be the future life-blood of the business (see Figure 21.8).

Many organizations have turned to merger and acquisition in pursuit of growth and shareholder value. While this strategy may provide short-term performance improvements, it is unlikely to generate long-term shareholder value. The reason is that sustainable growth generated by continuous innovation is based on the capabilities and attitudes of the people within the company, and depends on a culture that encourages entrepreneurship and processes that enable individual and team-based creativity to surface and flourish. At 3M, which invests over 7 per cent of its turnover in research and development, the link between its astonishing growth in sales and shareholder value is very clearly based on a vision that identifies innovation as a core company process.

Figure 21.8 Cultural blockages to new product initiatives

Engaging

Every company should endeavour to be attractive and enticing at every customer touch point – not just to customers, but also to its current and future workforce and wider supply chain network. Happy employees and other company representatives tend to indicate that the organization's

policies on employee recruitment and selection, employment, and retention, in addition to those surrounding business operations, are sound
and acceptable. In other words, a corporate culture that demonstrates
integrity and is consistently engaging in its various expressions, will
generally reveal an employer whose 'true colours' include openness,
fairness, equality, diversity, and a work opportunity well worth taking.

Inclusive

Creating an organizational culture which ensures that thoroughness
and innovation go into developing the value proposition and communicating it throughout the organization, is not easy, but once the
culture is right it is very difficult to for competitors to replicate it, and
as such it becomes a source of sustainable competitive advantage.
Cross-functional co-operation and company-wide involvement in
steering the business towards appropriate goals can be obtained
through well-considered and established procedures.

Chapter 4 referred to the enormous potential in terms of information and insight contained within the organization itself, in its people,
information systems and operational approaches, that could be har-
nessed usefully in business development activities. Chapter 12 outlined
some of the areas for developing the role of key account managers and
their range of competencies, while Chapter 15 touched on the various
business 'hats' worn by salespeople. These discussions highlight the
wealth of internal potential that can be exploited through employee
development and internally inclusive business practices.

Rewarding

Issues of remuneration and motivation in respect to managing the sales
force were covered in Chapter 15. However, creating an organizational
culture that rewards its members justly for their contributions to the
business can be seen to encompass all stakeholders, including employees, distributors, shareholders, and even customers. Indeed, corporate
culture is reflected in company partnership programmes as well as customer loyalty and affinity schemes. For example, in some strategic
alliances, working partners are offered special access to company information in return for their willingness to share ideas. Companies which
value customer feedback often stimulate customer comment by inserting
questionnaires in regular communications or as part of online-ordering
processes, or by offering prizes for the best responses to statements such

as: 'I like this product because. . .' in competitions. While promotional inducements seek to attract new business, information-gathering incentives support value-building activities.

Empowering

A challenging and exciting corporate climate is produced by the culmination of the above characteristics, together with a heavy dose of empowerment and entrepreneurial spirit. The need for balance between control and creativity was mentioned earlier in the chapter. Organizations that can reach and maintain a productive equilibrium will benefit from the strength provided by disciplined practices and the energy derived from positive reinforcement of individual and collective creativity.

Employees need the knowledge and 'breathing space' that allow them to understand and contribute to organizational performance, as well as the power to take decisions that influence organizational direction and performance. Au Bon Pain, a chain of bakery cafés on the east coast of the USA, illustrates empowerment in practice; see Case study 21.1.

Case study 21.1 How Au Bon Pain empowers employees

Au Bon Pain has focused on empowerment as a means of growing employee value in its bakery café chain. Managers were empowered to make significant alterations to processes, procedures, store layout and other policies, in order to develop service quality and marketing activities designed to build stronger relationships with frequent customers.

These changes led to significant performance improvements. Staff turnover in one of the Boston stores has dropped to 10 per cent per annum for entry-level jobs compared with an industry norm of about 200 per cent. Absenteeism has plummeted, and sales have soared as customers develop a relationship with counter staff. Productivity has increased greatly, and employee headcount has been considerably reduced. Under the Partner-Manager Programme at Au Bon, employees can earn double the industry average wages, and the manager of an outlet can earn up to U.S. $160 000 a year. The type and quality of employee has changed radically, and word of mouth creates strong demand for jobs at all levels in the chain.

As mentioned in Chapter 13, the fundamental aims of internal marketing are to develop awareness among employees of both internal and external customers, and to remove functional barriers to organizational effectiveness. By regarding every employee and every department as internal customer and/or an internal supplier, it is possible to ensure that every individual and department provides and receives high standards of internal service. It also promotes internal buy-in to the organization's mission, strategy and goals, which produces a more collaborative and cohesive working environment.

Summary

An organization's ability to strengthen the level and scope of its professionalism lies clearly with its skill and dedication to assimilating learning. Organizations that are unwilling or unable to recognize the lessons inherent in their own experience or that of others will never be the leading-edge companies of tomorrow. In contrast, those that have responded appropriately to the need for organizational revision as result of more integrated and interactive processes have secured, or are the way to securing, enhanced value through organizational capability and operational capacity.

The essential feature of marketing organization and control is that it 'closes the loop' and connects marketing plans to marketing actions. Ultimately, therefore, the way we manage marketing is the major determinant of commercial success or failure.

The structure of the organization can impede the enhancement of value seriously, and therefore also the development of customer relationships. For example, traditional vertical organizations with a hierarchical structure and functional orientation often favour individual functions at the expense of the whole business and the customer. Cross-functional marketing, as advocated by a relationship marketing approach, focuses instead on the processes that create and deliver customer value, drawing together multi-disciplinary teams which marshal resources to achieve customer-based objectives. An organizational culture imbued with collaborative and empowering practices and a marketing orientation will promote the kind of innovation and inspiration required for such relationship-building.

The ongoing search to find the 'right' structure stems from the ever-changing nature of the business environment. Demand patterns alter, new technology emerges, new legislation is introduced, there is an economic crisis, and so on. However, experimentation with the different types of structure has shown that, in certain circumstances, some types are going to be more successful than others. For example, the joint, rather than separate, supervision of sales and marketing tends to make it easier to ensure a sensible co-ordination between planning and doing. However, what is most crucial to any organizational structure or culture is leadership – founded in and fighting for the creation and delivery of superior customer value.

Further reading

Achrol, R. (1991) Evolution of the marketing organisation: new forms for turbulent environments. *Journal of Marketing*, **55(4)** pp. 77–94.

Piercy, N. (1999) Marketing implementation, organisational change and internal marketing strategy; in M. Baker (ed.), *The Marketing Book*, Butterworth-Heinemann, Oxford.

Webster, F. (1997) The future role of markets in the organization, in D. Lehmann and K. Jocz (eds), *Reflection on the Futures of Marketing*, Marketing Science Institute, Cambridge, Mass. pp. 39–66.

References

Greiner, L. E. (1972) Evolution and revolution as organizations grow. *Harvard Business Review* (July/August).

McDonald, M., Christopher, M., Payne, A. and Knox, S. (2001) *Creating a Company for Customers*, Financial Times/Prentice-Hall, London.

22 Corporate ethos and ethics

Marketing in the postmodern era

A book entitled *Marketing: A Complete Guide*, would not be complete without a section on the ethos and ethics of marketing. In today's tumultuous times, the way in which businesses conduct themselves with respect to accepted conventions on issues such as human rights and social responsibility, environmental and ecological stewardship, and global capitalism has a resounding effect on their presence, and indeed, future in the market place. So, what *is* happening, and what *should* happen in marketing's sphere of influence?

As the debate continues, let us consider a few points in respect to marketing's role from an ethical perspective. The old model of marketing *is* changing and *is* responding, albeit imperfectly, to the challenges posed by the postmodern consumer. No one could argue with the notion that society changes over time, and that commerce is affected by (and, of course, affects) such changes. But those who remain in an outdated paradigm gradually disappear. Responsive organizations adapt to the subtle changes taking place about them, and this is reflected in best practice. This best practice is manifested in evolving managerial systems and these state-of-the-art developments are indeed reflected in the research agendas and curricula of the world's top business schools.

Another fundamental point is that best practice is no longer about doing things *to* consumers. The interactionist school has grown in strength on the observation that successful and profitable relationships today have to be dyadic. Best practice today already separates the processing of information about products from the products themselves, by helping customers to search for, find and evaluate products independently of those who sell them, and by providing consumers with as much information about themselves as they traditionally had about them.

Another point concerns consumer behaviour models. Figure 22.1 (already seen as Figure 11.7 on page 259) compares the traditional (old, out-of-date) model of consumer and industrial buying and supplier behaviour with the interactionist reality of modern best

Figure 22.1 A comparison of traditional and modern models of consumer behaviour

Supplier perspective		Interaction perspective		Buyer perspective	
Advertising	Selling	Marketing activity	Interaction	Decision theory	Consumer behaviour
		Define markets/ understand value Create value proposition	Recognize exchange potential	Problem recognition	Category need
Brand awareness					Awareness
	Prospecting	Initiate dialogue			
Brand attitude				Information search	Attitude
Info re: benefits Brand image Feelings Peer influence	Provide information	Exchange information			
	Persuade	Negotiate/tailor		Evaluation of alternatives	Information gathering and judgement
Trial inducement	Close sale	Commit		Choices/ purchase	Purchase process
Reduce cognitive dissonance	Deliver	Exchange value			
	Service		Monitor	Post-purchase behaviour	Post-purchase experience

practice. The interactionist perspective, in the middle of the table, is based on observations of leading-edge companies.

Through educational resources and marketing guides such as this, some authors are trying to help organizations to relate to the postmodern consumer. Of course, it is impossibly difficult to understand a consumer who goes into a retail store on a Saturday, buys on the internet at home on Sunday, uses a WAP phone on Monday, uses a Palm Pilot on Tuesday (possibly from more than one country!), uses interactive TV on Wednesday, uses interactive broadband PC on Thursday, and goes to the cinema on Friday, in the meantime reading the *Sun* newspaper, the *Financial Times* and a trade journal. How is a company to go about understanding such a person's profile and preferences, and to adapt its marketing to maximize the value to both supplier and receiver? But marketing processes, such as market segmentation and strategic marketing planning *are* being adapted to take into account such complexity. Leading edge companies *are* attempting to understand and respond to the atomistic nature of society at the start of the twenty-first century, as are leading academics.

Finally, the last section of this chapter was written by one of the authors around the late 1980s, when all manner of criticisms were being levelled at marketing in the wake of the consumerist movement. But, as you will see from the line of argument then, exactly the same approach must be taken to those who attack marketing today in the context of postmodernism.

Is marketing unethical?

In recent years, dissatisfaction has been expressed by increasingly large numbers of people at the structure of a society that seems to have consumption as both its means and its end. Capitalism presents an unacceptable face, some believe, inasmuch as it promotes the growth of an acquisitive and materialistic society.

In the late 1960s and early 1970s there was a growing consciousness of the problems that the age of mass consumption brought with it, and a new awareness of alternatives that might be possible, indeed necessary, became apparent. This movement quickly found its chroniclers: books such as Charles Reich's *The Greening of America*, Alvin Toffler's *Future Shock* and Theodore Roszak's *The Making of a Counter Culture* appeared on book shelves throughout the world. The message articulated in these and other testaments of the movement was basically a simple one: that people could no longer be thought of as 'consumers', as some aggregate variable in the grand design of market planning. They were individuals intent on doing their own bidding.

Feelings such as these led in the late 1980s and early 1990s to a critical examination of commercial activity of all kinds. As one of the more visible manifestations of such activity, marketing has been singled out for special attention. One criticism frequently levelled against marketing is that it plays on people's weaknesses. By insidious means, it is claimed, marketing attempts to persuade consumers that they must smoke this brand of cigarette or use this brand of deodorant; and that without them their lives are somehow incomplete. This argument involves the notion of the defenceless consumer, a person who is like clay in the hands of a wily marketer, and thus in need of protection. Such a view of marketing tends to exaggerate the influence the marketer can bring to bear on the market place. It implies that consumers' powers of perception are limited in the extreme, and that consumers' intelligence is minimal. It further suggests that skilful marketing can create needs.

This last point deserves close examination. Marketing may well be able to persuade people that they want a product; but that process should not be confused with creating a need. The sceptic might respond to this view by claiming, for example, that, 'Nobody wanted television before it was invented; now it is a highly competitive market. That market must have been created.' This argument confuses needs and wants. Clearly, nobody wanted television before it was invented; but there has always been a need for home entertainment. Previously, that need had been met by a piano, a book, parlour games, or something of that kind. Now technology has made available a further means of satisfying the basic need for domestic entertainment – television. Many consumers find that television better satisfies their need for home entertainment than did the piano.

Any argument that depends on a view of the defenceless consumer must be rejected by a scrupulous marketer. The consumer is still sovereign as long as he or she is free to make choices – either choices between competing products, or the choice not to buy at all. Indeed, it could be argued that by extending the range of choices that consumer have available to them, marketing is enhancing consumer sovereignty rather than eroding it. It should be noted, too, that while promotional activity may persuade an individual to buy a product or service for the first time, promotion is unlikely to be the persuasive factor in subsequent purchases, when the consumer is acting from first-hand experience of the product. Although promotion may sell an unsatisfactory product the first time round, it cannot do so on future occasions.

Nevertheless, as we have observed, commercial activities of all kinds, including marketing, have evolved in the light of societal changes. As we move deeper into the new millennium, It is necessary, therefore, that we look very closely at both the kinds of roles that marketing assumes, and the social and economic systems that are supporting them.

Some ethical concerns

Several specific issues have formed the focus of the debate on the ethics of marketing. The main issues to be discussed include marketing's contribution to materialism; rising consumer expectations as a result of marketing pressure; and the use of advertising to mislead or distort. Let us look at some of the arguments involved in these discussions.

Marketing, it has been suggested, helps to feed, and in turn feeds on, the materialistic and acquisitive urges of society. Implicit in such criticism is the value judgement that materialism and acquisitiveness are, in themselves, undesirable. Whether or not one agrees with this view, there would seem to be a case here for marketing to answer. The prosecution in this case would argue that marketing contributes to a general raising of the level of consumer expectations. These expectations are more than simple aspirations: they represent on the part of the consumer a desire to acquire a specific set of gratifications through the purchase of goods and services. The desire for these gratifications is fuelled by marketing's insistent messages. Further, if the individual lacks the financial resources with which to fulfil these expectations, then this inevitably adds to a greater awareness of differences in society, and to dissatisfaction and unrest among those in this situation.

The counter-argument that can be used here is that marketing itself does not contribute to rising expectations, and thus to differences in society; it merely makes people aware of, and better informed about, the differences that already exist in society. Indeed, the advocates of the cause of marketing could well claim that, in this respect, its effects are beneficial, since it supports, even hastens, pressures for redistribution. The defence in this case could also usefully point out that materialism is not a recent phenomenon, correlated with the advent of mass marketing.

Much of the criticism levelled at marketing is in fact directed at one aspect of it: advertising. Advertising practitioners themselves are fully conscious of these criticisms. One booklet published by the advertising agency, J. Walter Thompson, was entitled: 'Advertising – is this the sort of work that an honest man can take pride in?' Within that publication were summarized six of the major arguments used by critics of advertising:

► Advertising makes misleading claims about the product or service advertised.
► By implication or association it offers misleading promises of other benefits which purchase and use of the product will bring.
► It uses hidden, dangerously powerful techniques of persuasion.
► By encouraging undesirable attitudes it has adverse social effects.
► It works by the exploitation of human inadequacy.
► It wastes skills and talents which could be better employed in other jobs.

Supporters of advertising would point to the fact that advertising in all its forms is heavily controlled in most Western societies, either by self-imposed codes (such as the British Code of Advertising Practice) or by legislation (such as the Trade Description Act). It could also be claimed, on behalf of advertising, that a company might be able to persuade people to buy something once through subtle advertising claims, but that sustained patterns of repeat purchase cannot be built up if the product itself is not perceived by consumers to provide the gratifications they seek. For example, we might be persuaded that Martini is indeed 'The Right One', as its promoters claim, and we might give it a trial. However, if it fails to do the things we want it to do (that is, meet the needs we wish to satisfy) we will quickly turn to drinking something else and/or seek to gratify our needs in another way.

The debate about the ethics of marketing often confuses marketing institutions with the people who work in them. Clearly, there are dishonest business people who engage in activities that are detrimental to their fellow citizens. These activities include dubious trade practices, misleading advertising, unsafe products, and various unethical practices that are harmful to consumers. However, it seems a grave error to criticize marketing institutions because of the practices of a small number of unethical marketers. It is clear, for example, that there are advertisers who engage in deceptive practices designed to mislead and possibly defraud consumers. Nevertheless, the institution of advertising can be used not only to inform consumers about potentially beneficial new products, such as new, energy-saving technologies, but also to promote non-profit community services, such as theatres and orchestras. This argument can, of course, be applied to all marketing activities.

Marketing and society

Any critical appraisal of marketing as an activity must take place within the context of the social and economic systems in which it is practised. A leading marketing scholar, the late Wroe Alderson, suggested the concept of marketing ecology as a useful approach to interpreting marketing's wider role. By this, he meant the study of the continual adaptation of marketing systems to their environments; his suggestion was that the marketing systems in existence at any one time are simply reflections of the contemporary value system dominant in society. In systems technology, this approach would involve seeing marketing as an 'organized' behavioural system that sustains itself by drawing on the resources of the environment, and survives only by adapting to changes in that environment. The environment represents not only the immediate surroundings of our customers and suppliers, but also the wider phenomena that are embodied in technological, ideological, moral and social dimensions.

The environment exerts a number of continuing pressures on a marketing system. Technology alone demands constant change in any marketing activity – shortening life-cycles in all product fields bear witness to its clamorous effects. Many commentators have claimed that the rate of technological development is one of the most forceful catalysts for marketing change. Even greater, perhaps, than this pressure, however, has been the impetus for change provided by a radically different moral and ideological climate in society at large. The basic purpose of business activities today has come to be questioned, and not only by those committed to alternative systems of exchange.

As has already been discussed briefly, marketing has been caught up in the broader issue of the social responsibility of business. Although there is a wide range of opinion about the meaning of 'social responsibility', the implication is always that the organization must look beyond the profit motive. Recent studies have shown that the vast majority of company executives acknowledge the interests of employees and consumers as well as the interests of shareholders. Executives are now being asked to acknowledge the interests of a 'fourth estate' – that is, society.

Although unlikely to abandon the profit motive as the primary focus of their attention, company executives are now increasingly exploring ways of conducting business where 'social responsibility' is a salient criterion of success. The positive acknowledgement of the social dimension of corporate activity is likely to result in the deliberate use of marketing and marketing technology as an agent of social change. We have already seen the adoption of a marketing approach by government agencies in attempts to gain participation in local planning decisions, to care for the countryside, to discourage the smoking of cigarettes and so on.

When we talk about marketing, we are referring to more than just a set of techniques and procedures. We are alluding to an organized behavioural system that is changing constantly as it adapts to the evolving requirements of society. It is indeed the case that society gets the sort of marketing systems that it needs.

Closely connected to the issue of ethics of marketing is the issue of consumerism.

Caveat emptor

In a perfectly competitive market place, all the products or services offered by an organization would meet the needs of its customers and consumers at the requisite level of profits. As the situation is at the time of writing, however, consumers complain with increasingly strident voices about the way businesses operate. What conclusions are to be drawn from this? Are the major companies not based soundly on a marketing philosophy? Or are the strident voices not representative of the wishes of the vast majority of customers?

Consumerism, the name given to a wide spread of activities in the 1990s, focuses our attention on the problem. Is marketing failing to do its job well, or are a small collection of agitators making something out of nothing? The truth in most cases is probably to be found in the 80/20 rule: 80 per cent of the problem is poor marketing, and 20 per cent is populist agitation.

Traditionally, it has been argued that a bad product will sell only once. Its customers will reject it after unsatisfactory performance, and any organization that persists in offering such products or services cannot survive for long. Consumerists argue increasingly that a passive approach of this kind amounts to shutting the stable door after the horse has bolted. They usually want to see it made illegal for such products or services to be offered on the market in the first place. Most countries have passed a significant amount of legislation in support of this position. Up to the end of the nineteenth century the doctrine of 'caveat emptor' or 'let the purchaser beware' was widely accepted, although customers and consumers had always enjoyed a certain amount of protection as a result of regulations imposed on traders. However, since the end of the nineteenth century, the responsibility for the quality of the product or service sold has fallen more and more on the shoulders of the vendor.

Caveat venditor

In most countries within the European Union (EU), at the time of writing, customer groups have succeeded in obtaining massive legislative support. Sweden is perhaps the most extreme example, with its consumer ombudsman and market court. However, the UK has its own Director of Fair Trading and an impressive array of legislation, including the Competition Act, which became law in April 1980 and gives the Director of Fair Trading increased powers of intervention. As an illustration of legislation that supports customers' rights, we can perhaps take the concept of 'implied terms of sale'. In 1973, a statutory responsibility was laid on a supplier of goods in the UK to ensure that any goods were indeed good for the purpose for which they were promoted and sold. This reversed the dictum 'caveat emptor' to 'caveat venditor', or 'let the seller beware'.

Although many business people resisted this trend, it is difficult to see why they should feel that a change of this kind damaged their interests. No marketer, surely, would doubt that trust was an important element in his or her relationship with a customer. That customer groups, or politicians, with or without populist agitation, had to lobby to have laws passed to secure this sort of relationship with suppliers is an indictment of marketing activities throughout Europe and beyond.

The marketing of children's toys provides an example of how customers, consumers and company objectives can all be satisfied by careful business practice. The successful toy companies now are those that inform parents that their products are not potentially dangerous, not coated with lead paint, and will not be destroyed the hour after they are first pressed into active service. Fisher-Price is one of the most successful toy manufacturers. Since 1968 it has eschewed child-manipulative promotion, tested its products carefully with children for durability, safety and purposeful play, and charged the prices necessary to make and market 'good' toys. Sales and profit margins are impressively good.

Consumerism's better way to marketing

Consumerism is pro-marketing; it wants the marketing approach to business implemented in a sincere rather than a cynical spirit. The cynical implementation that consumerists claim has been all too widely practised is no better than high-pressure salesmanship or misleading puffery. The sincere implementation of the marketing approach entails respect for each individual customer. Indeed, the consumerist argues eloquently that the sort of relationship found between a manufacturer and a customer in, say, a capital-goods market, should be created in consumer markets. And, in so far as that is both economically feasible and what the consumer really wants, marketers must surely want it also.

Broadly, consumerists argue that recognition of the following consumer rights would ensure that a more satisfactory relationship would be built up between organization and customer: the right to be informed; the right to be protected; and the right to ensure quality of life.

These are highlighted in Figure 22.2.

The right to be informed of the facts involved in any buyer–seller relationship is clearly a fundamental right. Some of the key aspects, which have already been subject to legislation or regulation in

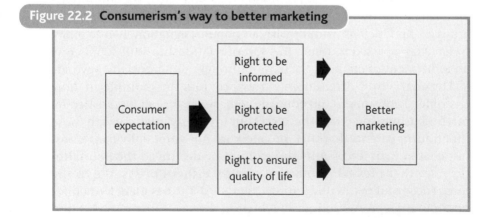

Figure 22.2 **Consumerism's way to better marketing**

Europe, include the full cost of credit/loans taken up, often known as 'truth-in-lending'; the true cost of an item, under the slogan 'unit pricing'; the basic constituent elements of products, known as 'ingredient informative labelling'; the freshness of foods, discussed generally as 'open-dating'; and 'truth-in-advertising'.

The case against producers is that they either mislead through exaggerated claims, or fail to tell the whole truth about their products or services. Consumerists believe that individuals have the right to know these truths. Again, who can doubt that this demand, if sincerely felt, should be met? Who would be unwilling to tell an industrial purchaser the answer to basic questions about any merchandise offered for sale? What other information would customers like?

The right to be protected is also a major plank in the consumerist platform. All too often now, consumerists argue, consumers' trust in organizations is abused. Safety standards (which are monitored by government agencies) and the quality of medicines (which are subject to statutory controls) are exceptions that all businesses could learn from. It is certainly the case that the trend within the EU is for many more product fields to be affected by legislative controls. The consumerists' argument that manufacturers should assume liability for any malfunctioning of products offered in the market place would appear to have overwhelmed the opposition. In most cases, however, good marketing will go well beyond the minimum standards required – and will not be slow to tell the customer that it does so.

Concerns about the security and privacy of information is another major issue. The use of the Internet for placing orders or requesting further information is being restrained by worries about how personal information will be used, and who will have access to it. Incidents of computer fraud, hacking and theft justify such concerns. A number of security initiatives have been undertaken in response, such as the SET protocol, an Internet security standard developed by credit card firms, which works with established Internet encryption standards. While these measures help to protect customers from data abuse, continuing anxiety is likely to bias Internet sales in the direction of relatively low-value items, and in favour of suppliers with strong brands trusted by the consumer.

The right to ensure quality of life is perhaps the most difficult demand for the marketing activity to satisfy. None the less, if a meaningful segment of the market needs to perceive the products it purchases as furthering the quality of life, then that is a need that should be respected. The non-biodegradability of packaging, for example, has been shown on occasion to offend substantial numbers of customers. If a sufficiently large group of these customers is prepared to meet an organization's research and development costs, along with the costs involved in changing to a preferred alternative, then good marketing should lead the organization to work with these customers towards a change in its methods of packaging.

It should be emphasized that none of these rights is unfamiliar to marketers of industrial or consumer products. They have become accustomed to responding to similar demands. What is different now is that the process of marketing is no longer done on the initiative of the marketer in a framework of caveat emptor. The framework is no longer paternalistic. At the time of writing, customers works through representative institutions, even unions – and the cry is caveat venditor.

Consumerism will affect marketing by bringing into being a more informative approach to all forms of marketing communication. It must, and will, give rise to a greater integrity in the advertising and promotional puffery of the profession, without, one hopes, making life too dull, too much like a company share-issue prospectus. It will give rise to a greater concern among all levels of business management with the long-term social implications of the materialistic bias of Western society. Does the continual emphasis on immediate material expectations bear some responsibility for the level of delinquency in Western society? What are the implications for tomorrow of our present pattern of usage of raw materials or pollution of the environment?

The consumerist argues that in present-day Europe we can certainly afford to trade off some of today's advantages in favour of the longer-term interests of society.

Consumerism as an opportunity

The social emphasis of consumerism, particularly its demands for an enhanced quality of life, is no threat to profitable enterprise. In considering this point, organizations might find it helpful to draw an analogy with changing attitudes to social factors at work. From the mid-nineteenth century, manufacturers were compelled by law to ensure that unsafe machinery was fitted with guards, and considerable cost was, of course, incurred in carrying this out. Within the office, modern times have seen a concern to obtain office furniture and equipment designed to promote comfort at work; again, the introduction of such equipment has been an expensive business. It may well be that, in the long term, fewer accidents and a happier work force will help improve an organization's overall profitability. Even if this does not happen, however, the organization should bear in mind that society expects the cost of safety at work to be included in the price of a product or service. Consumerism, like safety at work, presents an opportunity to adjust its approach in accordance with changing social standards. As an articulate expression of customer needs, consumerism demands a marketing response.

Consumerism calls out for the reformulation and development of products and services to meet the requirements both of short-term satisfaction and longer-term benefits. A closer look must be taken at the system of marketing values that asserts that immediate consumer satisfaction and longer-term consumer welfare may be opposing goals for an organization's marketing activity. It is now necessary – and good marketing practice – to promote products that provide consumers with both short- and long-term satisfaction.

In consumer-goods markets, for example, marketing specialists have devoted most of their efforts to promoting desirable and pleasing products, and they have tended to ignore the long-term disadvantages to society that often accompany such products. Consumerism has reminded us vociferously of these disadvantages and, in a very real sense, has given us the opportunity to be better citizens. It is possible now to design and sell a motor car that is considerabley safer than its equivalent in 1960. At that time, attempts to sell safety were conspicuously unsuccessful, even though car makers emphasized safety factors in their promotional literature. It is possible now to design and sell an effective flameproof fabric for children's wear because an awareness of the need for it has been created. Consumerism, in other words, opens up market opportunities that the astute marketing-based organization will wish to take up. Other examples that can be cited are phosphate-free detergents, lead-free petrol, degradable plastics containers for a host of products, synthetic tobaccos, new nutrient-based breakfast cereals, and low-polluting manufacturing systems.

The articulate customer movement known as consumerism is here to stay as a force acting on organizations in their market place. If used respectfully, it can provide a significant further input of information in the process of matching the resources of the organization with the needs of its customers.

Summary

Traditionally, marketing was thought by many to be just another word for 'selling' or, at best, an activity that was appropriate for fast-moving consumer goods, but not for the world of industrial products or the growing services sector. More recently, however, this attitude has changed, and there is now a greater recognition of the fundamental importance of marketing to business success. Marketing, as we have seen, is more than simply 'giving the customer what he or she wants'. Marketing requires a clear understanding of the asset value of the business and the means whereby it can differentiate itself from competitors.

The process of marketing is universally applicable, irrespective of whether it takes place in consumer, service or international contexts. There are merely some important differences in emphasis to be noted.

From this discussion of marketing ethics and consumerism, the conclusion reached is that consumerism offers nothing but opportunities to the organization that puts the interests of the customer at the centre of its business philosophy. Marketing is a prime candidate for carrying the torch!

Further reading

Hunt, S., Chonko, L. and Wilcox, J. (1984) Ethical problems of marketing researchers. *Journal of Marketing Research*, **21**, pp. 309–24.

Smith, C. (1999) Marketing ethics, in M. Baker (ed.) *IEBM Encyclopaedia of Marketing*, Thomson International Press, London.

References

McDonald, M. and Wilson, H. (2002) *The New Marketing: Transforming the Corporate Future*, Butterworth-Heinemann, Oxford.

Reich, Charles A. (1970) *The Greening of America*, Random House, New York.

Roszack, Theodore (1969) *The Making of a Counter Culture: Reflections on the Technocratic Society and its Youthful Opposition*, Anchor Books, New York.

Toffler, Alvin (1970) *Future Shock*, Bodley Head, London.

Conclusion

The marketing concept

In 1776, when Adam Smith said that consumption was the sole end and purpose of production, he was in fact describing what in recent years has become known as the *marketing concept*. The marketing concept implies that all the activities of an organization are driven by a desire to satisfy customer needs. Indeed, the central idea of marketing is of a matching process between a company's capabilities and the wants of customers in order to achieve the objectives of both parties. It is about providing goods or services for which there is a known demand, as opposed to selling what the company likes to produce. By focusing on customers and their wants, the company is better positioned to make a profit and thus to be sustainable in the longer term.

Defining a market orientation

Companies that 'live and breathe' the marketing concept are said to be market-led, or to have a *market orientation*. While the exact definition of 'market orientation', and whether it is something distinct from or synonymous with a 'marketing orientation', remains the subject of debate, a market-orientated business can be seen to possess the following characteristics:

- ▶ a concern for customers;
- ▶ an interest in the business environment;
- ▶ a focus on competitors;
- ▶ a curiosity about the future;
- ▶ an entrepreneurial spirit; and
- ▶ a zeal for action.

To be consistent with modern writers, this book uses the expression 'market orientation' as a generic term for the organizational attributes that together comprise the features of a market, marketing or customer-focused enterprise. The number of closely related terms that can be collated under the umbrella of 'market orientation' indicates the multi-dimensional nature of the concept, rather than any serious disagreement about the fundamentals of its meaning.

This multi-dimensional quality of market orientation can be illustrated by reference to the ways in which different writers have gone about explaining and exploring the concept. For some, market orientation is essentially a *philosophy*, representing a body of thought that can be applied to an organization or used to underpin the way in which a business is conceptualized or run. Others view market orientation as an aspect of organizational *culture*, where attention is focused on the values, attitudes and beliefs held collectively by an organization's members. Still others conceive the concept as a *process*: a series of actions or activities that constitutes the heart of what it means to be market-orientated.

Given this diversity of perception, one way of moving towards a better understanding of market orientation is to identify common themes within the various usages of the term. What becomes strikingly apparent from such an exercise is the emphasis each approach places on the interaction between an organization and its external environment, and the myriad of relationships this interaction generates. Thus, while the substance of a market orientation may vary from one observer to another, the object of a market orientation remains the same. Market orientation, therefore, embodies:

The ability and willingness of an organization to take account of external factors which will affect the possibility of it developing profitable exchanges (however profit is defined by the organization), both now and in the future, and the ability and willingness of the organization to take action as a result of these factors to strengthen important relationships.

This definition of market orientation acknowledges the constraints placed on organizations by internal factors (their 'ability and willingness' and their need for certain outcomes or 'profit'), and emphasizes the key activity of effective marketing organizations: understanding and acting on the dynamic of the markets in which they operate, concentrating on critical relationships – namely, the relationships with their customers.

Market-orientated organizations will therefore be interested in the acquisition of intelligence about customers, competitors, market trends and opportunities, and, of course, existing and potential relationships. More important, they will also be interested in the response this intelligence suggests, and the actions it prompts.

Engendering a market orientation

Instilling a market orientation into an organization is a difficult job. It is easy to accept that long-term survival depends on creating and keeping customers, whether they are paying customers or otherwise, but it is quite another matter to introduce this philosophy into managerial processes. This is because people are subject to a large number of influences and pressures in their work, which will tend to counter the pursuit of marketing principles.

Other orientations that can exist side by side with marketing include: production, design, technology, financial, sales, and social orientations. These are not 'wrong', and are all needed at certain times to a greater or lesser extent. If, for example, an organization has profitability problems, it will be important that a financial orientation should emerge as a priority to enable the short-term survival of the business. Alternatively, an organization that relies on product innovation and development for its success in the market place should encourage a technology orientation within its ranks.

The problem with these various types of orientation is achieving the right balance between them to match the environmental conditions within which the organization operates. Successful organizations are good at matching, not only in terms of the four 'P's, but also in terms of the ways in which they set priorities for themselves. In good times, marketing tends to be forgotten and other priorities dominate, but in bad times marketing becomes the way forward, but by that point it is often perceived as a threat to the other traditional values already embedded in the organization. The point is that, as with other disciplines, marketing needs to exist in an organization. Whether or not it stems from a formal marketing department is irrelevant.

The marketing function

In addition to understanding the marketing concept, it is also necessary to be clear about the difference between the marketing concept (often referred to as 'market orientation') and the marketing function, which is concerned with the management of the *marketing mix*. The management of the marketing mix involves using various tools and techniques in order to implement the marketing concept.

Managing the marketing mix

The marketing mix is the name given to the main demand-influencing variables available to the organization. The classic description of the marketing mix, although something of a simplification, is the as the four 'P's:

1 *Product*: What type and range of product or service should we provide?
2 *Price*: What price should be set for each product or service?
3 *Promotion*: How do we best communicate with our target customers and persuade them to buy our offer? and
4 *Place*: What channels of distribution and what levels of service are appropriate?

More recently, some commentators have advocated the expansion of the marketing mix to include additional 'P's, such as Physical evidence (customer service), People, and Process.

When developing policies for the various elements of the marketing mix, it is important to be comprehensive, but also to identify those areas that are significant in the markets in which an organization operates. Thus, some organizations use an expanded marketing mix for managerial and planning purposes. This can involve isolating sales plans, processes, people or customer service for special attention. Whatever the case, the key task of the marketing manager is to ensure that the marketing mix is internally consistent and offers superior customer value.

Delivering customer value

There are a number of definitions of marketing. For the purpose of clarification, this book has used the following definition:

> marketing is a process for understanding markets, for quantifying the present and future value required by the different groups of customers within these markets, for communicating this to all other functions with responsibility for delivering this value, and for measuring the value actually delivered. For marketing to be effective, all other functions should be 'market driven'.

The notion of customer value is intrinsic to marketing's role within the business. It can be seen to encompass both the value delivered to the customer by the supplying organization (the 'package' of benefits), and the value received by the supplying organization from the customer (the return on investment). This return on investment, in its broadest sense, includes the actual business profit generated by the customer relationship, and the wider customer insight gained from it. Clearly, the revenue-producing capacity of the organization depends on the accuracy with which it is able to define and meet customer need.

Achieving corporate objectives

What causes business success in the long run, by which we mean a continuous growth in earnings per share and in the capital value of the shares, has been shown by research to depend on four ingredients:

1 An excellent core product or service and all the associated research and development.
2 First-rate, world-class, state-of-the-art operations, where marketing contributes to defining operational efficiency in customer satisfaction terms.
3 A culture that encourages and produces an infrastructure conducive to creativity and entrepreneurialism.
4 Proficient marketing departments, staffed by qualified professionals (not failures from other functions).

Given these ingredients and, above all else, a corporate culture that is not dominated (because of its history) by production, operations or financial orientation, all the evidence shows that marketing as a function makes a contribution to the achievement of corporate objectives. Its principal role is to spell out the several value propositions demanded by different customer groups, so that everyone in the organization knows what their responsibility is in creating and delivering this value.

The creation of winning (suitable, superior and sustainable) value propositions demands a synthesis of knowledge and expertise. An in-depth understanding of customer needs and preferences, and of organizational strengths and weaknesses, is the bedrock of saleable products and services. To be successful, offers must also represent a mutually beneficial arrangement, whereby both parties obtain an acceptable gain for their respective investment.

The regular and ongoing monitoring of marketing planning and performance is therefore necessary to check whether the creation and delivery of value is 'hitting the mark' and doing so cost-effectively. Is meaningful information being gathered and employed to optimal effect? Are markets being segmented in such a way that the 'right' customers are targeted? Are resource levels and allocations appropriate and sufficient? Is management providing the inspiration and leadership required to ensure that the whole organization is pulling in the same (correct), direction? These are just some of the questions that organizations need constantly to ask themselves in order to remain valid and viable businesses.

Securing customer centricity

A primary concern of the marketing task within a business is to seek to innovate through product and market development, and to strive to enhance competitive performance. Opportunities for productivity improvement tend to be self-limiting in the sense that costs can only be cut so far, and price and product mix adjustments can only be made with limited frequency. On the other hand, the opportunities for innovation and improved competitiveness are limited only by imagination and creativity.

In both cases, it is only by placing the customer at the centre of the business that success can be achieved. Innovation that is not based on the satisfaction of a customer need, either existing or latent, will not succeed – the world is littered with 'better mousetraps'. Similarly, the search for competitive advantage will only be successful if based on a strategy of meeting customer needs more effectively than can competitors. This concept of *differential advantage* lies at the heart of strategic marketing. It could even be argued that the primary task of marketing management is to achieve and maintain maximum positive differentiation over and above the competition in the eyes of customers.

Ultimately, therefore, the role of marketing in the organization is, first, to ensure that the orientation of the business is towards the customer, and second, to seek to marshal the resources of the business in such a way as to be perceived by the market as providing benefits superior to those available elsewhere.

There are thus two aspects to marketing. One is about corporate value and culture, and the other about strategy and execution. It is important to recognize that to have a marketing orientation and to achieve competitive advantage it is not necessary to have a marketing department, or even a single marketing executive. What is essential is that every move the organization makes is guided by the principles of marketing, and that a customer orientation pervades the organization.

Many books and articles have appeared which have sought to explain the factors that determine business success. Books like *In Search of Excellence* by Peters and Waterman, have all drawn the same conclusion: put very simply, it is that those companies where customer satisfaction is an article of faith rather than a convenient slogan will tend to succeed. The surprising thing is that it has taken so long for such a simple concept to gain widespread acceptance!

Marketing in transition

For many years, marketing was considered to be just another word for 'selling'. As the weight of this book will testify, marketing today is clearly about much, much more. The growth in understanding and appreciation of marketing's role in business has led to the greater realization of its current and future potential. The case for marketing being a major contributor to organizational performance no longer needs to be made. What remains a challenge is the application of marketing principles within a market place of unprecedented character and momentum.

Moving from transactions to relationships

In the past, it was more often the case that organizations were structured and managed on the basis of optimizing their own operations, with little regard for the way in which they interfaced with suppliers and, indeed, customers. The business model was essentially 'transactional', meaning that products and services were bought and sold 'at arm's length' and that there was little enthusiasm for the concept of long-term, inter-allied relationships.

The new competitive paradigm that is now emerging is in stark contrast to the conventional model. It suggests that in the challenging global markets of the twenty-first century, the route to sustainable advantage lies increasingly in managing the complex web of relationships that link together partners in a mutually profitable 'value chain'. These relationships span multiple markets, including customer markets; referral markets; internal markets; recruitment markets; influencer markets; and supplier and alliance markets. This relationship marketing (RM) approach extends the marketing concept beyond traditional marketing and embraces the entire supply chain to achieve greater customer value at every level in the chain.

Emphasizing customer acquisition and retention

Unlike the transactional, functionally-orientated approach, RM is a cross-functional process concerned with balancing marketing efforts among key markets. A critical issue within the customer market domain is to ensure that customer retention as well as customer acquisition is emphasized. Recognition of the significant link between customer retention and profitability is leading to new and better strategies for strengthening customer satisfaction and loyalty.

More sophisticated use of channels and media, for example, is helping marketers to develop profitable, *long-term* relationships with customers. Successful channel management highlights the importance of managing channel relationships well, from the minimization of channel conflict and risk, to the maximization of channel integrity and relevance. Companies can build customer value by offering customers both a wider range of channels, and more personalized treatment through the integration of channels. Channel strategy now might include direct sales, sales through indirect channels such as distributors or brokers, and Internet sales using electronic commerce (e-commerce). Individualized services can be provided via a range of media, including telephone, facsimile (fax), mail, the Internet, various mobile devices, and face-to-face interaction. The opportunities for reaching and connecting with specifically targeted customers have never been greater – nor have customer expectations been so high.

The advent of customer relationship management (CRM) is a response to the need to meet heightened customer expectations and face intensified market competition. CRM emphasizes the use of information technology in managing customer relationships. Advances in database technology has made it possible to know and segment customers in ever more creative ways. Data warehouses can be used to store and search vast amounts of data. Data mining and modelling techniques can reveal otherwise 'invisible' patterns of customer behaviour, which can be translated into customer-specific marketing strategies. With its foundations in RM, CRM reinforces the view that marketers manage – and businesses win/lose – customer relationships, not customers.

Balancing customer and commercial interests

As we have seen already, managing customer relationships effectively is a complex and challenging task. Although firms need to be in tune with their markets, customers and competitors, an excessive focus in external matters can distract from the achievement of the returns required for long-term business survival. For many organizations, these returns are measured as profits in one form or another, while for others they may be the achievement of social, charitable or artistic objectives.

Internal factors obviously affect profitability, or the achievement of other types of objective, and should consequently have an equal influence on the practice of marketing. Thus marketing managers must have an appreciation of such areas as resource availability, cost generation and organizational capability, as well as an in-depth knowledge of customer wants and purchase behaviour. Without the former, it becomes difficult to gauge the attractiveness of different marketing opportunities; and without the latter, the business is unfocused.

Offering benefits, not features

Customers buy products and services because they seek the benefits derived from them, not their inherent features. In this sense, products and services are problem-solvers. For example, customers buy aspirin to solve the problem of headaches, and they buy drills because they need to make holes. Not every product or service benefit will have equal appeal to all customers, or groups of customers. However, through customer dialogue or market research it is possible to establish which benefits customers perceive as being important.

The marketing of services should not call for a different philosophy from that underlying the marketing of physical products. Rather, it calls for an even greater emphasis on availability, particularly given the 'perishability' of the service product. Nevertheless, both service and tangible products are increasingly dependent for their success on the suppliers' ability to enhance their appeal though the 'added value' of customer service. Customer service comprises a host of value-adding activities that provide time and place utilities for the customer.

Becoming a beacon, not a bolt-on

The stature and position of marketing within organizations is clearly changing. Marketing is increasingly being seen more as a business 'beacon' and less as a business bolt-on. From the days when marketing meant simply advertising the same message to a mass audience about what research and development, and production and engineering were doing, it has evolved into a pan-company, collaborative expertise that is capable of interactive and individualized dialogue with customers. Its role is no longer confined merely to winning customers and generating sales, but to keeping those customers and developing enduring, mutually beneficial relationships with them.

As stated earlier, marketing is essentially a matching process between an organization's capabilities and the wants of customers. By an organization's capabilities, we mean the unique set of resources and management skills that a particular firm has, which are not necessarily capable of taking advantage of *all* market opportunities as effectively, and hence as competitively, as other firms. This matching challenge is compounded further by the context in which the organization operates, or 'the marketing environment', which is both complex and ever-changing. It is crucial, therefore, that an organization is able to identify market needs, and to exploit internal competencies and the marketing environment in order to satisfy those needs. In short, the marketing process is fundamental to commercial success.

Reference

Peters, T. and Waterman, R. (1982) *In Search of Excellence*, Warner Books, New York.

Index